The Bedford Companion to Shakespeare

An Introduction with Documents

>←

The Bedford Companion to Shakespeare

An Introduction with Documents

><

RUSS McDONALD

University of North Carolina at Greensboro

Bedford Books of St. Martin's Press

BOSTON ✷ NEW YORK

For Bedford Books
President and Publisher: Charles H. Christensen
General Manager and Associate Publisher: Joan E. Feinberg
Managing Editor: Elizabeth M. Schaaf
Developmental Editor: Karen S. Henry
Editorial Assistant: Andrea Goldman
Production Editor: Lori Chong
Copyeditor: Kathryn Blatt
Text Design: Claire Seng-Niemoeller
Cover Design: Hannus Design Associates
Cover Art: Detail of *A Fête at Bermondsey*, c. 1570 by Joris Hoefnagel. Courtesy of the
   Marquess of Salisbury.

Library of Congress Catalog Card Number: 95-80798

0   9   8   7   6

f   e   d   c   b

For information, write: St. Martin's Press, Inc.
175 Fifth Avenue, New York, NY 10010

Editorial Offices: Bedford Books *of* St. Martin's Press
75 Arlington Street, Boston, MA 02116

ISBN: 0-312-10075-2 (paperback)
ISBN: 0-312-15857-2 (hardcover)

Published and distributed outside North America by:

MACMILLAN PRESS LTD.
Houndmills, Basingstoke, Hampshire RG21 2XS and London
Companies and representatives throughout the world.

ISBN: 0-333-63833-6

Acknowledgments

CHAPTER I
The House Known as Shakespeare's Birthplace. Reprinted by permission of the Folger Shakespeare
   Library.
Record of Shakespeare's Baptism. Reprinted by permission of Vicar and Churchwardens, Holy Trin-
   ity Church, Stratford-upon-Avon.

*Acknowledgments and copyrights are continued at the back of the book on pages 355-56, which constitute an ex-
tension of the copyright page. It is a violation of the law to reproduce these selections by any means whatsoever
without the written permission of the copyright holder.*

This book is dedicated to five great teachers

Avis Hartley

George Walton Williams

Robert Y. Turner

Cyrus Hoy

Stephen Booth

Preface

Teachers of Shakespeare face an acute version of a problem that vexes most English professors: how to do justice both to the literary works on the syllabus and to the culture that helped to generate them. *Hamlet*, to take a familiar example, begs to be studied in light of Elizabethan anxiety about the health of the queen, the problem of royal succession, and early modern ideas about subjection and power. However, *Hamlet* itself is such a rich and complex work of art that class time spent talking about Elizabeth, Essex, and James or about sixteenth-century political theory can be seen as class time stolen from such major topics as Hamlet's language, the parallel structures of action, the effects of tragedy, and the play's metadramatic brilliance. The increased historical awareness characteristic of recent scholarship has sharpened our sense that an understanding of a play depends on familiarity with multiple contexts, and yet such a conviction does not cancel our obligation to teach principles of literary analysis that reveal the pleasures of the text. For Shakespeareans, this dilemma is compounded by modern students' difficulties with the early modern idiom. It's all very well to talk loftily about Renaissance politics, but if readers can't comprehend the words in the first two scenes of *Hamlet*, the result is frustration and disappointment both for instructor and class members. Then there is the further problem that *Hamlet* exists in three different texts, two of them "good" and one of them "bad." Instructors and students need help with the multitude of textual and extratextual matters that the study of William Shakespeare entails.

The Bedford Companion represents an attempt to put the Shakespearean text into cultural perspective without causing it to disappear. The book is designed as a vehicle for efficiently conveying facts and ideas that will inform class discussion and enhance students' comprehension of Shakespearean drama. First, the chapters themselves contain an abundance of introductory information on which instructors can build. The treatment of Elizabethan performance in Chapter 2, for example, should generate questions about the staging of crucial episodes not specifically examined in the chapter, such as the tomb scene of *Romeo and Juliet*. Further, coming to terms with the spareness of the original staging leads easily to an appreciation of the opulent poetry in the same scene. Second, the documents that follow each chapter lend themselves to correlation with a wide range of plays. The excerpts from *Patriarcha*, Sir Robert Filmer's defense of royal authority, and from King James's 1610 speech to Parliament should stimulate students to hear the rhetoric of Richard II, Claudius, King Lear, and Prospero in terms of contemporary political writing. Or certain chapters might be profitably considered in relation to particular plays, such as the chapter on the family in connection with *As You Like It*. The combination of introduction and primary materials offers students something unavailable elsewhere. Shakespeare criticism abounds, but students need critical readings much less than they need contextual data about early modern society, religion, literary theory, economics, politics, printing, language, and theater.

The feature that distinguishes this volume is its collection of documents and illustrations. These comprise a broad range of primary materials: maps of London and Stratford, excerpts from Elizabethan diaries, selections from Holinshed's *Chronicles*, facsimiles of pages from Shakespearean quartos, royal proclamations, portraits of Elizabeth and James, excerpts from contemporary literary criticism, passages from handbooks on courtship, political treatises, and an acerbic commentary on urban fashion. These examples constitute a partial introduction to early modern English culture, and students and instructors who find themselves fascinated with a passage can seek out more such material as well as additional or contradictory examples in modern texts, facsimiles, or microfilm versions of the originals. For a discussion of editorial policy—a glance through the book will reveal that some excerpts are modernized and some not—see the Introduction. (Several other notes are included in the section titled "To the Reader," which follows this preface.)

Although my professional bias leads me to favor the poetic over the historical, this book is not a receptacle for extraliterary, contextual information that students need to know but that I don't want to talk about. On the contrary, to exploit the metaphor contained in the title, it is a genuine companion, a book that goes along with a volume of Shakespeare and carries on a dialogue with it. I will employ it in my own classes as a means of allowing students to consider questions that require explanation and reflection: the instability of the Shakespearean text, the problematic definition of a literary "source," early modern dogma about the family (and challenges to it), the religious controversies of the late sixteenth century, changing critical notions of literary modes, and so on. I hope other instructors will do the same. The publisher and I would welcome responses from instructors about how they use the book. Likewise, we would appreciate being informed of errors that, despite the efforts of many, I have allowed to creep into the finished volume.

By a rough estimate, about half the living Shakespeareans in the United States and England have helped with this book, and I wish to express my profound gratitude for the assistance received.

Staff members at several libraries have responded helpfully to requests: Jackson Library at the University of North Carolina at Greensboro, especially Nancy Fogarty and Mark Schumacher; the Folger Shakespeare Library, particularly Elizabeth Walsh; Perkins Library at Duke University; the Huntington Library; and the British Library. The English Department at Greensboro has generously provided me with course relief and research assistance, for which I thank James Evans and my colleagues.

I gladly acknowledge my undergraduate and graduate students at Greensboro and the University of Rochester for helping to shape the contents and the form of *The Bedford Companion*. In effect, they are its collective parents.

At the beginning of the project, almost two hundred members of the Shakespeare Association of America answered a questionnaire about their teaching habits and preferences, and that detailed information has been enormously useful. My thanks to all who took the time to reply.

Albert Braunmuller, James Longenbach, Catherine Loomis, Gail McDonald, and Michael Warren read the entire manuscript, correcting factual errors, adjusting faulty emphases, making valuable suggestions about coverage, and improving my prose style. Others performed similar service in reading one or more chapters: Thomas Berger, Stephen Booth, William Carroll, Maurice Charney, Miriam Gilbert, Christopher Hodgkins, Arthur Kinney, Carole Levin, Margaret Maurer, Robert Miola, Gail Kern Paster, Russell Peck, Bruce Smith, Susan Snyder, Valerie Traub, Paul Werstine, and George Walton Williams. I deeply appreciate the efforts of all these kind and careful readers.

For guidance in choosing the documents and illustrations, I am grateful to most of those listed above, as well as to Roslyn Knutson and Debora Shuger. Both generously supplied me with copies of primary materials and helped me to locate difficult items. Gratitude for advice, illuminating conversation, and scholarly favors goes to Peter Blayney, Susan Cerasano, Alan Dessen, Frances Dolan, Andrew Gurr, Frank Melton, Hugh Parker, Mary Tonkinson, Gina Wilkins, and Perez Zagorin.

Since this book is designed chiefly for the classroom, I take pleasure in thanking Peggy O'Brien and Jeanne Addison Roberts for involving me in the NEH-sponsored Teaching Shakespeare Institute at the Folger Library. For ten years the Institute served me as a Shakespearean pedagogical laboratory: many sections of this book were first devised for its participants, and its workshops and small groups permitted the testing of various practices in the teaching of Shakespeare. I learned not only from the hundreds of high-school teachers, but also from the master teachers and resident and visiting scholars associated with the program.

Karen Henry of Bedford Books deserves to have her name on the front of this volume. For three years, since we first met on a bus at a meeting of the Shakespeare Association of America, she has labored tirelessly and cheerfully to help me get a confused heap of materials into print. What makes her an extraordinary editor is her pedagogical sensitivity. A teacher without a classroom, she knows instinctively what students need and is able to help an author fulfill those needs. Thanks also to many others at Bedford, especially Charles Christensen, Joan Feinberg, Lori Chong, Andrea Goldman, Verity Winship, and Joanne Diaz. I also gratefully acknowledge the assistance of Katie Blatt with copyediting and Jacob Molyneux with proofreading.

The length of these lists notwithstanding, there are a few people I have forgotten to thank. To them, apologies and thanks.

Thanks to Cate and Michael Parker for their friendship, which I prize. Gail McDonald and Jack McDonald have been indulgent and helpful during the making of this book, and I want to declare publicly that I love and appreciate them.

To the Reader

><

A few notes having to do with early modern conventions may be helpful.

In Shakespeare's England, the new year officially began not on January 1 but on March 25 (the feast of the Annunciation, or "Lady Day"). Apparent inconsistencies in dates sometimes arise from this feature of the early modern calendar; diaries and legal documents can be particularly confusing. For example, King James's payment to the King's Men recorded in February 1603 was actually made in the year we call 1604. When a document printed here contains such a date, the inconsistency is signified with a slash mark—in the example above, 1603/04. When a document does not contain the date itself, as with King James's speech to Parliament (March 21, 1609), the year has been silently modernized (here, to 1610).

Several of the facsimiles and unmodernized documents presented here contain "y^e" or "y^t." These signs are simply abbreviations for the words *the* and *that*. The *y* derives from the Old English letter **Þ** and served the printer as an economy, since the *t* and *h* which it replaced were common letters often needed elsewhere. *Y* is pronounced "th" (never "ye," as in the modern "Ye olde gifte shoppe").

Some financial records contain the monetary abbreviations £ (or *l*), *s*, and *d*. £ stands for pound (from the Latin *libra*), *s* for shilling (from the Latin *solidus*), and *d* for pence (from the Latin *denarius*). Other abbreviations and peculiarities can lead to confusion. In monetary sums recorded in Henslowe's *Diary*, for example, the last *i* is printed as *j*, as in the figure "iiij s" (four shillings). Elizabethan spelling made no distinction between *i* and *j*, although they were pronounced differently.

In reproducing selections from sixteenth- and seventeenth-century printed texts, I have mostly used original editions (or microfilm copies of them) as copy text. All quotations from Shakespeare, unless otherwise noted, are taken from *The Riverside Shakespeare* (1974), edited by G. Blakemore Evans.

Contents

—✦—

151-2
162-66

→ CHAPTER 2
Performances, Playhouses, and Players   *40*

➔ CHAPTER 5
Theater à la Mode: Shakespeare and the Kinds of Drama   151

➔ CHAPTER 6
"To What End Are All These Words?": Shakespeare's Dramatic Language   180

→ CHAPTER 7
Town and Country: Life in Shakespeare's England   221

The Bedford Companion to Shakespeare

to Shakespeare

An Introduction with Documents

Introduction

><-

From the time Shakespeare's plays first began to appear, they have not only attracted people to the theater but also led many to want to read the texts. Many of the plays were printed during the dramatist's lifetime, some more than once, and seven years after Shakespeare's death his theatrical colleagues published a nearly complete collection of his plays in one volume, the book we know as the First Folio of 1623. For the better part of the next three centuries, people continued to attend performances or read Shakespeare for pleasure (privately and in groups), and many literate households owned editions of his works. But Shakespeare became a subject of academic study in Britain and America only at the end of the nineteenth century, when English literature was established as a discipline and British and American poetry, fiction, and drama began to displace classical literature written in Greek and Latin. The works of William Shakespeare were quickly and properly installed at the center of the canon of literature written in English, and they still occupy this prominent position, whatever additions and modifications the canon may have undergone. More people are studying William Shakespeare today than at any other point in the last four hundred years.

Shakespeare in Our Time

The rapid expansion of the Anglo-American college and university system after the Second World War introduced millions of new students to Shakespeare's plays, but methods of study have undergone important changes in the past fifty years, and these developments help to account for the publication of the book you are now reading. In the 1950s and 1960s, Shakespeare study was dominated by a style of literary analysis called new criticism, which focused on the verbal details of poetry, drama, and prose fiction. Close reading of the Shakespearean passage has by no means been abandoned, but the past two decades have seen an adjustment in the relative importance of literary text and historical context. According to recent thinking, the cultural forces to which any Renaissance writer was inevitably subject demand greater notice: civic, court, and international politics; religious controversy; economic prosperity or depression; scientific discoveries; fashions in clothing, architecture, furniture, gardening, and music; tensions among social and economic classes; developments in legal practice; changes in literary taste; and the effects of plague and weather, to name some of the most powerful determinants. This broader concept of literary study is sometimes referred to as new historicism, or cultural poetics. But whether we accept such labels or not, critics today are reluctant to think of the play or poem as a verbal icon and thus to regard the culture from which it emerged merely as background, a niche in which to display the literary object. Although Shakespeare the author has scarcely disappeared, he now looks less like a free agent.

The complex process of artistic production and response also entails the conditions of another culture, however—that of the respondent. What we call "Shakespeare" is an artistic phenomenon resulting from an interaction between an early modern playwright's words and the environment in which they are heard or read. The performance of *Hamlet* that Shakespeare's original audience witnessed, with Richard Burbage playing the Prince of Denmark on the open stage of the Globe Playhouse in the suburbs of Elizabethan London, is a very different phenomenon from the performance that New Yorkers are seeing (as these words are being written) inside the Belasco Theater with Ralph Fiennes in the title role. The branch of study known as performance criticism has recently begun to explore the assumptions and decisions that inform every production of a Shakespeare play. Yet another proof of the dynamic relation between the literary object and those who receive it appears in the unprecedented growth of feminist criticism. Twenty-five years ago such a critical school scarcely existed, and certainly not by that name. Now it is without question one of the most influential modes of Shakespeare study. In the words of Jeanne Addison Roberts, "One of the most beneficial effects of feminism is that it has given us a new Shakespeare." But what does this mean, to possess a "new" Shakespeare? What happened to the old one? And how many are there?

Recognition that who we are determines what Shakespeare is need not imply critical chaos nor generate undue anxiety in the student who comes to study him for the first time. We have the texts, problematic though they may be, of thirty-four plays that Shakespeare seems to have written alone, of three or four others on which he probably collaborated, and of 154 sonnets, two narrative poems, and a handful of lyrics. These furnish a practically inexhaustible source of study, discovery, and pleasure. But how are they to be approached?

As literary artifacts? theatrical scripts? dramatic poems? documents in English political history? records of a power struggle among social classes? depictions of ongoing gender conflicts? archival evidence in the history of ideas? The answer to all these questions is "yes." Every critic, every instructor, every student will address the texts differently, and that is as it should be. But the most successful encounter with Shakespeare's works occurs when the person confronting them is well informed about the texts, their creator, and the culture from which they arose.

The Uses of a Companion

This book is designed to supply information, ideas, and contextual material that will promote such a productive encounter. Its nine chapters cover three general areas. The first (Chapters 1–3) introduces the writer and his career by surveying the facts about Shakespeare's life, the theatrical world he inhabited, and the physical process by which his plays moved from pen to stage to print. The second section (Chapters 4–6) takes up literary matters. It considers a few of the books Shakespeare read and their influence on his choice of theatrical subjects and stories; the dramatic modes of comedy, history, tragedy, tragicomedy, and romance that he inherited and reshaped; and some of the features of early modern English and Shakespeare's distinctive use of it. The last section (Chapters 7–9) expands the scope, offering a broadly sketched picture of the cultural milieu of which Shakespeare was a product and which he helped to produce. These last chapters provide details of daily life in early modern England; information about marriage customs, the family unit, and larger social communities; and, finally, a glance at the political players and ideological issues that concerned the subjects of Queen Elizabeth and King James.

Each of these chapters is inevitably incomplete. The topics treated in each of the early ones have been the subject of a number of excellent books. For the later chapters, on early modern social and political life, the issues are so vast and complex that they have inspired shelves of books. Readers are encouraged to seek additional information and opinions, and the supplementary bibliography at the end of the book is designed to promote further investigation. On the subject of Shakespeare's biography, for example, Samuel Schoenbaum's excellent *William Shakespeare: A Documentary Life* can supply further details and fill in gaps that result from the spatial limitations of this book. Also inevitably, each chapter is partial in its presentation of the topic, reflecting my personal sense of those facts and ideas most relevant to Shakespeare study at the end of the twentieth century. My own bias is toward Shakespeare as artist, a predisposition that prizes language and its arrangement into patterns, but I attempt to keep it from eclipsing other topics and approaches. Occasionally, as with the authorship controversy, contrary views are deliberately included within the chapter discussions. And the primary documents at the end of each chapter make available a wealth of material on a broad range of issues.

The Illustrations and Documents

This book is distinguished chiefly by its presentation of illustrations and documents, so a word is in order about what they are, how they were selected, and how they might best be used. Simply speaking, the documentary materials are meant to illustrate or clarify the topics discussed within each chapter. To take an example from the first chapter: in a paragraph on the fortunes of the house in which William Shakespeare was born, the reader is parenthetically directed to page 29, where the first illustration is an eighteenth-century drawing of that structure. For a different kind of example, Chapter 7 contains a brief discussion of Elizabethan clothing (pp. 233–35) that sends the reader to the last document in the chapter, an excerpt from William Harrison's *Description of England* of 1587, in which the Elizabethan commentator surveys what Londoners are wearing and remarks acidly on the follies of fashion.

Most chapters offer several types of documentary material, from illustrations and maps to facsimiles of pages from early modern texts to excerpts from pertinent books and records. The nature of the accompanying material depends to a great extent on the subject of the chapter. Chapter 3, for instance, which outlines the transmission of the text from Shakespeare's manuscript to a stage version to a printed copy to a modern edition, is followed by several photographs of pages from quarto versions and from the 1623 Folio. As the subject of inquiry widens to social and political issues, the primary materials become more discursive. Chapter 9, "Politics and Religion: Early Modern Ideologies," presents a passage from the early modern political theorist Sir Thomas Smith, a generous excerpt from *An Homily against Disobedience and Willful Rebellion*, a letter and parts of a speech and treatise by King James I, a section of an inflammatory Puritan pamphlet addressed to Parliament, and other such polemical writing.

Most of this material is well known to the specialist, and some of it familiar even to the beginning student of Shakespeare. A few illustrations, such as the copy of Johannes de Witt's drawing of the Swan Playhouse or the title page of the 1623 Folio, are reproduced everywhere. The frequency with which such items reappear in studies of Shakespeare attests to their explanatory value, and it would have been perverse not to provide them. Certain selections are quite new, such as the photograph of the foundations of the Rose Playhouse, unearthed in 1989. Many of the documents exist in modern editions but are not immediately accessible to the student. Examples of this type include the excerpts from Edward Hall and Raphael Holinshed, on which Shakespeare based his history plays, and the passage from a translation of the Scriptures that Shakespeare would have known, the Geneva Bible of 1560. A few of the documents, such as William Gouge's *Of Domesti-*

cal Duties: Eight Treatises, a Jacobean marriage manual with a decidedly Christian, patriarchal slant, have rarely been reprinted since the seventeenth century.

It is difficult to articulate a single criterion for the selection of primary materials. In considering what to include, I sought, and usually took, advice from specialists in each of the nine major areas treated here, although in no case was it possible to print all the materials recommended. In general my goal has been to negotiate a middle way between the obvious and the arcane. Certain documents—such as the list of theatrical costumes from Henslowe's papers—have been chosen to illuminate topics treated in the chapter; others—such as John Foxe's compelling report of the execution of two Protestant martyrs—are included because the interest of the narrative far outweighs the document's relevance to the specific concerns of the chapter. The doubts and complaints about the documentary materials that will arise in some readers' minds are probably just: it may be objected that the excerpts and illustrations are idiosyncratically chosen, that there are too few of them, and that the few selected are too brief. In response, I would plead the limitations of space and reply that the book contains almost a hundred items offering an imaginative thoroughfare into Shakespeare's world. It is doubtful that any two experts could agree on an ideal list. Instead, this is one scholar-teacher's idea of what would be helpful.

That said, however, this selector would still urge the student confronting these chunks of early modern thought and experience to be cautious. In the first place, the materials reproduced in this book offer a selective and minuscule sampling, the tip of the tip of the iceberg. We have inherited a partial and perhaps unrepresentative view of life in sixteenth- and seventeenth-century England, a view shaped and colored by what has come down to us in written form. Moreover, the surviving legacy was originally determined by what was printed and sold during the period, or by what was deemed worthy of preservation. For example, royal documents are more likely to have survived than a tailor's daily account books.

Second, much of the material available to us, notably political writing and handbooks on conduct, must be approached warily because of its prescriptive character. In other words, the claims of these various writers must not be taken as gospel. Many of the documents are presented not as proof of how things were in the period, but as expressions of how certain people thought things ought to be. One of the clearest instances of this difference would be James I's speech to Parliament in 1610 on the role of the monarchy. In that oration the king proclaims the divine basis of royal authority, but the modern reader must not therefore assume that such a position was universally accepted. Quite the opposite. That the speech was given at all implies considerable resistance to the monarch's argument, and independent sources confirm the strength of such tensions between James and Parliament in just those years. In other words, every document must be examined with a question about its context and its conditionality. Even the maps and illustrations, which would seem to be safe enough, are potentially misleading: the copy of the de Witt drawing of the Swan may have been the worst of ten such sketches from the period, but because this is the one that has survived, we have latched onto it.

With these provisos in mind, the reader may elect to use the chapter discussions and documents in several ways. As indicated, the chapters have been arranged in a pattern moving from the specific to the general, from Shakespeare's life through his working habits to the culture he inhabited. They need not be studied in this order, of course. In fact, the nine chapters might with equal profit be approached in reverse, so that acquaintance with early modern ideology and society precedes and prepares the reader for study of Shakespeare's place in that milieu. Since most of the documents and illustrations have been chosen to accompany information or clarify concepts discussed in the chapters, readers will find their understanding enhanced if they refer, as directed in the text, to the appropriate item at the end of the chapter.

Some of the primary materials can be employed independently of the chapters to which they are attached. To mention the most obvious of possibilities, many of the excerpts from Shakespeare's sources—Hall, Holinshed, Cinthio, and Strachey, for example—might serve as the basis for class discussion or as the starting point for an essay about the particular plays deriving from the sources. But more general uses present themselves as well: *An Homily of the State of Matrimony,* for instance, or the advice on prudence and passion given in Whetstone's *Heptameron of Civil Discourses* might be studied in conjunction with the representation of marriage in many of the comedies (most obviously *The Taming of the Shrew*) and some of the tragedies as well. The excerpt from Filmer's *Patriarcha* may be employed to illuminate the conflicts in *As You Like It, King Lear,* and other plays. Or the selections in Chapters 7 through 9 might be read on their own as a kind of crash course in early modern English history.

Examining these documents alongside Shakespeare's plays, students may begin to wonder about the nature of influence. Throughout the nineteenth century and well into the twentieth, scholars spent considerable energy identifying and scrutinizing texts that Shakespeare must have read and relied on in the creation of his dramas and poems. Chapter 4 makes use of much of this labor, and the documents that follow afford a glimpse of some of the major sources. Recently, however, scholarship has come to adopt a more relaxed understanding of influence, first recognizing that an author need not have read a particular text to be familiar with its ideas, and, second, that the existence of such a book means that the author's audience would have been aware, either directly or indirectly, of its contents. Gouge's marriage pamphlet, for example, was published after Shakespeare's retirement, but its treatment of the theory, history, and practice of matrimony records what a substantial portion of Shakespeare's contemporaries thought about such issues. Thus it furnishes us with a set of opinions (and, implicitly, contrary ideas) that were circulating in Shakespeare's culture and that audiences would have brought with them to performances of such marriage plays as *Much Ado about Nothing* or *Othello.*

Three Troublesome Topics:
Terminology, Modernization, and Money

A comment about terminology. The period under scrutiny, the end of the sixteenth and beginning of the seventeenth century, goes by at least two names, the traditional *Renaissance* and the more recent *early modern*. Those who prefer the second name believe that *Renaissance* privileges the period unfairly by endorsing the notion of "awakening" and thus implying an unwarranted superiority to the preceding "dark ages." Partisans of the term *Renaissance* sometimes claim that to speak of early modern England is to appropriate for our own purposes a period of history distinct and in significant ways alien from our own. It is probably fair to say that *Renaissance* looks to the past, since it acknowledges the rebirth of classical learning in sixteenth-century England, whereas *early modern* looks forward, locating there the origins of capitalism and other forms of modernity. To my way of thinking, each term has its virtues and its limitations, and so this book uses both (as well as the more specific Tudor, Elizabethan, Jacobean, and Stuart). I have tried to employ each as context would seem to dictate: hence, *Renaissance* tends to dominate at the beginning of the book, where literary matters are central, while *early modern* becomes more frequent as attention shifts to social and political institutions.

I have also avoided a slavish consistency in modernizing the form of primary materials. Most of the texts are presented here using modern American spelling and punctuation. Chief among the many reasons for this choice is that, since comprehension of an argument or narrative is of paramount importance for most of the documents, modernized spelling makes the passage easier to read, understand, and remember. Not to modernize would be to estrange the reader from the text unnecessarily, and in the wrong ways. One wants to preserve the historical strangeness of the ideas being presented, and retention of old spelling would make the distinctiveness of those ideas harder to see, not easier. Moreover, original spelling interposes a screen between the modern reader and the historical text that Shakespeare's contemporaries would not have had to look through. The sixteenth-century reader's eye processed the original spelling as automatically as a modern eye does modern spelling. Looked at in this way, the decision to modernize constitutes a paradoxical form of historicism. Another determinant is that virtually everyone today reads Shakespeare's plays in modern-spelling editions. Thus, not to modernize collateral documents would be to make Shakespeare seem more accessible and familiar than his contemporaries, more like us than like them, and that would be a falsification. In a very few cases, with short passages or documents of a particular kind—the list of costumes belonging to the Lord Admiral's Men, for example—the original spelling has been preserved to expose the reader to the conventions of early modern spelling and punctuation, especially their fluidity and inconsistency. Glosses of potentially unfamiliar words appear in brackets in the text; footnotes, it was felt, would be disruptive (although a few footnotes are included for definitions that extend beyond a word or two).

A final vexing question concerns money and how to think about it. Readers of the following chapters will occasionally come across a monetary figure and wonder what it means. They should probably not seek to translate the amount into modern terms, since the number of variables involved makes it virtually impossible to provide equivalents for what things cost in Shakespeare's day. Even though records of prices survive, they are misleading. In the first place, most people didn't purchase many of the same commodities we buy, such as loaves of bread, which were baked at home, or fruits and vegetables, which came from people's gardens. Second, technology has altered the cost of making and distributing other necessities, and thus has changed their value in relation to other articles: suits of clothing, those not made at home, were exceedingly expensive to purchase because they were not available off the rack but tailored individually. Third, the cash economy was much more thoroughly developed in London than in villages or the countryside, where shops were scarce and a system of barter and exchange was widespread. Finally, the changes in value brought on by inflation, which was especially fierce toward the end of the sixteenth century, practically defeat any effort to contextualize prices and wages in any given year. Instead of seeking modern equivalents, we will do better to compare the price of a given item with the cost of other commodities and services at roughly the same time. This topic is treated at greater length in Chapter 7, where some such equivalents can be found.

A Final Word

Shakespeare has continued to sell—in bookstores, theaters, and schools. His appeal seems in no danger of diminishing, but as the world changes, readers need more help comprehending certain features of his work and his culture. This book was conceived as a tool for reuniting text and context, for bringing the work of art into closer proximity with its formative conditions. *The Bedford Companion* will have served its purpose if the reader is able to connect the words, characters, actions, and ideas of Shakespeare's texts with the political institutions, social practices, theatrical milieu, discursive habits, literary scene, and printing process that contributed to their creation. It reflects some of the changes in recent thought described at the beginning of this introduction, specifically the return of historical criticism, because its assemblage of documents permits the reader to situate the text culturally. But it also seeks, even while admitting the inescapable connection between scholarship and the era that produced it, to avoid a single critical dogma or agenda. This book does not survey the major schools of critical thought; such guides are available elsewhere. Nor is there a section on stage history and performance beyond the Renaissance, as the emphasis here is on Shakespeare in his own age. Those who wish to know about such matters will find assistance in the bibliography. Most of the time, and insofar as possible, I leave the task of literary interpretation to the reader.

Having argued that people study Shakespeare in multiple ways and for a variety of reasons at different times, I would qualify that claim by suggesting the presence of a constant factor in human responses to the plays: the pleasure his works afford. To be sure, the conditions of reception determine the kinds of satisfaction—aural, intellectual, theatrical, social, economic. But usually people study Shakespeare because they like to. The main purpose of this book is to amplify those pleasures. When I first went to England as a student, I spent a weekend in Oxford and then hitched a ride to Stratford-upon-Avon for the day. After attending a performance at the Royal Shakespeare Theatre, I found myself unwilling to leave the town, and so I stayed for a week, going to every play in the repertory, and to some more than once. They were the most beautiful things I had ever seen. This book is one product of a lifelong effort to remain in Shakespeare's world and to entice others into it.

CHAPTER I

Shakespeare, "Shakespeare," and the Problem of Authorship

———————————————— ›‹ ————————————————

The playwright William Shakespeare was born in Stratford-upon-Avon, a market town about a hundred miles northwest of London, in April 1564. A Tudor building that stands today in Henley Street is shown to millions of visitors as the house in which the playwright was born, and that building (illustrated on p. 29) may serve as an emblem for the problems of Shakespearean biography. In structure and appearance it seems to be Elizabethan, and parts of it may even be original, but the house is substantially different from the way it was in the middle of the sixteenth century. Originally there were two buildings, an eastern and a western structure, that John Shakespeare, the playwright's father, purchased at different times and that have since been joined to make the present one. In 1552 there was a midden heap outside the house, an illegal garbage dump for which the authorities levied a fine. Part of the ground floor housed the leather business in which John Shakespeare was engaged. The playwright inherited the buildings upon the death of his father and may have rented the eastern structure as a coaching inn. In the eighteenth century, as Shakespeare's reputation grew, a birth room was identified and efforts were made to save and memorialize the building. Now the house is a primary exhibit in the tourist industry that has come to dominate life in Stratford. In Shakespeare's day there was no gift shop. Even mildly skeptical visitors will find themselves wondering about the authenticity of "the birthplace" and about how faithfully modern appearances are able to convey historical truth.

So it is with the story of William Shakespeare's life. The narrative that most of us know bears some resemblance to the facts, but myths and distortions have accumulated over the centuries, and the uneasy mixture of fact and legend has prompted contradictory reactions to the problem of Shakespearean biography. On the one hand, many people still relish and repeat the colorful, sentimental tales that originated in the hundred years or so following Shakespeare's death—that he delivered rousing speeches while helping his father butcher animals; that he left Stratford a fugitive after being caught poaching deer at Charlecote, the nearby estate of Sir Thomas Lucy; that he got his start in the London theaters taking care of the horses of gentlemen who arrived for performances—in other words, he served as a kind of parking attendant—and then joined the company and became its principal playwright. On the other hand, the spuriousness of many of these tales has led some people to dismiss not only the myths but also the facts that scholars have carefully and certainly established about Shakespeare's life in London and Stratford. A further product of this skepticism has been the urge to propose more suitable candidates for authorship of the works traditionally assigned to Shakespeare.

Both of these extreme positions, sentimental credulity and radical disbelief, are mistaken. We do not know as much as we would like about William Shakespeare the man, but we do know much, and what we know makes a convincing case for a glover's son from a small town in Warwickshire going to London in his young manhood, finding his way into the theatrical world by acting and writing, and producing the plays and poems that have captured the imagination of the world. This chapter will offer a brief survey of Shakespeare's life, seeking to separate fact from fiction and, insofar as possible, to give a human face to the celebrated figure from the distant past and a different culture. This much might have been done fifty years ago. Two recent developments demand further consideration, however. In the past few years the proponents of the earl of Oxford as the author of Shakespeare's plays have been pressing their claims with unusual volume, and thus the legitimacy of that case needs to be examined. Second, recent literary theory has begun to reshape our sense of authorship: we have been reminded that works of art are the products not merely of an individual writer's genius but also of the culture that produced that writer. This principle is especially pertinent to that author of authors who made his name in the Elizabethan theater, where more than in most artistic arenas the final product was the result of a collaborative process involving writers, copyists, actors, censors, audiences, and printers. We need to do as much as possible to learn the facts about William Shakespeare's life, but finally the life is less important than the work.

Early Life

William Shakespeare was born to Mary and John Shakespeare in April 1564, their third child and first son. The infant was baptized on April 26, and since by ecclesiastical order the sacrament had to be performed within a few days of birth, his birthday has traditionally been assigned to April 23. Already we have entered the realm of myth and sentiment: April 23 is St. George's Day, the date given over to celebration of England's patron saint and therefore appropriate for the birth of England's greatest poet; April 23 is also the date of Shakespeare's death fifty-two years later, and so it offers tempting symmetry.

That the precise hour and day of Shakespeare's birth are unknown is insignif-
icant compared to the relative abundance of detail that survives about his family, thanks to town records and the parish register of Holy Trinity Church: we
know that he was probably born in late April 1564 because he was baptized on
Wednesday the 26th, as indicated in the church record reproduced on page 30;
that his parents were John and Mary Shakespeare of Stratford; that he grew
up with four younger siblings, brothers named Gilbert, Edmund, and
Richard, and a sister named Joan; that three other sisters, two older and one
younger than he, died in infancy or youth;[1] and that the family lived in the
house in Henley Street throughout Shakespeare's boyhood. The historical
records of the town itself are relatively full as well. Stratford had been a center
of trade since the twelfth century, when Richard I licensed its Thursday market, and the basic street plan, depicted in the eighteenth-century map on
page 31, was laid out in medieval times and has not changed much.

John Shakespeare, having moved to Stratford from a nearby village and
found a wife, Mary Arden, in another neighboring village, became a prominent
citizen of the town. Turning his back on the agricultural pursuits of his own
family, he became a glover, or *whittawer*, one who treated the hides of animals
and made and sold soft leather goods such as gloves, belts, and purses. He
quickly became involved in town government, serving in several responsible positions, ranging from ale-taster (an officer who ascertained that loaves of bread
weighed what they were supposed to and that ale was up to standard) to constable to burgess to alderman and finally to bailiff, the small-town equivalent of
mayor. When William was about twelve years old, John Shakespeare's fortunes
began to decline: he failed to attend town council meetings, began to sell property apparently to raise cash, was fined for failing to make a court appearance,
was replaced as alderman in 1586 for shirking his responsibility, and in 1592 was
reprimanded "for not comminge monethlie to the churche . . . [i]t is sayd . . . for
feare of processe for debtte" (qtd. in Halliday 442). Some scholars attribute these
absences to recusancy, a religiously motivated unwillingness to conform to the
practices of the Church of England: there is some slight evidence that John
Shakespeare and his family may have held Catholic sympathies, as did many
English people less than half a century after Henry VIII's break with Rome.
Financially and socially, things improved at the very end of his life, perhaps as a
result of his son's professional success in London. In 1596 the playwright
petitioned for and was granted a family coat of arms, apparently on behalf of his
father, whose application had been denied some years earlier, and in 1601, the
year of his death, John Shakespeare again occupied a place on the town council.
The story of Shakespeare's parents is representative of many small-town tradesmen in the sixteenth century—success in business, modest social prominence,
and public service. In this case the fruits of hard work were imperiled by adversity, but in the end balance was restored. Their eldest son would achieve even

---

[1] The Shakespeares' first child, Joan, died sometime between her birth in 1558 and the christening of her
sister, also named Joan, in 1569; the second, Margaret, died in infancy in 1562; and the last, Anne, died
at age seven in 1579.

greater financial success and social prominence, but the means to those ends lay in London, where he ventured probably in his mid-twenties.

Shakespeare's youth in Stratford requires a good deal of speculation, since much biographical information from the period is based on legal records in which children were not mentioned. But it is fairly safe speculation, given what we know of his family. As the son of a prominent citizen, he probably attended the Stratford grammar school, an institution established for the male offspring of just such people; sons of burgesses attended free. There he would have learned Latin and begun a rigorous course of reading in the great Roman authors.[2] We may assume that he attended church. Even if the Shakespeare family were secretly loyal to Rome, they apparently adhered to the law and conformed to Anglican practice (perhaps excepting John Shakespeare's 1592 lapse mentioned earlier). We may also conclude that, at least in some small way, Shakespeare helped his father in his business and developed an acquaintance with the agricultural and mercantile practices of the region in which he spent his first twenty years.

As Shakespeare comes of age, the record becomes more ample. In November 1582 the young man married the not-so-young Anne Hathaway, eight years older than her eighteen-year-old groom and three months pregnant at the wedding. In May of the next year, their daughter Susanna was christened, followed in 1585 by twins named Hamnet and Judith. Most biographers thus assume that Shakespeare resided in Stratford through his twenty-second year. Concerning the next seven years, until Shakespeare surfaced in London in 1592, the record is virtually silent; this is the period known to biographers as "the Lost Years." Theories abound as to what the young man might have been doing during this phase. The tale that he fled town to escape punishment for poaching was first mentioned nearly a century after his death. It is possible that he joined a troupe of players touring the provinces and thus made his way into the margins of the theatrical world centered in London. One of the earliest biographers (John Aubrey) reports that Shakespeare "had been in his younger years a schoolmaster in the country"; one of the latest (E. A. J. Honigmann) claims to have identified the Catholic family in Lancashire who employed the teenaged Shakespeare. There is scant documentary evidence to support any of these stories, and that which does exist is open to dispute. Wherever he went upon leaving Stratford, he must have arrived in London toward the end of the 1580s, just as the public theaters were beginning to flourish.

London: The First Decade

That Shakespeare is mentioned in 1592 as a presence to be reckoned with on the London theatrical scene indicates that he had been active there for some

---

[2]See Chapter 6 for more on Shakespeare's education.

time. This first reference—a dig at a newcomer—seems to derive from professional jealousy. Robert Greene was a university-educated rake, pamphleteer, and playwright who obliquely attacked Shakespeare in a piece written just before Greene's death:

> [F]or there is an upstart Crow, beautified with our feathers, that with his *Tygers hart wrapt in a Players hyde,* supposes he is as well able to bombast out a blanke verse as the best of you: and beeing an absolute *Iohannes fac totum,* is in his owne conceit the onely Shake-scene in a countrey.

Scholars have made much of the images and allusions herein, some of their surmises probably justified, some of them probably not. That the "upstart Crow" implies a novice or parvenu seems obvious, but it may also refer to Shakespeare's lack of a university education; Greene was proud of his. The second phrase, "beautified with our feathers," has been taken to mean that Shakespeare the young actor depended on playwrights like Greene for his lines; it could also depict Shakespeare as the adapter or thief of others' plays and dramatic ideas. The charge of vicious hypocrisy is cloaked in a phrase twisted from Shakespeare's own *Henry VI, Part 3,* where York assails Queen Margaret as a "tiger's heart wrapp'd in a woman's hide." And Greene concludes with another jab at pretension, attacking a young theatrical jack-of-all-trades (*Iohannes fac totum*) who presumes to think himself an artist.

If Shakespeare had provoked envy by the early 1590s, he had also attracted favorable attention. In the same year as Greene's attack, another London writer, Thomas Nashe, referred to the uncommon success of the *Henry VI* plays, noting that tens of thousands of spectators had thrilled to the heroics of one of its characters. But success arrived in another guise as well. In 1593 Shakespeare first appeared in print with the narrative erotic poem *Venus and Adonis* dedicated to Henry Wriothesley, the third earl of Southampton. The nature of the relationship between poet and dedicatee is unclear: was it personal, or a conventional case of patronage? Whichever it was, the connection seems to have been durable and important, for a year later Southampton found himself the recipient of Shakespeare's second narrative poem, *The Rape of Lucrece.* The two poems may owe their existence to the outbreak of plague in 1593: the sixteenth-century London historian John Stow reports that almost 11,000 people died in London between December 1592 and December 1593—this in a city of 200,000 residents—and the proportions of the epidemic led to the closing of the theaters. Thus Shakespeare may have used the idle days away from the playhouse to seek more remunerative literary work. Eighteenth-century legend has it that Southampton gave Shakespeare a thousand pounds in recompense for the poems. Further, Southampton is sometimes identified with the comely young man of the sonnets, which Shakespeare may have begun to compose during this period of theatrical inactivity. Whatever the terms of the Southampton connection, it adds color and detail to our understanding of Shakespeare's extraordinary literary and social success.

The sequence of 154 sonnets divides into two groups, 1–126 and 127–54, and contains characters and implied narratives. In the first series, an older poet affectionately praises a beautiful young man, sometimes longingly, and urges him to marry. In the later group, the speaker confesses passion for and anguish at a mistress, a faithless "Dark Lady." If the earl of Southampton was not the young man of the first group of sonnets, who was? Who is the Dark Lady? Does the adjective *dark* refer to her hair color, her complexion, or her shady character? Who is the rival poet who makes an occasional entrance? When were the sonnets written? These primary questions are usually accompanied by others about the ordering of the poems, the circumstances of their publication, the sexual proclivities of the poet, and (above all) whether the implied narrative in the sequence represents poetically the lived experiences of actual persons. To some extent, of course, the sonnets must be a record of their creator's emotional biography, as is the case with every work of art by every artist; but when the amorous and sexual energies are as various and complex as those exhibited here, and when the poet is as celebrated as Shakespeare, the temptation to speculate, and even to assume a direct relationship between the work and the life, becomes nearly irresistible. However, scholarship (both historical and interpretive) has been notoriously unsuccessful in its attempts to solve the mysteries of the sonnets, and thus it seems prudent, given the limited space available here, to confine commentary to the place of these poems in Shakespeare's artistic output.

Although arguments about the dating of the poems are almost as numerous and contradictory as those about who is dating whom *in* the poems, most of the sonnets were probably written in the 1590s, as part of the Elizabethan vogue for sonneteering that reached its apogee in these years. English poets had been writing sonnets for decades, many of them in the style of the Italian poet Petrarch, but the publication of Sir Philip Sidney's sonnet sequence *Astrophil and Stella* in 1591 generated a rush of similar verse. (It might be added that the obvious historical identities of the characters in that collection have helped to encourage the inspection of Shakespeare's sonnets for similar evidence.) Shakespeare was to some extent following literary fashion, and presumably the closing of the theaters in the period 1592–94 gave him leisure for lyric as well as narrative verse. Whether or not the poems were written for publication, initially they circulated in manuscript: Francis Meres, a literary commentator writing in 1598, refers in his *Palladis Tamia* (see p. 32) to Shakespeare's "sugared sonnets among his private friends." Versions of two of the sonnets were printed in a poetry anthology of 1599; in 1609 the 154 that exist were published together, along with Shakespeare's short poem "A Lover's Complaint." Whether the poet authorized or oversaw the publication of the volume, we do not know. Whether he or someone else is responsible for the arrangement of the poems, we do not know. Whether the poet's sexual biography is relevant to the narrative in the sequence, we do not know. These questions are tantalizing, and it is vain to discourage speculation. But as compelling as the story of the sonnets seems to be, and as beautiful as the sonnets are as poems, Shakespeare was by trade a playwright. When the plague abated around May 1594, he returned to theatrical production.

The reopening of the theaters coincided with, and perhaps to some degree produced, a shuffling of personnel and leadership in the London acting companies. Scholars have been unable to ascertain which theatrical company (or companies) first employed Shakespeare as actor and playwright—the Queen's Men, Pembroke's Men, and Lord Strange's Men are frequently mentioned possibilities—but in 1594 he joined Richard Burbage and six other players to form a new company under the sponsorship of Henry Carey, Lord Hunsdon, who at that time served as lord chamberlain. The formation of this theatrical troupe occurred at the point when Shakespeare the playwright was attaining artistic maturity, and so 1594 ushered in a period of relative stability: with Burbage taking the leading roles and Shakespeare providing scripts such as *Richard II* (the first installment of what would become the great second cycle of English history plays), *A Midsummer Night's Dream*, and *Romeo and Juliet* in 1595–96, the company began playing regularly at the Theatre just north of the city walls, and within a few years became the most successful theatrical troupe in England. They began to appear at court, playing at Greenwich Palace (presumably for Queen Elizabeth herself) during the Christmas season of 1594 and eventually giving more royal performances than any other contemporary theatrical company.

"Stability," however, was as evanescent in the theater then as it is now. Two years later, in 1596, the actors experienced troubles with their lease when the owner of the land on which the Theatre stood got sticky about his terms, and the company was forced to find another playing space. This crisis ended happily, leading ultimately to the construction of the Globe and, after a series of complicated transactions, the acquisition of a second theater, the indoor Blackfriars. By the time James I came to the throne in 1603, Shakespeare's was unquestionably the premier English theatrical company, and the new king, hoping to associate his name with success, chose to patronize it, as the royal license (p. 33) indicates. Renamed the King's Men, the troupe continued to perform for almost four decades, surviving Shakespeare's death in 1616 and Burbage's in 1619; they succumbed finally, as did all such enterprises, to Parliament's closing the theaters in 1642. It is fair to say that Shakespeare's contribution as author helped to secure the prominence and endurance of the company.

The year 1594 also saw the first publication of a Shakespeare play, *Titus Andronicus*, although his name was not listed on the title page. Such neglect of the writer by the publisher was not uncommon unless the author was sufficiently well known to increase sales, which at this point Shakespeare apparently was not. Famous or no, playwrights rarely had much say in the publication of their plays, since the script legally belonged to the theatrical company that produced it.[3] What did sell books, apparently, was the record of performances: the title page of *Titus Andronicus* (reproduced on p. 92) advertises that "it was Plaide by the Right Honourable the Earle of Darbie, Earle of Pembrooke, and Earle of Sussex their Seruants." Similarly, five more

---

[3] Some of the complexities of the publication process will be clarified in Chapter 3, "What Is Your Text?"

of Shakespeare's plays were published over the next four years (*Romeo and Juliet* in two versions) without his name attached, although the names of the companies that performed them do appear. In 1598, with the quarto publication of *Love's Labor's Lost,* the title page attributes the work to Shakespeare, as is the case for most of the plays published subsequently (including some that he apparently did not write). By the end of the 1590s Shakespeare had written most of his history plays and many of his most popular comedies. Francis Meres, the critic who mentions the private circulation of the sonnets, compares him in the same passage to the Roman masters of comedy and tragedy, Plautus and Seneca, naming several of Shakespeare's comedies and histories, the two tragedies written so far, and the narrative poems. (See the excerpt from Meres's *Palladis Tamia* on p. 32.) By the turn of the seventeenth century Shakespeare had become the most successful playwright in London.

He had not broken his ties with his hometown, however, as various financial and other documents attest. His wife and children apparently remained in Stratford while he lived in London, and it seems likely that he made regular trips back and forth during the twenty years or so that he worked in the capital. The journey would have taken four days on foot, perhaps two on horseback. Shakespeare's only son, the twin Hamnet, died in August 1596. In that same year the College of Heralds granted the Shakespeares the coat of arms that had been denied John Shakespeare almost thirty years before. In May 1597 William Shakespeare purchased New Place, the second-largest house in Stratford; the spread also included two barns, two gardens, and two orchards. In London during the mid-1590s, he lived near Bishopsgate, fairly near the Theatre, where his company played; in 1600 he is known to have lived on the South Bank of the Thames River, probably as a result of the company's having built the Globe there in 1599; in 1604 he lodged with a French family, the Mountjoys, in Silver Street near St. Olave's Church. The map of London on page 34 indicates the exact location of the Mountjoy house.

Although his growing fame as a playwright made him a valuable asset to the company and he maintained his normal rate of production, writing an average of two plays each year, he also continued to perform, acting in Ben Jonson's *Every Man in his Humour* in 1598 and again in Jonson's *Sejanus* in 1603. He may have acted in other plays as well, although these are the only two in which surviving records indicate that he took a role. Given the familiar conception of Shakespeare the natural genius transcending the vicissitudes of the material world—as in Milton's description of "sweetest Shakespeare, fancy's child, / Warbl[ing] his native woodnotes-wild"—it is worth emphasizing the hands-on quality of his professional activity. He was actively engaged, as actor, shareholder, and supplier of scripts, in the financial affairs of the company. It is true that the nature of the documents that survive—court records, details of lawsuits, transfers of property—tends to highlight the commercial side of the man's life at the expense of the artistic. But in our rush to celebrate the art we have tended to slight the revelatory value of these mundane financial details: Shakespeare was a businessman as well as an artist.

London: Maturity

Shakespeare's growing prosperity is attributable not so much to his writing as to his status as a shareholder in the Lord Chamberlain's Men. When the Globe was erected from the timbers of the original Theatre in 1599, Shakespeare was listed as one of the ten "housekeepers," or shareowners. He is also recorded as one of the seven housekeepers of the indoor playhouse at Blackfriars in 1608, when the company obtained the right to use the building as a theater. (James Burbage, Richard's father, had acquired Blackfriars in 1596, perhaps out of concern for the difficulties with the landlord of the Theatre, but neighborhood protest prevented its theatrical use at that time.) If the investments in property that Shakespeare continued to make in Stratford are a reliable guide, his profit from these enterprises was handsome. He bought 127 acres of land in Old Stratford (a suburb of the town) for £320 in May 1602 and then a cottage opposite New Place later that same year; in 1605 he invested £440 in "a lease of tithes"—something like stock in an agricultural enterprise—for property in and around Stratford. Interestingly enough, although most biographers think he had by this time retired to Stratford, he purchased a house in London in 1612, near the theater in the Blackfriars district. Perhaps he was following the example of his colleague Richard Burbage, who had made similar investments, or it may be that he did not deem his theatrical career finished. Shakespeare kept a close eye on his account books, and during the last twenty years of his life, beginning with the purchase of New Place, there was a lot to count. To note these financial transactions and to acknowledge Shakespeare's keen business sense is not to discount his imaginative gifts and literary achievement. Rather, it is to modify the portrait of the otherworldly artist and to admit that art and commerce are often productive partners.

Around 1600, after a decade of writing mostly comedies and histories, Shakespeare changed artistic direction. Thus began the great tragic phase, starting with *Julius Caesar* in 1599 and *Hamlet* shortly thereafter and continuing through *Macbeth* in 1606 and *Antony and Cleopatra* and *Coriolanus* about 1607 or 1608. Although he continued to write comedies, the comic spirit informing the plays is noticeably altered. *All's Well That Ends Well* (c. 1603) and *Measure for Measure* (1604), although their endings are technically "happy," deal with problematic subjects: in the first case a young woman insists on marrying an immature, unworthy man who doesn't want her, and in the second a novice must defend herself against the sexual harassment of a corrupt civic official as she seeks to save her brother from being executed for fornication. These plays exhibit tonal ironies so bitter and representations of human activity so unflattering that at times it is difficult to remember that they are comedies. Another problematic play from these years, *Troilus and Cressida*, is even more difficult to classify. In its dark assessment of human experience and achievement it more nearly resembles *Othello* or *King Lear* than *Much Ado about Nothing* or *As You Like It*. And yet it is not clearly a tragedy either.

The impetus for this shift of direction remains one of the great mysteries of Shakespeare's career, for which various explanations have been offered. Psychological: Shakespeare the man experienced some kind of personal crisis brought on perhaps by the death of his son and his father or by some unrecorded emotional event. Practical: perhaps performances of tragedies drew audiences in greater numbers. Formal: Shakespeare had tired of writing the kinds of plays to which he had devoted the previous ten years and sought to experiment with the theatrical possibilities of tragedy. Literary: tragedy had long been considered the more important mode, superior to comedy in its themes and range. Cultural: Shakespeare's darkening vision reflects the increasing pessimism of his society about politics, economics, and the social structure. We are not likely to learn the actual reason for this artistic reversal, if there was only one, and even if we did, we would need a corresponding explanation for yet another change, the shift that occurs around 1608 and leads to the creation of the late romances. The Jacobean Shakespeare differs from the Elizabethan Shakespeare, but to seek the man in the work is to court frustration and uncertainty.

Shakespeare's second decade in the theater differed from the first in a number of meaningful ways. First, he enjoyed professional security, remaining with the company he had helped to found until his retirement from the theater and return to Stratford. Second, he became, practically speaking, an unofficial court dramatist. As principal playwright for the King's Men, Shakespeare saw much of his contemporary work performed for King James and the royal family—notably *Measure for Measure, Othello,* and *King Lear*—and many of the earlier plays that they would have missed before their arrival in London in 1603 were revived for court performance. *Macbeth* must have been written with James's experience and taste in mind: the Scottish king took pride in his legendary descent from the family of Banquo, had narrowly escaped assassination in the Gunpowder Plot of 1605 (when a group of radical Catholics planted explosives that would detonate at James's opening of Parliament), had published a treatise on witchcraft, and was known to like short plays, which *Macbeth* conspicuously is. Third, with the company's acquisition of a second theater in 1608, Shakespeare found himself writing not only for the usual spectators at the Globe but also for a more exclusive audience. The indoor house at Blackfriars, although frequently referred to as a "private theater" from the days when children's companies had performed there, was in fact as public as the Bankside amphitheaters. But it was smaller, the absence of natural light meant that performances could be held at night and lit by candles, and the admission price was higher. Thus Blackfriars is thought to have attracted a more aristocratic, fashionable crowd. Finally, Shakespeare's rate of productivity slowed down slightly, to about one play each year, perhaps an understandable consequence of his success and increasing age but probably also of reduced opportunities for playing. The plague had returned to London with a vengeance: between 1603 and 1610 the public theaters were closed almost as much as they were open. The authorities prohibited public gatherings when the number of deaths per week in London and its suburbs reached a certain level, usually forty but sometimes thirty or fifty. The reduction in business caused by the plague was perhaps counterbalanced by the increased receipts from two theaters instead of one, and certainly the payments for royal performances must also have helped offset losses. In any case, Shakespeare and his colleagues dominated the English theatrical scene, and by the end of his career in London he was rich and famous.

Exactly when the end of his London career came and why he elected to end it are difficult to determine. The turn to romance that occurred around 1608 needs to be assessed with the same restraint appropriate to the shift into tragedy. Despite the wishful claims of nineteenth-century Shakespeare worship, or bardolatry, Shakespeare's theatrical career does not conclude with a glorious, autobiographical farewell disguised as a play (*The Tempest*). He was experimenting up to the end, sometimes successfully, sometimes not. *Cymbeline*, for example, written about 1609–10, a year or two before *The Tempest* and probably before *The Winter's Tale*, is a fascinating, beautiful, and at times bizarre piece of work, for the dramatist was stretching himself in ways that critics and audiences have sometimes found baffling. And even if we could see the last plays as a progression of affirmative steps leading to the triumph of *The Tempest*, we would still have three texts to deal with, *Henry VIII*, *The Two Noble Kinsmen*, and *Cardenio* (this last one now lost). These unusual plays were written with John Fletcher, who was to be Shakespeare's successor as chief dramatist of the King's Men. Some believe that Shakespeare had retired to Stratford by about 1611 and composed his portions of these plays while living in retirement, and it could be that *The Tempest* or even earlier plays were written under such conditions. But we have few historical details to flesh out the bare skeleton of his final years as an artist.

Shakespeare's last years in the theater should probably be considered representative of his career as a whole. He did what a good professional might have been expected to do, what he had always done, inventing or at least developing new dramatic forms to suit his tastes and please audiences. This was an especially useful gift to a company needing to attract spectators to two theaters, and Shakespeare at the last, as at the first, was sensitive to the opportunities of theatrical space: the magical tone and effects of the late plays bespeak a deliberate effort to exploit the resources of the new indoor theater. Even on the verge of retirement he was still helping the company by collaborating with Fletcher. Whether this was a relationship of mentor to pupil or merely a practical arrangement is uncertain: Fletcher was hardly a novice, having had several successes with Francis Beaumont. Presumably Shakespeare's name on a play helped to bring in customers, although it may be that the younger Fletcher, developer of the new and fashionable tragicomedy, was by 1612 the greater draw. Businessman that he was, Shakespeare would have remained interested, in every sense, in the company's financial health.

Retirement

The available information about Shakespeare's last few years is mostly financial or legal. Presumably he lived at New Place with his wife and in proximity to his two daughters, one of them now married, and the other surviving members of his family. His mother died in 1608, seven years after his father; in 1612 and 1613 his brothers Gilbert and Richard were buried; his sister Joan lived in the western half of the Henley Street property. Although an enormous fire ravaged much of Stratford in July 1614, Shakespeare seems to have suffered no direct loss. A heated controversy over property occurred in that same summer, however, when two powerful landowners in town attempted to enclose a large meadow at Welcombe, just outside Stratford, a common area in which many citizens, Shakespeare among them, had a financial interest. Since the enclosure would apparently have converted farmland to pasture for grazing sheep, thus reducing employment, diminishing the tithe-profits of investors, and possibly increasing claims on civic charity, fierce resistance arose in the town council, with Thomas Greene, a kinsman of Shakespeare, leading the effort to block the project. The enclosers actually began to dig up the earth with the intent of planting hedges, but men, women, and children from the town came into the meadow with spades and set about to fill the ditches. Although Shakespeare's name is listed in several of the surviving documents, no one has been able to determine satisfactorily where he stood on the issue. Perhaps his sympathies were divided, or perhaps he was attempting to placate both parties by refusing to take a firm position. As often happens in such matters, the case lasted longer than some of the litigants. The Welcombe controversy made its way slowly through the legal system until it reached the king's chief justice, Sir Edward Coke, who denied the attempt to enclose; that was in April 1616, the same month and year that Shakespeare died.

The lack of solid information about Shakespeare's last years has left a gap that legend has been eager to fill. For example, the cause of Shakespeare's death is unknown, but John Ward, the vicar of Stratford in the mid–seventeenth century, supplies a tantalizing story of a party in which Shakespeare, drinking with his literary friends Ben Jonson and Michael Drayton, contracted a fever that led to his death. (In his play *Bingo,* the modern English playwright Edward Bond depicts an imagined version of this occasion, along with an unflattering view of Shakespeare's participation in the Welcombe enclosure dispute.) This anecdote, recorded in Ward's diary entry given on page 35, is typical of the ambiguous nature of biographical evidence: it occupies one sentence in a series of entries in a notebook; it is cryptic and medically questionable; and it is possibly true nonetheless. Although Ward was not born until twelve years after Shakespeare's death, he was well connected in Stratford, knew the playwright's daughter personally, and presumably was familiar with local gossip. We may wish to believe some version of this nearly contemporary story, but where do we draw the line between legend and fact?

In March 1616 Shakespeare seems to have known that his life was nearing its close because he sent for his attorney to alter his will, probably in reaction to his daughter Judith's recent marriage. (Shakespeare ensures that Judith's new husband, Thomas Quiney, does not take advantage of her for her portion. A man of dubious reputation, Quiney pleaded guilty to impregnating another woman not long before his marriage to Judith; a month after the wedding, the woman and infant died in childbirth.) The will, of which a transcription and a photograph are provided on pages 35–38, has occasioned much debate: eighteenth-century admirers of its author found the testament cold and unpoetic, and many have been disturbed by the one ambiguous reference to his wife, Anne. (He bequeaths her his "second best bed" and its linens.) The dry quality of the will's language need not trouble us, since many of the sentences were formulaic, standard legal wording supplied by the attorney and found in numerous similar documents. In *Shakespeare: A Biographical Handbook*, Gerald Eades Bentley persuasively contends that the will is typical of a comfortable landowner at the beginning of the seventeenth century (Bentley 61). The dying Shakespeare left remembrances and gifts to various relations, friends, and colleagues—his fellow actors were to receive money to buy memorial rings—but most of the estate devolved to his daughter Susanna and her husband, the local physician John Hall. His books would have gone to them and thus remained at New Place. Of Shakespeare's theatrical manuscripts there is no mention, but this is as it should be, since the plays belonged technically to the company that had produced them. In the eyes of the law, the handwritten manuscripts would have had no value.

We cannot be sure why Shakespeare did not provide specifically for his wife, and too little is known about local practice to be certain whether, as in some parts of England, she would have automatically inherited one-third of her husband's estate, the "widow's portion." The most plausible suggestion is that Anne Shakespeare, who in 1616 was about sixty years old, would naturally have remained a resident of New Place and would have been provided for by her inheriting daughter. But what about the "second best bed"? In this case, as Samuel Schoenbaum says pointedly, we have a "choice between cynicism and sentiment" (*William Shakespeare: A Compact Documentary Life* 304). Other contemporary wills refer to pieces of furniture in their order of value, specifically to second-best beds, and it may be that the second-best bed would have been the one shared by husband and wife, the best being reserved for guests. Yet the phrase does not seem entirely innocent. Across the gap of time, the legacy appears to have been either a kind of mordant joke hinting at marital difficulty or an affectionate sexual souvenir.

Shakespeare was buried where he was baptized, in Holy Trinity Church in Stratford, beneath a stone slab carved with the following verse:

Good Frend for Jesus Sake Forbeare,
To Digg the Dust Encloased Heare:
Bleste Be Y^e Man Y^t Spares Thes Stones,
And Curst Be He Y^t Moves My Bones.

The dead man's wishes have been respected: the tomb remains undisturbed in the chancel of the church, although the number of pilgrims walking across the grave led to such deterioration by the eighteenth century that the authorities had to replace the stone and inscription. Early in the seventeenth century a monument was erected, a painted bust of the poet done in the conventional funerary style, that has lasted to this day.

Seven years after his death, the book we know as the First Folio—its actual title is *Mr. William Shakespeares Comedies, Histories, & Tragedies*—was published in London. John Heminges and Henry Condell, two of the fellow actors remembered in the will with rings, assembled manuscripts and earlier published versions of Shakespeare's plays and arranged for them to be collected into a single printed volume containing thirty-six plays, half of them published for the first time. Although the book did not appear until 1623, the idea for such a volume must have arisen several years before, and the actual printing took more than a year. Heminges and Condell may have been inspired by the example of Ben Jonson, who in 1616 had published a folio volume consisting of his plays, masques, and poems, called *Workes*. As the compilers seem to have been aware, and as the prefatory verse contributed by Jonson himself enunciates, this book is Shakespeare's everlasting monument.

The Anti-Stratfordians

A question frequently asked by the general public is whether the works attributed to Shakespeare were in fact written by the man from Stratford. Such skepticism is fueled from time to time by those who cannot bring themselves to accept that a glover's son from a small provincial town could have written the plays, and who have spent a great deal of energy attempting to convince the world that the real author of the Shakespeare canon is someone else. Although a slew of nominees have been proposed over the last two centuries, from Christopher Marlowe to Queen Elizabeth, the favorites are Francis Bacon and Edward de Vere, earl of Oxford. What these two men have in common is their aristocratic status, and it is on this ground that the Baconians and Oxfordians usually stake their claim. (It is probably worth mentioning that, while both Bacon and de Vere were titled, de Vere's status was much higher than Bacon's. The latter was knighted in 1603 and much later became an earl, whereas de Vere, the descendant of an old and distinguished family, inherited the title of seventeenth earl of Oxford.) The doubters do not question the existence of William Shakespeare of Stratford, and some even acknowledge his participation in the London theatrical scene; but he is reckoned to be a front man for an aristocratic writer who would not permit his name to be linked to the popular theater.

The anti-Stratfordian argument is based in two areas: education and class, with the first being a less inflammatory version of the second. No one, it is said, could have attained the learning and sophistication required to write Shakespeare's comedies, histories, and tragedies without the benefit of a university education. In order to strengthen this contention, its proponents sometimes characterize William Shakespeare not only as lacking a university education but as actually illiterate. Since most Englishmen who attended universities in the sixteenth century were members of the nobility, the argument about education is in fact an argument about class. To some, it is intolerable to suppose that a person from the lower middle class—and from the country, at that—produced the works that are considered the pinnacle of Western literary achievement. Thus it is necessary to propose an aristocratic substitute as the author.

In the nineteenth century, Francis Bacon was the choice of the anti-Stratfordians as the true author of "Shakespeare's" plays. Far outstripping other pretenders, he even inspired the production of a journal, *Baconiana,* in which the plays were meticulously scrutinized for secret clues to Bacon's authorship. But recently Bacon's fortunes have waned while those of another candidate have waxed. Edward de Vere lived from 1550 to 1604, spent much of his time at the court of Elizabeth, wrote some poetry, associated with most of the major figures in politics and the arts, and in midcareer retired to the country with an annual pension from the Crown. His candidacy has benefited lately from the advocacy of one of his descendants, who has assumed direction of the Shakespeare-Oxford Society and devoted a great deal of time to polemics about the authorship question. Given this degree of attention, Oxford's candidacy may serve to represent the claims of all the pretenders and the conspiracy theories attached to them.

In brief, the Oxfordians propose that the plays exhibit such a detailed knowledge of court politics and of social practices at the highest echelons that their creator must have had firsthand knowledge of such a milieu. According to this view, a tradesman's son from the provinces could not have had access to such people and customs, and thus the plays' author must have been a courtier-poet such as de Vere. The accompanying postulate is that, given the rigid power structures of the Tudor court and the hypersensitivity of an aging monarch, the regime would never have permitted such an insider to take credit for dramas such as *Richard III, Richard II,* and *Love's Labor's Lost.* Whether or not they were deemed to comment on recognizable persons and events, the plays concern themselves with such sensitive issues as the abuse of royal power, political hypocrisy, courtly vanity, monarchical madness, and regicide. And since Elizabeth's watchful councillors would not have tolerated potentially negative representations of royal concerns, two stratagems were employed. First, all traces of aristocratic origins and connections were expunged from the plays and poems so as to maintain the fiction of humble authorship, a task accomplished by the supreme authority of Elizabeth's chief ministers, the Cecil family. Second, a decoy, a beard, was required to play the role of playwright: enter William Shakespeare of Stratford.

This is hardly the place for a lengthy refutation of the Oxfordian or Baconian position, but some instances of stretched logic and special pleading ought to be noticed. To begin with, the doubts about Shakespeare's education are hardly decisive. Although the Stratford archives do not supply us with William Shakespeare's report card, we may be reasonably sure that, as the son of a town burgess, he attended the local school and earned over some ten years a thorough grounding in Latin grammar and literature. He received the kind of classical education, in short, that would have given him a taste for fiction, history, and poetry, and would have stimulated and enabled him to continue his education on his own. Moreover, English literature is replete with examples of young people from modest beginnings who had no university training but who made distinguished contributions to literature. In fact, Shakespeare's contemporary Ben Jonson did not attend a university but, diligently building on his excellent grammar school education, became one of the most learned and creative figures of his age.

Since Oxford died in 1604, there are chronological bars to his candidacy. The historical record indicates that *Macbeth* and *The Tempest* were written circa 1606 and 1611, respectively, and more important, they depend explicitly on events that occurred after Oxford's death, notably the Gunpowder Plot of 1605 and the circulation in 1610 of pamphlets about the New World. Many other obstacles present themselves, such as books that Oxford could not have known before his death but that indisputably served as sources for the plays.

Perhaps the most damning refutation of the various pretenders' claims is the ingenuity needed to demonstrate that the real author has secretly encoded his name in various Shakespearean works and that such signals can be revealed only through complicated cryptographic schemes. As recently as 1987 an attorney named Penn Leary published a book called *The Cryptographic Shakespeare: A Monograph Wherein the Poems and Plays Attributed to William Shakespeare Are Proven to Contain the Enciphered Name of the Concealed Author, Francis Bacon.* And, as the excerpt on page 39 discloses, the earl of Oxford's supporters are hardly less fanciful, finding "E-d-w-a-r-d d-e V-e-r-e" peppered among the sonnets, the poems, and even the prefatory "To the Reader" that begins the First Folio.

The strongest case against Oxford or Bacon or Marlowe or anyone, however, arises not from a barrage of negative arguments but rather from the positive evidence placing William Shakespeare of Stratford in London between 1592 and 1612, connecting him to the theatrical scene there (specifically his membership in the King's Men), and identifying him with the published texts that derived from public performances and that bear his name.

What Is an Author?

The authorship question has taken a new turn in the past two decades owing to changes in theory and criticism that have affected the study of literature. Scholars and critics have challenged the romantic image of the artist as an individual and transcendent genius and supplanted it with a broader, culturally based model of authorship. Much attention is given to the writer's social and institutional affiliations, a primary goal being to identify as specifically as possible the conditions and details of the writer's participation in a discursive community. In poststructuralist criticism, the earlier notion of authorial autonomy has yielded to a keen alertness to the embeddedness of dramatic texts in social, economic, and political structures. To some extent, the artist is a subject, inescapably responsive ("subjected") to the local forces of history, politics, and literature.

The work of Stephen Greenblatt and Louis Adrian Montrose, both writing under the influence of the French theorist Michel Foucault, has been especially influential in prompting revision of our comfortable notion of the imaginative master working in splendid isolation. As Greenblatt puts it, "There may be a moment in which a solitary individual puts words on a page, but it is by no means clear that this moment is the heart of the mystery and that everything else is to be stripped away and discarded. Moreover, the moment of inscription, on closer analysis, is itself a social moment" (*Shakespearean Negotiations* 4–5). In other words, the literary productions of a writer such as Shakespeare are conditioned and determined by historical and social forces that vastly complicate simple notions of authorship and artistic responsibility. Whereas earlier scholars sought to identify books that a writer might have known or to describe scientific debates or economic practices incorporated into a work, recent critics have relaxed the definition of artistic influence. Now major political figures or particular social practices are seen as contributing to the creation of the literary text whether any direct relation to that text can be demonstrated or not. Thus an author becomes something of a channel for a flood of cultural forces, and authorial control over the process of creation—the creator's *authority*—tends to be spread into the culture at large.

Montrose, for example, sees *A Midsummer Night's Dream*, a play celebrating within its fiction the royal marriage of Theseus and Hippolyta and perhaps performed as part of the celebration of an aristocratic wedding, as shaped to a large degree by the cultural presence of Elizabeth I.

> Whether or not Queen Elizabeth was present at the first performance of *A Midsummer Night's Dream*, her pervasive *cultural presence* was a condition of the play's imaginative possibility. This is not to imply that *A Midsummer Night's Dream* is merely an inert "product" of Elizabethan culture. The play is rather a new *production* in Elizabethan culture enlarging the dimensions of the cultural field and altering the lines of force within it. Thus, in the sense that the royal presence was itself represented within the play, it may be said that the play henceforth conditioned the imaginative possibility of the Queen.   (" 'Shaping Fantasies' " 62)

This reciprocity between the cultural field and the literary artifact is one of the primary tenets of what has come to be called new historicist analysis of early modern literature. Although the passage illustrates the new historicist concern with how dramatic texts work to change the culture that produced them, what is especially important for our purposes is Montrose's insistence on the dispersal of responsibility for the creation of the play. Thus, Queen Elizabeth, in one sense, participates in the authorship of *A Midsummer Night's Dream*. In the postmodern critical climate, the author of Shakespeare's plays is perceived to have a slightly lesser role in the process of literary creation than would have been true fifty years ago.

The diminution of individual agency in recent theory coincides with a fundamental truth about the stage, one that has always been recognized but that has assumed greater importance in recent years—the collaborative nature of the theatrical enterprise. In some ways the theater is the most socially embedded of all the arts, depending as it does upon a direct process of exchange between performer and spectator and thus subordinating the contribution of the writer. Moreover, Shakespeare's plays are the products of a complex process of creation, realization, and transmission. Even if we hold to the notion of the solitary artist scribbling in a garret, we must recognize that the script of *King Lear* as it was delivered to the company on the first day of rehearsals in the 1605–06 season may well be very different from the version that we confront when we sit down to read it in a modern edition. The text of the play probably underwent changes at several junctures: in the hands of the scribe who copied out the parts for the actors, in the company's progress from first rehearsal to public presentation, between the opening and subsequent performances or even revivals, in the making of a copy to send to the printer, and in the compositorial labor that finally produced the printed text. *King Lear* is a particularly telling example of the complex stages of production because there are two versions, one that appears in the Quarto of 1608 and another in the Folio of 1623, and the discrepancies between them have led scholars to detect an act of revision that further complicates the notion of an "authorized" text.

These theoretical and critical developments help to put the mysteries of biography in perspective. Finally it matters less who wrote the plays than that they were written and that we continue to admire and enjoy them. This is not to say, however, that our curiosity about literary creativity is illegitimate and the identity of the playwright irrelevant. We know that life informs art, and we continue to learn how that transaction occurs. In her fascinating psychological study *Shakespeare the Actor and the Purposes of Playing*, Meredith Skura proposes that William Shakespeare's experience as a performer—the familiar narcissism of the actor—forcefully influenced the forms and ideas of his dramas, particularly in the creation of such figures as Richard III and Iago. Finally, it is important to remember that the case is never entirely closed. Shakespearean biography has been painstakingly constructed from the most detailed and mundane forms of evidence, and while we should not expect astounding revelations—a signed note in Shakespeare's hand, turned up in a Warwickshire barn, claiming authorship of plays from *The Comedy of Errors* to *Cardenio*—it is possible that new discoveries will help to answer some of the questions that continue to tease us.

→ The House Known as Shakespeare's Birthplace   *c. 1762*

This drawing, from a watercolor by Richard Greene, depicts the house in Henley Street, Stratford-upon-Avon, in which Shakespeare's parents lived at the time of his birth. Despite alterations over the past four centuries, the house is still standing.

→ Record of Shakespeare's Baptism   *1564* ➤

This page from the baptismal record of Holy Trinity Church, Stratford-upon-Avon, shows the original notation of Shakespeare's baptism on April 26, 1564. The relevant phrase is in Latin: *Gulielmus filius Johannes Shakspere* (William son of John Shakspere). The "xxx" was added later to designate the famous name.

October 26	Ffrancisca filia Johannes Bromwych de addomchefton notch...
28	Elizabeth filia T Boyers
November 5	Agnes filia Stephani Burman
11	Thomas filius Guliehmi Smith
11	Agnes filia Thome Dirkes
17	Johanna filia Richardi Roberts
27	Richardus filius Rogeri Banister
December 1	Richardus filius Johannes Hemming
5	Gulielmus filius Gulielmi Hearing
7	Henricus filius Henrici ffeild
14	Rodolphus filius Richardi Castell
15	Antonius filius Gulielmi Braford
22	Johannes filius Thome Bayspes
24	Maria Rogeri Paxepoynte
Januari 5	Robertus filius Richardi Marden
5	Richardus filius Humfredy Pindar
9	Ffrancisca filia Johannes Stanley
13	Nicholaus filius Richardi Barbar de draxton
13	Helena filia Nicholai Cope
14	Johanna filia Roberti Archar
23	Elizabeth filia Thome Hunde
28	Richardus filius Johannes ffrey
30	Maria filia Davidis Cateby
30	Anna filia Henrici Wagftaff
Februari 2	Maria filia Gulielmi Bray
14	Gulielmus filius Rogeri Bull
23	Maria filia Rodolphi Cawdrey
23	Catarina filia Brandi Pixtrot
27	Maria filia Richardi Greenway
28	Agnes filia Thome Horne de Bufhopton
28	W filius Richardi Horbarht

1564

April 3	Edwardus filius Thome Shefeld
6	Benedicta filia Thome Fflemming
22	Johannes filius william Brooks
26	Gulielmus filius Johannes Shakspere XXX
may 3	Humfredus filius william furge
4	Maria filia Johannes Rogers de bufhopton
12	Johannes filius Johannes Golford
21	Richardus filius Gulielmi Ball de Bufhopton

⇢ Map of Stratford-upon-Avon   *c. 1768*

This plan of Shakespeare's hometown was made by Samuel Winter around 1768. Despite the late date of the map, the layout of the town was essentially the same in the eighteenth century as it was in Shakespeare's day, and as it is now. Note particularly the location of the birthplace (#18) in Henley Street and New Place (#16) at the corner of Church Street and Chapel Lane.

PLAN of STRATFORD
— On Avon —

SCALE

Gunter's Chains

7 Ely Street or Swine Street
8 Scholars or Tinkers Lane
9 Bull Lane
10 Street called Old Town
11 Church Street
12 Chapel Street
13 High Street
14 Market Cross
15 Town Hall
16 New Place
17 Chapel Public Schools &
18 House where Shakespeare was born

19 Back Bridge St
20 Fore Bridge Street
21 Sheep Street
22 Chapel Lane
23 Street called Waterside
24 Sou . . . Lane
25
26 White Lion

RIVER AVON

→ FRANCIS MERES

From *Palladis Tamia: Wit's Treasury* 1598

Meres's book, a compendium of philosophical and literary observations, evaluates England's literary scene at the end of the sixteenth century by comparing modern writers with their ancient counterparts. Shakespeare appears as the master of several genres and dramatic modes, and his repeated mention is one of the first and strongest indicators of his prominence at the end of the 1590s. The principal Roman writers invoked are Ovid, the poet whose stories of mythological transformation appear in his *Metamorphoses;* Plautus, the dramatist whose comedies Shakespeare adapted directly in *The Comedy of Errors;* and Seneca, the touchstone for classical tragedy.

A comparatiue discourse of our English Poets,
with the *Greeke, Latine, and Italian Poets.*

. . . [T]he English tongue is mightily enriched, and gorgeouslie inuested in rare ornaments and resplendent abiliments by sir *Philip Sidney, Spencer, Daniel, Drayton, Warner, Shakespeare, Marlow* and *Chapman.* . . .

As the soule of *Euphorbus* was thought to liue in *Pythagoras:* so the sweete wittie soule of *Ouid* liues in mellifluous & hony-tongued *Shakespeare,* witnes his *Venus and Adonis,* his *Lucrece,* his sugred Sonnets among his priuate friends, &c.

As *Plautus* and *Seneca* are accounted the best for Comedy and Tragedy among the Latines: so *Shakespeare* among ye English is the most excellent in both kinds for the stage; for Comedy, witnes his *Gentlemen of Verona,* his *Errors,* his *Loue labors lost,* his *Loue labours wonne,*[1] his *Midsummers night dreame,* & his *Merchant of Venice:* for Tragedy his *Richard the 2. Richard the 3. Henry the 4. King Iohn, Titus Andronicus* and his *Romeo* and *Iuliet.*

As *Epius Stolo* said, that the Muses would speake with *Plautus* tongue, if they would speak Latin: so I say that the Muses would speake with *Shakespeares* fine filed phrase, if they would speake English. . . .

As *Pindarus, Anacreon* and *Callimachus* among the Greekes; and *Horace* and *Catullus* among the Latines are the best Lyrick Poets: so in this faculty the best among our Poets are *Spencer* (who excelleth in all kinds) *Daniel, Drayton, Shakespeare, Bretton.* . . .

. . . [T]hese are our best for Tragedie, the Lorde *Buckhurst,* Doctor *Leg* of Cambridge, Doctor *Edes* of Oxforde, maister *Edward Ferris,* the Authour of the *Mirrour for Magistrates, Marlow, Peele, Watson, Kid, Shakespeare, Drayton, Chapman, Decker,* and *Beniamin Iohnson.* . . .

. . . [T]he best for Comedy amongst us bee, *Edward* Earle of Oxforde, Doctor *Gager* of Oxforde, Maister *Rowley* once a rare Scholler of learned Pembrooke Hall in Cambridge, Maister *Edwardes* one of her Maiesties Chappell, eloquent and wittie *Iohn Lilly, Lodge, Gascoyne, Greene, Shakespeare, Thomas Nash, Thomas Heywood, Anthony Mundye* our best plotter, *Chapman, Porter, Wilson, Hathway,* and *Henry Chettle.* . . .

---

[1] *Love's Labor's Won* is the puzzling title that scholars have not been able to trace. It may be either the title of a lost play or an alternate title for an existing comedy such as *The Taming of the Shrew.*

. . . [T]hese are the most passionate among us to bewaile and bemoane the perplexities of Loue, *Henrie Howard* Earle of Surrey, sir *Thomas Wyat* the elder, sir *Francis Brian*, sir *Philip Sidney*, sir *Walter Rawley*, sir *Edward Dyer*, *Spencer, Daniel, Drayton, Shakespeare, Whetstone, Gascoyne, Samuell Page* sometimes fellowe of *Corpus Christi* Colledge in Oxford, *Churchyard, Bretton*.

✦ The Royal License for Shakespeare's Company   *1603*

From its formation in 1594 until 1603, Shakespeare's company was known as the Lord Chamberlain's Men. King James assumed patronage of the troupe in a document dated May 19, 1603, from which this passage is taken. The new title, the King's Men, was retained until the closing of the theaters in 1642.

We . . . do license and authorize these our Servants Lawrence Fletcher, William Shakespeare, Richard Burbage, Augustine Phillips, John Heminges, Henry Condell, William Sly, Robert Armin, Richard Cowley, and the rest of their associates freely to use and exercise the art and faculty of playing comedies, tragedies, histories, interludes, morals, pastorals, stageplays, and such others like as they have already studied or hereafter shall use or study as well for the recreation of our loving subjects as for our solace and pleasure when we shall think good to see them during our pleasure.

✦ Detail from the "Agas" Map of London   *c. 1604* ➤
With Shakespeare's Lodging Indicated

This detail from the "Agas" map of London (drawn c. 1553–59) shows the house where Shakespeare lived around the time he wrote *Othello* and *Measure for Measure*. According to testimony in a 1612 trial, Shakespeare apparently rented a room ("one Mr Shakespeare that lay in the house") from Christopher Mountjoy and his family. The house, indicated by a circle, stands near the northern wall of the city, on the northeastern corner of Silver ("Sylver") and Monkswell ("Muggle") Streets.

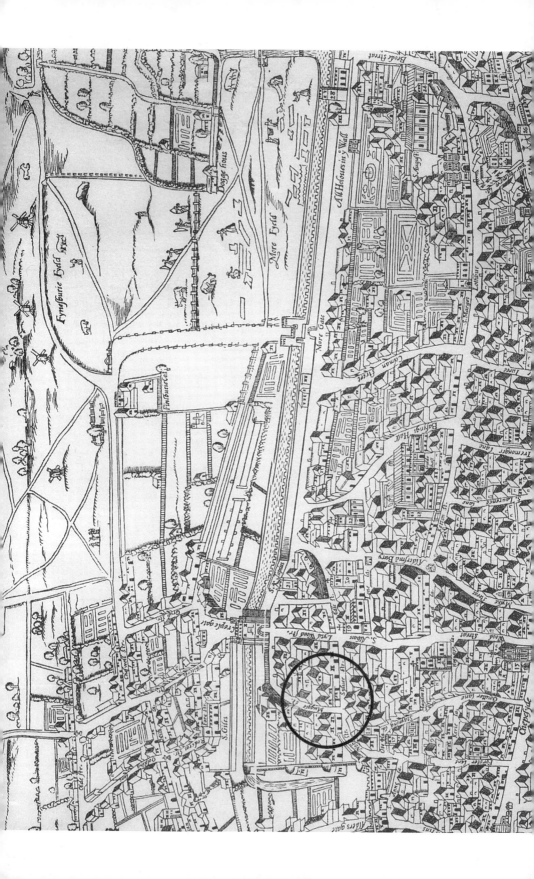

→ JOHN WARD, VICAR OF STRATFORD

From His Diary

These remembrances are taken from the diary of John Ward, vicar of Stratford (1662–81). Although Ward was born after Shakespeare's death, his diary offers reported details about Shakespeare's life and death, as well as references to his descendants.

Shakespeare had but two daughters, one whereof Mr. Hall, the physician, married, and by her had one daughter, to wit, the Lady Bernard of Abingdon. . . .

I have heard that Mr. Shakespeare was a natural wit, without any art at all; he frequented the plays all his younger time, but in his elder days lived at Stratford, and supplied the stage with two plays every year, and for that had an allowance so large, that he spent at the rate of £1,000 a year, as I have heard.

Remember to peruse Shakespeare's plays, and be versed in them, that I may not be ignorant in that matter. . . .

Shakespeare, Drayton, and Ben Jonson had a merry meeting, and it seems drank too hard, for Shakespeare died of a fever there contracted. . . .

→ Shakespeare's Will

This complete transcription of Shakespeare's last will and testament dated March 25, 1616, is followed by a facsimile of the last page, which includes the playwright's autograph ("By me William Shakspeare"); the text of the manuscript would have been written by a clerk. Some of the changes, such as "Ianuarij" (January) to "martij" (March) and the cancelled section that originally began page two, indicate a revision of an earlier version. The alterations appear to reflect the dying man's concern about the recent marriage (February 10, 1616) of his daughter Judith to the disreputable Thomas Quiney.

T*estamentum willel*mij Shackspeare[1]

Vicesimo Quinto die [I<anuar>ij][2] {martij} Anno Regni D*omi*ni n*os*tri Iacobi nunc R*egis* Anglie &c decimo quarto & Scotie xlixo Annoq*ue domini* 1616[3]

In the name of god Amen I William Shackspeare of Stratford vpon Avon in the countie of warr*wick* gent*leman* in p*er*fect health & memorie god be praysed doe make & Ordayne this my last will & testam*ent* in mann*er* & forme followeing That ys to saye ffirst I Comend my Soule into the hand*es* of god my

---

[1]The editors who transcribed Shakespeare's will used the following symbols:

italic	editorial expansions of abbreviated forms
[. . .]	material deleted in manuscript
{ . . . }	material inserted in manuscript
< . . . >	material illegible in manuscript
(. . .)	parentheses in manuscript.

[2][*I<anuar>ij*] interpreted thus by Chambers, etc.; read by Malone and others as *Februarij* (Chambers, *William Shakespeare: A Study of Facts and Problems*, 2 vols, Oxford, 1930, II, 175).

[3]*Vicesimo . . . 1616:* "On the twenty-fifth day of March, in the fourteenth year of the reign of our lord King James now King of England, etc., and of Scotland the forty-ninth, in the year of our lord 1616."

Creator hoping & assuredlie beleeving through thonelie merittes of Iesus Christe my Saviour to be made partaker of lyfe everlastinge And my bodye to the Earth whereof yt ys made Item I Gyve & bequeath vnto my [sonne in L] Daug<ht>er Iudyth One Hundred & ffyft<ie po>undes of lawf<ull> English money to be paied vnto her in manner & forme followeing That ys to saye One Hundred Poundes {in discharge of her marriage porcion} within one yeare after my Deceas with consideracion after the Rate of twoe shillinges in the pound for soe long tyme as the same shalbe vnpaied vnto her after my deceas & the ffyftie poundes Residewe thereof vpon her Surrendring {of} or gyving of such sufficient securitie as the overseers of this my Will shall like of to Surrender or graunnte All her estate & Right that shall discend or come vnto her after my deceas or {that shee} nowe hath of in or to one Copiehold tenemente with thappurtenaunces lyeing & being in Stratford vpon Avon aforesaied in the saied countie of warrwick being parcell or holden of the mannour of Rowington vnto my Daughter Susanna Hall & her heires for ever Item I Gyve & bequeath vnto my saied Daughter Iudith One Hundred & ffyftie Poundes more if shee or Anie issue of her bodie be Lyvinge att thend of three Yeares next ensueing the daie of the Date of this my Will during which tyme my executours to paie her consideracion from my deceas according to the Rate afore saied And if she dye within the saied terme without issue of her bodye then my will ys & I doe gyve & bequeath One Hundred Poundes thereof to my Neece Elizabeth Hall & the ffiftie Poundes to be sett fourth by my executours during the lief of my Sister Iohane Harte & the vse & proffitt thereof Cominge shalbe payed to my saied Sister Ione & after her deceas the saied l li shall Remaine Amongst the children of my saied Sister Equallie to be Devided Amongst them But if my saied Daughter Iudith be lyving att thend of the saied three Yeares or anie yssue of her bodye the<n> my Will ys & soe I devise & bequeath the saied Hundred & ffyftie poundes to be sett out {by my executours & overseers} for the best benefitt of her & her issue & {the stock} not {to be} paied vnto her soe long as she shalbe marryed & Covert Baron [by my executours & overseers] but my will ys that she shall have the consideracon yearelie paied vnto her during her lief & after her deceas the saied stock and consideracion to bee paied to her children if she have Anie & if not to her executours or assignes she lyving the saied terme after my deceas Provided that if such husbond as she shall att thend of the saied three Yeares be marryed vnto or attaine after doe sufficientle Assure vnto her & thissue of her bodie landes Awnswereable to the porcion by this my will gyven vnto her & to be adiudged soe by my executours & overseers then my will ys that the saied Cl li shalbe paied to such husbond as shall make such assurance to his owne vse Item I gyve & bequeath vnto my saied sister Ione xx li & all my wearing Apparrell to be paied & Deliuered within one yeare after my deceas And I doe Will & devise vnto her {the house} with thappurtenaunces in Stratford wherein she dwelleth for her naturall lief vn<der> the yearelie Rent of xij d. Itm[4] I gyue & bequeat<h>[5] (fo. 2) vnto her three sonns William Harte ⁶ hart &

---

[4] *Itm:* Mark of abbreviation omitted, rightly *Item.*
[5] Signed bottom left *Willi<a>m <Shakespear>e.*
[6] Blank in manuscript; rightly *Thomas.*

Michaell Harte ffyve pound*es* A peece to be payed w*i*thin one Yeare after my deceas [to be sett out for her w*i*thin one Yeare after my Deceas by my executo*urs*
w*i*th thadvise & direc*c*ions of my overseers for her best pro ffitt vntill her Marriage & then the same w*i*th the increase thereof to be paied vnto her]⁷ It*em* I
gyve & bequeath vnto [her] {the saied Elizabeth Hall} All my Plate {(except my
brod silver & gilt bole)} that I now<e> have att the Date of this my Will Itm I
gyve & bequeath vnt<o> the Poore of Stra<tf>ord aforesaied tenn pound*es* to mr
Thomas Combe my Sword to Thomas Russell Esquier ffyve pound*es* & to
ffrauncis Collins of the Borough of Warr*wick* in the countie of War<r*wick*> gen-
t*leman* thirteene pound*es* Sixe shilling*es* & Eight pence to be paied w*i*thin one
Yeare after my Deceas Itm I gyve & bequeath to [mr Richard Tyl<..>⁸
theld*er*] {Hamlett Sadler} xxvj s viij d to buy him A Ringe {to William
Raynold*es* gent*leman* xxvj s viij d to buy him A Ringe} to my godson Willi*a*m
Walker xx s in gold to Anthonye Nashe gent*leman* xxvj s viij d & to mr Iohn
Nashe xx{vj s viij d} [in gold] {& to my fellows Iohn Hemyn*n*ges Richard
Burbage & Henry Cundell xxvj s viij d A peece to buy them Ring<*es*>} It*em* I
Gyve Will bequeath & Devise vnto my Daughter Susanna Hall {for better en-
abling of her to p*er*forme this my will & toward*es* the p*er*formans thereof} All
that Capitall messuage or ten*eme*nt w*i*th thapp*ur*ten*au*nces {in Stratford afore-
saied} Called the newe place Wherein I nowe Dwell & twoe messuag*es* or ten-
*eme*ntes w*i*th thapp*ur*ten*au*nces scituat lyeing & being in Henley streete w*i*thin
the borough of Stratford aforesaied And all my barnes stables Orchard*es* gardens land*es* ten*eme*ntes & hereditam*en*tes Whatsoeu*er* scituat lyeing & being or
to be had Receyved p*er*ceyved or taken w*i*thin the townes Hamlett*es* villag*es*
ffield*es* & ground*es* of Stratford vpon Avon Oldstratford Bushopton & Welcombe or in anie of them in the saied countie of warr*wick* And alsoe All that
Messuage or ten*eme*nt w*i*th thapp*ur*ten*au*nces wherein one Iohn Robinson
dwelleth scituat lyeing & being in the blackfriers in London nere the Wardrobe
& all oth*er* my land*es* ten*eme*ntes & hereditam*en*tes Whatsoeu*er* To Have & to
hold All & sing*u*ler the saied p*re*misses w*i*th their App*ur*tenaunces vnto the saied
Susanna Hall for & During the terme of her naturall lief & after her Deceas to
the first son<n>e of her bodie lawfullie Yssueing & <to the> heires males of the
bodie of the saied first Sonne lawfullie Yssueinge & for defalt of such issue to
the second Sonne of her bodie lawfullie issueinge & [fr] to the heires males of
the bodie of the saied Second Sonne lawfullie yssueinge & for defalt of such
heires to the third Sonne of the bodie of the saied Susanna Lawfullie yssueing
& of the heires males of the bodie of the saied thir<d> sonne lawfullie yssueing
And for defalt of such issue the same s<oe> to be & Remaine to the ffourth
[sonne] ffyfth sixte & Seaventh sonnes of her bodie lawfullie issueing one after
Anoth*er* & to the heir<*es*>⁹ (fo. 3) Males of the bodies of the saied ffourth fifth
Sixte & Seaventh sonne<s> lawfullie yssueing in such mann*er* as yt ys before
Lymitted to be & Remaine to the first second & third Sonns of her bodie & to
their heires males And for defalt of such issue the saied p*re*misses to be & Re-

---

⁷[*to be sett . . . her*]: Originally began new page; what precedes on folio 2 probably added when will revised.
⁸*Tyl* . . : ? Tyler.
⁹Signed bottom right *Willm Shakspeare.*

maine to my sayed Neece Hall & the heires Males of her bodie Lawful<lie> yssueing for Defa<lt of> such issue to my Daughter Iudith & the heires Males of
her bodie lawfullie issueinge And for Defalt of such issue to the Right heires of
me the saied William Shackspere for ever {Itm I gyve vnto my wief my second
best bed with the furniture} Item I gyve & bequeath to my saied Daughter Iudith my broad silver gilt bole All the Rest of my goodes Chattel<les> Leases
plate Iewels & household stuffe Whatsoeuer after my dettes and Legasies paied
& my funerall expences discharged I gyve Devise & bequeath to my Sonne in
Lawe Iohn Hall gentleman & my Daughter Susanna his wief Whom I ordaine
& make executours of this my Last Will & testament And I doe intreat & Appoint {the saied} Thomas Russell Esquier & ffraunci<s> Collins gentleman to be
overseers hereof An<d> doe Revoke All former wills & publishe this to be my
last Will & testament In Wit<nes> Whereof I have her<e>vnto put my [Seale]
{hand} the Daie & Yeare first aboue Written./   By me William Shakspeare
witnes to the publishing hereof Fra: Collyns Iulyus Shawe Iohn Robinson
Hamnet Sadler Robert Whattcott

→ GEORGE FRISBEE

From *Edward de Vere, A Great Elizabethan*   *1931*

The Oxfordian Challenge

Some who attribute Shakespeare's plays to Edward de Vere, seventeenth earl of Oxford, believe that his name is encoded throughout the texts of the plays. This excerpt is taken from George Frisbee, *Edward de Vere, A Great Elizabethan*, pages 135–36.

The poem, by Ben Jonson [B.I.], comes from the 1623 Folio of Shakespeare's plays.

Beneath the poem are printed instructions for cracking the code. The letters in boldface and in italics are said to indicate the cryptographic figuration of "Ed. Devere."

The sums listed at the bottom of the page derive from yet another kind of secret code, a cipher scheme which assigns a number to each of the twenty-four letters in the Elizabethan alphabet (*i* and *j* count as one letter; *u* and *v* count as one letter): *a* = 1, *b* = 2, *c* = 3, and so forth. The detective then totals the numerical values of letters, as indicated in the guides, to reveal the arithmetical equivalents of, for example, "Ed. Oxenforde."

To the Reader.

> This Figur**e**, that thou here seest put,
> It was for gentle Shakespeare cut:

> Wherein the Grauer ha**d** a strife
> with Nature, to out **d**oo the life:

> O, could he but ha*ve* d*r*awn*e* his wit
> As well in brasse, as he hath hit   <
> His face, the Print woul*d* th*e*n surpasse
> All, that was euer writ in brasse.   <
> But, since he cannot, Rea*d*er, looke
> Not on his Picture, but his Book*e*.   <

B.I.

Begin on "e" in "figure," read L[eft] to R[ight], spell "Ed. Devere," end on "e" in "drawne."

Begin on "e" in "booke," read R[ight] to L[eft], spell "Ed. Devere," end on "e" in "drawne."

Total; words, and capital letters	95	Oxenford	95
Total first letter each first word	109	Ed. Oxenforde	109
Total first letter each last word	109	Ed. Oxenforde	109
Total last letter each first word	157	E. Vere E. Oxenforde	157
"This figure it"	146	E. Ver Edward Vere	146
"Gentle Shakespeare"	163	Edw. Devere Oxford	163

CHAPTER 2

Performances, Playhouses, and Players

———————————— ✕ ————————————

Going to a Play, Circa 1595

Let us imagine ourselves transported back to the London of Queen Eliza-beth, where we are attending the first performance of *Romeo and Juliet*. The date is sometime in 1595 or 1596, probably in the autumn or summer, just be-fore two o'clock in the afternoon. We are seated on benches in a gallery of the Theatre, one of the first permanent structures built for drama in Eng-land; constructed in 1576 by James Burbage, it is located just north of the walls of the City of London in a district called Shoreditch. The Curtain, an-other public theater that stands nearby, was built a year later. We are not at-tending the Globe because it has not yet been built. (All of these playhouses are indicated on the map printed on p. 58.) Today's play was written by William Shakespeare, a poet (as dramatists are known) who has made his name with a series of comedies (*The Comedy of Errors* and *Love's Labor's Lost* being two of his successes) and history plays based on the Wars of the Roses. The company preparing to perform, resident at the Theatre, is known as the Lord Chamberlain's Men, a group of players who left other companies in 1594 to join under the patronage of Henry Carey, Lord Hunsdon, and has rapidly become the most successful troupe in England. William Shake-speare is a permanent member of this company, a shareholder, as is its lead-ing actor, Richard Burbage, son of the carpenter-entrepreneur who built the Theatre. Musicians are warming up, actors are rushing around in the *tiring-house* ("attiring house," or dressing room) behind the stage, refreshments are being sold in the playhouse by vendors who move among the crowd, and spectators — having paid their admission in cash to *gatherers*, the early modern equivalent of ticket takers or ushers — are filling the seats in the galleries or standing in the yard in front of the platform or stage. (Laurence Olivier's 1944 film version of *Henry V* opens with a visual reconstruction of this preperformance activity.)

Once the play has begun we quickly notice that some of the conventions and performance practices common in the Elizabethan theater differ markedly from our own. To begin with, the stage is bare, without pictorial scenery; there is no souvenir program to introduce the characters; we must deduce such information as setting and time from the dialogue. The Prologue informs us that the play will last about two hours and that the action will occur in Verona. When the characters Sampson and Gregory enter, we know that they are outdoors because they are carrying swords and shields, which are customarily removed on entering a building. We gather that the area is public since they encounter their enemies, the Montagues ("I will frown as I pass by"), and citizens rush in with clubs and spears. The Prince's judgment confirms our conclusion: "If ever you disturb our streets again . . ." This first scene has much coming and going and falls into several sections, but it does not end until Romeo and Benvolio exit together at line 238, and the stage is momentarily empty. But only momentarily. Without delay "*Enter* CAPULET, COUNTY PARIS, *and the Clown*" — they may even be entering from one door as Benvolio and Romeo go out the other — and the second scene begins. But we are not necessarily in the same place.

Scene in Elizabethan usage refers not so much to a unit of dramatic organization as to a location ("In fair Verona, where we lay our scene . . ."), a place where characters meet and converse: when the place changes, the scene changes. On occasion the scene will change — or slide to an adjoining location — even with characters still on the stage, as occurs between what modern texts call scenes 4 and 5 of the first act. In scene 4, the Montagues are clowning and listening to Mercutio's account of his Queen Mab dream in the street, presumably in front of the Capulet house; they then "*march about the stage*" and presumably stand to one side. Next the Capulet servants enter to prepare for the party (scene 5), and the host and guests enter at line 16; thus, the Montagues have crashed the party without moving. The indoor scene has come to them.

The point of all this detail is to demonstrate that the Elizabethan stage is what the great modern director Peter Brook, speaking of his ideal stage, refers to as "the Empty Space." Although large scenic properties such as beds, scaffolds, and tents were used, the public theaters did not employ backdrops or sets in the modern sense. There was no front curtain to raise and lower between scenes. The stage was bare so that it could be filled imaginatively and then instantaneously emptied and refilled. This nonpictorial theatrical style creates flexibility and a rapid pace. It also requires that the spectators activate and exercise their curiosity and intelligence, as the Prologue to *Henry V* states explicitly: "Suppose that you have seen," "O, do but think / You stand upon the rivage [shore] and behold a city . . . ," "Work, work your thoughts," and "eche out [supplement] our performance with your mind." As audience members we must participate by "playing along."

Such engagement also permits us to mark the passage of time. Since the drama is being performed in full daylight — this being London, full sunlight is infrequent — the dramatist gives verbal and visual codes for day and night. The play apparently begins in the morning — "You, Capulet, shall go along with me, / And, Montague, come you this afternoon" (1.1.99–100) — a point clarified by Benvolio's "But new strook nine" (161). If we are attentive, we can chart the passage of the day. As scene 2 begins, Capulet has already had his interview with the Prince, and perhaps Montague has too — "But Montague is bound as well as I, in penalty alike" — although the Prince may merely have promised Capulet that Montague would be so warned. In any case, we move through the day as the first act proceeds. Scene 3, the discussion of Juliet's possible marriage to Paris, ends with the Nurse's bawdy "Go, girl, seek happy nights to happy days." The women exit, whereupon night arrives immediately with scene 4: "*Enter* ROMEO, MERCUTIO, BENVOLIO, *with five or six other* MASKERS; TORCH-BEARERS." Ironically, the illuminating presence of torches serves to indicate darkness on stage. Night continues through several scenes — during the Capulet party (1.5), as Romeo escapes from his friends after the party (2.1), as he enters the Capulet orchard and woos Juliet (2.2). There are more torches at the party ("she doth teach the torches to burn bright"); the Montagues very likely carry them in searching for Romeo, who in order to elude his pursuers does not carry one; perhaps one burns at Juliet's window. In a play that exploits the imagery of dark and light, day and night, and black and white, the presence of such stage props would enrich the text as well as serve as signals to the audience. At the end of Romeo and Juliet's "balcony scene" (2.2), morning approaches, or at least threatens to: "Good night, good night! Parting is such sweet sorrow, / That I shall say good night till it be morrow" (2.2.184–85). Four lines later, at the beginning of 2.3, the dawn has indeed arrived with Friar Lawrence's entrance: "The grey-ey'd morn smiles on the frowning night." The remainder of the play continues the pattern: we are told about the passage of time when it is helpful for us to know about it, but if such knowledge would be confusing, we are discouraged from thinking about the clock.

The bare stage is peopled with actors in sumptuous clothes. In fact, eye-popping costumes were one of the great attractions of the English stage, provoking comment from foreign visitors and Puritan critics. Wealthy citizens in their wills sometimes left their best clothing to favorite servants who, not legally allowed to wear it, sold it to the players. Clothing was so expensive that the Elizabethans carefully recycled it, creating a vigorous trade in secondhand apparel. The Prince in *Romeo and Juliet* would most likely wear rich robes of velvet or another plush fabric, trimmed perhaps in fox or rabbit or ermine; doublets were often embroidered in silver and gold; ladies' gowns were made of taffeta, silk, cloth of gold, and satin, and then finished with sleeves in complementary fabrics. Hats, gloves, boots, ruffs, cloaks, jerkins, chopines (high-heeled shoes), stockings, handkerchiefs, and other such accessories would be equally impressive.

Whether the costumes were appropriate to the Veronese setting of *Romeo and Juliet* appears to have been less important than their magnificence. In other words, credibility and cultural specificity were outweighed by the claims of spectacle for its own sake and the impracticality of faithfully representing the proper apparel of ancient Rome, ancient Greece, ancient Britain, Elsinore, Venice, the Forest of Arden, and Illyria. The crude sketch by Henry Peacham, reproduced on page 59, may represent a contemporary production of *Titus Andronicus*. The drawing gives a sense of the visual eclecticism that must have characterized the staging of virtually any play with a non-English, noncontemporary setting. Apparel could be employed specifically, however, to fulfill the same semiotic function as torches and other such props: nightgowns signified a late hour or surprised awakening, riding gear a journey, and various kinds of headwear the social or economic status of the wearer. Color could also be indicative, as we know from Hamlet's "customary suits of solemn black." The spectrum of colors reflected the rage for novelty characteristic both of the age of discovery and of fashion in most ages: some of the popular hues included carnation, puke (dark brown), tobacco, and goose-turd green.

A theatrical troupe's wardrobe of magnificent costumes was one of its most valuable assets. Careful expense records were kept, as we know from the transcription of a handwritten list of costumes given on page 60. This inventory was prepared by Edward Alleyn, chief actor of the Lord Admiral's Men and son-in-law to Philip Henslowe, the theatrical manager. A glorious costume stolen by a disgruntled actor could be very costly to the company. For a production of Thomas Heywood's *A Woman Killed with Kindness* in 1603, the Lord Worcester's Men paid the author six pounds for the play, but spent six pounds, thirteen shillings, for the gown worn by the heroine (see Schoenbaum, *Shakespeare: His Life, His Language, His Theater* 52). The cost and brilliance of costumes served as a primary target of Puritan attacks on the stage, such as the ranting in William Prynne's *Histriomastix* (1633): "Those plays which are usually acted and frequently in over-costly effeminate, strange, meretricious, lust-exciting apparell, are questionlesse unseemely, yea unlawfull unto Christians" (qtd. in Barish 86). Into this assault on costume Prynne manages to smuggle a favorite complaint about the sexual indeterminacy associated with the theater: young men were wearing dresses in public.

Women did not act on the English stage until after the Restoration of Charles II in 1660. In our imaginary performance, the roles of Juliet, the Nurse, Lady Capulet, and Lady Montague, as well as some of the extras at the Capulet party and in the street, are probably being played by boys, although some scholars contend that certain female parts, especially older women, may have been taken by men. London offered a few theatrical companies made up exclusively of boys, the "little eyases" [unfledged hawks] referred to in the gossip between Hamlet and Rosencrantz and Guildenstern. Some of these, like the company called Paul's Boys, were associated with schools or cathedrals and offered public performances intermittently over several decades. But in the major troupes most of the boy actors were apprenticed to members of the company and played women's roles until their voices changed or their physical growth made them no longer credible. This transvestite theater, as it has come to be known, had a palpable effect on the playwrights' creative choices; for example, it could limit the number of female parts called for and help to shape those roles. Moreover, it encouraged playwrights generally and Shakespeare in particular to develop the thematic possibilities of cross-dressing.

Writing with a certain group of actors in mind and with a financial stake in suiting his matter to his means, Shakespeare usually created only three or four female roles for each play. In *Julius Caesar* there are thirty-four men's roles, not counting messengers, senators, attendants, and spear-carriers, but only two women's parts. To some degree this paucity of female characters is a function not just of personnel but also of subject: historically, the assassination of Caesar was committed by men. And yet it may be that since the company consisted primarily of adult males Shakespeare dramatized stories without large numbers of female roles. Even in comedy, where the topic is courtship, men outnumber women: of the twenty-one named characters in *A Midsummer Night's Dream*, only four are female. If he had especially gifted boy actors, as he must have had in at least two phases of his professional career, Shakespeare exploited their talents by writing challenging parts for them. At the end of the 1590s, for example, the company probably included two exceptionally talented boys for whom Shakespeare wrote such parts as Portia and Nerissa (*The Merchant of Venice*), Beatrice and Hero (*Much Ado about Nothing*), and Rosalind and Celia (*As You Like It*). Then around 1606 he must have found an actor with star quality, one who partly inspired the creation of three of Shakespeare's greatest parts — Lady Macbeth, the irrepressibly talkative Volumnia in *Coriolanus*, and the monumental role of Cleopatra. Although these parts may have been performed by one or more adult males, the actor was probably a gifted juvenile. If so, his youth would have added even greater irony to the Egyptian queen's fears, expressed in her speech to Iras near the end of the play, of being taken captive to Rome and made to watch "Some squeaking Cleopatra boy my greatness / I' th' posture of a whore" (5.2.220–21).

The convention of boys dressed as girls led early modern playwrights to explore ideas of sexual roles and deceptive appearances. Often Shakespeare elected to return the boy actor to doublet and hose by disguising the female character as a boy, as when Rosalind in *As You Like It* disguises herself as Ganymede, taking the name of the beautiful, androgynous cupbearer of Jove. The layers of reality become dizzying in the wooing scenes of acts 3 and 4, where Rosalind as Ganymede plays Rosalind allowing herself to be courted by Orlando. Thus a boy actor plays a female character who plays a boy who pretends to be a girl. Recent scholarship has emphasized the homoerotic implications of these conventions, suggesting that the relationship between adult and apprentice actors may have been sexual, and that the dressing up of pretty boys as pretty girls had a frankly sexual appeal to the males in the audience.[1]

[1] See several of the essays in *Erotic Politics: Desire on the Renaissance Stage*, ed. Susan Zimmerman, particularly those by Lisa Jardine and Peter Stallybrass.

Thus the Puritan opponents of the theater may have had a point in complaining about the erotic atmosphere and the "effeminacy" of stage practices. In *Twelfth Night*, Orsino describes his new manservant Cesario (actually Viola disguised) in erotic terms:

> For they shall yet belie thy happy years,
> That say thou art a man. Diana's lip
> Is not so smooth and rubious; thy small pipe [throat, voice]
> Is as the maiden's organ, shrill and sound,
> And all is semblative a woman's part.   (1.4.30–34)

Whatever the strength of the sexual charge, whether powerful or muted, Shakespeare was aware of it and eager to exploit the ironic discrepancies it generated. And modern directors have been quick to highlight these ironies as well. In Ian Judge's 1994 production of *Twelfth Night* at Stratford-upon-Avon, Orsino kissed Cesario on the lips at the end of act 2, scene 4, well before the public revelation of the character's gender in the final scene.

The Playhouses

As recently as 1989 a construction crew working on the south bank of the Thames, demolishing one office building to replace it with another, uncovered the architectural remains of the Rose Playhouse. What they found embedded in the mud was not much to look at: the foundations of pillarlike corner supports for the polygonal building's sides, the foundational outline of the original and the redesigned stage, a narrow trench or drip line made by rainwater falling off the thatched roof, bits of mortar and hazelnut shells that served as flooring in the yard in front of the stage, and evidence of a major reconstruction project apparently undertaken to increase the capacity of the building. A photograph of the foundations and a conjectural drawing of the outlines of the building are found on pages 63–64. This new tangible evidence, limited though it is, has been enormously helpful to scholars' efforts to ascertain the size and shape of the building before and after renovation, the dimensions of the stage, and other structural details that have a bearing on what the building looked like and how it was used for the presentation of stage plays. The original building was a fourteen-sided polygon about 72 feet in diameter, with an inner yard measuring not quite 50 feet in diameter; the stage was not very deep, only about 15 1/2 feet, and 35 1/2 feet across at the rear, tapering to about 27 1/2 feet at the downstage end. The roof was thatched.

The importance of the Rose find encouraged archeologists to dig just a few yards away, across Park Street, where they promptly unearthed (in October 1989) some of the remains of the Globe: a small section of outer wall, the foundations of a turret stairwell attached to that wall, and a small section of the gallery wall (an inner wall facing onto the yard). More may yet be uncovered: some of the ruins seem to extend under existing buildings,

which will have to be moved or removed before further excavation can occur. As incredible as it may seem, it took almost four hundred years to un-
cover the foundations of two of the most important buildings in British
history. Now that we have studied them, we know considerably more about
these structures and the plays that they housed than we did ten years ago;
however, there is still much to learn. None of the public playhouses is still
standing, and the archeological and pictorial evidence is sketchy and often
conflicting.

The surviving drawings from the period, for example, often contradict
what we know about the size of the theaters or seem inconsistent with
recorded details of their structure. The Globe foundations discovered in Park
Street are, after all, a physical record of the second Globe Playhouse, built immediately after the first Globe burned to the ground during a performance of
Shakespeare's *Henry VIII* in June 1613. The second playhouse, about which we
know a little, was said to have been built on the foundations of the first structure, in which many of Shakespeare's plays were originally performed, but we
cannot be sure whether changes or improvements were introduced as the
building was reconstructed. C. Walter Hodges's drawing on page 65 provides
a conjectural view of the second Globe. The survey of the playhouses that follows, therefore, offers a useful lesson in the problems of theater history: much
of it is speculative, details are still emerging, and even now there is detective
work to be done.

In the 1590s several outdoor playhouses, what we tend to call public theaters, were operating around London. Indoor playhouses, or private theaters, had been in use in the 1570s and '80s; after the turn of the century they
became increasingly important. (A leading theater historian, Andrew Gurr,
regards the distinction between public and private as misleading, the main
differences being the presence of a roof and the price of admission, so he
calls the first type *amphitheaters* and the second *hall theaters*.) The outdoor
playhouses were designed as theaters and located outside the City walls because they were thus beyond the reach of the London authorities, who
tended to have Puritan sympathies and were therefore opposed to theatrical
performances. The indoor playhouses were converted spaces within existing
buildings. Their presence within the City was ambiguous, since the Blackfriars district where the main indoor playhouse stood was geographically
within the walls but was legally known as a *Liberty*, a site not subject to City
statutes.

The convenient notion that the Theatre was the first permanent playhouse
in England — a sentimental choice, given its appropriate name and its connection with Shakespeare's plays — has recently been superseded by awareness
that the Red Lion had been built as a playhouse for James Burbage almost ten
years earlier. The principal outdoor playhouses were the Theatre (built 1576),
the Curtain (1577), the Rose (1587), the Swan (1595), the Globe (1599), and the
Fortune (1600). The Theatre and the Curtain, along with others such as the
Fortune and the Red Bull (c. 1604), stood north of the City; the Rose, the
Swan, and the Globe to the south just across the Thames, on the Bankside. A

fascinating historical footnote concerns the connection between the Theatre and the Globe. In 1596 Burbage lost his lease on the property where the Theatre stood, and so the Lord Chamberlain's Men were unable to play in their accustomed place. After renting spaces and moving around for two seasons, the company devised a scheme: they hired workmen to dismantle the Theatre, hauled the timbers and ironwork across the river in January 1599, and engaged a contractor named Peter Street to use the materials to construct the Globe.

The major indoor playhouse was Blackfriars. It took its name from the old monastic neighborhood where in 1594 James Burbage purchased the Priory, a building that had been used as a theater between 1576 and 1584. His attempts to convert it for use by the Lord Chamberlain's Men were blocked by an early modern version of a neighborhood alliance that feared the effects of traffic and mischief. Over a decade later, in 1608, the space came into its own when the King's Men were authorized to use it as a theater. A year or so later they began to play there regularly while continuing to perform at the Globe.

Understanding the London playhouses and their function as performing spaces must begin with the so-called de Witt drawing of the Swan on page 66. The sketch we have was actually made circa 1596 by the Dutch scholar Arend van Buchell: he copied it into his notebook from a drawing sent him by his friend Johannes de Witt, who had just visited London. To some scholars the sketch raises more questions than it answers — the perspective is off, there are no spectators except perhaps a few above the stage, and there is no "inner stage" — but it does provide an introduction to sixteenth-century theater architecture and stagecraft. Another important picture that helps us to visualize these spaces is Wenceslas Hollar's 1644 engraving known as the *Long View of London* (p. 67), although one error in it demands correction: the arenas labeled "The Globe" and "Beere bayting [bearbaiting]" have been mistakenly reversed. Other relevant information comes from builders' contracts, financial details recorded in Henslowe's *Diary*, and the excavations of the last decade.

The amphitheater stage was elevated several feet and protruded into the center of the arena, jutting out from the housing that contained the backstage area and extended to the outside circular wall. The size of the stage at the Fortune was about 43 feet wide and 27 feet deep, larger than the Rose's platform described on page 45. Two columns on the stage itself supported a roof that partly covered the playing area; this canopy, known as the *heavens*, was adorned with paintings of the sun, moon, and stars visible from below. The *heavens* corresponded to the *hell* beneath the stage. A trapdoor in the stage gave access to the area beneath the stage so that in plays like Christopher Marlowe's *Doctor Faustus*, Faustus could be taken into hell. The hidden area under the stage platform also allowed for special effects: at a mysterious moment in *Antony and Cleopatra*, the stage directions stipulate that the "*Music of the hoboys [oboes] is under the stage*"; in *Hamlet*, the Ghost disappears through the trapdoor and then speaks from "the cellarage." Andrew Gurr has brilliantly concluded that, in the de Witt drawing, what appear to be curved trestles or pilings supporting the stage are in fact gaps in the curtains that concealed the below-stage area from the audience's view.

At the back of the stage were doors, from which entrances and exits were made. The number of doors is much disputed and may have varied from theater to theater. Some stage directions include the words "*at the other door,*" which would seem to specify two. On the other hand, certain texts obviously require a *discovery space* at the rear of the stage, an area hidden by a curtain or perhaps a door similarly covered: such a place could conceal Polonius when he hides behind the arras in the closet scene of *Hamlet,* or hide Desdemona's bed until it was thrust forward in the final scene of *Othello.* In other words, some playhouses may have had a middle door or hidden space; even in the Swan, with its two doors, such a concealed area could have been rigged up temporarily with curtains. Scholars still debate the existence and importance of the discovery space, but the most recent thinking suggests two kinds of spaces, one of them, according to Gurr, "permanent, a curtained alcove or discovery-space in the tiring-house wall, which served as a shop, tomb, cell, study or closet," the other "a special property, a raised platform, or even a curtained 'booth' set up on stage" that served as a tent (in the history plays) or Cleopatra's monument or an executioner's scaffold (*Shakespearean Stage* 149).

Above the stage in the de Witt drawing we see a gallery or a series of windows or rooms that may have served, like expensive boxes in a modern sports stadium, as private viewing rooms for the wealthy; known as the *tarras,* this section may also have been "the lords' rooms" referred to in a contemporary play script. One or more of these gallery rooms may have housed musicians for performances in which their services were wanted. The tarras was also used for plays in which two levels were specified, such as the balcony scene in *Romeo and Juliet.* Perhaps one of the above-stage rooms was reserved for such action in plays that required it, or perhaps the spectators were temporarily pushed aside. Higher still, above the tarras and the heavens, was the *hut,* an enclosed space that permitted hidden stagehands to create special effects, such as shaking sheets of metal for thunder, and to operate machinery for "flying" immortal or magical characters, such as Ariel in *The Tempest,* onto the stage. In the Swan drawing, a trumpeter makes use of a small platform attached to the hut, perhaps to announce the beginning of a performance. Most of the outdoor playhouses seem to have been constructed more or less according to this model, with minor variations. The key to theater architecture in this period is that its relative uniformity — a bare stage with heavens, hell, a trap, doors leading to the tiring-house, and a tarras — promotes the flexible, nonspecific nature of the staging implicit in the play texts that survive. In *Twelfth Night,* for example, the stage can represent a sumptuous room in Orsino's house at one moment, the deserted Illyrian seacoast at the next, and Olivia's garden immediately thereafter. In *Antony and Cleopatra,* the action moves fluidly back and forth among various indoor and outdoor locations from Egypt to Rome to Athens. The playing areas of the hall theaters may have been slightly smaller or different in detail, but they probably resembled those in the amphitheaters, for the King's Men performed the same repertory at both the Globe and Blackfriars.

What we call the *auditorium*, the area for the spectators, differed significantly in the outdoor and indoor theaters. The amphitheaters were large structures, much bigger than the faulty perspective of the Swan drawing suggests. The Globe was a polygon with perhaps as many as twenty sides (i.e., virtually round), a diameter of about 100 feet, and a capacity of some 3,000 spectators. The dimensions of the Swan were similar. The inside gallery walls were about 10 feet from the outer walls, which means that the diameter of the yard must have been about 80 feet (Gurr, *Shakespearean Stage* 143). The Rose, before its enlargement in 1592, was considerably smaller, about two-thirds the size of the Globe. Spectators would have entered at a single door and paid a gatherer one penny to be admitted to the yard, where they then stood around the base of the stage. Those who wanted to watch the play in greater comfort would have sought entry into one of the galleries, at the price of another penny; a seat in the higher galleries with a more expansive view would have cost a third penny. (See p. 8 in the Introduction as well as pp. 235–37 in Chapter 7 for contexts and equivalents of these prices.) The best seats in the house were located in the *lords' rooms*, those private portions of the gallery nearest the stage (and perhaps even over the stage itself) which cost sixpence. One benefit of the recent archeological discoveries is that they reveal the different forms of entry at the Rose and the Globe: at the Rose, a spectator entered the yard first and then the gallery; at the Globe, as the presence of outer stair turrets indicates, people entering the gallery did so directly from the back, without going through the yard (Gurr, *Shakespearean Stage* 134).

Who were the spectators entering the yard and the galleries? The makeup of the audience at the outdoor playhouses is much contested because such demographic information is hard to obtain. One view holds that Shakespeare's plays drew spectators from all but the lowest economic and social strata, that the audience was truly heterogeneous: merchants and their wives, aristocrats, whores, lawyers from the Inns of Court, laborers, visitors from the country and from abroad, apprentices, servants. Another account describes a more privileged crowd made up of people who could afford not only the price of admission but also time for pleasure in the middle of a workday. Such a view also relates attendance to literacy, noting that drama would have first attracted the educated, who would have been comparatively well-off. The repertories of particular theaters apparently drew different audiences: James Wright, writing a century later in 1699, reports that the Fortune and the Red Bull "were mostly frequented by Citizens, and the meaner sort [lower classes] of People" (qtd. in Gurr, *Playgoing in Shakespeare's London* 251). Whatever the majority at any given house, the evidence suggests that most social classes, from apprentices to gallants, were represented in the amphitheaters. If a woman was respectable, she was necessarily escorted by a man; if not, not. Men outnumbered women — once again literacy may be a factor — but there was a substantial number of women among the 3,000 people who packed the Globe for Shakespeare's most popular plays.

The indoor playhouses were considerably smaller, although the price of admission was higher, so they were at least as profitable to the companies as the larger amphitheaters. Blackfriars, the private theater about which we have the most information, comprised one large upper room in a large building, much like a giant ballroom or other public space at the top of a modern structure. The room's dimensions were about 66 feet by 46 feet. The stage stood at one of the smaller ends of the room, with a tiring-house behind it. Galleries curved around the length of the other three walls, with benches rather than standing places in the central area in front of the stage, here known as *the pit*. Whether there were boxes at the back of the Blackfriars stage is uncertain. In structure and detail, the stage apparently resembled that in the amphitheaters, with a trap, doors leading from the stage to the tiring-house, space for musicians, and a mechanism for flying.

The stage at Blackfriars had one feature that the amphitheaters probably lacked — spectators.[2] About ten stools around the edges could be hired by fashionable theatergoers who wished to see well and be seen. These gallants paid two shillings (twenty-four pence) for such a privilege. The price for entry into the hall, guaranteeing a place in an upper gallery, was six pence. An additional shilling purchased a bench in the pit, and the expensive boxes, partitioned sections of the gallery, cost half a crown (two shillings and six pence). These prices meant that ordinary citizens did not usually patronize the indoor theaters, and this exclusivity contributed, of course, to their popularity. Their location in town rather than in the suburbs or across the river also gave them special appeal for the socially and economically prominent (and those who coveted such prominence). Their sudden vogue was mainly attributable, however, to their location indoors, away from sources of natural light: since all illumination was supplied by candles and torches, it was possible to play at night.

Shakespeare appears to have noticed the prosperity and fashionability of his evening audiences. In *The Winter's Tale*, when Time, the Chorus, enters to announce the passage of some sixteen years, he also declares his familiarity with recent customs and modes of behavior.

> I witness to
> The times that brought them in; so shall I do
> To th' freshest things now reigning, and make stale
> The glistering of this present, as my tale
> Now seems to it.   (4.1.11–15)

Thus Time asserts the irresistibility and constancy of change, and this passage may have had a particularly chilling effect on the sophisticated Blackfriars audience of 1610. Adorned in their most glittering clothing and jewelry, having paid dearly for their admission, and conscious of their superiority (whether social, political, or financial), the members of this chic crowd are warned that their days are numbered, that the darlings of fashion are always supplanted by

---

[2] Although some scholars believe that spectators may have sat on the stage at the Globe, the evidence is so far inconclusive.

others who are wealthier, more beautiful, more powerful. When Shakespeare began his career around 1590, these social considerations were not as meaningful as they unquestionably were by its end. The rise of indoor playing spaces helped to establish the link between attendance at the playhouse and social prominence, to give the theater the function that in some quarters it still maintains, that of social barometer.

The Companies

The fortunes of the London theatrical companies should probably be seen as an episode in the history of economics as well as the history of literature: a professional troupe was a company in both the financial and the theatrical senses. Groups of players had been touring the countryside and performing in town squares and London innyards since the fifteenth century; and as London grew in size and importance in the sixteenth century, the companies naturally began to gravitate toward it. Since actors were low on the social ladder, occupying the same level as vagabonds and beggars, the law required that troupes of players be sponsored by aristocratic patrons, men who accepted nominal responsibility for the companies (although in practice this connection was fairly remote). Throughout the 1570s, '80s, and '90s, many groups of professional players formed, merged, dissolved, and reconstituted themselves under a variety of patrons: Lord Strange's Men, Lord Pembroke's Men, Lord Worcester's Men, the Lord Admiral's Men, and the Lord Chamberlain's Men. (This list does not include the companies of boy actors, mentioned earlier, that were associated with educational institutions and that sometimes performed in the hall theaters.) By the middle of the 1590s, however, the many groups had distilled themselves down to two dominant companies, the Lord Admiral's Men and the Lord Chamberlain's Men. In 1598 an order from the Privy Council (the queen's executive committee) established these two as the only adult companies licensed to play in London.

Regular playing in a single location by the same group of actors is largely responsible for the maturing of English drama in this period and thus for the dramatic output of William Shakespeare. The success of these companies owes much to their connection with two strong theatrical families, headed by Philip Henslowe and James Burbage. The Lord Admiral's Men prospered thanks to the business acumen of Philip Henslowe, landlord, moneylender, theatrical promoter, and the father-in-law of Edward Alleyn, the celebrated actor who originated heroic roles such as Marlowe's Tamburlaine and Doctor Faustus for the Admiral's Men. In 1587 Henslowe built the Rose, in partnership with John Cholmley, and then in 1592 enlarged it to increase profits. When the Lord Chamberlain's Men disassembled the Theatre north of town and opened the Globe in 1599 just next to the Rose on the Bankside, Henslowe responded to this competitive threat by arranging with the builder of the Globe, Peter Street, to build a new theater, the Fortune, in the neighborhood just vacated by the Lord Chamberlain's Men.

Henslowe's passion for minute financial detail has been invaluable to theatrical historians. He kept a daily record of loans, expenditures, losses, money collected from performances, and the cost of business lunches. He also kept a log of plays performed on specific dates (see p. 68).[3] From Henslowe's *Diary* we learn, for example, that in the 1590s the usual fee paid to a playwright for a new play was five to eight pounds (the fee rose to ten to twelve pounds after 1600); that costumes were exceedingly expensive; that it generally took about three weeks from delivery of the manuscript for a company to mount a production of a play; that his company had among its properties "i [one] Hell mought [mouth]" (presumably for Faustus to be dragged into), "i bores head & Serberosse [Cerberus's] iii heads," and "i lyone; ii lyone heades; i great horse with his leages [legs]"; and that the average wage for a minor actor was ten shillings (or one-half of a pound) per week.

Henslowe's counterpart in the rival company was James Burbage, the carpenter-turned-impresario who arranged to build the Red Lion in 1567 and the Theatre in 1576, who purchased the Blackfriars building in 1595, and whose sons, Cuthbert and Richard, were his partners in his later theatrical dealings. Richard, the principal actor for the troupe, played such parts as Richard III, Shylock, and most of the great tragic figures from Brutus and Hamlet through Antony and Coriolanus. Links obtained among all the major theatrical figures and companies: Edward Alleyn had acted under Burbage's sponsorship at the Theatre in 1591 until the two fell out over money. James Burbage's principal achievement was probably the consolidation in 1594 of the Lord Chamberlain's Men from members of various other companies. This company became the greatest of all the early modern theatrical troupes and the vehicle for the production of all Shakespeare's plays from 1594 to the end of his career in 1612 or 1613. In 1603 the company came under royal patronage and was known thereafter as the King's Men. The company performed at court more than any of its rivals, in fact as often as all the other companies combined, and it continued its domination of the theatrical scene by producing the plays of Ben Jonson, John Webster, Thomas Middleton, and, after the retirement of Shakespeare, John Fletcher, Philip Massinger, John Ford, and James Shirley. Even after Shakespeare's death in 1616 and Richard Burbage's in 1619, the company carried on until the closing of the theaters in 1642.

Theatrical promoters like Henslowe and Burbage were influential but not all-important, for the permanent adult companies such as the Admiral's Men and the Chamberlain's Men were in fact cooperatively owned and run. The most important members were the shareholders, those men who held a financial interest in the company, jointly owned its assets (play texts, costumes, properties), and profited from its success. Being a shareholder in a London company was profitable, but it also entailed considerable responsibility: a

---

[3] Upon Henslowe's death these papers passed to Alleyn, who preserved them; they were discovered in the late eighteenth century by the great Shakespearean editor Edmond Malone and have been published in modern editions.

sharer had to commit his talents and services exclusively to the company, and could sell his share and leave the troupe only with the consent of his fellows. The company had eight shareholders in 1596, including William Shakespeare, Richard Burbage, the clown Will Kemp, Augustine Phillips, and John Heminges, one of the sponsors of the First Folio of Shakespeare's plays a quarter of a century later, in 1623. In 1603, when they became the King's Men, this number increased to twelve. The customary number for the major London companies seems to have been about ten. Although theatrical work was not a socially respectable profession, its financial rewards could provide a kind of social standing: in 1597, as we have seen in Chapter 1, Shakespeare used some of his shareholders' profits to buy the second-largest house in Stratford. Shakespeare also invested in the Globe Theater as a property. Such financial backers were known as *housekeepers*. In the season of 1598–99 the Lord Chamberlain's Men turned the disaster of their eviction into a financial bonanza when they moved the timbers of the Theatre across the Thames and built the Globe. The costs for this venture, which must have been enormous, were shared by the two Burbage sons, who put up half the sum, and by five shareholders, who together raised the other 50 percent. Thenceforth, instead of having to turn over to the landlord half of the gallery receipts from each performance, the company in its new location was its own landlord; with anywhere from 500 to 3,000 spectators paying at least a penny (many of them more than that), the receipts were considerable (Gurr, *Shakespearean Stage* 44–45).

The sharers formed the core of each company, taking major parts (as in the case of Richard Burbage) and supplying scripts (as in the case of William Shakespeare), but they needed help with the multitude of tasks involved in theatrical work. Hired men, paid by the week, filled out the company, taking less important stage roles, playing musical instruments, assisting with properties and costumes, and serving as gatherers. (Interestingly, there is evidence that women sometimes worked as gatherers.) In addition there were the boys who played women's parts, some of whom would have been apprentices to the sharers. Some of Shakespeare's plays could have been performed by as few as a dozen or so actors, but most required considerably more. The average size of a full London company, counting apprentices, hired men, and musicians, was between twenty and thirty; for certain major productions even more performers and helpers were probably engaged; and on tour the number would have been reduced substantially. Actors in each company were almost certainly typed according to their specialties, and Shakespeare wrote with these actors in mind. (In fact, certain surviving printed texts refer to the character by the actor's name.) Burbage assumed the great tragic roles; the other great type was the Clown, for which Shakespeare's specialist changed. Until 1599 Will Kemp, a shareholder in the Lord Chamberlain's Men, acted the Clown's parts, and Shakespeare seems to have had him in mind in writing the roles of Dogberry in *Much Ado about Nothing*, Peter in *Romeo and Juliet*, and perhaps Bottom in *A Midsummer Night's Dream*. Kemp's decision to sell his share and leave the company coincided with Shakespeare's increasing attraction to tragedy and to the darker shades of comedy, and so the Clown's parts, now written for Robert

Armin, became more mordant and reflective, roles such as Feste in *Twelfth Night* and the Fool in *King Lear*.

The disproportionate number of characters to actors — the thirty-six parts in *Julius Caesar* and a company of perhaps twenty-four actors — meant that in virtually every play many actors performed several parts. A player taking a major role such as King Lear or Rosalind would not have acted another part in the same production, but other cast members would have. This convention of doubling, combined with the absence of scenery, the lack of artificial lighting in the amphitheaters, and the proximity of the audience, fostered what is known as the *presentational*, as opposed to the *representational*, style of performance. In presentational theater, the illusion of a fictional narrative is maintained at the same time that the audience is reminded that a fiction is being performed. In other words, there is no strict pretense that this is Hamlet striding the battlements at Elsinore; rather, the audience is conscious that they are watching Burbage playing Hamlet on the stage of the Globe. And doubling can augment the spectators' pleasure, first by multiplying the instances of representation (one actor playing several parts) on which drama is based, and, second, by increasing the sense of virtuosity that any good actor brings to any single part.

Whether sharers or hirelings, the actors worked very hard. The major companies played every day except during Lent and on major church holidays, and their repertories were immense. The Lord Admiral's Men, in the season of 1594–95 (autumn to summer), presented thirty-eight plays, twenty-one of them new (Gurr, *Shakespearean Stage* 103). Even great favorites were not repeated too often lest their potential popularity be damaged. Apparently a new play was added every couple of weeks or so. This repertory system required the actors to do a quick run-through of the scheduled play in the morning and then perform it in the afternoon. After a play had been running for some time, less rehearsal time would have been necessary; but with long gaps between performances, inevitable changes of personnel, and other unpredictable events, touch-up rehearsals must have been needed. Sometimes scripts were altered for revival: Ben Jonson was paid for additions to Thomas Kyd's *The Spanish Tragedy* some fifteen years after its initial run. And then new plays would have to be rehearsed as well. Naturally the company sharers would want to perform as often as possible, but they could not play in Lent, during epidemics of plague, or when vile weather made outdoor performance impossible.

The Theater and the Authorities

The municipal government and the Crown were both attentive to the growing popularity of the theater in Elizabethan London. Prohibitions against playing were issued by the Privy Council to defend against the spread of disease in periods of plague. Since medical science had not yet identified the cause of bubonic plague — bites from fleas spread by rats — it was assumed that the presence of crowds would contribute to contagion, and so the theaters were closed. Virulent outbreaks of plague ravaged London between 1592 and 1594 and again in 1603, when over 30,000 people died (in a population of just over 200,000), and in both cases the theaters were closed for over a year. The authorities also closed the playhouses during Elizabeth's final illness in 1603. In fact, during the first decade of the seventeenth century, public playing was forbidden repeatedly and for very lengthy periods: had it not been for handsomely rewarded performances at court and additional royal largesse, Shakespeare's company could have suffered financial ruin.

Had regulation of the theater been left to the London authorities, the playhouses would have been closed permanently. The members of the City Corporation, if not Puritans themselves, were responsive to the pressures of their Puritan constituencies, and the Puritans were increasingly antipathetic to actors, the practice of cross-dressing, colorful costume of any kind, the pretense or hypocrisy inherent in acting, and imaginative literature in general. But the theaters, located as they were in those dubious neighborhoods known as the Liberties, fell under the scrutiny of the Crown, not the City, and Elizabeth's and James's governments were more tolerant of the pleasures of playing and concerned that the municipal authorities of London not become too powerful. Government regulation was officially in the hands of the Privy Council, but the agency that executed the monarch's will in the sphere of public entertainment was the Revels Office headed by the Master of the Revels. Henry VIII had created this office to provide courtly performances, and it continued to fulfill that function under Elizabeth and the Stuarts, as well as to ensure that the Crown's interests were protected at all times. The Revels Office, like most bureaucratic agencies, was in an ambiguous position toward those it regulated. The Master found the players to be an easy and relatively cheap source of courtly entertainment: rather than having to devise and fund an elaborate performance himself, he could buy one ready-made by bringing the players to court for a royal performance.

The primary duty of the Master of the Revels was to license plays for performance, so the theatrical companies were required to submit a new script to the Revels Office to be checked for offensive material. The Master received a fee (seven shillings) for this service, and additional payment (five to ten shillings) for licensing the playhouse. During James's reign the Master was also responsible for checking and approving plays for print, again for a fee. The Master of the Revels, in other words, was the government censor, and material considered seditious or irreligious was removed from the text. A few surviving theatrical manuscripts bear the marks of censorship, and the occasional printed text reveals such cuts: *Richard II*, for example, was originally printed, almost certainly for political reasons, without the section in act 4, scene 1, in which the king is actually deposed.

On certain points the government could be extremely sensitive. In February 1601 the earl of Essex led his followers into London in an ill-organized and unsuccessful attempt at seizing the throne. The day before that uprising the Lord Chamberlain's Men, paid specifically for the purpose by the supporters of Essex, mounted a performance of *Richard II*. Augustine Phillips, one of the shareholders of the company, was called before the Privy Council to explain. (An excerpt from his testimony is given on p. 71.) King James could be equally touchy. The satiric *Eastward Ho!*, a collaborative play by Ben Jonson, John Marston, and George Chapman, was presented in 1605 by a children's company at Blackfriars. It is full of topical jokes about the Scots, who had descended on England with their favorite son in 1603 and were purchasing knighthoods; it also ridicules City merchants and the Puritan economic ethic. The Crown was not amused, and Chapman and Jonson went briefly to jail, Marston having escaped arrest by leaving town. In 1606 Parliament passed legislation regulating the language of the stage, establishing a fine of ten pounds for anyone who should "jestingly or prophanely speake or use the holy name of God or of Christ Jesus, or of the Holy Ghoste or of the Trinitie." Although it could and sometimes did act punitively, the government for the most part maintained a hands-off policy toward the stage, and recently scholars have come to believe that this tolerance may itself have been a political act. In other words, by permitting a small degree of opposition to be expressed or enacted in the controlled space of the public playhouses, the government employed the theater as a kind of safety valve, an outlet for releasing political pressure before it increased to an explosion.

Governmental support of the theater had to do with pleasure as well as with politics: Elizabeth and James (and James's Queen Anne) liked plays. The monarch never attended the theater, however, no matter how fashionable it became or how aristocratic the audience. When the sovereign wished to see a performance, the players were summoned to the palace and paid for their services, as indicated in the records quoted on pages 71–72. The Lord Chamberlain's Men frequently performed Shakespeare's plays at the court of Elizabeth, and while we should be skeptical of the rumors to which the eighteenth and nineteenth centuries were susceptible — that Shakespeare wrote *The Merry Wives of Windsor* because Elizabeth wished to see Falstaff in love, or that Edward Alleyn returned to the stage after retirement because the Queen missed seeing him act — there is enough anecdotal evidence to suggest that Elizabeth encouraged the players not just because they were useful to her and to the Commonwealth but because she enjoyed their work. Scholars disagree on the extent to which James was engaged directly with the theatrical troupe that bore his name; J. Leeds Barroll has recently claimed that the company's connection with its patron was merely nominal (*Politics, Plague, and Shakespeare's Theater*). But whether or not James gave his players much thought, the company's participation in royal festivities increased markedly under the Stuarts, and court records attest that Shakespeare's plays were extremely popular at court. Performances during the holiday season — from early December through early February — were especially numerous. In addition, this was the age when the court masque flourished in the work of Ben Jonson and Inigo Jones. In such extravagant entertainments as *The Masque of Blackness* (1605) and *The Masque of Queens* (1609), players and dancers were often engaged to take minor roles, serving as foils to the mythical figures impersonated by Queen Anne and other noble members of the court. Whether Shakespeare participated in any of these royal performances is not known, but he was certainly aware of their visual magnificence, their immodest cost, and King James's fondness for the dancing that concluded the masques. This awareness may have stimulated him to develop the pageantry, music, and magic that characterize such late plays as *The Winter's Tale* and *The Tempest*.

The court, the amphitheaters, and the indoor theaters were the players' main performing locations, but there was one other venue — the provinces. The urban theatrical companies were descendants of the troupes of traveling players that moved from town to town throughout the fifteenth and sixteenth centuries; and even in the heyday of London theater, those actors who could not find work in town formed pickup groups that toured the countryside. Predictably, the major companies, having established themselves on the Bankside, in town, and at court, were not enthusiastic about returning to their peripatetic origins, as a letter from Edward Alleyn to his wife attests (p. 72). Road conditions were difficult, the number of spectators was reduced, and the profits were consequently smaller. Henslowe records paying an actor on tour half of what the man would have made in London. Sometimes, however, the players had no choice. The plague drove them out of London and into public squares or town halls. As is sometimes still the case today, the provinces probably didn't get quite the same show as the capital: the conditions of touring led to smaller casts and perhaps abbreviated scripts.

It is easy to imagine that in, say, 1595, when the threat of plague had subsided, Shakespeare and his fellows were gratified and relieved at having returned for a time to their commodious theater, its relatively urbane crowd, and a healthy box office. The actors playing Sampson and Gregory, the Capulets who begin *Romeo and Juliet*, must have felt particular relief and pleasure as they stepped on the stage to deliver their bawdy puns.

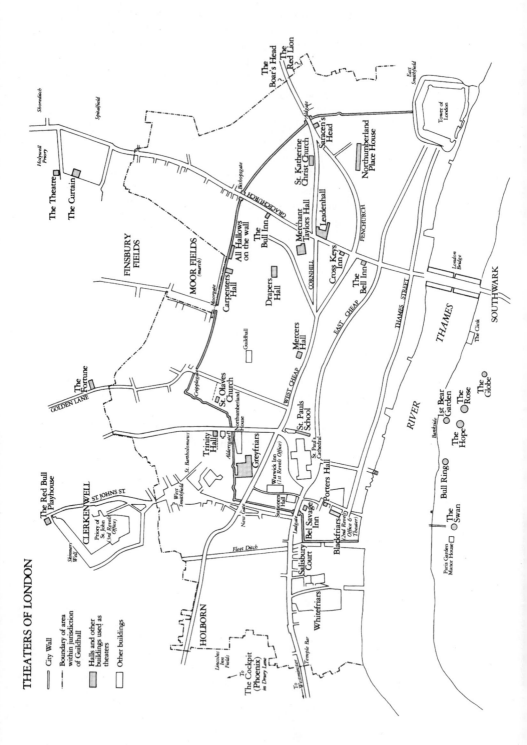

THEATERS OF LONDON

— City Wall
--- Boundary of area
    within jurisdiction
    of Guildhall
▨ Halls and other
    buildings used as
    theaters
☐ Other buildings

Shoreditch
Spitalfield
Holywell Priory
The Theatre
The Curtain
FINSBURY FIELDS
MOOR FIELDS (marsh)
Moorgate
Carpenters Hall
All Hallows on the wall
The Bull Inn
Merchant Taylors Hall
Leadenhall
St. Katherine Christ Church
Saracen's Head
Northumberland Place House
The Boar's Head
The Red Lion
East Smithfield
Tower of London
Bishopsgate
GRACECHURCH
CORNHILL
FENCHURCH
Drapers Hall
Cross Keys Inn
The Bell Inn
EAST CHEAP
THAMES STREET
London Bridge
SOUTHWARK
Mercers Hall
WEST CHEAP
Guildhall
The Fortune
GOLDEN LANE
Cripplegate
St. Olaves Church
Northumberland House
St. Pauls School
St. Paul's Cathedral
THAMES
RIVER
Bankside
1st Bear Garden
The Rose
The Globe
The Hope
The Swan
Bull Ring
Paris Garden Manor House
The Red Bull Playhouse
CLERKENWELL
ST JOHNS ST
Prior of St. John (3rd Revels Office)
Skinners Well
Aldersgate
Trinity Hall
St. Bartholomews
West Smithfield
New Gate
Greyfriars
Warwick Inn (1st Revels Office)
Stationers Hall
Porters Hall
Ludgate
Bel Savage Inn
Blackfriars (2nd Revels Office & Theater)
Salisbury Court
Whitefriars
Fleet Ditch
HOLBORN
Lincolns Inn Fields
Temple Bar
To Westminster
To The Cockpit (Phoenix) in Drury Lane
The Clink

ILLUSTRATIONS AND DOCUMENTS

≺ Map Showing the Playhouses in Shakespeare's Time

This modern map of London circa 1600 indicates the location of the principal Elizabethan and Jacobean theaters. The major "public playhouses," or the outdoor arenas, are situated outside the City to the north and across the Thames River to the south.

⇥ HENRY PEACHAM

Sketch of *Titus Andronicus*   *c. 1595*

This sketch by Henry Peacham is thought to represent a performance of Shakespeare's first tragedy. Shown slightly reduced, the drawing appears at the top of a manuscript page. Beneath it, lines from acts 1 and 5 (Tamora's plea for her sons' lives) have been transcribed. In the illustration, the Romans are on the left; Tamora, Queen of the Goths, and Aaron the Moor are on the right. The eclectic style of the costumes is noteworthy, with some classical and some contemporary.

→ ## Inventory of Theatrical Costumes

c. 1602

From Henslowe's Papers

This list of costumes, transcribed in the original spelling, was probably compiled about 1602. Most likely the apparel belonged to the Lord Admiral's Men, the troupe of players managed by Philip Henslowe, a theater owner and entrepreneur who kept meticulous records of his holdings and profits. The list is in the hand of Edward Alleyn, tragedian and Henslowe's son-in-law. Several items, indicated here by open parentheses at the left, are crossed out (in different ink) in the original.

1 A scarlett cloke wth ij [2] brode gould Laces: w^t [with] gould buttens of the sam downe the sids

2 A black velvett cloke

A scarlett cloke Layd (the)[1] downe w^t silver Lace and silver buttens

4 A short velvett cap clok embroydered w^t gould and gould spangles

5 A watshod [watchet, light blue] sattins clok w^t v gould laces

6 A pur(l)pell sattin w^telted [welted, bordered] w^t velvett and silver twist

7 A bla*ck*[2] tufted cloke   cloke

8 A damask cloke garded cloke garded [guarded, trimmed] w^t velvett

A longe blak tafata cloke

A colored bugell [beaded cloak?] for aboye

A scarlett w^t buttens of gould fact [faced, trimmed] w^t blew velvett

12 A scarlett fact w^t blak velvett

13 A stamell [red] cloke w^t (b)gould lace

14 blak bugell cloke

Gownes

(1 hary ye viij gowne

2 the blak velvett gowne w^t wight fure

3 A crimosin Robe strypt w^t gould fact w^t ermin

4 on of wrought cloth of gould

5 on of red silk w^t gould butt*ens*

(6 a cardinalls gowne

7 wemens gowns

---

[1] Parentheses indicate deletions or alterations.
[2] Italic letters indicate difficult readings, attenuated or blotted letters in the original.

8 i blak velvett embroyde

9 w^t gould

10 i cloth of gould candish [Cavendish?, an actor or role] his *stuf*

11 blak velvett lact and drawne owt w^t wight sarsnett [silk fabric]

12 A black silk w^t red flush

13 A cloth of silver for pan [Parr?, an actor]

14 a yelow silk gowne

(15 a red silk gowne

(16 angels silk

17 ij blew calico gowns

Antik sutes [clown suits, motley]

1 a cote of crimosen velvett cutt in payns and embryderd in gould

2 i cloth of gould cote w^t grene bases [skirts]

3 i cloth of goul*d* cote w^t oraingtawny bases

4 i cloth of go<..>^{3} silver cott w^t blewe silk & tinsell bases

5 i blew damask cote the more

6 a red velvett hors mans cote

7 A yelow tafata pd [?]

8 cloth of gould horsmans cote

9 cloth *of* bodkin [baudekin, rich fabric] hormans cote

10 orayngtany horsmans cot of cloth lact

11 daniels gowne

12 blew embroyderde bases

13 will somers [Will Summers, an actor] cote

14 wight embroyd bases

15 (g) gilt lether cot

16 ij hedtirs [head tires, tiaras] sett w^t stons

17

Jerkings and
dublets

1 A crymosin velvett pd w^t gould buttens & lace

2 a crymasin sattin case [fitted jacket] lact w^t gould lace all over

(3 A velvett dublett cut di*a*mond lact w^t gould lace and spang [small ornament]

---

^{3} Pointed brackets indicate letters or words that are illegible, mutilated, or cut away in the original.

4 a dublett of blak velvett cut [slashed ornamentally] on sillver tinsell

5 A ginger colored dublett

6 i wight sattin cute onwight

7 blak velvett w^t gould lace

8 green velvett

9 blak tafata cut on blak velvett lacte w^t bugell

10 blak velvett playne

11 ould wight sattin

12 red velvett for a boye

13 A carnation velvett lacte w^t silver

14 A yelow spangled case

15 red velvett w^t blew sattin sleves & case

16 cloth of silver Jerkin

17 faustus [Faustus, Marlowe's tragic character] Jerkin his clok

1 frenchose

blew velvett embr w^t gould paynes blew sattin scalin [unidentified garment]

2 silver paynes lact w^t carnation satins lact over w^t silver

3 the guises [masks]

(4 Rich payns [strips of cloth] w^t Long *stok*ins

5 gould payns w^t blak stript scalings of ca*nis* [?]

6 gould payns w^t velvett scalings

7 gould payns w^t red strypt scalings

8 black bugell

9 red payns for a boy w^t yelo scalins

10 pryams hoes [Priam's hose]

11 spangled hoes

venetians

(1 A purple velvett cut in dimonds Lact & spangels

2 red velved lact w^t gould spanish

(3 a purpell velvet emproydored w^t silver cut on tinse*l*

4 green velvett lact w^t gould spanish

5 blake velvett

6 cloth of silver

7 gren strypt sattin

8 cloth of gould for a boye

↝ Remains of the Rose Playhouse   *1989*

This photograph of the Rose foundations seen from above was taken in 1989, shortly after excavation. The group of pilings in the center should be ignored; they derive from a twentieth-century building.

→ Two Plans of the Rose Playhouse

These modern sketches by John Orrell depict the ground plan of the original Rose Playhouse built in 1587 (top) and after its redesign in the spring of 1592 (bottom). The owner of the playhouse, Philip Henslowe, probably undertook the renovation to accommodate more spectators. At the northern end of the building, the stage and gallery walls were taken down and rebuilt farther back, thus extending the gallery and enlarging the size of the yard.

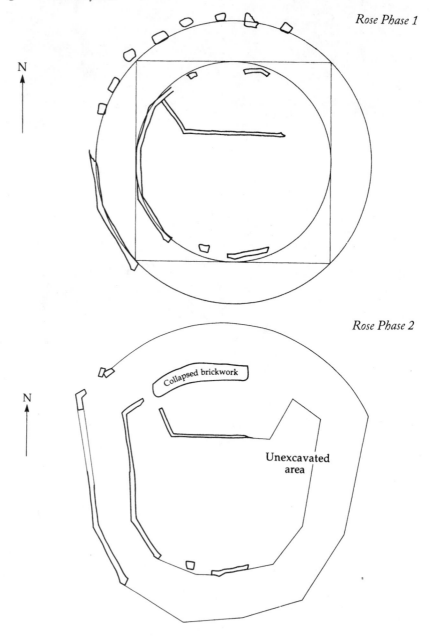

Rose Phase 1

N

Rose Phase 2

N

Collapsed brickwork

Unexcavated
area

→ C. WALTER HODGES

Illustration of the Second Globe

This modern speculative drawing by C. Walter Hodges indicates what the Globe probably looked like after its reconstruction in 1614. The original building burned to the ground on June 29, 1613, during a performance of Shakespeare's *Henry VIII*, when cannons set off during the play ignited the thatched roof. The event is recorded in a letter from Sir Henry Wotton dated July 2, 1613.

A Main entrance
B The yard
C Entrances to lowest gallery
D Position of entrances to staircase and upper galleries
E Corridor serving the different sections of the middle gallery
F Middle gallery ("twopenny rooms")
G Position of "gentlemen's rooms" or "lords' rooms"
H The stage
J The hanging being put up round the stage
K The "hell" under the stage

L The stage trap leading down to the hell
M Stage doors
N Curtained "place behind the stage"
O Gallery above the stage, used as required sometimes by musicians, sometimes by spectators, and often as part of the play
P Backstage area (the tiring-house)
Q Tiring-house door
R Dressing rooms
S Wardrobe and storage
T The hut housing the machine for lowering enthroned gods, etc., to the stage
U The "heavens"
W Hoisting the playhouse flag

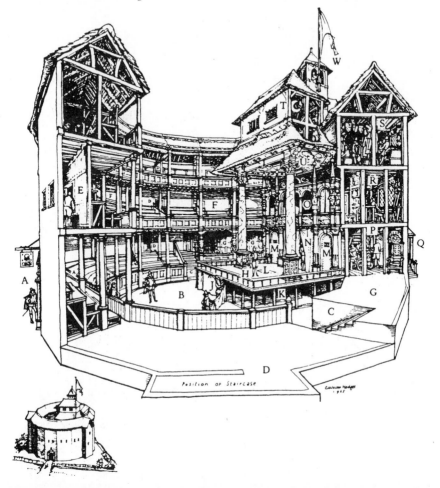

→ Copy of De Witt's Sketch of the Swan Playhouse 1596

This drawing, a copy of a sketch of the Swan Playhouse by Johannes de Witt, roughly suggests the structure of an Elizabethan outdoor playhouse. De Witt had visited London and included the original drawing in a letter to his friend Arend van Buchell, who copied it into his diary.

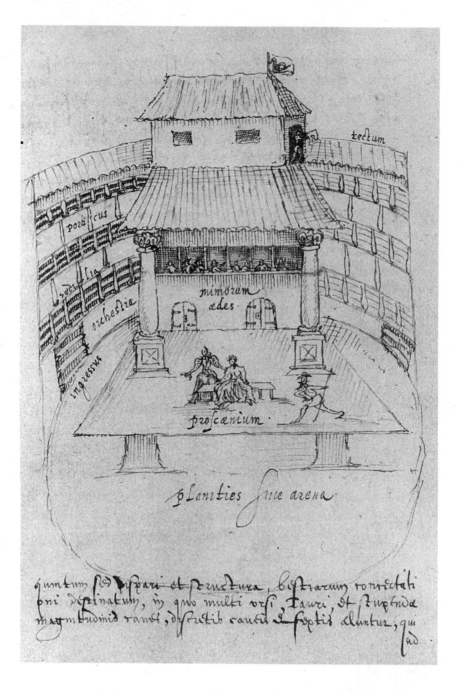

◄ WENCESLAS HOLLAR

Detail from *Long View of London* 1644

This detailed section from Wenceslas Hollar's engraving *Long View of London* depicts the south bank of the Thames River. The designations "The Globe" (over the amphitheater near the river) and "Beere bayting" (on the amphitheater to the left) are inaccurate and should be reversed.

⟶ PHILIP HENSLOWE ➤

Log of Plays from His *Diary* 1591/92

This log of plays performed comes from the handwritten financial accounts of Henslowe's company, consisting of actors under the sponsorship of Lord Strange and the Lord Admiral. (The list is transcribed on p. 70.) The *Diary*, which lists plays and dates of performance, receipts collected at each performance, money lent to actors, fees paid to writers, and the costs of materials used in construction, is one of the most instructive and valuable documents in theater history. The sheet reproduced includes such notable titles as Christopher Marlowe's *The Jew of Malta* (*the Jewe of malltuse*), Thomas Kyd's *The Spanish Tragedy* (*Jeronymo*), and *Henry VI* (*harey the vj*), which may possibly be one of Shakespeare's three plays of that name.

The date at the top of Henslowe's page, February 19, 1591, corresponds to February 1592 in our modern calendar: in the sixteenth century, the New Year began on March 25. (To complicate matters further, Henslowe uses 1591 even past March 25 in these entries, failing to correct himself until April 24.)

The lines in the left margin signify Henslowe's division of the record into weeks. The word *ne* means new, indicating the first performance of a play. *Ester* is Easter. In the sums listed at the right, Henslowe indicates monetary amounts with Roman numerals. The abbreviations that follow the sums are as follows: *li* stands for pounds, *s* for shillings, and *d* for pence (from the Latin *libra*, *solidus*, and *denarius*).

In the name of god Amen 1591
beginninge the 19 of febreary my
lord stranges mene as foloweth
1591

Rd at fryer bacone the 19 of febreary satterday	xvijs iijd
Rd at mvlomvrco the 20 of febreary	xxixs
Rd at orlando the 21 of febreary	xvjs vjd
Rd at spanes comody donne oracoe the 23 of febreary	xiijs vjd
Rd at sr John mandevell the 24 of febreary	xijs vjd
Rd at harey of cornwell the 25 of febreary 1591	xxxijs
Rd at the Iewe of malta the 26 of febreary 1591	ls
Rd at clorys & orgasto the 28 of febreary 1591	xviijs
Rd at mvlomvrco the 29 of febreary 1591	xxxiiijs
Rd at poope Ione the 1 of marche 1591	vs
Rd at matchavell the 2 of marche 1591	xiiijs
Rd at harey the vj the 3 of marche 1591	iijll xvjs 8d
Rd at bendo & Richardo the 4 of marche 1591	xvjs vjd
Rd at iiij playes in one the 6 of marche 1591	xxxjs vjd
Rd at harey the vj the 7 of marche 1591	iijll
Rd at the loockinglasse the 8 of marche 1591	vijs
Rd at senobia the 9 of marche 1591	xxijs vjd
Rd at the Iewe of malta the 10 of marche 1591	lvjs
Rd at harey the vj the 11 of marche 1591	xxxxvijs 6d
Rd at the comodey of doneoracio the 13 marche 1591	xxviijs
Rd at Ieronymo the 14 of marche 1591	xxxviijs
Rd at harey the 16 of marche 1591	xxxxvijs vjd
Rd at mvlo mvloco the 17 of marche 1591	xxxiiijs vijd
Rd at the Iewe of malta the 18 of marche 1591	xxxxiijs
Rd at Ieronymo the 20 of marche 1591	xxxviijs
Rd at constantine the 21 of marche 1591	xiijs
Rd at Ierusallem the 22 of marche 1591	xviijs
Rd at harey of cornwell the 23 of marche 1591	xxijs 6d
Rd at fryer bacone the 25 of marche 1591	xxvjs
Rd at the loockinglasse the 27 of marche 1591	xxs
Rd at harey the vj the 28 of marche 1591	iijll viijs
Rd at mvlomvloco the 29 of marche 1591	xxxiiijs
Rd at doneoracio the 30 of marche 1591	xxviijs
Rd at Ieronymo the 31 of marche 1591	xvs
Rd at mandevell the 1 of aprell 1591	xijs
Rd at matchevell the 2 of aprell 1591	xvjs
Rd at the Iewe of malta the 4 of aprell 1591	xxxxiijs
Rd at harey the vj the 5 of aprell 1591	xxxxjs
Rd at brandymer the 6 of aprell 1591	xxijs
Rd at Ieronymo the 7 of aprell 1591	xxvjs
Rd at mvlomvloco the 8 of aprell 1591	xxxvjs

I̶n the name of god A men 1591
beginge the 19 of febreary my
lord stranges mene A ffoloweth

1591

Rd at fryer bacvne the[1] 19 of febreary … satterdaye …. xvij s iij d[2]

Rd at mvlomvr*co* the 20 of febreary … xxix s

Rd at orlando the 21 of febreary … xvj s vj d

Rd at spanes comodye donne oracioe the 23 of febreary .. xiij s vj d

Rd at sy^r John mandevell the 24 of febreary … xij^s vj d

Rd at harey of cornwell the 25 of febreary 1591 … xxxij^s

Rd at the Jewe of malltuse the 26 of febrearye 1591 … l s

—— Rd at clorys & orgasto the 28 of febreary 1591 … xviij s

Rd at mvlamvlluco the 29 of febrearye 1591 … xxxiiij s

Rd at poope Jone the 1 of marche 1591 … xv^s

Rd at matchavell the 2 of marche 1591 … xiiij s

ne — Rd at harey the vj the 3 of marche 1591 … iiij^li xvj^s 8 d

Rd at bendo & Richardo the 4 of marche 1591 … xvj s

—— Rd at iiij playes in one the 6 of marche 1591 … xxxj s vj d

Rd at harey the vj the 7 of marche 1591 … iij li

Rd at the lockinglasse the 8 of marche 1591 … vij^s

Rd at senobia the 9 of marche 1591 … xxij s vj d

Rd at the Jewe of malta the 10 of marche 1591 … lvj s

Rd at harey the vj the 11 of marche 1591 … xxxxvij^s vj^d

—— Rd at the comodey of doneoracio the 13 march 1591–x– .. xxviiij^s

Rd at Jeronymo the 14 of march 1591 … iij li xj s

Rd at harey the 16 of marche 1591 … xxxj s vj d

Rd at mvlo mvllocco the 17 of marche 1591 … xxviiij s vj^d

Rd at the Jewe of malta the 18 of marche 1591 … xxxix s

—— Rd at Joronymo the 20 of marche 1591 … xxxviiij s

Rd at constantine the 21 of marche 1591 … xij s

Rd at Q Jerusallem the 22 of marche 1591 … xviij s

Rd at harey of cornwell the 23 of marche 1591 … xiij s vj d

Ester<.> Rd at fryer bacon the 25 of marche 1591 … xv^s vj^d

—— Rd at the lockinglasse the 27 of marche 1591 … lv^s

Rd at harey the vj the 28 of marche 1591 … iiij^li viij s

Rd at mvlimvlucko the 29 of marche 1591 … iiij^e ij s

Rd at doneoracio the 30 of marche 1591 … xxxix s

Rd at J*o*ronymo the 31 of marche 1591 … iij li

Rd at mandefell the 1 of ap^rell 1591 … xxx s

—— Rd at matchevell the 3 of ap^rell 1591 … xxij s

Rd at the Jewe of malta the 4 of ap^rell 1591 … xxxxiij s

Rd at harey the vj the 5 of ap^rell 1591 … xxxxj s

Rd at brandymer the 6 of ap^rell 1591 … xxij s

Rd at Jeronymo the 7 of ap^rell 1591 … xxvj s

Rd at mvl*e* mvloco the 8 of ap^rell 1591. J. h.–01–10–00 … xxiij s

---

[1] Italic letters indicate difficult readings, attenuated or blotted letters in the original.

[2] In this example, "xvij s iij d" equals seventeen shillings and three pence.

→ Testimony about a Performance of *Richard II*   *1600/01*

This excerpt from Elizabethan state papers describes the testimony of Augustine Phillips, a shareholder in the Lord Chamberlain's Men, who was summoned to account for the company's performance of *Richard II* in February 1600/01. Supporters of Robert Devereux, earl of Essex, commissioned the performance of a play in which a usurper takes the throne from a monarch deemed unfit to rule, arranging that it be performed the day before the earl's march on London in an attempted coup d'état.

T he Examination of Augustyne Phillypps servant vnto the L Chamberlyne and one of hys players taken the xviij^th of Februarij 1600 vpon hys oth

He sayeth that on Fryday last was sennyght or Thursday Sr Charles Percy Sr Josclyne Percy and the L. Montegle with some thre more spak to some of the players in the presans of thys examinate [person being examined, i.e., Phillips] to have the play of the deposyng and kyllyng of Kyng Rychard the second to be played the Saterday next promysyng to gete them xl*s*. more then their ordynary to play yt. Wher thys Examinate and hys fellowes were determyned to have played some other play, holdyng that play of Kyng Richard to be so old & so long out of vse as that they shold have small or no Company at yt. But at their request this Examinate and his fellowes were Content to play yt the Saterday and had their xl*s*. more then their ordynary for yt and so played yt accordyngly

Augustine Phillips

→ Record of King James's Payment to the King's Men   *1603/04–1604/05*

The Chamber Accounts kept by the Treasurer of the Chamber, one of the king's chief financial officers, record payments for performances at court by Shakespeare's company, as well as monetary gifts to support the company while the theaters were closed due to the plague.

116a   T o Richard Burbadg one of his ma^te [majesty's] Comedians vppon the Councelle warraunte dated at Hamptoncourte viij^o die [eighth day of] Februarij 1603 for the mayntenaunce and releife of himselfe and the rest of his Company being prohibited to p^rsente any playes publiquelie in or neere London by reason of greate perill that might growe throughe the extraordinary Concourse and assemblie of people to a newe increase of the plague till it shall please god to settle the Cittie in a more pfecte health by way of his Maties free gifte

xxx^li [30£]

116a   To Iohn Hemynge one of his ma^te players vppon the Councelle warraunte dated at the Courte at Whitehall vltimo die [last day of] Februar' 1603 for himselfe and the rest of his Company for two playes p^rsented before his ma^tie viz the one on Candelmas Day at night and the other on Shrouesonday at night the some of thirtene poundes six

shilling and eight pence and[1] way of his ma^{te} rewarde for the same twoe
playes six poundes thirteene shilling and iiij^{or} pence in all the some of
$$xx^{li}$$

137b To Iohn Hemynges one of his Ma^{te} players vppon the Counselle warraunte dated at the Courte at Whitehalle xxj^{mo} die \Ianuarij/ 1604 for
the paines and expences of himselfe and his companie in playinge and
presentinge of sixe Enterludes or plaies before his Matie viz on all
Saintes daie at nighte the Sonday at nighte followinge beinge the iiijth
of November 1604 S^{t}. Stephens daie at nighte Innocente day at nighte
and on the vijth and viijth daies of Ianuarie for everie of the saide plaies
accordinge to the usualle allowaunce of vj^{li} xiij^{s} iiij^{d} the peece xl^{li} and lxvj^{s}
viij^{d} for everie plaie by waie of his Ma^{te} rewarde xx^{li} in all the some of
$$lx^{li}$$

[1] Scribal slip.

→ EDWARD ALLEYN

Letter to His Wife   1593?

In August 1593, Edward Alleyn, the great tragedian and interpreter of Christopher
Marlowe's heroic characters, wrote from Bristol to his wife in London while he was
touring the provinces with the Lord Admiral's Men. The playhouses in the capital
were closed for much of 1592 and 1593 owing to an epidemic of plague.

M$_y$ good sweett mouse I comend me hartely
to yo^u And to my father my mother & my
sister bess hoping in god thought [though] the siknes
beround about you yett by his mercy itt may
escape yor house wch by y^e grace of god it
shall therfor vse this corse [course] kepe yor house
fayr and clean wch I knowe you will
and every evening throwe water before yor dore
and in yor bakcsid and haue in yor windowes
good store of rwe and herbe of grace and
w^t all the grace of god wch must be obtaynd
by prayers and so doinge no dout but ye lord
will mercyfully defend yo^u: now good mouse
I haue no newse to send you but this thatt
we haue all ou^r helth for wch the lord be praysed
I reseved yor letter att bristo [Bristol] by richard couley
for the wich I thank you   I haue sent yo^u by this
berer Thomas popes kinsman my whit [white]
wascote because it is a trobell to me to cary it

reseave it w^t this letter And lay it vp for
me till I com   if you send any mor letters
send to me by the cariers of shrowsbery or to west
chester or to york to be keptt till my lord
stranges players com and thus sweett hartt
w^t my harty comendā [commendations] to all o^r [our] frends I sess [cease]
from bristo this wensday after saynt Jams his day
being redy to begin the playe of hary of cornwall
mouse do my harty comend to m^r grigs his wif
and all his houshould and to my sister phillyps
        Yo^r Loving housband E Alleyn

mouse you send me no newes of any things
you should send of yor domestycall matters
such things as hapens att home as how yor
distilled watter proves or this or that or any
thing what you will

[*vertically in left-hand margin*]
and Jug I pray yo^u lett my orayng tawny stokins [stockings] of wolen
be dyed a very good blak against I com hom to wear in the
winter   yo^u sente me nott word of my garden but next tym you will
but remember this in any case that all that bed wch was parsley
in the month of september you sowe itt w^t spinage for then is the tym:
I would do it my self but we shall nott com hom till allholand tyd [All Saints'
    Day, November 1]
and so swett mouse farwell and broke [brook, endure] ou^r long Jorney w^t
    patienc

[*addressed:*]
This be delyvered
to m^r hinslo on [one] of the
gromes of hir ma͞ıst [majesty's]
chamber dwelling
on the bank sid
right over against
the clink

CHAPTER 3

"What Is Your Text?"

————————————————————— ✕ —————————————————————

Because Shakespeare has become, for many who study him and even for many who do not, an object of veneration or a cultural idol, his works have almost assumed the status of religious documents. A quick look at two modern editions of Shakespeare, however, will reveal variations in this sacred text, numerous and sometimes major differences in the words that constitute it. In the 1986 Oxford edition of *Hamlet*, for example, Hamlet in his first soliloquy wishes that his "too too solid flesh would melt, / Thaw, and resolve itself into a dew"; in the Riverside edition, that flesh is "too too sallied" (*sallied* is a variation of *sullied,* meaning "stained"). This inconsistency, a famous instance of a textual *crux,* or problem, raises a question that every student of Shakespeare needs to be aware of: how can we tell what Shakespeare wrote? Whether we read from a collection of the complete works such as *The Riverside Shakespeare* or *The Complete Pelican Shakespeare,* or a single-play volume from a popular series such as the Folger or Signet editions, the excellence and familiarity of modern Shakespeare texts have made it easy to read the plays. But this same convenience distances us from the difficulties of the original texts and protects us from the problems and uncertainties attendant on the laborious process of establishing that text. It is worthwhile to spend some time defamiliarizing our modern books, to move away from them temporarily so as to examine the nature and origins of the Shakespearean text. What is it, and how did it get to be the way that it is?

What Is a Shakespearean Text?

The central problem in textual scholarship is one of authority, a problem related, as the etymology suggests, to that of authorship. Textual scholars seek to establish as accurately as possible the words that the author wrote. But as any-one who has ever used a word processor to produce a revised version of a doc-ument will recognize, this is not an easy matter. Is it immediately clear which is the original and which the revision? Is there a longhand version against which the printed copies can be checked? For works composed some four hundred years ago, these difficulties are compounded, and there are different problems as well. No manuscripts for any of Shakespeare's plays have survived. (A possible exception to this broad statement is a set of additions to a collab-orative play called *Sir Thomas More*; some scholars believe that a section of this manuscript, shown on p. 91, is in Shakespeare's handwriting.) His plays have come down to us in the form of books printed from lost manuscripts, either authorial drafts or copies of them. Furthermore, the printing process that gave us those books was in a relatively early state of development, making its prod-ucts highly vulnerable to error. Even the author who supervised the printing of his works and checked proofs directly from the press, which Shakespeare apparently did not do for his plays, found that mistakes inevitably made their way into the final versions. Spelling and punctuation were flexible and irregu-lar: the surviving signatures imply that Shakespeare spelled even his own name in different ways.

But the problems associated with textual authority derive not only from an evolving orthographic system and an imperfect mechanical process. An even greater source of confusion is the genre in which Shakespeare wrote. Of all forms of writing, drama is probably the one in which the author's identity is hardest to establish because theater, as we observed in Chapters 1 and 2, is es-sentially a collaborative art. An Elizabethan lyric poet's words may have been accidentally misread in the printing house, but the dramatist's words were subject to modification well before the printing process even began. The scribe who copied out the parts for the actors, for example, may have misunderstood the author's penmanship and thus introduced errors. An actor may have found a particular line difficult to deliver and requested a change — or simply made the change himself. Actors frequently misremember or alter lines, and some-times these erroneous versions become a permanent part of the play text. The prompter, or "book-keeper," needing more time to get an actor on stage, may have contributed a line or two himself to stall the action until the required character could appear. If the play were running overtime in rehearsal, the au-thor or perhaps the book-keeper might have made cuts. The rehearsal scenes in *A Midsummer Night's Dream*, in which the mechanicals prepare their play *Pyramus and Thisbe* for Duke Theseus, humorously depict how changes might have been introduced into a theatrical script.

Still another obstacle to textual authority is Shakespeare's apparent indif-ference to publishing. Only about half of his plays were printed during his life-time, and he seems not to have been directly involved in their publication. On the other hand, he may have overseen the printing of his early narrative po-ems, *Venus and Adonis* and *The Rape of Lucrece*. As strange as it may seem to us, such authorial distance was not uncommon in the theater of early modern England. To a Renaissance playwright, "publication" meant presentation of the work to the public on a stage; it did not necessarily imply preservation in the form of a printed book. Copyright laws as we know them did not exist, and prevailing notions of intellectual or artistic property had little to do with the author. Normally a play belonged to the dramatic company, the Lord Admiral's Men or the King's Men, for example, that produced it on the stage, or else to the bookseller or printer who had purchased it from that company.

When a playwright finished a script, he delivered it to the theatrical company for which he worked (or which had commissioned or purchased it) and thus relinquished his rights to the play. ("He" is the appropriate pronoun: there were no female professional playwrights.) Only one or two complete copies of the script existed, the author's original and perhaps another copy; one of these served as "the book of the play," the master copy used for the stage production. Transcripts were expensive to produce, of course, since the entire play had to be copied over by hand with quill pen and ink. Actors were never given complete versions of the script, as is the practice in the modern theater, but were provided with only their own parts, known as *sides,* consisting of their lines with cues and instructions for entrances and exits. (In the second scene of *A Midsummer Night's Dream,* the mechanicals' first rehearsal, Peter Quince distributes the "parts" to the actors and urges them to learn their lines.) A theatrical company carefully guarded its copies of the script to prevent theft and subsequent performance of the play by another theatrical troupe. After a number of performances, when a play had ceased to draw audiences and was to be taken out of the repertory, the company may have sold the script to a publisher, who then printed and sold copies to the public. It was not in a company's interest to publish a popular play that might warrant revival, since the fewer copies in circulation the better.

The record of publication for Shakespeare's plays during his active career offers some insight into the economics of the Renaissance theatrical companies and their dramatic properties. The first of his plays to be published was *Titus Andronicus* in 1594; as the title page (reproduced on p. 92) reveals, the author went unnamed. At about the same time there appeared a version of one of the *Henry VI* plays — unattributed, with a different title, and textually very different from the one we know. From 1597, when Shakespeare was becoming one of the most popular and productive dramatists in London, more and more of his plays began to see print: *Richard II* in 1597; *Love's Labor's Lost* and *Henry IV, Part 1* in 1598; *A Midsummer Night's Dream, The Merchant of Venice, Much Ado about Nothing,* and *Henry IV, Part 2* in 1600. In addition, versions of *Romeo and Juliet* and *Henry V* that differ substantially from those printed later were issued in 1598 and 1600 respectively. During the second decade of Shakespeare's career, however, fewer of his plays appeared in bookshops: some of those we rank among his most important (*As You Like It, Julius Caesar, Twelfth Night, Macbeth, Antony and Cleopatra, The Winter's Tale,* and *The Tempest*) were printed only after his death, in the 1623 collected edition known as the First Folio. (See the title page and catalogue reproduced on pp. 93–94.) This publishing record suggests that as Shakespeare became famous and a potential source of income for the new theatrical troupe that he and his associates had established in 1594, some of his scripts were sold to publishers in an effort to capitalize on his name and the popularity of his recent work. As their principal playwright's reputation grew and as the King's Men consolidated their theatrical sovereignty in Jacobean London, the frequency of publication began to diminish, as if the company no longer needed to make a few pounds off old scripts and was less inclined to dispose of them.

The complexities of this route from playwright to actors to printer, and the number of stops along the way, make it extremely difficult for modern scholars to determine the accuracy of a Shakespearean text. Some of the most perplexing questions arise from the existence of different texts for some plays. The First Folio contains thirty-six plays; of these, eighteen had already been printed in single-play editions called quartos. Thus, for about half of the plays we have two versions, and for some of these we have multiple versions because the quartos were reprinted to meet demand. It is important to keep in mind that reprinting in the Renaissance meant something different from what it does now, when a popular text can simply be copied photographically. At the turn of the seventeenth century, reprinting a play meant starting over, perhaps correcting mistakes found in the earlier version and probably introducing new errors. Thus a reprinted Renaissance text may actually be a new version of the play. In some cases, notably *King Lear*, the differences between the two texts, the Quarto of 1608 and the Folio of 1623, are so numerous and significant that the hazards of reprinting alone cannot account for them; as we shall see, some scholars now believe that Shakespeare himself may have revised his initial version so that both texts are "authorial."

When you open a modern edition of *King Lear*, which text are you reading? How will you know? Which one is "Shakespeare's"? Who decided? On what grounds? Does it matter? What is at stake in the attempt to certify the text as "Shakespeare's" alone, rather than Shakespeare's and Nicholas Rowe's, or Alexander Pope's, or David Bevington's, or one of the many other editors who have attempted to establish the text over the past four centuries? To such questions this chapter will attempt to provide at least partial answers, but the effort to do so has been complicated by recent developments in critical theory. The postmodern urge to think of authorship as collective rather than individual and the concomitant challenge to authorial intention have altered the entire enterprise of textual scholarship. In particular, uncertainty about definitions of authorship makes it virtually impossible to establish an authoritative text. In the face of such complications, it makes sense to gather as many facts as possible, and thus a brief introduction to the printing process at the turn of the seventeenth century is in order.

From Pen to Press: The Printing of Renaissance Plays

An account of early modern printing must begin with the author's original manuscript. A dramatist who wrote a play did so in longhand, producing a manuscript sometimes known as the author's *foul papers*. Before the play was submitted for performance, either the dramatist himself or a professional scribe probably made a transcript suitable for theatrical use. This second manuscript is now known as a *fair copy*. Then a member of the company marked up that copy, specifying theatrical business that the author might have left unclear and attending to textual details that affected the process of theatrical realization. This adjusted version became known as *the book of the play;* to the company that owned it, it was the most valuable form of the text. Of these three manuscript versions — foul papers, fair copy, or the book of the play — one (and sometimes more than one) was used by the publisher as the copy text for printing; all were in different ways problematic. The paradigm I have described is necessarily simplified. Numerous variations of these three categories of handwritten texts probably existed. And as Paul Werstine reminds us, "These texts were open to penetration and alteration not only by Shakespeare himself and by his fellow actors but also by multiple theatrical and extra-theatrical scriveners, by theatrical annotators, adapters and revisers (who might cut or add), by censors, and by compositors and proofreaders" (86).

Foul papers probably represented the version closest to the author's intentions, although such a manuscript might not include authorial changes introduced into the fair copy or, during the course of rehearsal, into the book of the play. Foul papers, as the name connotes, were often difficult to read. The penmanship, what is known as secretary hand, is not easy for the modern eye to decipher; and while a contemporary reader would have had less trouble than we do, the writing still exhibits certain orthographic features that could make it confusing even to the practiced reader. Foul papers by definition offer an early version of the play and would have contained deletions, marginal and interlinear additions, and other instances of second thoughts or false starts. Inconsistencies, as we know from the rough drafts of our own papers, were manifold: in one of the early printed versions of *Romeo and Juliet,* which appears to have been set from foul papers, the stage directions refer to Juliet's mother variously as "Mother," "Capulet's Wife," "Lady," and "Lady of the house"; the prefixes to the character's speeches vary from "Wife" to "Mo." to "M." to "La." to "Capu. Wi." to "Cap. Wi." to "Old La." Some of the speech prefixes in manuscript originals even shift from the name of the character to the name of the actor for whom Shakespeare wrote the part.

Fair copy might be easier to read and thus to transcribe and set into type, but it, too, would presumably contain mistakes, especially if it were made not by the author but by a hired copyist. Mistakes aside, the copyist's own linguistic and orthographic biases could intrude. Ralph Crane, a professional scribe whose transcripts of several plays were used in the printing of the First Folio, had certain preferences in punctuation (he appears to have been inordinately fond of parentheses, for example) that have made their way into our modern texts but probably do not reflect Shakespeare's practice. The book of the play can be especially perplexing because it may remove us even further from the author's original script. Again, however, the term *original* is indefinite and unreliable when used in reference to a dramatic text, given its collaborative nature. It is difficult to know whether certain characteristics of a text deriving from the book of the play result from an author's design or from the conditions of a theatrical process with which the author may have had little or even nothing to do. Any of these potentially faulty documents might have served as copy text for the printer who made the play available for public sale and thus preserved it for posterity. And still more errors would be introduced in the print shop.

For understanding the printing of Renaissance books the first important term to grasp is *sheet*, denoting the large piece of paper with which the printer began and which was pressed onto the inked type. (This sheet was probably at least 18 by 14 inches in size; paper was handmade, and the size of printing sheets may have varied. Moreover, it is difficult to speculate based on existing folios: these vary significantly in size, and many would have been cut down for purposes of binding and perhaps cut down again years later for rebinding.) To make a folio — the large form used for the collected edition of Shakespeare's plays — the printer folded the sheet once, making two leaves, or four pages front and back; the book was thus about 9 by 14 inches. To make a quarto — the form in which a single play was usually published — the printer folded the sheet twice, making four leaves (hence the name *quarto*), or eight pages front and back; this book was thus about 7 by 9 inches, or the size of a large modern paperback. For a folio, the folded sheets were gathered into groups and sewn together. With the First Folio, they were gathered "in sixes," that is, three folded sheets were placed within one another at the fold, producing a *gathering*, or *quire*, of six leaves, or twelve pages. For a quarto, the single folded sheet, producing eight pages, was the unit of sewing. The folding, sewing, and binding were the last steps in the process.

Whatever the size of the book, folio or quarto, pages were not printed in numerical order. One entire sheet was placed flat onto the printing press, first on one side and then on the other. The printing was done according to the size of the gathering, so that for a folio-in-sixes, twelve pages (or three sheets, front and back) were being prepared for a single gathering. This system required that the pages be set up according to the way that the sheet would finally be folded: with the folio format, for example, pages one and twelve were printed on one side of a sheet, and then pages two and eleven on the reverse side. The illustration on page 80 illustrates this process. Two compositors would have set the type simultaneously, one of them beginning on page six and working backward to page one, the second beginning on page seven and working forward to page twelve. Thus the side of the sheet containing pages six and seven was set first and printed first, and then pages five and eight on the other side was set and printed. As awkward as the process may seem, this was the most economical way to print a text. Beginning not at the beginning but in the middle of a gathering that contained three entire sheets, or twelve pages of a finished book, the printer had to estimate the amount of text that would fill each of the twelve pages. This process of estimation was called *casting off* copy.

Once the copy had been cast off, normally by an experienced printer accustomed to the task, the compositors (from *com-pose*, or "put together") began

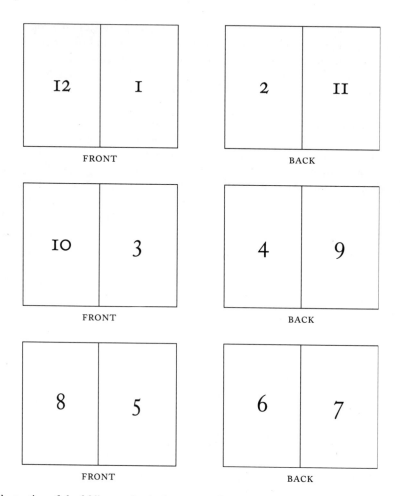

Illustration of the folding and printing process for a gathering of twelve folio pages, re-produced from G. B. Harrison, Introducing Shakespeare, *p. 208*

the process of setting type. Reading the portion of the manuscript assigned to them by the person who had cast it off, they selected pieces of metal type, taking each one from large cases divided into small boxes containing each letter and punctuation mark. They then placed the pieces of type, formed into the words of the text, into the frame that was locked into the bed of the press. (A seventeenth-century illustration of a printing press is found on p. 95.) The blank sheet was pressed onto the bed and imprinted; it was then removed and proofread, after which the pieces of type were extracted from the frame and sorted and returned to their cases.

This process of casting off copy and then printing pages out of numerical order saved time and type, but it could also create serious problems for the printing house. For example, the last page of the Quarto text of *King Lear* (1608), shown on page 96, presents a case in which the printer apparently had to squeeze text onto the last page available to him. Consequently we see evidence of corner-cutting: two short speeches are run together on the same line; the Duke of Albany's sympathetic tribute to Lear is converted from verse to prose, which takes less space. The need for economy may also explain why a word is dropped ("great" in "this great decay") and the stage direction for Lear's death omitted. These and other such compromises saved the printer the expense of having to use another sheet.

The chaos that must have reigned in the London print shops of the late sixteenth century is hard to exaggerate. To start with, the noise emanating from the machinery must have been overwhelming, as the wooden and iron parts of the printing presses banged against each other in the process of setting paper to type. Printing was a dirty job as well, considering the quantities of ink required. The leather print balls used to apply the ink had to be kept supple, so English pressmen soaked the leather overnight in human urine. It is thus likely that the print shops were plagued with flies. Sometimes compositors were working on more than one book at the same time; likewise, a single book was sometimes printed by various houses and then bound together. The organizational challenges must have been enormous. In view of these physical difficulties, it is to be expected that errors would appear in the printed versions of Shakespeare's plays — dropped lines, perhaps even larger omissions, the misreading of handwriting, the wrong letter substituted for the right one, blunders in casting off copy. We should be surprised only that the texts we have do not contain more obvious mistakes than they do.

Shakespeare's Plays in Print

Of the eighteen Shakespeare plays printed in quarto, a majority were printed more than once. Some of these reprints signify the popularity of a particular play: it was reprinted because the first printing sold out and a demand for it still existed. Some of the plays, however, may have been reprinted because the first issue represented an unusually faulty text. These peculiar and problematic versions are sometimes known as "bad quartos." Many of them may have been published illicitly, a result of theft or some other irregularity; and in a few cases the appearance of a bad quarto seems to have stimulated Shakespeare's company to arrange for the printing of a more accurate version of the text.

Hamlet is the classic instance of such a scenario. The first printed version, or First Quarto (Q1), appeared in 1603, and it differs radically from the version we read now. In Q1 the text is very short, about half the length of the later versions; scenes and speeches are placed in an order different from the sequence we know; the figure familiar to us as Polonius is called Corambis; and certain well-known passages are barely recognizable. Consider the beginning of the play's most famous speech:

To be, or not to be, I [ay] there's the point,
To Die, to sleepe, is that all? I all:
No, to sleepe, to dreame, I mary there it goes . . .

As these three lines attest, the differences between this passage and the familiar Folio (F) version are not minor, and additional variations appear in the complete versions of the speech from Q1 and F on pages 98 and 99. Once the Quarto text had appeared for sale in London, the King's Men evidently arranged for a corrected version to be made available. Q2, published in 1604 (although some copies read 1605), is advertised as being "Newly imprinted and enlarged to almost as much againe as it was, according to the true and perfect Coppie."

The status of such different versions is now the subject of fierce debate. Some textual scholars believe that a bad quarto derived from a reconstructed version of the play by a person or persons only slightly familiar with it; some of these pirated texts are thought to have been concocted by actors who had played small parts in the production and who then sought, with varying degrees of success, to re-create the play from memory. Thus the poor texts of the bad quartos are said to result from "memorial reconstruction." Although this theory is sometimes disputed on the grounds that evidence is slim, nineteenth-century theatrical practice attests to feats of memory no less impressive. Moreover, the Spanish playwright Lope de Vega, a contemporary of Shakespeare, speaks of professional dramatic pirates who went to the theater deliberately to memorize and reproduce plays for print (see Potter 21). In the case of *Hamlet*, it looks as if the text was recited to a scribe by the actor who played the tiny parts of Marcellus and Lucianus. Some form of memorial reconstruction appears to be the most plausible way of accounting for the wildly discrepant texts of certain plays.

Strong resistance has arisen to the pejorative nature of the term *bad quarto*, and some scholars argue that modern editors have been too quick to dismiss these versions as corrupt and un-Shakespearean. One new theory — actually an old theory revived — came to prominence in the 1970s and '80s: that some of the bad quartos may in fact be early Shakespearean versions of the plays, akin to rough drafts, and that the differences between two texts of a play are attributable to Shakespeare's own rewriting of the initial text. The controversy over the two texts of *King Lear*, described below, has prompted scholars to reassess several quarto texts formerly condemned as inferior, such as the 1597 Quarto of *Richard III* and the 1602 Quarto of *The Merry Wives of Windsor*; Steven Urkowitz, whose arguments about the revision of *King Lear* have gained considerable favor, has sought to rehabilitate even the bad quarto of *Hamlet*. According to one witty scholar, there is now no such thing as a bad quarto, only a misunderstood quarto or an unloved quarto.

Most of those who stop short of attributing to Shakespeare the peculiar version of "To be or not to be" found in Q1 of *Hamlet* will admit the legitimacy of two Shakespearean versions of *King Lear*. The existence of two different texts of *King Lear*, the 1608 Quarto and the 1623 Folio, has always puzzled scholars, who naturally want to know which was the "real," the authoritative, the "Shakespearean" form of the play. Although the 1608 printing has not generally been considered a bad quarto, the discrepancies between it and the Folio often led editors to posit the existence of a prior ideal text. Now, however, both versions are held to be legitimate and authorial, the Folio constituting Shakespeare's later revision of the Quarto. Q is a relatively good text, and it contains certain lines and episodes that do not appear in F but that seem indisputably Shakespearean, not the invention or the faulty recollection of a pirate reporter. F contains about one hundred lines absent from Q, while Q contains about three hundred lines not found in F. Until recently most modern editors of *King Lear*, believing each text to be a corruption of a lost original, conflated Q and F, even though such a synthesis creates some redundancy. Even more troubling, such a conflation offers the reader a dramatic work Shakespeare apparently never conceived. The revision theory has Shakespeare himself revising Q into F, expanding the earlier text in some places but also cutting so as to achieve greater speed in the second half of the play. These scholarly debates have begun to have a significant impact on what we read: the Oxford edition of the complete works, prepared in the 1980s by editors who fueled the debate over *King Lear*, prints both versions as if they were separate plays. Even the original titles vary, one being *The Historie of King Lear* (Q), the other *The Tragedie of King Lear* (F).

Uncertainties about the alternative versions of a play point to an important shift in modern thinking about textual scholarship and what it can achieve. Shortly after the beginning of the twentieth century, bibliographical scholars such as W. W. Greg, R. B. McKerrow, and, later, Fredson Bowers and Charlton Hinman began to study the process by which Shakespeare's texts came into physical being and thus to develop the tools of analytical bibliography, methods that have taught us how to judge the texts that have survived. Professor Hinman, who published his detailed investigations in *The Printing and Proof-Reading of the First Folio of Shakespeare*, compared each page of fifty-five copies of the First Folio at the Folger Shakespeare Library and even identified individual pieces of type that had become damaged in the printing process. He and other scholars distinguished the work of five compositors who set the pages of the First Folio, discerning their spelling preferences, propensity for certain kinds of errors, and varying degrees of skill. Compositor B, for example, a thorough professional, set over half the pages of the book. Compositor E, on the other hand, was an apprentice, probably a teenager, who joined the project late, worked mainly on the tragedies, and made an enormous number of mistakes in reading copy and setting type. The spelling practices of Compositors A and B are illustrated in the facsimiles on page 97.

The precision of this research and the fascinating historical picture it produced imparted a spirit of optimism and potential certainty to the enterprise of textual scholarship. Fredson Bowers, writing in 1958, articulated the guiding principles of textual criticism:

> May we not lay this down as a doctrine? In all cases when a definitive edition is proposed for a dramatist, or other author, of no matter what century, we should insist (*a*) that it be critically edited, and (*b*) that in its texture of accidentals, as well as in its words, it conform to the closest approximation to the author's own linguistic and orthographic characteristics that can be recovered. (141)

At the risk of oversimplifying, we can say that this first wave of twentieth-century textual criticism was based on two assumptions: that an ideal text of a Shakespeare play did exist, and that a scientific approach would permit the scholar, with persistence and luck, to recover that text as the author wrote it.

Postmodern editing has rejected the first of these premises. It is now generally conceded that there was no such thing as a final perfected version of, say, *Hamlet;* that Shakespeare probably reworked and altered the text continuously during its theatrical life; and that the problem of dramatic authorship, with actors, prompters, and scribes all contributing to the creation of the play, makes it naive to fetishize a single text. Such thinking can be taken too far: it is probably wrongheaded to defend Q1 of *Hamlet* as just one among several legitimate versions. Nevertheless, these doubts about the perfect text point us in the right direction. They remind us that the words before us, as solid and authoritative as they may look, are unstable and open to question, and they should lead us to recognize that we cannot approach any Shakespeare play fairly without being aware of the complex and curious process by which it came into existence.

The Folio seems more solid and reliable than most of the quartos (especially the bad ones), and whatever its inherent textual problems, it is the only source we have for almost half of the plays. As a volume of collected works, it was very nearly anticipated by another publisher three years after the playwright's death. Thomas Pavier, a Londoner who had obtained the rights to a few of the plays already in print, made a shady effort to amass and sell a volume of previously published quartos. His scheme was foiled by defensive action on the part of the King's Men (although a few Pavier quartos were printed and sold). It is unclear whether Shakespeare's former colleagues had already planned such a book, or whether Pavier's entrepreneurial efforts stimulated them to undertake a collected edition. (Furthermore, we are not certain whether the primary impetus was commemorative, and so initiated by the players, or commercial, and so initiated by the publishers; almost certainly the motives were mixed.) Whatever the sequence, two of Shakespeare's fellow actors, John Heminges and Henry Condell, joined with the London publishers Edward Blount and Isaac Jaggard to produce a volume that contained not only the plays already in print but most of the hitherto unprinted works as well. They sought to acquire the rights to the plays already in print — these texts were owned by the men who had registered and then printed them — and to assemble usable manuscripts of those never published. This was a formidable task, and the contents of the volume were determined by whether rights could be secured. In the case of *Troilus and Cressida,* for example, it appears that the two people who had registered and published the Quarto of 1609, at first unwilling to yield their rights to the play, came to terms at the eleventh hour, when the Folio was almost completely printed; when they did agree, the contents were rearranged slightly in order to facilitate the last-minute inclusion of *Troilus.* The negotiations were concluded so hastily and late that a few copies of the Folio seem to have been sewn and placed on sale before *Troilus* was entirely printed and bound into the book.

The Folio, known now as the First Folio, was offered for sale in London in November 1623 for one pound. (For a complicated set of reasons, there may have been some flexibility in the price.) It contains thirty-six plays, eighteen of which had never seen print before, some of them among Shakespeare's greatest achievements (e.g., *Macbeth, Twelfth Night,* and *The Tempest*). Not every play in which Shakespeare had a hand is present. Two on which he worked with John Fletcher, *The Two Noble Kinsmen* (printed later in quarto) and *Cardenio* (now lost), are absent, as is *Pericles*, a late play with similarly uncertain authorship. Yet *Henry VIII*, also a late collaboration with Fletcher, does appear in the volume. Considering that the playwright was dead when the Folio project was begun and that some of the plays had been printed before, the vital question concerns the nature of the various materials that were to be printed in it. To ascertain as exactly as possible the words that Shakespeare wrote, it is important to know what sources the printers used as copy to set the type for each play in the Folio.

The sources for the works printed in the Folio are: (1) Shakespeare's own manuscripts, (2) scribal transcripts of those manuscripts, some of them from the playhouse, (3) quarto versions already in print, or (4) some combination of these. For plays already printed in reasonably accurate form, the quarto version was used as copy text, often corrected or annotated with reference to a manuscript, either authorial or scribal, of the same play. *A Midsummer Night's Dream*, for example, falls into this category, having been printed from Q2 but supplemented with readings from another copy. For plays never printed, different kinds of manuscripts were consulted. Sometimes Shakespeare's own draft (foul papers) was used as the source: *The Comedy of Errors* exhibits characteristics that indicate a direct authorial origin. Sometimes the source is a scribal transcript prepared with the aim of achieving a clean, legible copy, although for whom the transcript was prepared is not always clear (the acting company? the printers themselves?). Manuscripts prepared by Ralph Crane (the professional scribe) served as copy texts for several plays in the Folio, such as *The Two Gentlemen of Verona* and *The Tempest*. Occasionally a copy that had been used as the book of the play became the basis for the Folio text, as with *Macbeth;* this may explain why the Scottish play is notably shorter than most of the tragedies, since the book of the play may have been a transcript designed for a particular kind of performance. Or it may be that *Macbeth* is brief because Shakespeare's artistic sense so dictated.

All these complexities are germane to the inescapable question of textual authority. To approach the problem microscopically, how can we be sure that the word we admire in a favorite speech was written by Shakespeare and not supplied by a scribe who could not decipher the original, or invented by a stage manager whose place in the text was smudged and who needed a word right away, or mistakenly set down by a compositor who was momentarily woolgathering? To put the matter in macroscopic terms, if a New York publishing house wishes to offer a modern-spelling edition of *Hamlet* and engages an editor to prepare it, which early version should be used for copy text? The problematic Q1 might be dismissed easily, except that it contains one scene (between the Queen and Horatio, near the end of act 4) found in no other contemporary text. What about the second Quarto, which has been thought to derive from authorial foul papers? It is usually considered the best choice. But then the Folio version contains many useful directions for stage practice absent from Q2: should some of these be included? Shouldn't the editor simply choose the readings that seem most authoritative from each version and combine them into a single text? But what is the basis for deciding on "the readings that seem most authoritative"? And isn't the *Hamlet* produced by such compromises the creation of the editor more than the author? But once again, in the case of early modern plays, what is an author?

Some Examples of Textual Instability

A glance at some famous textual problems in Shakespeare transports us quickly from the abstract to the concrete and reveals how contingent and problematic our texts can be. Here is the conclusion of *Titus Andronicus*, Shakespeare's earliest tragedy, as printed in the Folio of 1623:

> See Iustice done on *Aaron* that damn'd Moore,
> From whom, our heauy happes had their beginning:
> Then afterwards, to Order well the State,
> That like Euents, may ne're it Ruinate.

Many readers have condemned these last four lines — as heavy-handed morally as they are poetically — as too crude to be worthy of the world's most celebrated playwright. At the same time, however, all of *Titus* has struck many readers and audiences as coarse and un-Shakespearean, and the lines are consistent with its raw theatricality (hands cut off; severed heads exhibited onstage; a tongue cut out; and, at a banquet near the end of the play, a mother invited to feast on a pie made with the flesh of her two sons). Indeed, the play seems to have been composed by a young dramatist still learning his craft and responsive to the sensational revenge plays of the early 1590s. So it is with this last verse passage, which strikes the ear perhaps as crude but not completely uncharacteristic, not unlike, for example, the two lines that precede these in the Folio: "Her life was Beast-like, and deuoid of pitty, / And being so, shall have like want of pitty." As it turns out, these two lines are authentic, but the last four lines were in fact not written by Shakespeare at all — they appear to have been composed by a printer.

Using the techniques of analytical bibliography, scholars have determined that the Folio text of *Titus Andronicus* was prepared from the third Quarto (1611) of the play, which was reprinted from the second Quarto of 1600. All of these texts are substantially alike, and all contain (with minor variations) the last four lines about Aaron's villainy and the restoration of order in Rome. In 1904, however, the textual picture changed radically with the discovery in Sweden of a copy of the first printing of *Titus*, Q1 (1594). (Still the world's only surviving copy, it now resides in the Folger Shakespeare Library in Washington, D.C.) What is important here is that Q1 does not contain the four lines quoted above, and scholarly detective work has thus created a fascinating story of how the new ending of *Titus* came into being.

The evidence suggests that the text for Q2 — the basis for the Folio and all subsequent texts until this century — was prepared from a copy of Q1, but that the physical book used as the source was defective, with the last three leaves damaged at the bottom and the words obscured. G. Blakemore Evans describes what must have happened as the printer approached the end of his job and found himself confronted with defective copy:

> Instead of obtaining another copy of Q1, somebody (almost certainly in the printing house) "restored" the missing words or lines as best he could by guesswork. On the last page (sig. K4v) he outdid himself. Misled by the fact that the text as he found it did not fill out the page and by the chance that the original compositor of Q1 had placed the final *Exeunt.* (now missing because of the damage to the leaf) two lines below the last line of the play, he invented four new and feeble lines relating to Aaron and the disposing of the state. (*Riverside Shakespeare* 1051)

Modern editions therefore omit these last lines. The end of *Titus* provides a rare glimpse at how spurious lines made their way into a Shakespeare text and, until new information became available, were considered authorial. The text, in other words, is never definitive, and it is possible that additional facts will surface and cause us to alter our assumptions about other passages, perhaps even cherished lines in familiar plays.

In the case of *Titus* it is relatively easy to decide which text is more nearly Shakespearean, but other conflicts between a quarto and the Folio versions of a play are less easy to resolve. *A Midsummer Night's Dream*, for example, appeared in quarto in 1600, four or five years after the initial stage performances. In the Quarto text, Egeus, Hermia's angry father who resists her marriage to Lysander, is overruled by the Duke and leaves the stage in act 4 without having agreed to her marriage or having blessed it. He does not appear again for the wedding festivities in act 5. In the Folio, however, Egeus does reemerge in act 5, scene 1, to present Theseus with the list of proposed after-dinner entertainments, a task assigned in the Quarto to Philostrate, the master of the revels. Whether Egeus attends or does not attend his daughter's wedding feast need not seriously alter the ending of the play, but his presence there can augment the sense of reconciliation and harmony and thus lighten the tone of the final scene. Did Shakespeare revise the play with this conciliatory motive? Possibly, but an alternative explanation is practical or financial. The Folio text may derive from a theatrical prompt-book, thus opening a window onto theatrical history: in his first appearance in act 1, scene 1, Philostrate doesn't speak and isn't strictly necessary to the action. It could be that the company gave Philostrate's lines in the last act to Egeus and thus managed with one fewer actor by doubling the two parts. There is a textual lesson here: in attempting to establish the authority of Shakespeare's lines, it is sometimes helpful to check the bottom line.

One of the most famous textual cruxes is the conflict in *Hamlet* between F's "too too solid flesh" and Q2 through Q4's "too too sallied flesh," mentioned at the beginning of this chapter. (Q1 prints "too much griev'd and sallied flesh.") The crux results from competing texts: Q2 and F both have some claim to authority. The choice is not only between Q2's "sallied" and F's "solid," however. "Sallied" appears to be an early version of "sullied," or stained, and therefore editors usually select either "sullied" or "solid." Some editors — such as Irving Ribner in his revision of Kittredge's edition (1936) — have chosen the Folio's "too too solid," possibly because it seems logically consistent with "melt, thaw, and resolve" in the following line. On the other hand, the second Quarto apparently represents the version of the play closest to Shakespeare's own manuscript — if there was only one manuscript version — so other editors (Harbage in the Pelican [1969], Barnet in the Signet [1972], and Bevington in the complete HarperCollins edition [1992]) print "sullied," the modernized form of Q2's "sallied." Stanley Wells and Gary Taylor, in the recent Oxford edition (1986), use Q2 as their copy text but depart from it to print "solid." In cases like this, the choice is very technical, depending on the editor's view of the competing authority of the early texts, and so modern readers have little choice but to trust the editor while remaining aware that decisions are being made for them.

An even trickier case occurs when a play exists in only one early text and yet a reading seems to demand emendation. In the third scene of *Measure for Measure*, the Duke explains to a Friar his own failure to enforce Viennese laws against fornication:

> We have strict statutes and most biting laws,
> The needful bits and curbs to headstrong weeds,
> Which for this fourteen years we have let slip;   (1.3.19–21)

The problem here is the word "weeds" or, as the Folio spells it, "weedes." The statutes and laws are described figuratively as bits and curbs designed to rein in or control human passion or desire, here expressed as weeds. This reads suspiciously like a mixed metaphor: it requires no extraordinary literary sensibility to recognize that bits and curbs have little effect on weeds. What can it mean that "weeds" have been "let slip"? Or have the bits and curbs been allowed to slip? There is no quarto, no alternative text, against which to check the Folio reading. The apparent imagistic incompatibility led Lewis Theobald, the eighteenth-century editor, to alter the word on logical grounds, so "weeds" became "steeds." Not satisfied with either F's original or with Theobald's proposed substitution, later editors have made other suggestions: "wills," which mediates between the figurative and the literal (since "will" is a synonym for sexual desire in the period); and "jades," meaning horses, which (like "steeds") is logically consonant with the metaphorical context.

Which of these did Shakespeare write? Considerations of figurative language would seem to call for "steeds" or "jades," and yet "weeds" may have a poetic claim: it has been pointed out that in at least two other plays Shakespeare metaphorically associates "curbs" with "weeds." (See Wells and Taylor, *William Shakespeare: A Textual Companion* 470.) Moreover, "weeds" would seem to have the paleographic edge. Elizabethan handwriting is difficult to decipher and risky to make judgments about, but it is unlikely that a compositor or scribe would have misread so badly as to print "w" when "st" or "j" was written in the manuscript, especially since "steeds" or "jades" seems so immediately appropriate.

Which of these should a modern editor print? The Riverside edition retains "weeds," as does the New Penguin; the Pelican and the Arden editors emend to "jades"; Kittredge chooses "steeds," as does a recent editor, David Bevington. In brief, the theoretical question is this: when, and on what grounds, should the editor emend? Or, how bad must the poetry be before an alternative reading is sought? Bibliographical history is crammed with editors, particularly in the eighteenth century, who disgraced themselves by attempting to tidy up what seemed to them messy or irregular and therefore unacceptable texts; in the attempt to enforce scientific principles, it is easy to forget that irregularity is a characteristic of genius.

Yet sometimes emendation is unavoidable. In fact, many of the same editors who emended mistakenly also made an inspired guess that suddenly clarified an obscure passage. For the Hostess's tearful narration of the death of Falstaff in *Henry V*, Lewis Theobald (again) offered just such a brilliant reading. In the Folio text — the only text, since the Quarto omits the questionable line — the Hostess describes the dying man as follows: "for after I saw him fumble with the Sheets, and play with Flowers, and smile vpon his fingers end, I knew there was but one way: for his Nose was as sharpe as a Pen, and a Table of greene fields." That last phrase, "and a Table of greene fields," seems hopelessly puzzling until one sees, as Theobald suggested, that "a" is a sixteenth-century contraction ('a) of "he" — it also appears earlier in the speech — and that "Table" is probably an error in transmission for "babbled." Thus the green fields represent the heavenly region, the Elysian Fields that the Hostess imagines Falstaff preparing to enter. Gary Taylor, in his recent Oxford edition of *Henry V*, briefly summarizes the four reasonable alternatives: "to retain the Folio reading, to emend *and* to *on* (Collier) [so that the Pen lies on a green Table], emend *Table* to *talkd* (as proposed by Theobald's anonymous 'gentleman sometime deceased'), or to emend *Table* to *babeld* (Theobald)" (293). Should an editor print "babbled"? Almost certainly; like virtually all modern editors, Taylor does. It is true that to do so is to tamper with a text, but in these lines the case for accepting Theobald's guess seems nearly irresistible.

Shakespeare's Texts and the General Reader

The problems of textual transmission can seem absurdly pedantic and interesting only to specialists. But I hope it is clear that an awareness of this process is vital to an understanding of Shakespeare's plays and of "Shakespeare" as a cultural presence. The optimism of editorial theory in the first half of the twentieth century, marked by confidence that a text of each of Shakespeare's plays could be established and trusted, has yielded in recent times to skepticism in the face of multiple versions, the apparent irrecoverability of authorial intention, and the recognition that every text, even the earliest quartos and Folio, is an edited text. Although scholars need access to all the available versions of a play, no matter how minute the differences, the complexities and frustrations caused by these variations should not incapacitate the nonspecialist. To extend the multiplicity theory too far, printing every collected edition of Shakespeare with two texts of *King Lear*, three of *Hamlet*, and competing versions of other plays, would be self-defeating. At some point an editor must choose which reading of a line to print, and an actor must decide which word to speak. For the general reader, the appropriate response to textual uncertainty should combine skepticism and faith.

◁ Facsimile of a Part of the Play Script
of *Sir Thomas More*

c. 1593–c. 1601

The text of the collaborative play *Sir Thomas More* is one of the few Elizabethan theatrical manuscripts to have survived, and some scholars believe this portion to be in Shakespeare's handwriting. The collaborators and/or revisers probably included Anthony Munday, Henry Chettle, Thomas Heywood, Thomas Dekker, and William Shakespeare. As F. E. Halliday puts it, this passage was written by someone who "is either Shakespeare or an author whose writing, spelling, psychology, verse and imagery closely resemble his" (457).

⇥ Title Page of *Titus Andronicus*

1594

First Quarto

The first of Shakespeare's plays to appear in print, though without his name on the title page, was the Roman tragedy *Titus Andronicus*. Only one copy of the Quarto survives. It was discovered in Sweden in 1904 and is now housed in the Folger Shakespeare Library in Washington, D.C.

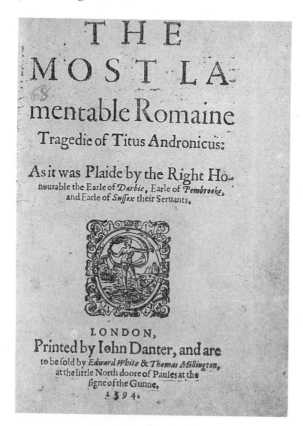

THE
MOST LA-
mentable Romaine
Tragedie of Titus Andronicus:

As it was Plaide by the Right Ho-
nourable the Earle of *Darbie*, Earle of *Pembrooke*,
and Earle of *Suffex* their Seruants.

LONDON,
Printed by Iohn Danter, and are
to be sold by *Edward White* & *Thomas Millington*,
at the little North doore of Paules at the
signe of the Gunne.
1594.

→ Title Page and Catalogue of the First Folio $\quad$ *1623*

Seven years after Shakespeare's death, a collected edition of his plays, the book we know as the First Folio, was published in London through the cooperation of a group of his former colleagues. It should be noted that the plays are grouped into just three categories: comedies, histories, and tragedies. Modern editions classify *Cymbeline, The Winter's Tale,* and *The Tempest* (along with *Pericles,* not published in the Folio) as romances. *Troilus and Cressida* is not listed in the catalogue, since it appears to have been added late; it is placed between *Henry VIII* and *Coriolanus. The Two Noble Kinsmen,* a collaboration with John Fletcher, is not included in the collection; nor are the sonnets, lyrics, or the narrative poems, *Venus and Adonis* and *The Rape of Lucrece.*

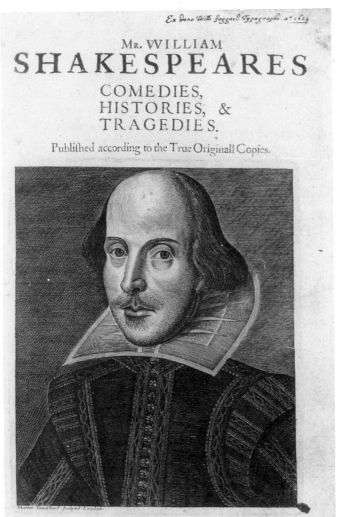

A CATALOGVE

of the seuerall Comedies, Histories, and Tragedies contained in this Volume.

→ Illustration of a Seventeenth-Century Printing Press

This drawing of a printing press was published by Joseph Moxon in his *Mechanic Exercises* (1683). Although the illustration is from the late seventeenth century, the technology had not significantly changed since Shakespeare's plays were printed.

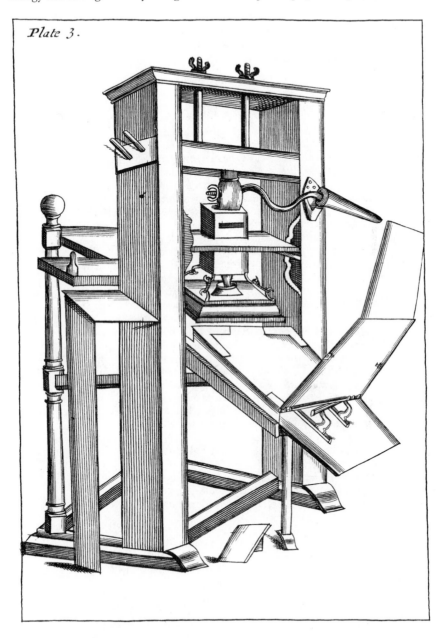

Plate 3.

→ Facsimile of the Last Page of *King Lear*   *1608*

First Quarto

This facsimile of the last page of *King Lear* shows the printer's attempt to crowd text onto the page so as not to have to use another sheet. Some lines are crowded together, for example, and subsequent texts suggest, in their more complete version of the scene, that the compositor of this first printing may have been forced to omit lines. (See p. 81 for a more detailed discussion of this textual matter.) The cuts could have resulted, however, from authorial revision.

The Historie of King Lear.

Kent. That from your life of difference and decay,
Haue followed your sad steps.   *Lear.* You'r welcome hither.
   Kent. Nor no man else, als chearles, darke and deadly,
Your eldest daughters haue foredoome themselues,
And desperatly are dead.   *Lear.* So thinke I to.
   Duke. He knowes not what he sees, and vaine it is,
That we present vs to him.   *Edg.* Very bootlesse,   *Enter*
   Capt. Edmund is dead my Lord.   *Captaine.*
   Duke. Thats but a trifle heere, you Lords and noble friends,
Know our intent, what comfort to this decay may come, shall be
applied: for vs we wil resigne during the life of this old maiesty,
to him our absolute power, you to your rights with boote, and
such addition as your honor haue more then merited, all friends
shall tast the wages of their vertue, and al foes the cup of their de-
seruings, O see, see.
   Lear. And my poore foole is hangd, no, no life, why should a
dog, a horse, a rat of life and thou no breath at all, O thou wilt
come no more, neuer, neuer, neuer, pray you vndo this button,
thanke you sir, O, o, o, o.   *Edg.* He faints my Lord, my Lord.
   Lear. Breake hart, I prethe breake. *Edgar.* Look vp my Lord.
   Kent. Vex not his ghost, O let him passe,
He hates him that would vpon the wracke,
Of this tough world stretch him out longer.
   Edg. O he is gone indeed.
   Kent. The wonder is, he hath endured so long,
He but vsurpt his life.
   Duke. Beare them from hence, our present busines
Is to generall woe, friends of my soule, you twaine
Rule in this kingdome, and the goard state sustaine.
   Kent. I haue a iourney sir, shortly to go,
My maister cals, and I must not say no.
   Duke. The waight of this sad time we must obey,
Speake what we feele, not what we ought to say,
The oldest haue borne most, we that are yong,
Shall neuer see so much, nor liue so long.

FINIS.

Rich. I, good leaue haue you, for you will haue leaue,
Till Youth take leaue, and leaue you to the Crutch.

King. Now tell me, Madame, doe you loue your
Children?

Wid. I, full as dearely as I loue my selfe.

King. And would you not doe much to doe them
good?

Wid. To doe them good, I would suftayne some
harme.

King. Then get your Husbands Lands, to doe them
good.

Wid. Therefore I came vnto your Maieftie.

King. Ile tell you how thefe Lands are to be got.

Wid. So fhall you bind me to your Highneffe feruice.

King. What feruice wilt thou doe me, if I giue them?

Wid. What you command, that refts in me to doe.

King. But you will take exceptions to my Boone.

Wid. No, gracious Lord, except I cannot doe it.

King. I, but thou canft doe what I meane to aske.

Wid. Why then I will doe what your Grace commands.

Rich. Hee plyes her hard, and much Raine weares the

Prouoke vs hither now, to flaughter thee.

Cla. If you do loue my Brother, hate not me:
I am his Brother, and I loue him well.
If you are hyr'd for meed, go backe againe,
And I will fend you to my Brother Gloufter:
Who fhall reward you better for my life,
Then *Edward* will for tydings of my death.

2 You are decciu'd,
Your Brother Gloufter hates you.

Cla. Oh no, he loues me, and he holds me deere:
Go you to him from me.

1 I fo we will.

Cla. Tell him, when that our Princely Father **Yorke**,
Bleft his three Sonnes with his victorious Arme,
He little thought of this diuided Friendfhip:
Bid Gloufter thinke on this, and he will weepe,

1 I Milftones, as he leffoned vs to weepe.

Cla. O do not flander him, for he is kinde.

1 Right, as Snow in Harueft:
Come, you deceiue your felfe,
'Tis he that fends vs to deftroy you heere.

Cla. It cannotbe, for he bewept my Fortune,

A Comparison of the Work of Compositors A and B on the 1623 Folio

The two passages reproduced here from Peter Blayney's *The First Folio of Shakespeare* (1991) exhibit the different spelling habits of two of the printers, or compositors, who set type for the Folio. Scholars have been able to use the idiosyncrasies of early modern spelling and other such clues to ascertain a great deal of information about the printing of Shakespeare's plays.

The passage above, from Henry VI, Part 3 *(Histories, page 159), was set by Compositor A and shows a cluster of his characteristic* doe *spellings. Neither* goe *nor* here *is illustrated (neither word is used as often as* do*), but A's preference for using an "a" in* deare *or* dearely *is also shown.*

This passage, from Richard III *(Histories, page 181), was set by Compositor B and includes four of his best-documented preferential spellings:* do, go, heere, *and* deere.

→ Facsimile of "To be or not to be" from
Hamlet, Prince of Denmark   *1603*

First Quarto

This version of "To be or not to be" differs radically from the speech that modern actors usually perform, which derives from later published versions (1604 and 1623).
Scholars are uncertain about the origins of the differences, although most attribute
them to a faulty copy text for the 1603 Quarto.

To leaue vs here?
  Que. With all my hart.   *exit.*
  Cor. And here *Ofelia,* reade you on this booke,
And walke aloofe, the King fhal be vnfeene.
  Ham. To be, or not to be, I there's the point,
To Die, to fleepe, is that all? I all:
No, to fleepe, to dreame, I mary there it goes,
For in that dreame of death, when wee awake,
And borne before an euerlafting Iudge,
From whence no paffenger euer retur'nd,
The vndifcouered countiy, at whofe fight
The happy fmile, and the accurfed damn'd.
But for this, the ioyfull hope of this,
Whol'd beare the fcornes and flattery of the world,
Scorned by the right rich, the rich curffed of the poore?
                                              The

Prince of Denmarke
The widow being oppreffed, the orphan wrong'd,
The tafte of hunger, or a tirants raigne,
And thoufand more calamities befides,
To grunt and fweate vnder this weary life,
When that he may his full *Quietus* make,
With a bare bodkin, who would this indure,
But for a hope of fomething after death?
Which pufles the braine, and doth confound the fence,
Which makes vs rather beare thofe euilles we haue,
Than flie to others that we know not of.
I that, O this confcience makes cowardes of vs all,
Lady in thy orizons, be all my finnes remembred.
  Ofel. My Lord, I haue fought opportunitie, which now
I haue, to redeliuer to your worthy handes, a fmall remem-
brance, fuch tokens which I haue receiued of you.
  Ham. Are you faire?
  Ofel. My Lord.
  Ham. Are you honeft?

The Harlots Cheeke beautied with plaift'ring Art
Is not more vgly to the thing that helpes it,
Then is my deede, to my moft painted word.
Oh heauie burthen!

Pol. I heare him comming, let's withdraw my Lord.

                               Exeunt.

          Enter Hamlet.

Ham. To be, or not to be, that is the Queftion:
Whether 'tis Nobler in the minde to fuffer
The Slings and Arrowes of outragious Fortune,
Or to take Armes againft a Sea of troubles,
And by oppofing end them: to dye, to fleepe
No more; and by a fleepe, to fay we end
The Heart-ake, and the thoufand Naturall fhockes

That Flefh is heyre too? 'Tis a confummation
Deuoutly to be wifh'd. To dye to fleepe,
To fleepe, perchance to Dreame; I, there's the rub,
For in that fleepe of death, what dreames may come,
When we haue fhuffiel'd off this mortall coile,
Muft giue vs pawfe. There's the refpect
That makes Calamity of fo long life:
For who would beare the Whips and Scornes of time,
The Oppreffors wrong, the poore mans Contumely,
The pangs of difpriz'd Loue, the Lawes delay,
The infolence of Office, and the Spurnes
That patient merit of the vnworthy takes,
When he himfelfe might his *Quietus* make
With a bare Bodkin? Who would thefe Fardles beare
To grunt and fweat vnder a weary life,
But that the dread of fomething after death,
The vndifcouered Countrey, from whofe Borne
No Traueller returnes, Puzels the will,
And makes vs rather beare thofe illes we haue,
Then flye to others that we know not of.
Thus Confcience does make Cowards of vs all,
And thus the Natiue hew of Refolution
Is ficklied o're, with the pale caft of Thought,
And enterprizes of great pith and moment,
With this regard their Currants turne away,
And loofe the name of Action. Soft you now,
The faire *Ophelia?* Nimph, in thy Orizons
Be all my finnes remembred.

    Ophe. Good my Lord,

Facsimile of "To be or not to be" from *Hamlet, Prince of Denmark*

1623 Folio

This familiar version of "To be or not to be," printed in the Folio, more nearly resembles the speech as it appeared in all printings except the first. This is also substantially the version of the speech printed in the Second Quarto of 1604, which appears to have been published as a corrective to the problematic Q1.

CHAPTER 4

"I Loved My Books": Shakespeare's Reading

---–⋆–---

For almost four centuries Shakespeare has been stereotyped as the "natural" artist, the unlettered genius whose inspired creations owe hardly anything to learning and almost everything to inherent imaginative genius. Only fifteen years after Shakespeare's death John Milton, in "L'Allegro," commemorated his achievement by imagining a theater in which one might hear "sweetest Shakespeare, fancy's child, / Warble his native wood-notes wild." Milton here opposes Shakespeare's imaginative talents to the scholarly bent of his contemporary, Ben Jonson: Milton's alternative to the "native wood-notes wild" is "Jonson's learned sock," a reference to the slipper worn by the classical actor of comedy. Even *native,* meaning English as opposed to Roman or Greek, is a code word for the nonclassical, the unpedantic.

In fact it was Jonson who, both during Shakespeare's lifetime and after his death, promulgated this distinction between learned playwrights like himself, devoted to classically sanctioned forms, and the natural and even barbarous creators of improbable fictions. These stereotypical oppositions cloud our understanding of what Shakespeare knew and how he came to know it. Surely what Shakespeare knew was not limited to the information he gathered from books, but because he made his living by the word, it seems worthwhile to consider what he was able to learn from other writers.

Scholars have meticulously studied the mass of material that the dramatist employed in composing his plays, from ancient comedies and tragedies to Italian novels and English narrative poems. In 1753–54 Charlotte Lennox published *Shakespeare Illustrated; or the Novels and Histories on which the Plays are founded,* a work that identified the sources of more than half the plays; as late as our own time, scholarly journals print articles with titles such as "A New Source for *Hamlet,* 1.3."

The simplest way to discover what Shakespeare read is to examine the printed sources of his work. This chapter begins with a review of the Greek and Roman literature that Shakespeare first encountered as a schoolboy ("Shakespeare and the Classics"). It then offers a brief catalog ("Major Influences") of the principal literary influences. (The three books that Shakespeare used most extensively — Ovid's *Metamorphoses*, Plutarch's *Lives of the Noble Grecians and Romans*, and Holinshed's *Chronicles of England, Scotland, and Ireland* — are here mentioned briefly in the context of similar sources and then given special treatment at the end of the chapter.) These first two sections are designed to provide an overview of what Shakespeare found appealing and useful when he set to work.

But such a survey, if it did no more than describe the texts that Shakespeare certainly or probably or possibly consulted in writing a play, would surely be an inadequate register of Shakespeare's reading. To take the most obvious example, the Bible has a claim to being the most important book Shakespeare knew, even though it did not serve as a major source for any of his plots. So it is with Elizabethan poetry, some of which had a palpable effect on the development of his dramatic verse. It will be useful, in other words, to expand our definition of *source*, to look beyond the indisputable originals of the plays into less obviously influential books and especially into non-canonical forms of writing such as pamphlets and ballads. The Scriptures also complicate the definition of "reading." We know, for instance, that Shakespeare knew the Bible, but he need not have "read" it religiously or systematically. Law-abiding English citizens at the turn of the seventeenth century went to church every Sunday and on religious holidays, where they heard the Scriptures read from the pulpit and homilies based on biblical examples. Similarly, we know that Shakespeare knew the plays of Christopher Marlowe and Ben Jonson and other contemporary playwrights. Did he read them? Did he hear them spoken from the stage? Or did he learn them by heart, from the experience of acting in them? The third section of this chapter ("Indirect Sources") addresses some of these questions.

A few of Shakespeare's favorite books merit special attention, not only because it is fascinating to discover what the playwright particularly enjoyed reading but also because the nature of his artistic achievement is closely tied to his literary tastes. A work that he especially loved was Ovid's *Metamorphoses*, which he read in both the original Latin and in an Elizabethan translation by Arthur Golding (1567). Ovid's collection is valuable as an indicator of the kind of stories Shakespeare liked. He obviously relished the Roman poet's fantastic world of tranformation and magic, but he also responded to the actual deeds of human heroes in the classical world. His basic text for such stories was Plutarch's *Lives of the Noble Grecians and Romans*. For accounts of colorful figures closer to his own time, Shakespeare turned repeatedly to Raphael Holinshed's recently published *Chronicles of England, Scotland, and Ireland*. A discussion of these works concludes the chapter ("Shakespeare's Favorites"). A brief analysis of their principal appeals will help to define the artistic sensibility that has endowed Shakespeare's work with its own enduring power.

Shakespeare was indisputably an enthusiastic and wide-ranging reader. But an investigation of his reading requires awareness that any conclusions we reach must be indefinite and partial. For example, we do not know where Shakespeare obtained the books he read or how many he owned — books were expensive. Perhaps at the beginning of his career he borrowed from a wealthy friend or patron, possibly the earl of Southampton, or had the use of his library. No one is sure about the extent to which the theatrical community intersected with the more conventional literary circles, and so information about Shakespeare's access to poetry and fiction in manuscript is uncertain. The temporal distance impedes our ability to discover the full range of his literary and nonliterary influences. Much of the printed material from the sixteenth and seventeenth centuries has perished. Moreover, it is not easy to draw absolute distinctions between printed and nonprinted texts: Shakespeare may have seen performances of many of the plays that nourished his work, but not read them. It is also important to remember that the world Shakespeare inhabited was much more of an oral culture than ours. But finally, even if we could identify all of Shakespeare's sources with absolute certainty, this knowledge would still be less important than recognition of his unparalleled capacity for adapting, combining, and transmuting what he read.

Shakespeare and the Classics

Shakespeare's command of the classics, those works of Greek and Roman antiquity reborn in England with the arrival of sixteenth-century humanism, was for a long time the subject of intense debate. A primary question was whether his connection was direct or oblique: did Shakespeare read the originals of the stories and dramas that he appropriated, or did he rely mainly on translations? Ben Jonson started the trouble, in his commemorative verses for the First Folio, when he declared that although Shakespeare had "small Latin and less Greek," such ignorance didn't matter because he still deserved to be ranked with the greatest classical authors. This debate was sustained throughout the eighteenth and nineteenth centuries by commentators who sought either to defend Shakespeare's learning and thus safeguard his artistic status, or else to defend his ignorance and thus emphasize his natural genius. In the second half of the eighteenth century, for example, a Cambridge University scholar named Richard Farmer was able, by means of verbal echoes in the plays, to identify the Elizabethan translations of Plutarch and Ovid that Shakespeare consulted. On the basis of these discoveries he insisted that the dramatist's learning did not include Greek and Latin originals: "He remembered perhaps enough of his schoolboy learning to put the *Hig, hag, hog* [the proper Latin is *hic, haec, hoc*] into the mouth of Sir Hugh Evans; and might pick up in the writers of the time, or the course of his conversation, a familiar phrase or two of French or Italian; but his *studies* were most demonstratively confined to *nature* and *his own language*" (qtd. in Halliday 162).

Modern scholarship has overturned these conclusions. We now know that while Shakespeare often used translations, he could and did read sources in Latin, French, and probably Italian. In scrutinizing a celebrated speech from Ovid that shows up in *The Tempest* as Prospero's "Ye elves of hills, brooks, standing lakes, and groves" (5.1.33ff), scholars have been able to demonstrate just how and where Shakespeare uses the translation and where he reverts to the original. Then what of Jonson's left-handed compliment? It needs to be put in context: Jonson was one of the most learned men of his age, a master of ancient and modern languages, a proud scholar who larded his classically derived tragedies with marginal quotations from and footnotes to the models and originals that he imitated. Compared to Jonson's mastery of Latin, Shakespeare's was perhaps "small." But considered on its own terms, Shakespeare's classical learning was respectable for the age in which he lived, and for the age in which *we* live, it was formidable.

Grammar schools in the sixteenth century were devoted to instruction in Latin grammar, and as a student at the King's New School in Stratford, Shakespeare would have spent much of his boyhood translating Latin. The Latin grammar text of William Lyly, grandfather of the playwright John Lyly, was supplemented by exercise books and composition manuals designed to inculcate the principles of rhetoric and style. Having mastered the fundamentals, pupils moved on to translation: for most of the day, six days a week, for about ten years, they rendered Latin texts into English and then retranslated the English back into Latin. The graduated curriculum of reading began with the relatively easy Latin of Aesop (translated from the original Greek) and Caesar. This introduction prepared them for the work of the great poets, historians, orators, and essayists: Cicero, Virgil, Ovid, Horace, Suetonius, Livy, Seneca. They also encountered Roman drama, especially the work of Terence, the favorite of the Renaissance humanists. The comedies of Plautus and tragedies of Seneca were studied less often in schools, but Shakespeare clearly read them, perhaps on his own.

The exact degree of Shakespeare's proficiency is difficult to ascertain, but we do know that he was able to read fairly sophisticated Latin in the original. In addition to the documented cases in which a Shakespearean passage departs from Arthur Golding's English version of the *Metamorphoses* in favor of a phrase or trope from the original, scholars have discovered other evidence. For example, in *The Rape of Lucrece* Shakespeare borrows certain details directly from a story in Ovid's *Fasti* that was available to him only in its Latin version. Apparently Shakespeare did not know Greek. It was less frequently studied than Latin in Renaissance England, and those who read the monuments of Greek literature usually depended on Latin translations. A major exception, Plutarch's *Lives*, was written in the author's native Greek (although composed during the Roman empire); it became widely known, however, through the English translation of Sir Thomas North, who used a French translation by Jacques Amyot. For the Renaissance reader, "classical" meant primarily Latin.

Major Influences

Not only was Shakespeare able to read Latin literature in the original, but he also seems to have liked it and to have decided that theater audiences would too. Thus Roman authors provided the material for many of his plays, early and late. Near the beginning of his career, about the time that he converted Ovid's story into *The Rape of Lucrece,* he turned to antiquity for what may have been his initial efforts in tragedy and comedy. Scrutiny of these classical texts and of the use Shakespeare made of them reveals two overriding characteristics of his practice as an adapter: first, his eclecticism, his genius for combining classical stories with other materials, both ancient and modern, to form new creations; and second, his ability to expand and multiply characters, episodes, and effects in order to surpass the classical models.

The plot of *Titus Andronicus* apparently derives from an English story of the Roman general and not from classical history. In order to represent its horrors more vividly, however, Shakespeare enriched the narrative with material taken from the *Thyestes* of Seneca, the Roman playwright whose vengeful ghosts and tormented heroes made him the acknowledged master of passion and violence; and he also drew on the *Metamorphoses,* adapting for his own story of rape and revenge Ovid's tale of Philomela, Tereus, and Procne. In creating *The Comedy of Errors,* Shakespeare combined two plays by the Roman dramatist Plautus: *Menaechmi,* an identity comedy in which twins are mistaken for each other; and *Amphitruo,* in which Jupiter, disguised as Amphitruo, assumes the husband's place in bed, while Mercury, disguised as Amphitruo's servant, shuts both husband and servant out of the house. Shakespeare immediately perceived the appeal of these plays and set about to reproduce and augment their attractions in his own farce: he re-creates Plautus's twins as the Antipholus brothers and then gives them twin servants, the Dromios, thus multiplying the opportunities for comic confusion. Having observed the effectiveness of this formula, he returned to it in his second twin comedy, *Twelfth Night.* There he developed romantic sentiments not present in Roman comedy, but he did not sacrifice delight in the hilarious consequences of mistaken identity. These Roman plays taught Shakespeare a great deal about dramatic construction and about the affective possibilities of comedy and tragedy. But he moved quickly to adapt other kinds of ancient writing, particularly Ovid's *Metamorphoses* and Plutarch's *Lives.* The influence of both these authors on Shakespeare is so pervasive that they demand separate treatment, along with Shakespeare's other favorite, Raphael Holinshed.

Holinshed's *Chronicles of England, Scotland, and Ireland,* however, is only one of the many books that fed Shakespeare's vision of England's past. Almost as influential was Edward Hall's *The Union of the Two Noble and Illustre Families of Lancaster and York* (second edition, 1548), particularly in the creation of Shakespeare's first group of history plays, the First Tetralogy (*Henry VI, Parts 1, 2, and 3* and *Richard III*). The *Union* was the most ideologically pointed of the major sixteenth-century chronicles, for Hall frankly conceived of himself as an apologist for the Tudor monarchy. In dedicating the work to King Edward VI, he acknowledged previous historians' diligence but lamented their lack of moral purpose. To him the Wars of the Roses were a nightmare from which Henry VII, Edward's grandfather, had mercifully awakened his country; the villainous characterization of Henry's enemy, Richard III, is apparent in the excerpt given on page 118. Hall saw it as his duty to instruct his contemporaries in the causes and effects of the chaos, tyranny, and bloodshed that had afflicted England in the previous century.

Other historians also furnished Shakespeare with information or inspiration. Published in 1559 and often reprinted and expanded, *A Mirror for Magistrates* is an anthology of verse narratives in which notorious figures from classical and English history recount their tragic stories and anatomize the vices that accompany power (see the account of Julius Caesar on p. 119). In 1595 Samuel Daniel published his long poem *The Civil Wars*, which was probably influenced by Shakespeare's First Tetralogy and in turn probably influenced the Second Tetralogy. The popular stage furnished historical dramas as well, such as the anonymous *Woodstock*, one of the sources for *Richard II*, and the (also anonymous) drama called *The Famous Victories of Henry V*.

Just as the dramatists borrowed characters and details from the English chronicles, the historians — in the absence of modern copyright laws — did not hesitate to appropriate one another's work. Holinshed borrowed liberally from Hall's *Union*, just as Hall had relied on the narratives of his illustrious predecessors, particularly Sir Thomas More on the life of Richard III and Polydore Vergil, author of *Anglica Historia*. This kind of piggyback history sometimes makes it hard to determine which source Shakespeare was reading when he composed his history plays, although occasionally a textual quirk affords a cherishable picture of William Shakespeare sitting at his desk with a specific edition of a particular book open before him. In *Henry IV, Part 1*, for example, the opening scene presents King Henry's report on the prisoners taken by Hotspur at the battle of Holmedon, including "Mordake Earl of Fife and eldest son / To beaten Douglas" (1.1.71–72). Mordake actually was the son of the earl of Albany, but a punctuation error in Holinshed misled Shakespeare: "and of prisoners among other were these, Mordacke earle of Fife, son to the governour Archembald earle Dowglas, which in the fight lost one of his eies" (see Bullough 4: 183). The lack of a comma after "governour" is responsible for the error. Such glimpses into the compositional process are relatively rare, however, and usually it is difficult to tell which historian Shakespeare was reading.

All of these historians shared common purposes: the justification of the Tudor line, the condemnation of what they saw as tyranny, and the exposition of history's lessons. Hall's work is governed by his conviction that "wryting is the keye to enduce vertue, and represse vice" (Bullough 3: 10), so he is keen to demonstrate that the virtuous thrive and the wicked suffer. Although Holinshed does not moralize so overtly, he appears to share Hall's belief and his method. Not everyone does, however. Much later in literary history, when

Miss Prism, the governess in Oscar Wilde's *The Importance of Being Earnest,* is asked to describe the ending of her romantic novel, she replies that "the good ended happily and the bad unhappily. That is what fiction means." As Shakespeare began the Second Tetralogy of histories, the great cycle including *Richard II, Henry IV, Parts 1 and 2,* and *Henry V,* he had come to accept the pessimism that underlies the Wildean irony, that only in books is virtue rewarded. Committed as he was to the value of order and the perils of discord, he nevertheless became increasingly conscious that the moral certainties of a Hall are not easy to sustain and that the writing of history, whether in dramatic or narrative form, is to a large extent a fictional enterprise. This is not to say that the First Tetralogy lacks irony about the transmission of historical events, as a quick reading of *Richard III* will attest. But the Second Tetralogy, particularly *Henry IV, Part 2,* urges a much more dubious view of the historian's task.

Another major literary group from which Shakespeare drew his plots was the fiction of his time, both European and English. These were mostly romances or adventure stories written in verse or prose. Many of them descend through various European languages from Greek originals, such as Apuleius's romance — actually an early version of a novel — called *The Golden Ass.* In a few cases, Shakespeare read translations of the Continental works; in other cases, he seems to have read the originals. Many of these narratives existed in multiple versions, having been retold in other forms and other languages, so Shakespeare's immediate source is not always obvious.

Romeo and Juliet offers a vivid example of Shakespeare's attraction to romantic tales that originated on the Continent and made their way into English. The play derives mainly from a long English poem, Arthur Brooke's *The Tragical History of Romeus and Juliet,* first printed about three decades earlier. Shakespeare knew this poem thoroughly (although he altered its thematic focus), but he may also have known the tale through its European sources, from which Brooke had derived his plot. Analogues of the story extend as far back as Greek romance of the third century, and several French and Italian versions, the details and themes of which vary widely, were produced in the hundred years before Shakespeare adapted it. In 1554 it appears in a form that we would recognize in Matteo Bandello's Italian prose *novella* (a long short story or a short novel, like its English equivalent); this version is retold by Boaistuau in French in 1559, and Brooke's three-thousand-line poem, a translation of Boaistuau, was published in 1562 and then reprinted in 1587. The flavor of Brooke's work can be suggested by a few of his couplets, which are written in "poulter's measure," a form in which lines of twelve and fourteen syllables alternate. Here is his account of the moment when Juliet discovers the dead Romeus: .

> But when she neither could her swelling sorow swage,
> Ne yet her tender hart abyde her sickenes furious rage,
> Falne on his corps, she lay long panting on his face,
> And then with all her force and strength, the ded corps dyd embrace,
> As though with sighes, with sobs, with force and busy payne,
> She would him rayse, and him restore from death to lyfe agayne. (2,725–30)

This passage provides a sample of the kind of writing that was popular in Eliz-abethan England and that Shakespeare found useful in seeking out dramatic subjects.

Such fictions from the Continent provided the basis for several of Shake-speare's plays, comic, tragic, and tragicomic. *The Two Gentlemen of Verona*, one of his earliest comedies, derives from a Portuguese prose romance, *Diana En-amorada*, by Jorge de Montemayor. About 1603, in midcareer, Shakespeare seems to have been reading *Gli Hecatommithi*, an anthology of short fiction by the Italian Giovanni Battista Giraldi Cinthio. It contains the story of the lust-ful civic official that Shakespeare reproduces in *Measure for Measure* and the tale of the jealous captain that Shakespeare converts into *Othello*. An excerpt from Cinthio's anthology is found on page 122. At the end of his career he re-turned to one of the fountainheads of this tradition, Giovanni Boccaccio, for the story of the wager in *Cymbeline*.

These European poets and romancers had English descendants who were working in the 1580s and '90s and whom Shakespeare also found stimulating and useful. In other words, he dramatized some of the most popular fiction of his own day. An appropriate analogy might be Hollywood: it is as if a screenwriter in our own time, unrestricted by laws of copyright, were to de-vise a script based on a novel by John Grisham or Stephen King. Thomas Lodge's *Rosalynde*, derived from a fourteenth-century English poem, was published in London in 1590, just as Shakespeare was beginning to write for the stage; about ten years later Lodge's prose pastoral served Shakespeare as a source for *As You Like It*, one of his experiments with romantic comedy. Sir Philip Sidney's *Arcadia*, also published in 1590, four years after the death of its author, was valuable to Shakespeare both directly and indirectly. As he wrote *King Lear*, developing the story of filial ingratitude and familial cru-elty found in Holinshed, he perhaps remembered Sidney's tale of the Pa-phlagonian king abused by his monstrous son and converted it into the parallel subplot of the Gloucester family. Or it may be that his reading of that grim story in the *Arcadia* returned him to the old chronicle play, *King Leir*, that he then used, alongside Holinshed, for the main plot of his tragedy. The more significant influence of Sidney's fiction, however, is on Shakespeare's later work. The extravagance of romance, its episodic and as-similative tendencies, its pattern of quest and deferral, its geographical and temporal sprawl, its devotion to extremes of behavior and experience, its ul-timately Protestant emphasis on the testing of human strength, its depen-dence on narrative and stylistic deviation or wandering — all of these qualities link the *Arcadia* with the romances of Shakespeare's final phase. In fact, late in his career Shakespeare seems to have been rereading a good deal of Elizabethan fiction. *The Winter's Tale* is a dramatization of a novella by Robert Greene called *Pandosto, or The Triumph of Time*, published in 1588 and then reprinted under a different title in 1607, three years before Shake-speare appropriated it. To read *Pandosto* alongside *The Winter's Tale* is to rec-ognize Shakespeare's theatrical gift for transforming his sources: whereas Greene's heroine dies, Shakespeare teases his audience with uncertainty and then revises the original ending, creating one of the most effective final scenes in all of drama.

This multitude of works from a variety of traditions illuminates Shakespeare's characteristic mode of composition. He rarely made up his own plots but instead adapted them from fictions, biographies, dramas, and even current events that fired his imagination. Invention and imitation were not two distinct processes in Renaissance artistic theory. First-time readers are sometimes disappointed to learn that Shakespeare was not "original," in the sense of originating entirely new plots. But the knowledge that the raw materials are borrowed should not diminish our sense of Shakespeare's artistic ability; instead, it should allow us to appreciate more exactly the nature of his genius for choosing subjects, a talent involving three main skills. The first was his knack for recognizing a potentially effective theatrical story when he saw one, a talent so obvious as to require no elaboration here: that so many of his plots existed in so many languages and verse forms over so many centuries is sufficient evidence of his nose for what would sell.

Second, Shakespeare early exhibited a talent for synthesis, for combining unlikely pairs of tales into a unified whole. In *The Comedy of Errors,* for example, he surrounds the two Roman comedies with a frame story, the narrative of a merchant, Egeon, searching the Mediterranean for his lost son; it is taken from the ancient tale of Apollonius of Tyre as retold in the *Confessio Amantis,* a book of stories by the medieval English poet John Gower, a contemporary of Chaucer. This unusual alliance affords Shakespeare a variety of tonal effects: while the farcical errors produce scornful laughter, the old man's narrow escape and reunion with his family contribute a sense of comic empathy. Even those plays that derive from one principal source — as *All's Well That Ends Well* does from one of Boccaccio's stories — benefit from the playwright's voracious reading, his eye for meaningful details, and his tendency to prefer histrionic effect to historical fact.

Third, Shakespeare excelled at identifying the dramatic heart of a story and presenting it in a way that especially suited the conditions of the Elizabethan theater. This unfailing sense of a story's theatrical core is best illustrated by *Richard III,* another early effort. Whereas Hall's account of the life of Richard of Gloucester is the fairly predictable work of a political apologist, Shakespeare's theatrical version is a vivid and complex portrait of a charismatic psychopath. What Shakespeare succeeds in doing, as none of his predecessors managed, was to make his subject a compelling stage presence and a self-conscious actor. The soliloquy that opens the play ("Now is the winter of our discontent"), in which Richard takes the audience into his confidence and gleefully outlines his scheme for disposing of his rivals and taking the crown, is the first of Richard's many histrionic strategies: witty asides, privately hatched theatrical schemes ("Plots have I laid, inductions dangerous," 1.1.32), staged scenes designed for public consumption, and periodic reviews of his own performances. The source narratives of More, Hall, and Holinshed all hint at the connection between politics and theater — action and acting, plots and plots — but only Shakespeare brilliantly explores the psychology of political tyrant as theatrical superstar.

Indirect Sources

The list of works that Shakespeare directly used, large as it is, represents only a fraction of the writing he must have read, and we must exert some effort to locate other subtler areas of his learning. The Bible is the most important of such texts. Stories from the Old and New Testaments are recalled by his characters; Christian doctrine is sometimes invoked as a context for interpreting dramatic action; and, perhaps most meaningfully, the cadences of the Elizabethan translations of the Bible are audible in his verse and prose. But Shakespeare's Bible was different from our own. The King James version (more properly called the Authorized Version) to our ears sounds "Shakespearean" because it was translated at the time that Shakespeare was writing. However, he could not have read it until he had virtually retired from the stage, for it was not published until 1611. Instead, he would have read the Geneva Bible (trans. 1560), an excerpt from which appears on page 123, or the Bishops' Bible (trans. 1568). The allusions in Shakespeare's work mostly echo these translations and sometimes their marginal notes as well. Into a similar category would fit *The Book of Common Prayer*, the guide to the rituals and sacraments of the Church of England composed in 1549; the public would have been almost as familiar with it as with the Scriptures themselves. (See "The Order for the Burial of the Dead" on p. 128). A final, indispensable document of this Protestant culture was John Foxe's *Acts and Monuments* (first published in 1563), a history of Catholic persecution and reformist virtue that went through numerous editions, was placed officially in every parish church, and ended up next to the Bible in many private homes. (An excerpt appears on p. 131.)

Although no newspapers existed in Shakespeare's England — printing was still in an early stage, and cheap paper was scarce — people hungered for news. Consequently, balladeers exploited the sorts of topics featured in our tabloid press — natural disasters, monstrous crimes, success stories — rapidly converting newsworthy events into rhymed narratives. These crude verses were printed on *broadside* sheets (sizable pieces of paper), set to a familiar tune named on the sheet itself ("To the Tune of 'Greensleeves'") and offered for sale. Sometimes preceded or accompanied by pamphlets in prose reporting on the same events, the broadside ballads were a familiar and important means of communication in London and especially in the countryside. Shakespeare's amused attitude toward some of these balladeers and their wares can be seen in his portrait of Autolycus, the combination con man, peddler, and ballad-seller in *The Winter's Tale* who hawks incredible stories to the country rubes. Still, as C. H. Firth puts it, "The ballads . . . supply evidence on the character of Shakespeare's audience. These remnants of the popular literature of the time show how the people lived, and what they thought, the stories with which they were familiar, and the allusions which they could understand" (qtd. in Lee and Onions 2: 511).

Since printed ballads had to be noted in the Register of the Stationers' Company, we have a fairly accurate record of many of these crude poems, although due to their ephemeral nature, many are lost. The Stationers' Register records some twenty-four ballads on the defeat of the Spanish Armada in 1588; the various conspiracies against Queen Elizabeth and King James gave rise to rhymed accounts of the traitors and their crimes; and fires, floods, and other such cataclysms invariably inspired the creation of new ones. A few generalizations can be made about these ballads when they are looked at collectively. First, they reveal a fierce patriotism that combines national pride with religious fervor, directing scorn at France, Spain, and especially Catholicism, as the following title indicates:

> A Letter to Rome, to Declare to the Pope
> John Felton, His Friend, Is Hang'd in a Rope,
> And Farther, Aright His Grace to Enform,
> He Died a Papist and Seem'd Not to Turn.

Second, in addition to politics and religion, sex is a major topic. Autolycus entices prospective buyers with a salacious story about a frigid woman turned into a (cold) fish. Third, the balladeers often moralized the atrocities they announced, with fires or storms treated as proof of God's judgment on the wicked. (See "The True Form and Shape of a Monstrous Child," p. 136.) Finally, some ballads offered, instead of a version of current events, a crudely versified retelling of a famous biblical or ancient narrative.

The broadside form was also used for public information and governmental propaganda. Accounts of the horrifying executions of criminals were popular, and such ballads served the government's ideological needs. Often the regime employed broadsides officially for admonition or regulation, issuing proclamations concerning public behavior ("A Proclamation against Unlawful Assemblies"), dress codes, the carrying of weapons, the number of deaths from plague, price-fixing, border disputes, and other such social and economic problems. Sometimes important public figures, such as Robert Cecil, Elizabeth's secretary of state, arranged for their likenesses to be distributed in broadside form, although Elizabeth herself disliked her broadside portrait and issued a proclamation (in broadside) forbidding the representation of her in that manner (see Firth in Lee and Onions 2: 536). Later royal figures seem not to have objected, however: broadside portraits exist of King James's consort, Queen Anne, and their son Prince Henry.

News of the New World — this was, after all, the end of the age of exploration and the beginning of the age of colonization — was available to the reading public through travel literature that was sometimes published and sometimes circulated privately. In *Twelfth Night*, Maria ridicules Malvolio's self-satisfaction by complaining that "He does smile his face into more lines than is in the new map, with the augmentation of the Indies" (3.2.78–80). Richard Hakluyt (1552–1616), archdeacon of Westminster and self-appointed geographer to the nation, kept the public informed about the triumphs of English explorers and colonizers, publishing his *Divers Voyages Touching the Discovery of America* in 1582 (and dedicating it to Sir Philip Sidney) and his *Principal Navigations, Voyages, and Discoveries of the English Nation* in 1589 (enlarged to three volumes in 1598–1600). After his death his work was carried on by Samuel Purchas, whose *Purchas His Pilgrims* (1625) contains Sir William Strachey's account (written in 1610) of the terrible events suffered by a group of colonists on a voyage to North America (see the excerpt on p. 137). Apparently Shakespeare read Strachey's *True Reportory of the Wreck* . . . in manuscript just after it was written and long before it was published, since in many details the narrative resembles the experience of the shipwrecked courtiers in *The Tempest*.

Plays from the public theater and the children's companies belong in a discussion of Shakespeare's reading, although he would have seen rather than read many of them. As he began his career in the theater, the available offerings were extremely varied, from old-style morality plays to the mystery cycles (which he might have seen in Coventry near his hometown) to romantic or pastoral comedies by John Lyly and George Peele to "chronicle histories" (*The Troublesome Reign of John, King of England*, for example) to Kyd's sensational *Spanish Tragedy*. Shakespeare learned about structure, character, and other points of stagecraft from all of these types of drama, but his ear must have been especially enchanted by Christopher Marlowe's heroic speeches, delivered by Edward Alleyn from the stage of the Rose Playhouse. The words written for such outsized characters as Tamburlaine, Doctor Faustus, and Barabas, the Jew of Malta, lie behind Shakespeare's creation of his mesmerizing Richard III, Richard II, and Shylock. (A passage from one of Tamburlaine's speeches, taken from a facsimile of the 1590 edition of Marlowe's play, is found on p. 140). We know, too, that Shakespeare acted in two of Ben Jonson's plays, the comedy *Every Man in his Humour* in 1598 and then *Sejanus*, Jonson's attempt at classical tragedy, in 1603. In fact, Shakespeare's position as shareholder with the King's Men meant that he would have been well acquainted with the numerous plays in the company's repertory from about 1594 to about 1610.

If Shakespeare, like his contemporaries, had a taste for the outrageous and crude offerings of popular literature, he also took pleasure in more elusive, less popular writing, perhaps most significantly the *Essays* of the French thinker Michel de Montaigne. Montaigne's work might well be considered a major source, since the *Essays* directly influenced Shakespeare in the creation of the plays. However, I treat it here among the less obvious stimuli because Montaigne offered the playwright not stories or characters but ideas and philosophical viewpoints. Just before Shakespeare's rise to prominence, Montaigne was earning notice among European readers for his two volumes of essays published in 1580 and expanded in 1595. A few titles give a sense of his concerns: "That Our Intention Judgeth Our Actions," "Of the Force of Imagination," "Of Friendship," "A Consideration upon Cicero," "Of Thumbs." The tone of these reflections is elusive and complex: Montaigne's persona adopts a skeptical view of experience, an attitude that can vary from bitterness to mild irony to remote amusement. The distance from which Montaigne regards all mortal activity generates a tolerant affection for human creatures with all their failings, a balance that we also recognize in the mature Shakespeare. The playwright may have felt a philosophical kinship with Montaigne and may in fact have absorbed directly some of the Frenchman's perspectivism, his understanding that what we see depends on where we stand. Shakespeare had probably read Montaigne by about 1601 or so, for *Hamlet* seems to refer to one of the most ambitious and darkest of the essays, "An Apology of Raymond Sebond." Most likely Shakespeare read the essay in French, for the first English translation, by John Florio, was not published until 1603 (although Shakespeare might have seen the translation in manuscript). In any case, he certainly read Florio's version. In a later play, *The Tempest,* the old counselor, Gonzalo, describes his vision of the perfect society in language that echoes Florio's translation of the essay "Of the Cannibals." Shakespeare's skepticism, in this case, is more pervasive than Montaigne's: whereas the philosopher idealizes the savages and condemns their conquerors, the dramatist seems dubious about both groups. Other philosophical writers probably held Shakespeare's attention, although none so firmly as Montaigne.

As a poetic dramatist, however, Shakespeare was especially attracted to poetry, and the recent works of his Elizabethan contemporaries were always on his desk or in his head. He probably read Edmund Spenser's sonnets, published as the *Amoretti,* as well as his vast allegory, *The Faerie Queene,* issued in two parts, Books 1–3 in 1590, 4–6 in 1596. We know from references in the plays that he was familiar with the work of the lesser poets of the age, such as Samuel Daniel and Michael Drayton, and he may have been aware of the vigorous satires that young John Donne was writing at the end of the 1590s. Shakespeare's sonnets indicate an attraction to the poetry of Sir Philip Sidney, whose sonnet sequence *Astrophil and Stella* was written around 1580 but not published until 1591. (Two poems appear on p. 140.) Sidney's brilliant lyrics very likely affected Shakespeare's efforts, both in the formal qualities of individual poems (wordplay, imagery, Petrarchan and anti-Petrarchan themes) and in the presence of a narrative loosely connecting the individual poems into a sequence, although the "characters" in *Astrophil and Stella* have proved less resistant to identification than the ghostly figures in Shakespeare's collection.

Other forms of writing popular in the period can only be mentioned. A primary source for poetry was the miscellany, an anthology of verses gathered by an editor or publisher and offered for sale under such titles as *A Gorgeous Gallery of Gallant Inventions* and *England's Helicon.* Probably the best known, *Songs and Sonnets,* the 1557 collection that we know as *Tottel's Miscellany,* receives a nod in *The Merry Wives of Windsor,* when the idiotic Slender wishes that he had brought his copy to impress the girl he hopes to win. Religious pamphleteers kept themselves busy, particularly in attacks on the theater like Stephen Gosson's *Plays Confuted in Five Actions.* The period saw major translations, such as Sir Thomas Hoby's rendering of Castiglione's elegant guide to aristocratic manners and success, *The Book of the Courtier,* and George Chapman's translations of Homer, which began to appear in 1598. Literary criticism appeared in such treatises as Sir Philip Sidney's *Defense of Poesy* and George Puttenham's *Art of English Poesy* (excerpts appear on pp. 171 and 209). And finally there were jokebooks, humorous equivalents to the poetic miscellanies, such as *A Hundred Merry Tales* and Robert Armin's *Nest of Ninnies.*

Shakespeare's Favorites

Most passionate readers have certain books to which they frequently return. For Shakespeare those books were Raphael Holinshed's *Chronicles*, Thomas North's translation of Plutarch's *Lives*, and Ovid's *Metamorphoses*. Each of these large, ambitious works involves the reader in a complete world — the realm of Britain from ancient to modern times, the two great European empires of Greece and Rome, and a prehistorical, mythological universe of deities and magic. Shakespeare valued each of these authors for different reasons, however, and it is important to notice those properties that attracted him to each of them.

Holinshed's *Chronicles of England, Scotland, and Ireland* was the most immediately helpful. It served as a source for a third of the plays — the ten histories as well as two tragedies (*King Lear* and *Macbeth*) and a romance (*Cymbeline*), all set in Britain. Shakespeare read the second edition of 1587 (the first appeared in 1577) and used it extensively. What was its attraction, and why did he compose with it open before him and return to it so often? Holinshed's prose is by no means distinguished, certainly not as elegant or vivid as North's rendering of Plutarch, for example. Nor did the historian arrange a compelling shape for most of the events he recounts, or for the episodic collection as a whole. What Holinshed did furnish was an absolutely comprehensive version of historical events that stimulated Shakespeare's imagination.

The scope of the *Chronicles* is captured in Stephen Booth's analysis of the length of the (enlarged) 1587 edition: "excluding blanks, scholarly apparatus, and seven title pages, the text runs to about three-and-a-half million words. That is roughly equal to the total of the Authorized Version of the Bible, the complete dramatic works of Shakespeare, *Clarissa*, Boswell's *Life of Johnson*, and *War and Peace* combined" (*The Book Called "Holinshed's Chronicles"* 1). The historical sweep afforded by such vast length can be thrilling, and apparently it excited Shakespeare, who seems not to have used the *Chronicles* merely as a reference tool but to have read widely and enthusiastically in it. In addition to range, Holinshed delivers mountains of detail. Much of this particularity results from the normal Tudor practice of incorporating and amplifying all the relevant work of one's professional predecessors. Shakespeare, by writing his dramas with the *Chronicles* before him, thus had access to the most recent and complete resources available, the latest model of the historian's product. The second edition of the *Chronicles*, published after Holinshed's death, had been augmented and annotated by (among others) Abraham Fleming, who added Latin tags to the margins and sought at every turn to put the recorded events in a moral context. Sometimes his moral squares with the episode to which it is attached; sometimes his interpretation seems flagrantly incompatible with the event. Fleming's prescriptive apparatus contributes yet another layer to the palimpsest of information and interpretation that Holinshed had devised.

Such complexity offered golden chances to a dramatist prospecting for theatrical conflict, and Shakespeare found it irresistible. The *Chronicles* should be regarded as a vast warehouse stuffed full of character studies, dates, details of battles, genealogical data, digressions on motives and consequences, Tudor political orthodoxy, and unintended subversions of that orthodoxy. Thus Shakespeare becomes a kind of shopper, a wholesale buyer passing up and down the aisles, scanning the shelves and surveying the merchandise, choosing items that he can then polish up and display for his own customers. Holinshed's book supplied the raw material to which Shakespeare gave theatrical shape, educing patterns and focusing ideas. For example, Holinshed only faintly delineates the parallelism that Shakespeare develops between Prince Hal and Hotspur in *Henry IV, Part 1.* Sometimes the dramatist wished to shroud rather than clarify the meaning of events, at least temporarily: in the opening scenes of the same play, the motives of the King and the Percy family are much less easy to discern than in the source. As the excerpt found on page 141 indicates, Holinshed emphatically establishes the "envy" of the Percy family and the King's fear of Mortimer's right to the throne. Shakespeare allows such emotions and motives to unfold slowly and indeterminately, as a means of investigating dramatically the ethics of rebellion, usurpation, and political loyalty. Similarly, he complicates the moral and political orthodoxy that emerges from the *Chronicles,* setting familiar conclusions against inconclusive facts and even prompting the audience to reflect on what it means to write history, in dramatic form or otherwise.

The historical biographies that make up Plutarch's *Lives of the Noble Grecians and Romans* offered the playwright heroic stories and characters, ready-made structures, and philosophical and stylistic pleasures. Shakespeare probably read the second edition (1595) of North's translation, using it as the basis for four tragedies: *Julius Caesar, Timon of Athens, Antony and Cleopatra,* and *Coriolanus.* Plutarch also contributed ideas about the classical world and innumerable historical details that turn up in other plays. Shakespeare compressed events, selected what he needed from the wealth of particulars, and drew on Plutarch's several versions of the episodes and persons, depending on what he needed at the moment. In composing *Julius Caesar,* for instance, he worked eclectically, choosing events that Plutarch records in three of his *Lives,* those of Brutus, Mark Antony, and Caesar himself. Shakespeare is faithful to his Plutarchan source in a way that he never is with Holinshed or his other models, and for three reasons.

First, Plutarch's biographical accounts, focused narrowly as they are on individual lives rather than on a historical panorama, present concentration and potential dramatic shape, as Holinshed's narratives do not. Second, as many commentators have pointed out, Shakespeare seems to have responded to the intellectual issues that occupy Plutarch — the relation of purpose to accident, the nature of heroism in an unheroic world, the interpenetration of the personal and the political. Such ideas suggest affinities among Shakespeare's books, for Plutarch was a favorite not only of Shakespeare but also of Montaigne, who declared, "Plutarch is my man." Shakespeare might have said the same. Third, Shakespeare's affection for Plutarch probably owes most to the power and elegance of North's prose style. A comparison of Enobarbus's speech about Cleopatra's royal barge (*Antony and Cleopatra* 2.2) with North's prose account of the same subject will illustrate Shakespeare's admiration for and indebtedness to his source: the dramatic speech is more or less versified North, whose account is reprinted on page 143. As I have pointed out, Renaissance ideas about imitation and originality differed from our own. What to us might look like literary theft was to early modern writers the creative reproduction of a favorite passage. But Shakespeare made changes as well. To study his appropriation of North, both here and in other passages, is to discern a multitude of subtle but significant alterations that illustrate the difference between history and theater.

Ovid is perhaps more important than either Holinshed or Plutarch, and it may even be true to say that the *Metamorphoses* was Shakespeare's favorite book. Ovidian originals influenced the two early narrative poems, *Venus and Adonis* and *The Rape of Lucrece*. Some of the comedies, notably *A Midsummer Night's Dream*, make explicit use of narrative material from the *Metamorphoses*. But Shakespeare did not regard Ovid's work as an object for slavish imitation; rather, it served as an imaginative stimulus, a source of inspiration. Shakespeare responded profoundly to the Roman mythographer's fantastic vision of human and divine experience, particularly to his all-encompassing theme of transformation. Sometimes Ovid's magical changes are for the better, as when Venus gratifies Pygmalion's yearning by giving life to the statue he has sculpted. Sometimes they are for the worse, as when Actaeon spies on the bathing Diana and is turned into a horned stag tormented by his own hounds. (See the sixteenth-century and modern translations of this tale on pp. 143 and 147.) Shakespeare invokes the Pygmalion myth at the end of *The Winter's Tale*, and the Actaeon story becomes Falstaff's humorous punishment in the final scene of *The Merry Wives of Windsor*. Ovid's presentation of change is fundamentally dramatic, and thus the transformational theme is to some extent responsible for shaping Shakespeare's theatrical structures. Finally, the allusive verbal texture of the plays is everywhere informed by Ovid's fantastic, memorable tales.

Ovid's shifting and elusive world appealed to and served Shakespeare in both his comic and tragic moods. The *Metamorphoses* lies behind Shakespeare's creation of a realm in which the impossible becomes possible, in which obstacles can be overcome and wishes fulfilled, in which change is beneficent and happiness attainable. For example, *The Taming of the Shrew*, packed with Ovidian references, depicts a world that seems constant in nothing but change. In the frame story, Christopher Sly is transformed into a rich lord and Bartholomew the page into his wife; in the play proper, "Tranio is changed into Lucentio" by means of disguise; Lucentio the student into Cambio the scholar; Hortensio the old suitor into Litio the music master; Petruchio on his wedding day into a kind of lunatic; an unsuspecting traveler into Vincentio, false father of the false Lucentio; Bianca the obedient daughter into an uncooperative wife; and, in the titular transformation, Katherina ("the curst") from an unhappy misfit into a seemingly contented spouse. Despite the heavy irony, these reversals and alterations intimate that human action is being guided by some providential force corresponding to Ovid's gods and goddesses. Conversely, Ovid's tales of disastrous alteration are consistent with the great Renaissance *topos* or theme of mutability, the impermanence of perfection. Thus his pattern of sudden decline informs the tragic reversal of fortune evident in, say, *Othello* and *King Lear*.

This attraction to metamorphosis is another manifestation of Shakespeare's commitment to the value of play, his pleasure in the beneficial effects of costumes, roles, impersonation, and all the other essentials and accidentals of the theater. To act is to inhabit the character of or to assume the persona of another in order to entertain, and the fictional realm created by performance affords the members of the audience, for the duration of the play, the chance to inhabit a world different from their own. Such a devotion to fiction accounts for Shakespeare's appreciation for the pleasures of storytelling, a taste satisfied by Ovid's compendium of exotic tales. Shakespeare's reverence for the theater and for fiction generally is part of a larger concern for the value of art in human affairs. In the Pygmalion section of book 10, Ovid asserts that "the best art . . . is that which conceals art." This insistence on the indistinguishability of the artificial and the natural, on art's equivalence and potential superiority to nature — the point of the Pygmalion episode — is a favorite Ovidian idea that pervades the Shakespearean canon as well. Always the idea is just beneath the surface, as in Shakespeare's sonnets, in Hamlet's instructions to Horatio to tell his story to future audiences, and in the comedies of identity, such as *As You Like It*. Occasionally that view breaks through the surface and declares itself explicitly. In *The Winter's Tale,* for example, it generates the debate between Perdita and Polixenes over the relative value of art and nature, and then later in the final scene when a statue comes to life.

The opposition of art and nature is only one of many that Shakespeare encourages his audience to consider, evaluate, and reevaluate, and his attachment to the principle of intellectual flexibility seems to reflect the Roman poet's fascination with various forms of transmutation. As he concludes the story of Diana and Actaeon with the voyeur's death, Ovid reports a divided reaction to Actaeon's fate:

> Much muttring was upon this fact. Some thought there was extended
> A great deale more extremitie than neded. Some commended
> *Dianas* doing: saying that it was but worthely
> For safegarde of hir womanhod. Eche partie did applie
> Good reasons to defende their case. (3.156–60, Golding translation)

Such conflicting assessments of dramatic action are built into Shakespeare's theatrical method: is *Henry V* a patriotic celebration of Christian kingship or a dark assault on militarism and royal vanity? Most sensitive readers see evidence for both claims, and this frequent Shakespearean opposition, known as *complementarity,* is likewise implicit in the *Metamorphoses*.

Much the same might be said of North's Plutarch and, perhaps to a lesser extent, the second edition of Holinshed's *Chronicles*. Shakespeare seems to have been attracted by stories and persons that were susceptible to plural and even contradictory readings. And having located such ambiguities, he exploited the inherent uncertainty of dramatic representation to develop them even further. He involved his audience in the complex process of interpretation to such an extent that interpretation becomes one of the principal themes of his plays.

Ultimately the study of Shakespeare's sources is the study of how Shakespeare treated his sources. What Keats refers to as Shakespeare's "negative capability," his gift for effacing himself entirely and entering imaginatively into the lives of his characters, is relevant to his transformation of his sources as well. He had an eye for the telling detail; he ignored history when necessary; he combined apparently incompatible narratives into something entirely new; he altered particulars that didn't suit him. But above all he had a genius for identifying the essence of a great story and retelling it theatrically. Some sixty versions of the Lear story were in circulation when Shakespeare set about to dramatize the tale of the old king in 1605. Nobody remembers these prior versions today. But *King Lear* continues to fill theaters.

➜ EDWARD HALL

From *The Union of the Two Noble and Illustre Families of Lancaster and York* *1548*

Edward Hall's *Union,* written during the reign of Henry VIII to promote the Tudor version of the nation's past, was one of Shakespeare's principal sources for the early history plays. This excerpt recounts Richard of Gloucester's plot to clear his path to the throne by arranging for James Tyrell to murder his nephews.

King Richard, after his coronation, taking his way to Gloucester to visit in his new honor the town of which he bare the name of old, devised as he rode [how] to fulfill that thing which he before had intended. And forasmuch as his mind gave him that his nephews living, men would not reckon that he could have right to the realm, he thought therefore without delay to rid them, as though the killing of his kinsmen might end his cause, and make him kindly [naturally] king. Whereupon he sent John Grene, whom he specially trusted, unto Sir Robert Brakenbury, constable of the Tower, with a letter and credence also, that the same Sir Robert in any wise should put the two children to death. This John Grene did his errand to Brakenbury, kneeling before our lady in the Tower, who plainly answered that he would never put them to death to die therefor. With the which answer Grene returned, recounting the same to King Richard at Warwick yet [still] on his journey, wherewith he took such displeasure and thought that the same night he said to a secret page of his: "Ah, whom shall a man trust? They that I have brought up my self, they that I went [weened, thought] would have most surely served me, even those fail me, and at my commandment will do nothing for me." "Sir," quoth the page, "there lieth one in the pallet-chamber [bedroom] without that I dare well say, to do your grace pleasure the thing were right hard that he would refuse," meaning this by [by this] James Tyrell, which was a man of goodly personage, and for the gifts of nature worthy to have served a much better prince, if he had well served God, and by grace obtained to have as much truth and good will, as he had strength and wit. The man had a high heart and sore longed upward, not rising yet so fast as he had hoped, being hindered and kept under by Sir Richard Ratcliff and Sir William Catesby . . . which thing this page had well marked and known: wherefore this occasion offered of very special friendship spied his time to set him forward, and such wise to do him good, that all the enemies that he had (except the devil) could never have done him so much hurt and shame, for upon the page's words, King Richard arose (for this communication had he sitting on a draft [a privy], a convenient carpet for such a counsel) and came out into the pallet-chamber, where he did find in bed the said James Tyrell and Sir Thomas Tyrell of person like and brethren of blood, but nothing of kin in conditions. Then said the king merely to them, "What, sirs, be you in bed so soon?" And called up James Tyrell, and broke to him secretly his mind in this mischievous matter, in the which he found him nothing strange [disaffected]. Wherefore on the morrow he sent him to Brakenbury with a letter by the which he was commanded to deliver to the said James all the keys of the Tower for a night, to the end that he might there accomplish the king's pleasure in such things as he there had given him in commandment. After which letter delivered and the keys received, James appointed the next night ensuing to destroy them, devising before and preparing the means. . . .

For James Tyrell devised that they should be murdered in their beds, and no blood shed. To the execution whereof he appointed Miles Forest, one of the four that before kept them, a fellow flesh-bred in murder before time. And to him he joined one John Dighton, his own horsekeeper, a big broad square and strong knave. Then all the other being removed from them, this Miles Forest and John Dighton about midnight, the sely [innocent] children lying in their beds, came into the chamber and suddenly lapped them up amongst the clothes [bedsheets] and so bewrapped them and entangled them, keeping down by force the featherbed and pillows hard unto their mouths, that within a while they smored [smothered] and stifled them, and their breaths failing, they gave up to God their innocent souls into the joys of heaven, leaving to the tormentors their bodies dead in the bed, which after the wretches perceived, first by the struggling with the pangs of death, and after long lying still, to be thoroughly dead, they laid the bodies out upon the bed, and fetched James Tyrell to see them, which when he saw them perfectly dead, he caused the murderers to bury them at the stair foot, meetly [appropriately] deep in the ground under a great heap of stones.

From *A Mirror for Magistrates* *1587 edition*

A Mirror for Magistrates was an influential collection of tragic narratives first published in 1559 and later supplemented. The 1587 edition contains forty-five versified stories chiefly concerned with the fall of corrupt rulers. The kind of moral history represented here by the life of Julius Caesar was extremely popular in early modern England; by 1610 eight editions of the *Mirror* had appeared.

CAIUS JULIUS CAESAR

But glory won, the way to hold and keep the same,
To hold good Fortune fast, a work of skill.
Who so with prudent art can stay that stately dame
Which sets us up so high upon her haughty hill,

And constant aye [always] can keep her love and favor still,   5
He wins immortal fame and high renown;
But thrice unhappy he that wears the stately crown,
If once misfortune kick and cast his scepter down.

    For when in Rome I was Dictator chose,
And Emperor or Captain sole for aye: 10
My glory did procure me secret foes,
Because above the rest I bare [bore] the sway.
By sundry means they sought my deep decay.
For why? There could no Consuls chosen be,
No Praetor [magistrate] take the place, no sentence have decree,   15
Unless it liked me first, and were approved by me.

    This they envied that sued aloft to climb,
As Cassius, which the Praetorship did crave,
And Brutus eke [also] his friend which bare the crime
Of my dispatch — for they did first deprave   20
My life, mine acts, and sought my blood to have —
Full secretly amongst themselves conspired, decreed
To be attemptors of that cruel bloody deed,
When Caesar in the Senate house from noble heart should bleed.

    But I forewarned was by Capis' tomb,   25
His Epitaph my death did long before foreshow.
Cornelius Balbus saw mine horses headless run
Without a guide, forsaking food for woe.
Spurina warned me that sooth [truth] of things did know:
A wren in beak with laurel green that flew   30
From woods to Pompey's court, whom birds there slew,
Foreshowed my doleful death, as after all men knew.

    The night before my slaughter, I did dream
I carried was, and flew the clouds above,
And sometimes hand in hand with Jove supreme
I walked, methought, which might suspicions move.   35
My wife Calphurnia, Caesar's only love,
Did dream she saw her crest of house to fall,
Her husband thrust through breast a sword withal;
Eke that same night her chamber doors themselves flew open all.   40

    These things did make me doubt that morning much,
And I accrazed was and thought at home to stay:
But who is he can void of [escape] destinies such,
Where so great number seeks him to betray?
The traitor Brutus bade me not delay,   45

Nor yet to frustrate there so great assembly sat:
On which to hear the public pleas I gate [went],
Mistrusting naught mine end and fatal fate.

There met me by the way a Roman good,
Presenting me a scroll of every name   50
And all their whole device [plot] that sought my blood,
That presently would execute the same.
But I supposed that for some suit he came,
I heedless bare this scroll in my left hand,
And others more, till leisure, left unscanned,   55
Which in my pocket afterwards they fand [found].

Spurina as I came, at sacrifices was,
Near to the place where I was after slain,
Of whose divinings I did little pass [care],
Though he to warn me oft before was fain [eager].   60
My haughty heart these warnings all disdain.
Quoth I, the Ides of March be come, yet harm is none;
Quoth he, the Ides of March be come, yet th'are not gone.
And reckless so to court I went, and took my throne.

As soon as I was set, the traitors all arose,   65
And one approached near, as to demand some thing;
To whom as I laid ear, at once my foes
Me compassed round, their weapons hid they bring.
Then I too late perceiv'd the fatal sting.
O this, quoth I, is violence: then Cassius pierc'd my breast;   70
And Brutus thou my son, quoth I, whom erst I loved best?
He stabbed me in, and so with daggers did the rest.

You princes all and noble men, beware of pride,
And careful will to war [i.e., ambition] for kingdom's sake:
By me, that set myself aloft the world to guide,   75
Beware what bloodshed you do undertake.
Ere three and twenty wounds had made my heart to quake,
What thousands fell for Pompey's pride and mine?
Of Pompey's life that cut the vital line,
Myself have told what fate I found in fine [ultimately].   80

Full many noble men, to rule alone, I slew,
And some themselves for grief of heart did slay;
For they ne would [would not] mine empire stay to view.
Some I did force to yield, some fled away,
As loath to see their countries quite decay.   85
The world in Afric, Asia, distant far,

And Europe knew my bloodsheds great in war,
Recounted yet through all the world that are.

    But sith [since] my whole pretense was glory vain,
To have renown and rule above the rest,   90
Without remorse of many thousands slain,
Which, for their own defense, their wars addressed,
I deem therefore my stony heart and breast
Receiv'd so many wounds for just revenge; they stood
By justice right of Jove, the sacred sentence good: 95
That who so slays, he pays the price, is blood for blood.

→   GIOVANNI BATTISTA GIRALDI CINTHIO

From *Gli Hecatommithi*   *1565*

The Principal Source for Othello   *Translated by Geoffrey Bullough*

Giovanni Battista Giraldi Cinthio's *Gli Hecatommithi* (1565) is an anthology of tales that Shakespeare apparently knew, probably in the original Italian. The passage reproduced here, in a modern translation by Geoffrey Bullough, is the story of the jealous captain that Shakespeare adapted as *Othello.* The use of Cinthio indicates that the playwright looked beyond his own nation and language for effective stories to dramatize.

Not long afterwards the Moor deprived the Corporal [the equivalent to Cassio] of his rank for having drawn his sword and wounded a soldier while on guard-duty. Disdemona was grieved by this and tried many times to reconcile the Moor with him. Whereupon the Moor told the rascally Ensign [the equivalent to Iago] that his wife importuned him so much for the Corporal that he feared he would be obliged to reinstate him. The evil man saw in this a hint for setting in train the deceits he had planned, and said: "Perhaps Disdemona has good cause to look on him so favourably!" "Why is that?" asked the Moor. "I do not wish," said the Ensign, "to come between man and wife, but if you keep your eyes open you will see for yourself." Nor for all the Moor's inquiries would the Ensign go beyond this: nonetheless his words left such a sharp thorn in the Moor's mind, that he gave himself up to pondering intensely what they could mean. He became quite melancholy, and one day, when his wife was trying to soften his anger towards the Corporal, begging him not to condemn to oblivion the loyal service and friendship of many years just for one small fault, especially since the Corporal had been reconciled to the man he had struck, the Moor burst out in anger and said to her, "There must be a very powerful reason why you take such trouble for this fellow, for he is not your brother, nor even a kinsman, yet you have him so much at heart!"

The lady, all courtesy and modesty, replied: "I should not like you to be angry with me. Nothing else makes me do it but sorrow to see you deprived of so dear a friend as you have shown that the Corporal was to you. He has not committed so serious an offence as to deserve such hostility.[1] But you Moors are so hot by nature that any little thing moves you to anger and revenge."

Still more enraged by these words the Moor answered: "Anyone who does not believe that may easily have proof of it! I shall take such revenge for any wrongs done to me as will more than satisfy me!" The lady was terrified by these words, and seeing her husband angry with her, quite against his habit, she said humbly: "Only a very good purpose made me speak to you about this, but rather than have you angry with me I shall never say another word on the subject."

The Moor, however, seeing the earnestness with which his wife had again pleaded for the Corporal, guessed that the Ensign's words had been intended to suggest that Disdemona was in love with the Corporal, and he went in deep depression to the scoundrel and urged him to speak more openly. The Ensign, intent on injuring this unfortunate lady, after pretending not to wish to say anything that might displease the Moor, appeared to be overcome by his entreaties and said: "I must confess that it grieves me greatly to have to tell you something that must be in the highest degree painful to you; but since you wish me to tell you, and the regard that I must have of your honour as my master spurs me on, I shall not fail in my duty to answer your request. You must know therefore that it is hard for your Lady to see the Corporal in disgrace for the simple reason that she takes her pleasure with him whenever he comes to your house. The woman has come to dislike your blackness."

[1] Cf. *Othello* 3.3.63–67.

→ # From the Geneva Bible   *1560* ➤

Named for its place of publication, a center of Calvinist thought, the Geneva Bible was one of the earliest and most influential English translations of the Scriptures. There was fierce debate in the sixteenth century about whether the Bible should be translated into English at all, and the success of the Geneva version helped to settle the question. The title page and map, both reduced, are reprinted from a facsimile edition. The map, which precedes Paul's Epistle to the Romans, depicts the territory covered by the disciples on their missionary journeys. Some of the place names used by Shakespeare include Illyria (*Twelfth Night*), Siracuse (*The Comedy of Errors*), Cyprus and the Pontick Sea (*Othello*), and Phillipi (*Julius Caesar*).

The facsimile text (slightly enlarged) on page 126 is from chapter 5 of the Gospel According to Matthew and contains the first part of the Sermon on the Mount. A transcription of the entire chapter follows.

THE BIBLE

AND
HOLY SCRIPTVRES

CONTEYNED IN
THE OLDE AND NEWE
Teſtament.

TRANSLATED ACCOR-
ding to the Ebrue and Greke, and conferred With
the beſt tranſlations in diuers langages.

WITH MOSTE PROFITABLE ANNOTA-
tions vpon all the hard places, and other things of great
importance as may appeare in the Epiſtle to the Reader.

FEARE YE NOT, STAND STIL, AND BEHOLDE
the ſaluacion of the Lord, which he wil ſhewe to you this day. Exod.14.13.

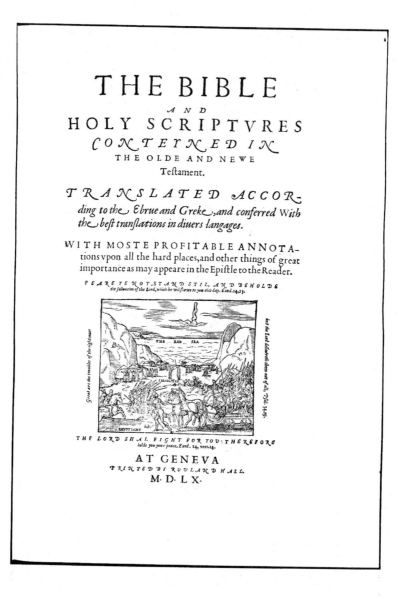

THE LORD SHAL FIGHT FOR YOV: THEREFORE
holde you your peace. Exod. 14, verſ.14.

AT GENEVA
PRINTED BY ROVLAND HALL
M. D. LX.

CHAP. V.

3 Christ teacheth who are blessed. 13 The salt of the earth & light of the worlde. 16 Good workes. 17 Christ came to fulfil the Law. 21 What is men: by killing. 25 Reconciliation. 27 Adulterie. 29 Offences. 31 Divorcement. 33 Not to sweare. 39 To suffer wrong. 43 To loue our enemies. 48 Perfection.

1 AND when he sawe the multitude, he went vp into a mountaine: and whē he was set, his disciples came to him. *Luk.6,20.*

2 And he opened his mouthe and taught them, saying,

3 *Blessed are the ªpoore in spirit, for theirs is the kingdome of heauen.

4 Blessed are they that ᵇ mourne: for they shalbe comforted.

5 *Blessed are the ᶜ meke: for they shal inherite the earth.

6 Blessed are they which ᵈ honger & thirst for righteousnes: for they shal be filled.

7 Blessed are the merciful: for thei shal obteine mercie.

8 Blessed are the ᵉpure in heart: for they shal se God.

9 Blessed are the peace makers : for they shalbe called the ᵉ children of God.

10 Blessed are they *which suffer persecutiō for righteousnes sake : for theirs is the kingdome of heauen.

11 *Blessed are ye when men reuile you, and persecute you, and say all maner of euil against you for my sake, falsely.

12 Reioyce and be glad , for great is your

a That feele them selues voide of all righteousnes that they may onely seeke it in Christ.
Isa.61,2.
luk.5,21.
b Which seele their owne miserie,&seeke their comfort in God.
Psal.73.11.
c Who rather wolde suffer all iniuries, then they wol de reuenge thē selues.
Psal.24,4.
d being in necessitie,desire it is vpright & godlie.
e For he is called ᶴ God of peace, 1. Cor 11,,3.
1.Pet.3,14.
1.Tet.4,14.
all.5,41.

rewarde in heauen: for so persecuted they the Prophets which were before you. *Mar.9,50, luk.14,34.*

13 *Ye are the ᶠ salte of the earth: but if the salte haue lost his sauour, wherewith shal it be salted? It is thenceforthe good for nothing, but to be cast out, & to be troden vnder fote of men.

14 Ye are the light of the worlde. A citie that is set on an hill, can not be hid.

15 *Nether do men light a candel, and put it vnder a bushel, but on a candelsticke , & it giueth light vnto all that are in the house.

16 *Let ᵍ your light so shine before men, that they may se your good workes, & glorifie your Father which is in heauen.

17 Thinke not that I am come to destroye the Law, or the Prophetes. ʰ I am not come to destroye them, but to fulfil them.

18 *For truely I say vnto you, Til heauen, and earth perish, one iote, or one title of the Law shal not scape, til ᶦ all things be fulfilled.

19 *Whosoeuer therefore shal breake one of ᵏ these least commandements, & teache men so, he shalbe called the least in the kingdome of heauen : but whosoeuer shal obserue and teache them , the same shal be called great in the kingdome of heauen.

20 For I say vnto you, except your righteousnes *excede the righteousnes of ᶴ ˡScribes and

f Your office is to season men with the salt of heauēlie doctrine.
Mar.4,21.
luk.8,16.
& 11,33.
g Because you are sene farre of, giue good example of life.
h The Gospel is the establi shing,& accōplishing of ᶴ Law.
1.Pet.2,12.
i The doctrine of the Law conteineth nothing vnprofitable or superfluous.
Luk.16,17.
Iam.2,10.
k Whosoeuer shal transgres se the least of the ten cōmandements in worde and example,he shal be cast out of the kingdome of God, except it be pardoned him in Christ.
Luk.11,39.
l Which nether expoūde the Law truely, nor obserue it is weл.

CHAPTER 5

3 Christ teacheth who are blessed. 13 The salt of the earth and light of the world. 16 Good works. 17 Christ came to fulfill the Law. 21 What is meant by killing. 23 Reconciliation. 27 Adultery. 29 Offenses. 31 Divorce. 33 Not to swear. 39 To suffer wrong. 43 To love our enemies. 48 Perfection.

1 And when he saw the multitude, he went up into a mountain; and when he was set, his disciples came to him.

2 And he opened his mouth and taught them, saying,

3 "Blessed are the poor in spirit, for theirs is the kingdom of heaven.

4 Blessed are they that mourn, for they shall be comforted.

5 Blessed are the meek, for they shall inherit the earth.

6 Blessed are they which hunger and thirst for righteousness, for they shall be filled.

7 Blessed are the merciful, for they shall obtain mercy.

8 Blessed are the pure in heart, for they shall see God.

9 Blessed are the peace makers, for they shall be called the children of God.

10 Blessed are they which suffer persecution for righteousness sake, for theirs is the kingdom of heaven.

11 Blessed are you when men revile you and persecute you and say all manner of evil against you for my sake falsely.

12 Rejoice and be glad, for great is your reward in heaven; for so persecuted they the Prophets which were before you.

13 You are the salt of the earth; but if the salt has lost his savor, wherewith shall it be salted? It is thenceforth good for nothing but to be cast out and to be trodden under foot of men.

14   You are the light of the world. A city that is set on a hill cannot be hid.

15   Neither do men light a candle and put it under a bushel, but on a candlestick, and it giveth light unto all that are in the house.

16   Let your light so shine before men that they may see your good works and glorify your Father which is in heaven.

17   Think not that I am come to destroy the Law or the Prophets. I am not come to destroy them, but to fulfill them.

18   For truly I say unto you, Till heaven and earth perish, one iota, or one tittle of the Law shall not escape, till all things be fulfilled.

19   Whosoever therefore shall break one of these least commandments and teach men so, he shall be called the least in the kingdom of heaven; but whosoever shall observe and teach them, the same shall be called great in the kingdom of heaven.

20   For I say unto you, except your righteousness exceed the righteousness of the Scribes and Pharisees, you shall not enter into the kingdom of heaven.

21   You have heard that it was said unto them of the old time, 'Thou shalt not kill; for whosoever killeth shall be culpable of judgment.'

22   But I say unto you, whosoever is angry with his brother unadvisedly shall be culpable of judgment. And whosoever sayeth unto his brother, 'Raca,' [a term of insult] shall be worthy to be punished by the Council. And whosoever shall say, 'Fool,' shall be worthy to be punished with hell fire.

23   If then thou bring thy gift to the altar, and there remember that thy brother hath ought against thee,

24   Leave there thine offering before the altar and go thy way; first be reconciled to thy brother, and then come and offer thy gift.

25   Agree with thine adversary quickly while thou art in the way with him, lest thine adversary deliver thee to the judge, and the judge deliver thee to the sergeant, and thou be cast into prison.

26   Verily I say unto thee, thou shalt not come out thence till thou hast paid the utmost farthing.

27   You have heard that it was said to them of old time, 'Thou shalt not commit adultery.'

28   But I say unto you that whosoever looketh on a woman to lust after her hath committed adultery with her already in his heart.

29   Wherefore, if thy right eye cause thee to offend, pluck it out and cast it from thee; for better it is for thee that one of thy members perish than that thy whole body should be cast into hell.

30   Also if thy right hand make thee to offend, cut it off and cast it from thee; for better it is for thee that one of thy members perish than that thy whole body should be cast into hell.

31   It hath been said also, 'Whosoever shall put away his wife, let him give her a testimonial of divorce.'

32   But I say unto you, whosoever shall put away his wife (except it be for fornication) causeth her to commit adultery; and whosoever shall marry her that is divorced committeth adultery.

33   Again, you have heard that it was said to them of old time, 'Thou shalt not forswear thyself, but shalt perform thine oaths to the Lord.'

34   But I say unto you, Swear not at all, neither by heaven, for it is the throne of God,

35   Nor yet by the earth, for it is his foot stool, neither by Jerusalem, for it is the city of the great King.

36   Neither shalt thou swear by thine head, because thou canst not make one hair white or black.

37   But let your communication be: Yea, yea; Nay, nay. [Let your yes be yes and your no be no.] For whatsoever is more than these, cometh of evil.

38   You have heard that it hath been said, 'An eye for an eye, and a tooth for a tooth.'

39   But I say unto you, Resist not evil; but whosoever shall smite thee on thy right cheek, turn to him the other also.

40   And if any man will sue thee at the law and take away thy coat, let him have thy cloak also.

41   And whosoever will compel thee to go a mile, go with him two.

42   Give to him that asketh, and from him that would borrow of thee, turn not away.

43   You have heard that it hath been said, 'Thou shalt love thy neighbor and hate thine enemy.'

44   But I say unto you, Love your enemies; bless them that curse you; do good to them that hate you, and pray for them which hurt you and persecute you,

45   That you may be the children of your Father that is in heaven; for he maketh his sun to arise on the evil and the good and sendeth rain on the just and unjust.

46   For if you love them which love you, what reward shall you have? Do not the Publicans [tax collectors] even the same?

47   And if you be friendly to your brethren only, what singular thing do you? Do not even the Publicans likewise?

48   You shall therefore be perfect, as your Father which is in heaven is perfect."

→ From *The Book of Common Prayer*   *1559*

The Order for the Burial of the Dead

This work replaced the Catholic liturgy and served as the basis for services in the Church of England. The 1559 version was a carefully worded compromise between the versions of 1549 and 1552, the first of which was more nearly Roman, the second more radically Protestant. Since attendance at church was mandatory in Elizabethan England, the words of the services would have been familiar to Shakespeare and his audience.

The priest meeting the corpse at the church stile, shall say or else the priests and clerks shall sing, and so go either unto the church, or toward the grave.

I AM the resurrection and the life (saith the Lord): he that believeth in me, yea, though he were dead, yet shall he live. And whosoever liveth and believeth in me, shall not die forever. [John 11.]

I KNOW that my redeemer liveth, and that I shall rise out of the earth in the last day, and shall be covered again with my skin, and shall see God in my flesh: yea, and I myself shall behold him, not with other, but with these same eyes. [Job 19.]

WE brought nothing into this world, neither may we carry anything out of this world. The Lord giveth, and the Lord taketh away. Even as it hath pleased the Lord, so cometh things to pass: blessed be the name of the Lord. [1 Tim. 6. Job 1.]

When they come at the grave, whiles the corpse is made ready to be laid into the earth, the priest shall say, or the priest and clerks shall sing.

MAN that is born of a woman hath but a short time to live, and is full of misery. He cometh up and is cut down like a flower; he flieth as it were a shadow, and never continueth in one stay. [Job 14.] In the midst of life we be in death: of whom may we seek for succor but of thee, O Lord, which for our sins justly art displeased. Yet, O Lord God most holy, O Lord most mighty, O holy and most merciful savior, deliver us not into the bitter pains of eternal death. Thou knowest, Lord, the secrets of our hearts, shut not up thy merciful eyes to our prayers: but spare us Lord most holy, O God most mighty, O holy and merciful savior, thou most worthy judge eternal, suffer us not at our last hour for any pains of death to fall from thee.

Then while the earth shall be cast upon the body by some standing by, the priest shall say.

FORASMUCH as it hath pleased Almighty God of his great mercy to take unto himself the soul of our dear brother here departed: we therefore commit his body to the ground, earth to earth, ashes to ashes, dust to dust, in sure and certain hope of resurrection to eternal life, through our Lord Jesus Christ, who shall change our vile body that it may be like to his glorious body, according to the mighty working, whereby he is able to subdue all things to himself.

Then shall be said or sung.

I HEARD a voice from heaven saying unto me, Write, From henceforth blessed are the dead which die in the Lord. Even so saith the Spirit, that they rest from their labors. [Rev. 14:13.]

Then shall follow this Lesson, taken out of the fifteenth chapter to the Corinthians, the first Epistle.

CHRIST is risen from the dead, and become the first fruits of them that slept. For by a man came death, and by a man came the resurrection of the dead. For as by Adam all die, even so by Christ shall all be made alive. But every man in his own order: The first is Christ, then they that are Christ's at his coming. Then cometh the end, when he hath delivered up the kingdom to

God the Father; when he hath put down all rule and all authority and power. For he must reign till he have put all his enemies under his feet. The last enemy that shall be destroyed is death. For he hath put all things under his feet. But when he saith all things are put under him, it is manifest that he is excepted, which did put all things under him. When all things are subdued unto him, then shall the Son also himself be subject unto him that put all things under him, that God may be all in all. Else what do they which are baptized over the dead, if the dead rise not at all? Why are they then baptized over them; yea, and why stand we alway then in jeopardy? By our rejoicing which I have in Christ Jesu our Lord, I die daily. That I have fought with beasts at Ephesus after the manner of men, what advantageth it me, if the dead rise not again? Let us eat and drink, for tomorrow we shall die. Be not ye deceived, evil words corrupt good manners. Awake truly out of sleep, and sin not. For some have not the knowledge of God. I speak this to your shame.

But some man will say, How arise the dead? With what body shall they come? Thou fool, that which thou sowest, is not quickened except it die. And what sowest thou? Thou sowest not that body that shall be, but bare corn, as of wheat or some other, but God giveth it a body at his pleasure, to every seed his own body. All flesh is not one manner of flesh, but there is one manner of flesh of men, and other manner of flesh of beasts, and other of fishes, another of birds. There are also celestial bodies, and there are bodies terrestrial. But the glory of the celestial is one, and the glory of the terrestrial is another. There is one manner glory of the sun, and another glory of the moon, and another glory of the stars. For one star differeth from another in glory: so is the resurrection of the dead. It is sown in corruption, it riseth again in incorruption. It is sown in dishonor, it riseth again in honor. It is sown in weakness, it riseth again in power. It is sown a natural body, it riseth a spiritual body. There is a natural body, and there is a spiritual body. As it is also written, The first man Adam was made a living soul, and the last Adam was made a quickening spirit. Howbeit, that is not first which is spiritual, but that which is natural, and then that which is spiritual. The first man is of the earth, earthy. The second man is the Lord from heaven, heavenly. As is the earthy, such are they that be earthy. And as is the heavenly, such are they that are heavenly. And as we have borne the image of the earthy, so shall we bear the image of the heavenly.

This say I brethren, that flesh and blood cannot inherit the kingdom of God, neither doth corruption inherit uncorruption. Behold, I show you a mystery. We shall not all sleep, but we shall all be changed, and that in a moment, in the twinkling of an eye by the last trump [trumpet]. For the trump shall blow, and the dead shall rise incorruptible, and we shall be changed. For this corruptible must put on incorruption, and this mortal must put on immortality. When this corruptible hath put on incorruption, and this mortal hath put on immortality, then shall be brought to pass the saying that is written, Death is swallowed up in victory. Death where is thy sting? Hell where is thy victory? The sting of death is sin; and the strength of sin is the law. But thanks be unto God, which hath given us victory, through our Lord Jesus Christ. Therefore my dear brethren, be ye steadfast and unmovable, always rich in the work of the Lord, forasmuch as ye know, how that your labor is not in vain in the Lord.

The Lesson ended, the priest shall say.

Lord have mercy upon us.
   Christ have mercy upon us.
Lord have mercy upon us.

OUR Father which art in heaven, etc.
And lead us not into temptation.
Answer. But deliver us from evil. Amen.

The Priest.

ALMIGHTY God, with whom do live the spirits of them that depart hence in the Lord, and in whom the souls of them that be elected, after they be delivered from the burden of the flesh, be in joy and felicity: We give thee hearty thanks, for that it hath pleased thee to deliver this   N.   our brother out of the miseries of this sinful world; beseeching thee, that it may please thee of thy gracious goodness, shortly to accomplish the number of thine elect, and to haste thy kingdom, that we with this our brother, and all other departed in the true faith of thy holy name, may have our perfect consummation and bliss, both in body and soul, in thy eternal and everlasting glory. Amen.

The Collect

O MERCIFUL God, the Father of our Lord Jesus Christ, who is the resurrection and the life, in whom whosoever believeth, shall live though he die, and whosoever liveth and believeth in him, shall not die eternally; who also taught us (by his holy Apostle Paul) not to be sorry, as men without hope, for them that sleep in him: We meekly beseech thee (O Father) to raise us from the death of sin unto the life of righteousness, that when we shall depart this life, we may rest in him, as our hope is this our brother doth; and that at the general resurrection in the last day, we may be found acceptable in thy sight, and receive that blessing which thy well-beloved Son shall then pronounce to all that love and fear thee, saying, Come ye blessed children of my Father, receive the kingdom prepared for you from the beginning of the world. Grant this we beseech thee, O merciful Father, through Jesus Christ our mediator and redeemer. Amen.

→ JOHN FOXE

From *Acts and Monuments*   *1563*

One of the most popular books in Renaissance England, John Foxe's *Acts and Monuments* relates in abundant and colorful detail the stories of Christians who suffered persecution. Particularly popular were the histories of Protestants victimized during the reign of Queen Mary (1553–58), who restored Roman Catholicism to Britain after Henry VIII's break with Rome. The excerpt here describes the martyrdom of Nicholas Ridley and Hugh Latimer, burned at the stake as heretics at Oxford in 1555.

The Behavior of Doctor Ridley at His Supper
the Night before His Suffering

The night before he suffered, his beard was washed and his legs; and as he sat at supper the same night at Master Irish's (who was his keeper) he bade his hostess and the rest at the board to his marriage. "For," saith he, "tomorrow I must be married." And so showed himself to be as merry as ever he was at any time before. And wishing his sister at his marriage, he asked his brother (sitting at the table) whether she could find in her heart to be there or no, and he answered, "Yea, I dare say, with all her heart." At which word he said he was glad to hear of her so much therein. So at this talk Mistress Irish wept.

But Master Ridley comforted her and said, "O Mistress Irish, you love me not now, I see well enough. For in that you weep it doth appear you will not be at my marriage, neither are content therewith. Indeed, you be not so much my friend as I thought you had been. But quiet yourself; though my breakfast shall be something sharp and painful, yet I am sure my supper shall be more pleasant and sweet, etc." When they rose from the table, his brother offered him to watch all night with him. But he said, "No, no, that you shall not. For I mind, God willing, to go to bed and to sleep as quietly tonight as ever I did in my life." So his brother departed, exhorting him to be of good cheer and to take his cross quietly, for the reward was great, etc.

The Behavior of Doctor Ridley and Master Latimer
at the Time of Their Death

Upon the north side of the town, in the ditch over against Bailliol College, the place of execution was appointed; and for fear of any tumult that might arise to let [hinder] the burning of them, my Lord Williams [the officer of the guard] was commanded by the queen's letters and the householders of the city to be there assistant, sufficiently appointed. And when everything was in a readiness, they were brought to the stake by the mayor and bailiffs: Master Ridley in a fair black gown, such as he was wont to wear when he was bishop, with a tippet [scarflike garment covering the shoulders] of sables about his neck, nothing undressed; Master Latimer in a poor Bristol frieze frock [coarse woolen gown] all worn, with his buttoned cap and a kerchief on his head all ready to the fire, a new long shroud hanging over his hose down to his feet, which at the first sight stirred men's hearts to rue upon them, beholding on the one side the honor they sometime [formerly] had, on the other the calamity whereunto they were then descended.

Master Doctor Ridley, as he passed towards Bocardo, he looked up where Master Cranmer [formerly Archbishop of Canterbury, also burned at the stake] did lie, and belike he would have seen him at the glass window, to have spoken unto him. But then Master Cranmer was busy with Friar Soto and his fellows, disputing together, so that he could not see him through that occasion. Then Master Ridley, looking back, espied Master Latimer coming after. Unto whom he said, "O, be you there?" "Yea," said Master Latimer, "have after, as fast as I can follow." So he following a pretty way off, at length they came both to the stake one after the other, where first Doctor Ridley entering the place, marvelous earnestly holding up both his hands, looked towards heaven, etc., and with a glimpse of his eye aside espying Master Latimer, with a wonderful cheerful look ran unto him, and embraced and kissed him, and as they that stood near reported, comforted him, saying: "Be of good heart, brother, for God will either assuage the fury of the flame, or else strengthen us to abide it." With that went he to the stake, kneeled down by it, kissed it, most effectuously prayed, and behind him Master Latimer kneeled, as earnestly calling upon God as he. After they arose, the one talked with the other a little while, till they which were appointed to see the execution removed themselves out of the sun. What they said, I can learn of no man. Then Doctor Smith began his sermon to them upon this text of Saint Paul in the thirteenth chapter of the first Epistle to the Corinthians: *Si corpus meum tradam igni, charitatem autem non habeo, nihil inde utilitatis capio,* which is thus much in English: "If I yield my body to the fire to be burnt, and have not charity, I shall gain nothing thereby." Wherein he alleged that the goodness of the cause nor the holiness of the person should not be judged by the order of the death, which he confirmed by the examples of Judas, and of a woman in Oxford that of late hanged herself, for that then they and such like (as he or two or three other recited) might be adjudged righteous, which desperately sundered their lives from their bodies, as he feared that those men that stood before him would do. But he cried still to the people to beware of them. For they were heretics and died out of the Church. And on the other side, he declared their diversity in opinions, as Lutherans, Oecolampadians [followers of Joannes Oecolampadius, German reformer and theologian], Zwinglians [followers of Huldreich Zwingli, Swiss theologian and reformer], of which sect they were, and that was the worst. But the old Church of Christ and the Catholic Faith believed far otherwise. At which place they lifted up both hands and their eyes to heaven, as it were calling God to witness of the truth.

The which countenance they made in many other places of his sermon, whereas they thought he spake amiss: he ended with a very short exhortation to them, to recant and come home again to the Church, and save their lives and souls, which else were condemned. His sermon was scant [hardly] in all a quarter of an hour.

Doctor Ridley said unto Master Latimer: "Will you begin to answer the sermon, or shall I?" Master Latimer said: "Begin you first, I pray you." "I will," said Master Ridley. Then the wicked sermon being ended, Doctor Ridley and Master Latimer kneeled down upon their knees, towards my Lord Williams of Tame, the vice-chancellor of Oxford, and divers [various] other commissioners appointed for that purpose, which sat upon a form [bench] thereby, unto whom Master Ridley said: "I beseech you, my lord, even for Christ's sake, that I may speak but two or three words," and whilst my lord bent his head to the mayor and vice-chancellor, as it appeared, to know whether he might give him leave to speak, the bailiffs and Doctor Marshall vice-chancellor ran hastily unto him, and with their hands stopped his mouth, and said: "Master Ridley, if you will revoke your erroneous opinions and recant the same, you shall not only have liberty so to do, but also the benefit of a subject, that is, have your life."

"Not otherwise?" said Master Ridley. "No," quoth Doctor Marshall. "Therefore if you will not do so, then there is no remedy but you must suffer for your deserts." "Well," quoth Master Ridley, "so long as the breath is in my body, I will never deny my Lord God and his known truth. God's will be done in me." And with that he rose up, and said with a loud voice: "Well, then, I commit our cause to Almighty God, which shall indifferently judge all." To whose saying Master Latimer added his old posy [motto], "Well, there is nothing hid but it shall be opened." And he said he could answer Smith well enough, if he might be suffered. Incontinently [immediately] they were commanded to make them ready, which they with all meekness obeyed. Master Ridley took his gown and his tippet, and gave it to his brother-in-law, Master Shepside, who all his time of imprisonment, although he might not be suffered to come to him, lay there at his own charges, to provide him necessaries, which from time to time he sent him by the sergeant that kept him. Some other of his apparel that was little worth he gave away; other the bailiffs took.

He gave away besides divers other small things to gentlemen standing by, and divers of them pitifully weeping, as to Sir Henry Lee he gave a new groat, and to divers of my Lord Williams' gentlemen some napkins, some nutmegs, and rasins [probably race, roots] of ginger, his dial, and such other things as he had about him to everyone that stood next him. Some plucked the points of his hose; happy was he that might get any rag of him. Master Latimer gave nothing, but very quietly suffered his keeper to pull off his hose and his other array, which to look unto was very simple. And being stripped into his shroud, seemed as comely a person to them that were there present as one should lightly [readily] see. And whereas in his clothes he appeared a withered and crooked sely [foolish] old man, he now stood bolt upright, as comely a father as one might lightly behold.

Then Master Ridley, standing as yet in his truss [close-fitting body garment], said to his brother: "It were best for me to go in my truss still." "No," quoth his brother, "it will put you to more pain; and the truss will do a poor man good." Whereunto Master Ridley said, "Be it in the name of God," and so unlaced himself. Then being in his shirt [undergarment], he stood upon the foresaid stone, and held up his hands, and said, "O heavenly Father, I give unto thee most hearty thanks for that thou hast called me to be a professor of thee, even unto death. I beseech thee, Lord God, take mercy upon this realm of England, and deliver the same from all her enemies."

Then the smith took a chain of iron and brought the same about both Doctor Ridley and Master Latimer's middles. And as he was knocking in a staple, Doctor Ridley took the chain in his hand, and shaked the same, for it did gird in his belly, and looking aside to the smith, said, "Good fellow, knock it in hard, for the flesh will have his course." Then his brother did bring him gunpowder in a bag, and would have tied the same about his neck. Master Ridley asked what it was; his brother said, "Gunpowder." Then said he, "I take it to be sent of God; therefore I will receive it, as sent of him. And have you any," said he, "for my brother?" — meaning Master Latimer. "Yea, sir, that I have," quoth his brother. "Then give it unto him," said he, "betime, lest you come too late." So his brother went and carried the same gunpowder unto Master Latimer. The meantime Doctor Ridley spake unto my Lord Williams and said, "My lord, I must be a suitor unto your lordship in the behalf of divers poor men, and especially in the cause of my poor sister. I have made a supplication to the queen's Majesty in their behalfs, I beseech your Lordship for Christ's sake to be a mean [mediator, advocate] to her Grace for them. My brother here hath the supplication and will resort to your Lordship to certify you thereof. There is nothing in all the world that troubleth my conscience, I praise God, this only excepted. Whiles I was in the See of London [religious office], divers poor men took leases of me and agreed with me for the same. Now I hear say the Bishop that now occupieth the same room will not allow my grants unto them made, but contrary unto all law and conscience hath taken from them their livings, and will not suffer them to enjoy the same. I beseech you, my Lord, be a mean for them. You shall do a good deed, and God will reward you."

Then brought they a faggot [stick] kindled with fire and laid the same down at Doctor Ridley's feet, and when he saw the fire flaming up towards him he cried with a wonderful loud voice, *"In manus tuas, Domine, commendo spiritum meum; Domine, recipe spiritum meum."* And after repeated this latter part often in English, "Lord, Lord, receive my spirit," Master Latimer crying as vehemently on the other side, "O Father of heaven, receive my soul," who received the flame as it were embracing it. After, as he had stroked his face with his hands, and as it were bathed them a little in the fire, soon died (as it appeared) with very little pain or none.

But Master Ridley, by reason of the evil making of the fire unto him, because the wooden faggots were laid about the gorse [prickly shrub], and over-high built, the fire burned first beneath, being kept down by the wood; which when he felt, he desired them for Christ's sake to let the fire come unto him. Which when his brother-in-law heard but not well understood, intending to rid him of his pain (for the which case he gave attendance), as one in such sorrow not well advised what he did, heaped faggots upon him that he clean covered him, which made the fire more vehement beneath, that it burned clean all his nether parts before it once touched the upper. And that made him leap up and down under the faggots, and often desire them to let the fire come unto him, saying "I cannot burn," which indeed appeared well. For after his legs were consumed by reason of his struggling with the pain (whereof he had no release, but only his contentation [contentment] in God) he showed that side toward us clean, shirt and all untouched with the flame. Yet in all this torment he forgot not to call unto God still, having in his mouth, "Lord, have mercy upon me," intermeddling this cry, "Let the fire come unto me, I cannot burn." In which pangs he labored till one of the standersby with his bill [blade or weapon] pulled off the faggots above, and where he espied the fire flame up, he wrested himself unto that side. And when the flame touched the gunpowder he was seen stir no more, but espied burning on the other side by Master Latimer. Which some said happened by reason that the chain loosed; others said that he fell over the chain, by reason of the poise of his body and the weakness of the nether limbs.

Some say that before he was like to fall from the stake, he defied them to hold him to it with their bills. Howsoever it was, surely it moved hundreds to tears, to behold the horrible sight. For I think there was none that had not clean exiled all humanity and mercy, which would not have lamented to behold the fury of the fire so rage upon their bodies. Signs there were of sorrow on every side.

↛ **A Moralized Ballad**   *1565*

"The True Form and Shape of a Monstrous Child" exemplifies the kind of macabre stories popular in early modern English culture. The original contains two drawings, beneath the title, giving front and rear views of the fused bodies. In the absence of newspapers, such ballads catered to the public taste for sensation, and many of them, like this one, justified their publication by offering a moral reading of the event. Shakespeare mocks such tales in the ballads sold by the peddler, Autolycus, in *The Winter's Tale*.

THE TRUE FORM AND SHAPE OF A MONSTROUS CHILD WHICH WAS BORN IN STONY STRATFORD IN NORTHAMPTONSHIRE THE YEAR OF OUR LORD MCCCCCLXV

This child was born on Friday, being the twenty-sixth day of January, betwixt six and seven of the clock in the morning, and lived two hours, and was christened by the midwife, and are both women children, having two bodies joining together, with four arms and four legs perfect, and from the navel upward one face, two eyes, one nose, and one mouth, and three ears, one being upon the backside of the head a little above the nape of the neck, having hair growing upon the head. Which child was born out of wedlock. The father's name is Richard Sotherne, who is now fled; and the mother is yet living in the same town. And this child was brought up to London where it was seen of divers worshipful men and women of the city, and also of the country. To

witness that it is a truth and no fable, but a warning of God to move all people
to amendment of life:

You that do see this child disfigured here,
　　Two babes in one, disguised [unnaturally altered] to behold,
Think with yourselves, when such things do appear,
　　All is not well, as wise heads may be bold.
But God that can in secrets show the sign
Can bring much more to pass by power divine.

And we that live to see this wonder, how
　　The gaze is given to make this mervail [marvel] great,
Let one by one that this beholdeth now
　　Be warned, as the wonder gives conceit,
To live to mend the wondrous shape we see,
Contrary much in all that ought to be.

For as we find this figure seemeth strange
　　Because it shows proportion not in ure [in performance or functions],
So bear in mind how time can chop and change,
　　Disguising works in wills that be unsure [weak].
From mean to more, from more to much excess,
Where Nature wills desire should be less.
　　　　　　　　　　　　Finis

　　　　　　　　　　　　W[illiam] Elderton

Imprinted at London in Fleet Street beneath the
Conduit at the sign of St. John Evangelist
by Thomas Colwell

SIR WILLIAM STRACHEY

From *A True Reportory of the Wreck and Redemption of Sir Thomas Gates*　　　　　*1610*

A Source for The Tempest

Sir William Strachey's *True Reportory of the Wreck and Redemption of Sir Thomas Gates, Knight, upon and from the Islands of the Bermudas, His Coming to Virginia, and the Estate of That Colony* was not published until 1625, but the account was written in July 1610 about an episode that occurred in the previous year. It exemplifies the marvelous tales brought back to England by travelers, especially those who had journeyed to the New World. Shakespeare seems to have read Strachey's report in manuscript and to have relied on it in composing *The Tempest*.

During all this time, the heavens looked so black upon us, that it was not possible the elevation of the Pole might be observed: nor a star by night, nor sun beam by day was to be seen. Only upon the Thursday night Sir George Summers, being upon the watch, had an apparition of a little round light, like a faint star, trembling, and streaming along with a sparkling blaze, half the height upon the mainmast, and shooting sometimes from shroud to shroud [a set of ropes], tempting to settle as it were upon any of the four shrouds; and for three or four hours together, or rather more, half the night it kept with us, running sometimes along the main-yard to the very end, and then returning. At which, Sir George Summers called divers about him, and showed them the same, who observed it with much wonder, and carefulness: but upon a sudden, towards the morning watch, they lost the sight of it, and knew not what way it made. The superstitious sea-men make many constructions of this sea-fire, which nevertheless is usual in storms: the same (it may be) which the Grecians were wont in the Mediterranean to call Castor and Pollux, of which, if one only appeared without the other, they took it for an evil sign of great tempest. The Italians, and such who lie open to the Adriatic and Tyrrhenian Sea, call it (a sacred Body) Corpo sancto; the Spaniards call it Saint Elmo, and have an authentic and miraculous legend for it. Be it what it will, we laid other foundations of safety or ruin, then in the rising or falling of it, but could it have served us now miraculously to have taken our height by, it might have strucken amazement and a reverence in our devotions, according to the due of a miracle. But it did not light us any whit the more to our known way, who ran now (as do hoodwinked men) at all adventures, sometimes north, and northeast, then north and by west, and in an instant again varying two or three points, and sometimes half the compass. East and by south we steered away as much as we could to bear upright, which was no small carefulness nor pain to do, albeit we much unrigged our ship, threw overboard much luggage, many a trunk and chest (in which I suffered no mean loss), and staved many a butt of beer, hogsheads of oil, cider, wine, and vinegar, and heaved away all our ordnance [ammunition or weapons] on the starboard side, and had now purposed to have cut down the mainmast, the more to lighten her, for we were much spent, and our men so weary, as their strengths together failed them with their hearts, having travailed now from Tuesday till Friday morning, day and night, without either sleep or food; for the leakage taking up all the hold, we could neither come by beer nor fresh water; fire we could keep none in the cookroom to dress any meat, and carefulness, grief, and our turn at the pump or bucket were sufficient to hold sleep from our eyes. . . . And from Tuesday noon till Friday noon, we bailed and pumped two thousand ton, and yet do what we could, when our ship held least in her (after Tuesday night second watch) she bore ten foot deep, at which stay our extreme working kept her on eight glasses, forbearance whereof had instantly sunk us, and it being now Friday, the fourth morning, it wanted little but that there had been a general determination to have shut up hatches and, commending our sinful souls to God, committed the ship to the mercy of the sea. Surely, that night we must have done it, and that night had we then perished; but see the goodness and sweet introduction of better hope, by our merciful God given unto us. Sir George Summers, when no man dreamed of such happiness, had discovered and cried "Land." Indeed the morning now three quarters spent, had won a little clearness from the days before, and it being better surveyed, the very trees were seen to move with the wind upon the shore side: whereupon our governor commanded the helmsman to bear up, the boatswain sounding at the first, found it thirteen fathom, and when we stood a little in seven fathom; and presently heaving his lead the third time, had ground at four fathom, and by this, we had got her within a mile under the southeast point of the land, where we had somewhat smooth water. But having no hope to save her by coming to an anchor in the same, we were enforced to run her ashore, as near the land as we could, which brought us within three quarters of a mile of shore, and by the mercy of God unto us, making out our boats, we had ere night brought all our men, women, and children, about the number of one hundred and fifty, safe into the island.

We found it to be the dangerous and dreaded island, or rather islands, of the Bermuda: whereof let me give your Ladyship a brief description, before I proceed to my narration. And that the rather, because they be so terrible to all that ever touched on them, and such tempests, thunders, and other fearful objects are seen and heard about them, that they be called commonly The Devils Islands, and are feared and avoided of all sea travelers alive, above any other place in the world. Yet it pleased our merciful God to make even this hideous and hated place both the place of our safety, and means of our deliverance.

And hereby also, I hope to deliver the world from a foul and general error: it being counted of most, that they [the islands] can be no habitation for men, but rather given over to devils and wicked spirits. Whereas indeed we find them now by experience to be as habitable and commodious as most countries of the same climate and situation; insomuch as if the entrance into them were as easy as the place itself is contenting, it had long ere this been inhabited, as well as other islands. Thus shall we make it appear, that Truth is the Daughter of Time, and that men ought not to deny everything which is not subject to their own sense.

The Bermudas be broken islands, five hundred of them in manner of an archipelago (at least if you may call them all islands that lie, how little soever into the sea, and by themselves) of small compass, some larger yet than other, as time and the sea hath won from them, and eaten his passage through, and all now lying in the figure of a crescent, within the circuit of six or seven leagues at the most, albeit at first it is said of them that they were thirteen or fourteen leagues, and more in longitude, as I have heard. For no greater distance is it from the northwest point to Gates's Bay, as by this map your Ladyship may see, in which Sir George Summers, who coasted in his boat about them all, took great care to express the same exactly and full, and made his draft perfect for all good occasions, and the benefit of such, who either in distress might be brought upon them, or make sail this way.

→ CHRISTOPHER MARLOWE

From *Tamburlaine the Great* 1590

This famous speech from Christopher Marlowe's play *Tamburlaine the Great* is reproduced (enlarged slightly) from the 1590 Quarto. The incantatory power of the verse and the hero's "high astounding terms" could be heard in the public playhouses shortly after Shakespeare's arrival in London. Verse such as this helped to shape the development of Shakespeare's poetic style.

Nature that fram'd vs of foure Elements,
Warring within our breasts for regiment,
Doth teach vs all to haue aspyring minds:
Our soules, whose faculties can comprehend
The wondrous Architecture of the world:
And measure euery wandring plannets course,
Still climing after knowledge infinite,
And alwaies moouing as the restles Spheares,
Wils vs to weare our selues and neuer rest,
Untill we reach the ripest fruit of all,
That perfect blisse and sole felicitie,
The sweet fruition of an earthly crowne.

→ SIR PHILIP SIDNEY

Two Sonnets from *Astrophil and Stella* c. 1579

Sir Philip Sidney's sonnet sequence was written about 1579 and published for the first time in 1591, five years after the author's death. Shakespeare appears to have known the sequence and to have been influenced by it in the composition of his own sonnets, particularly by Sidney's playfully skeptical response to Petrarchan conventions.

2

Not at first sight, nor with a dribbed shot,
    Love gave the wound which, while I breathe, will bleed;
    But known worth did in mine of time proceed,
    Till by degrees it had full conquest got.
I saw and liked, I liked but loved not,
    I loved, but straight did not what Love decreed. 5
    At length to Love's decrees I, forc'd, agreed,
    Yet with repining at so partial lot.
Now even that footstep of lost liberty
    Is gone, and now, like slave-born Muscovite, 10
    I call it praise to suffer tyranny;

And now employ the remnant of my wit
   To make myself believe that all is well,
   While, with a feeling skill, I paint my hell.

7

When Nature made her chief work, Stella's eyes,
   In color black why wrapp'd she beams so bright?
   Would she in beamy black, like painter wise,
   Frame daintiest luster mix'd of shades and light?
Or did she else that sober hue devise   5
   In object best to knit and strength our sight,
   Lest, if no veil those brave gleams did disguise,
   They, sunlike, should more dazzle than delight?
Or would she her miraculous power show,
   That, whereas black seems beauty's contrary,   10
   She even in black doth make all beauties flow?
Both so, and thus she, minding Love should be
   Placed ever there, gave him this mourning weed
   To honor all their deaths who for her bleed.

➔   RAPHAEL HOLINSHED

From *The Chronicles of England, Scotland, and Ireland*   *1587*

Second Edition

First published in 1577 and then amplified and revised a decade later, Raphael Holinshed's monumental history drew heavily on previous Tudor accounts. The 1587 version was a source for Shakespeare's plays on English history, as well as for *Macbeth, King Lear,* and parts of *Cymbeline.* The excerpt provided here describes the conflict between the recently crowned Henry IV and the members of the Percy family, events dramatized at the beginning of *Henry IV, Part 1.*

Henry, earl of Northumberland, with his brother Thomas, earl of Worcester, and his son, the lord Henry Percy, surnamed Hotspur, which were to King Henry in the beginning of his reign both faithful friends and earnest aiders, began now to envy his wealth and felicity; and especially they were grieved, because the king demanded of the earl and his son such Scottish prisoners as were taken at Holmedon and Nesbit: for of all the captives which were taken in the conflicts fought in those two places, there were delivered to the king's possession only Mordake, earl of Fife, the duke of Albany's son, though the king did divers and sundry times require deliverance of the residue, and that with great threatenings. Wherewith the Percys being sore offended, for that they claimed them as their own proper prisoners, and their peculiar preies [preys], by the counsel of the lord Thomas Percy, earl of Worcester, whose study was ever (as some write) to procure malice, and set things in a broil, came to the king unto Windsor (upon a purpose to prove [test] him) and there required of him that either by ransom or otherwise, he would cause to be delivered out of prison Edmund Mortimer, earl of March, their cousin germane [first cousin], whom (as they reported) Owen Glendower kept in filthy prison, shackled with irons, only for that he took his [the king's] part, and was to him faithful and true.

The king began not a little to muse at this request, and not without cause: for indeed it touched him somewhat near, sith [since] this Edmund was son to Roger, earl of March, son to the lady Phillippa, daughter of Lionel, duke of Clarence, the third son of King Edward the Third; which Edmund, at King Richard's going into Ireland, was proclaimed heir apparent to the crown and realm, whose aunt, called Elianor, the lord Henry Percy had married; and therefore King Henry could not well hear that any man should be earnest about the advancement of that lineage. The king, when he had studied on the matter, made answer that the earl of March was not taken prisoner for his cause, nor in his service, but willingly suffered himself to be taken, because he would not withstand the attempts of Owen Glendower and his complices, and therefore he would neither ransom him, nor relieve him.

The Percys with this answer and fraudulent excuse were not a little fumed [angered], insomuch that Henry Hotspur said openly: "Behold, the heir of the realm is robbed of his right, and yet the robber with his own will not redeem him." So in this fury the Percys departed, minding nothing more than to depose King Henry from the high type [summit] of his royalty, and to place in his seat their cousin Edmund, earl of March, whom they did not only deliver out of captivity, but also (to the high displeasure of King Henry) entered in league with the foresaid Owen Glendower. Herewith, they by their deputies in the house of the archdeacon of Bangor, divided the realm amongst them, causing a tripartite indenture to be made and sealed with their seals, by the covenants whereof, all England from Severn and Trent, south and eastward, was assigned to the earl of March; all Wales, and the lands beyond Severn westward, were appointed to Owen Glendower; and all the remnant from Trent northward, to the lord Percy.

→ PLUTARCH

From *Lives of the Noble Grecians and Romans*

Translated by Sir Thomas North, 1579

Thomas North's version of Plutarch was Shakespeare's major source for the classical tragedies. This excerpt records Cleopatra's appearance on the barge; the parallel passage in *Antony and Cleopatra* is Enobarbus's speech in act 2, scene 2. Shakespeare has versified North's prose and made numerous subtle changes, but many similarities of diction and imagery are apparent.

Therefore when she was sent unto by divers letters, both from Antonius himself, and also from his friends, she made so light of it, and mocked Antonius so much, that she disdained to set forward otherwise, but to take her barge in the river of Cydnus, the poop whereof was of gold, the sails of purple, and the oars of silver, which kept stroke in rowing after the sound of the music of flutes, oboes, citherns [guitars], viols, and such other instruments as they played upon in the barge. And now for the person of herself: she was laid under a pavilion of cloth of gold of tissue, appareled and attired like the goddess Venus, commonly drawn in picture; and hard by her, on either hand of her, pretty fair boys appareled as painters do set forth god Cupid, with little fans in their hands, with the which they fanned wind upon her. Her ladies and gentlewomen also, the fairest of them were appareled like the nymphs Nereides (which are the mermaids of the waters) and like the Graces, some steering the helm, others tending the tackle and ropes of the barge, out of the which there came a wonderful passing sweet savor of perfumes, that perfumed the wharf's side, pestered with innumerable multitudes of people. Some of them followed the barge all alongst the river's side: others also ran out of the city to see her coming in. So that in the end, there ran such multitudes of people one after another to see her, that Antonius was left post alone [entirely alone] in the marketplace, in his Imperial seat to give audience: and there went a rumor in the people's mouths, that the goddess Venus was come to play with the god Bacchus, for the general good of all Asia. When Cleopatra landed, Antonius sent to invite her to supper to him. But she sent him word again, he should do better rather to come and sup with her. Antonius, therefore, to show himself courteous unto her at her arrival, was contented to obey her, and went to supper to her: where he found such passing sumptuous fare, that no tongue can express it.

→ OVID

From *Metamorphoses*   *Translated by Arthur Golding, 1567*

The Roman poet's collection of mythological stories was written in Latin, circa 1 A.D. The story of Diana and Actaeon is presented here in two versions: the sixteenth-century translation by Arthur Golding, which Shakespeare knew, and a modern translation (p. 147). Shakespeare found Ovid useful less as a source of dramatic plots than as a storehouse of allusion and an inspiration for the ideas of transformation that inform the comedies.

Now *Thebes* stood in good estate, now *Cadmus* might thou say
  That when thy father banisht thee it was a luckie day.
To joyne aliance both with *Mars* and *Venus* was thy chaunce,
Whose daughter thou hadst tane to wife, who did thee much advaunce,
Not only through hir high renowne, but through a noble race   5
Of sonnes and daughters that she bare: whose children in like case

It was thy fortune for to see all men and women growne.
But ay the ende of every thing must marked be and knowne,
For none the name of blessednesse deserveth for to have,
Unlesse the tenor of this life last blessed to his grave. 10
Among so many prosprous happes that flowde with good successe,
Thine eldest Nephew was a cause of care and sore distresse.
Whose head was armde with palmed hornes, whose own hounds in ye wood
Did pull their master to the ground and fill them with his bloud.
But if you sift the matter well, ye shall not finde desart 15
But cruell fortune to have bene the cause of this his smart.
For who could doe with oversight? Great slaughter had bene made
Of sundrie sortes of savage beastes one morning, and the shade
Of things was waxed verie short. It was the time of day
That mid betweene the East and West the Sunne doth seeme to stay; 20
When as the Thebane stripling thus bespake his companie,
Still raunging in the waylesse woods some further game to spie.
Our weapons and our toyles are moist and staind with bloud of Deare:
This day hath done inough as by our quarrie may appeare.
Assoone as with hir scarlet wheeles next morning bringeth light, 25
We will about our worke againe. But now *Hiperion* bright
Is in the middes of Heaven, and seares the fieldes with firie rayes.
Take up your toyles, and ceasse your worke, and let us go our wayes.
They did even so, and ceast their worke. There was a valley thicke
With Pinaple and Cipresse trees that armed be with pricke. 30
Gargaphie hight this shadie plot, it was a sacred place
To chast *Diana* and the Nymphes that wayted on hir grace.
Within the furthest end thereof there was a pleasant Bowre
So vaulted with the leavie trees, the Sunne had there no powre:
Not made by hand nor mans devise, and yet no man alive, 35
A trimmer piece of worke than that could for his life contrive.
With flint and Pommy [lava] was it wallde by nature halfe about,
And on the right side of the same full freshly flowed out
A lively spring with Christall streame: whereof the upper brim
Was greene with grasse and matted herbes that smelled verie trim. 40
When *Phebe* [Diana] felt hir selfe waxe faint, of following of hir game,
It was hir custome for to come and bath hir in the same.
That day she having timely left hir hunting in the chace,
Was entred with hir troupe of Nymphes within this pleasant place.
She tooke hir quiver and hir bow the which she had unbent, 45
And eke hir Javelin to a Nymph that served that intent.
Another Nymph to take hir clothes among hir traine she chose,
Two losde [loosened] hir buskins from hir legges and pulled of hir hose.
The Thebane Ladie *Crocale*, more cunning than the rest,
Did trusse hir tresses handsomly which hung behind undrest. 50
And yet hir owne hung waving still. Then *Niphe* nete and cleene
With *Hiale* glistring like the grash [grass] in beautie fresh and sheene,

And *Rhanis* clearer of hir skin than are the rainie drops,
And little bibling *Phyale,* and *Pseke* that pretie Mops,
Powrde water into vessels large to washe their Ladie with.   55
Now while she keepes this wont, behold, by wandring in the frith [game
    preserve]
He wist not whither (having staid his pastime till the morrow)
Comes *Cadmus* Nephew to this thicke: and entring in with sorrow
(Such was his cursed cruell fate) saw *Phebe* where she washt.
The Damsels at the sight of man quite out of countnance dasht,   60
(Bicause they everichone were bare and naked to the quicke)
Did beate their handes against their brests, and cast out such a shricke,
That all the wood did ring thereof: and clinging to their dame
Did all they could to hide both hir and eke themselves fro shame.
But *Phebe* was of personage so comly and so tall,   65
That by the middle of hir necke she overpeerd them all.
Such colour as appeares in Heaven by *Phebus* broken rayes
Directly shining on the Cloudes, or such as is alwayes
The colour of the Morning Cloudes before the Sunne doth show,
Such sanguine colour in the face of *Phœbe* gan to glowe   70
There standing naked in his sight. Who though she had hir gard
Of Nymphes about hir: yet she turnde hir bodie from him ward [away].
And casting backe an angrie looke, like as she would have sent
An arrow at him had she had hir bow there readie bent:
So raught [reached] the water in hir hande, and for to wreake the spight, 75
Besprinckled all the heade and face of the unluckie Knight,
And thus forespake the heavie lot that should upon him light.
Now make thy vaunt among thy Mates, thou sawste *Diana* bare.
Tell if thou can: I give thee leave: tell heardly: doe not spare.
This done, she makes no further threates, but by and by doth spread   80
A payre of lively olde Harts hornes upon his sprinckled head.
She sharpes his eares, she makes his necke both slender, long and lanke.
She turnes his fingers into feete, his armes to spindle shanke.
She wrappes him in a hairie hyde beset with speckled spottes,
And planteth in him fearefulnesse. And so away he trottes,   85
Full greatly wondring to him selfe what made him in that cace
To be so wight [agile] and swift of foote. But when he saw his face
And horned temples in the brooke, he would have cryde alas,
But as for then no kinde of speach out of his lippes could passe.
He sight [sighed] and brayde: for that was then the speach that did remaine, 90
And downe the eyes that were not his, his bitter teares did raine.
No part remayned (save his minde) of that he earst [formerly] had beene.
What should he doe? turne home againe to *Cadmus* and the Queene?
Or hyde himselfe among the Woods? Of this he was afrayd,
And of the tother ill ashamde. While doubting thus he stayd: 95
    His houndes espyde him where he was, and Blackfoote first of all
    And Stalker speciall good of sent began aloud to call.

This latter was a hound of *Crete*, the other was of *Spart*.
Then all the kenell fell in round, and everie for his part,
Dyd follow freshly in the chase more swifter than the winde,   100
Spy, Eateal, Scalecliffe, three good houndes comne all of *Arcas* kinde.
Strong Kilbucke, currish Savage, Spring, and Hunter fresh of smell,
And Lightfoote who to lead a chase did beare away the bell.
Fierce Woodman hurte not long ago in hunting of a Bore
And Shepeheird woont to follow sheepe and neate [cattle] to fielde afore.   105
And Laund a fell [savage] and eger bitch that had a Wolfe to Syre:
Another brach [bitch] callde Greedigut with two hir Puppies by hir.
And Ladon gant as any Greewnd [greyhound] a hownd in *Sycion* bred,
Blab, Fleetewood, Patch whose flecked skin w^t sundrie spots was spred:
Wight, Bowman, Royster, beautie faire and white as winters snow,   110
And Tawnie full of duskie haires that over all did grow,
With lustie Ruffler passing all the resdue there in strength,
And Tempest best of footemanshipe in holding out at length.
And Cole, and Swift, and little Woolfe, as wight as any other,
Accompanide with a *Ciprian* hound that was his native brother,   115
And Snatch amid whose forehead stoode a starre as white as snowe,
The resdue being all as blacke and slicke as any Crowe,
And shaggie Rugge with other twaine that had a Syre of *Crete*,
And dam of *Sparta:* Tone [th' one] of them callde Jollyboy, a great
And large flewd [with large flews or jaws] hound: the tother Chorle who ever
    gnoorring went,   120
And Ringwood with a shyrle [shrill] loud mouth the which he freely spent,
With divers mo whose names to tell it were but losse of tyme.
This fellowes over hill and dale in hope of pray doe clyme.
Through thick and thin and craggie cliffes where was no way to go,
He flyes through groundes where oftentymes he chased had ere tho,   125
Even from his owne folke is he faine (alas) to flee away.
He strayned oftentymes to speake, and was about to say,
I am *Acteon:* know your Lorde and Mayster sirs I pray.
But use of wordes and speach did want to utter forth his minde.
Their crie did ring through all the Wood redoubled with the winde.   130
First Slo did pinch him by the haunch, and next came Kildeere in,
And Hylbred fastned on his shoulder, bote [bit] him through the skinne.
These came forth later than the rest, but coasting thwart a hill,
They did gainecope [trap] him as he came, and helde their Master still,
Untill that all the rest came in, and fastned on him to.   135
No part of him was free from wound. He could none other do
But sigh, and in the shape of Hart with voyce as Hartes are woont,
(For voyce of man was none now left to helpe him at the brunt)
By braying show his secret grief among the Mountaynes hie,
And kneeling sadly on his knees with dreerie teares in eye,   140
As one by humbling of himselfe that mercy seemde to crave,
With piteous looke in stead of handes his head about to wave.

Not knowing that it was their Lord, the huntsmen cheere their hounds
With wonted noyse and for *Acteon* looke about the grounds.
They hallow who could lowdest crie still calling him by name   145
As though he were not there, and much his absence they do blame,
In that he came not to the fall, but slackt to see the game.
As often as they named him he sadly shooke his head,
And faine he would have beene away thence in some other stead,
But there he was. And well he could have found in heart to see   150
His dogges fell deedes, so that to feele in place he had not bee.
They hem him in on everie side, and in the shape of Stagge,
With greedie teeth and griping pawes their Lord in peeces dragge.
So fierce was cruell *Phebes* wrath, it could not be alayde,
Till of his fault by bitter death the raunsome he had payde.   155
    Much muttring was upon this fact. Some thought there was extended
A great deale more extremitie than neded. Some commended
Dianas doing: saying that it was but worthely
For safegarde of hir womanhod. Eche partie did applie
Good reasons to defende their case.   160

→ OVID

From *Metamorphoses*   *Translated by Rolfe Humphries, 1955*

That was the city Thebes, and now the exile [Cadmus]
Might seem a happy man. Venus and Mars
Were parents of his bride, and there were children
Who turned out well, and children of the children,
Grown to maturity. But always, always,   5
A man must wait the final day, and no man
Should ever be called happy before burial.

One of these grandsons was the lad Actaeon,
First cause of Cadmus' sorrow. On his forehead
Horns sprouted, and his hound-dogs came to drink   10
The blood of their young master. In the story
You will find Actaeon guiltless; put the blame
On luck, not crime: what crime is there in error?

There was a mountain, on whose slopes had fallen
The blood of many kinds of game: high noon,   15
Short shadows, and Actaeon, at ease, and friendly
Telling his company: "Our nets and spears
Drip with the blood of our successful hunting.

To-day has brought us luck enough; to-morrow
We try again. The Sun-god, hot and burning,   20
Is halfway up his course. Give up the labor,
Bring home the nets." And they obeyed his orders.

There was a valley there, all dark and shaded
With pine and cypress, sacred to Diana,
Gargaphie, its name was, and it held   25
Deep in its inner shade a secret grotto
Made by no art, unless you think of Nature
As being an artist. Out of rock and tufa
She had formed an archway, where the shining water
Made slender watery sound, and soon subsided   30
Into a pool, and grassy banks around it.
The goddess of the woods, when tired from hunting,
Came here to bathe her limbs in the cool crystal.
She gave her armor-bearer spear and quiver
And loosened bow; another's arm received   35
The robe, laid off; two nymphs unbound her sandals,
And one, Crocale, defter than the others,
Knotted the flowing hair; others brought water,
Psecas, Phyale, Nephele, and Rhanis,
Pouring it out from good-sized urns, as always.   40
But look! While she was bathing there, all naked,
Actaeon came, with no more thought of hunting
Till the next day, wandering, far from certain,
Through unfamiliar woodland till he entered
Diana's grove, as fate seemed bound to have it.   45
And when he entered the cool dripping grotto,
The nymphs, all naked, saw him, saw a man,
And beat their breasts and screamed, and all together
Gathered around their goddess, tried to hide her
With their own bodies, but she stood above them,   50
Taller by head and shoulders. As the clouds
Grow red at sunset, as the daybreak reddens,
Diana blushed at being seen, and turned
Aside a little from her close companions,
Looked quickly for her arrows, found no weapon   55
Except the water, but scooped up a handful
And flung it in the young man's face, and over
The young man's hair. Those drops had vengeance in them.
She told him so: "Tell people you have seen me,
Diana, naked! Tell them if you can!"   60
She said no more, but on the sprinkled forehead
Horns of the long-lived stag began to sprout,
The neck stretched out, the ears were long and pointed,

The arms were legs, the hands were feet, the skin
A dappled hide, and the hunter's heart was fearful.   65
Away in flight he goes, and, going, marvels
At his own speed, and finally sees, reflected,
His features in a quiet pool. "Alas!"
He tries to say, but has no words. He groans,
The only speech he has, and the tears run down   70
Cheeks that are not his own. There is one thing only
Left him, his former mind. What should he do?
Where should he go — back to the royal palace
Or find some place of refuge in the forest?
Fear argues against one, and shame the other.   75
And while he hesitates, he sees his hounds,
Blackfoot, Trailchaser, Hungry, Hurricane,
Gazelle and Mountain-Ranger, Spot and Sylvan,
Swift Wingfoot, Glen, wolf-sired, and the bitch Harpy
With her two pups, half-grown, ranging beside her,   80
Tigress, another bitch, Hunter, and Lanky,
Chop-jaws, and Soot, and Wolf, with the white marking
On his black muzzle, Mountaineer, and Power,
The Killer, Whirlwind, Whitey, Blackskin, Grabber,
And others it would take too long to mention,   85
Arcadian hounds, and Cretan-bred, and Spartan.
The whole pack, with the lust of blood upon them,
Come baying over cliffs and crags and ledges
Where no trail runs: Actaeon, once pursuer
Over this very ground, is now pursued,   90
Fleeing his old companions. He would cry
"I am Actaeon: recognize your master!"
But the words fail, and nobody could hear him
So full the air of baying. First of all
The Killer fastens on him, then the Grabber,   95
Then Mountaineer gets hold of him by a shoulder.
These three had started last, but beat the others
By a short-cut through the mountains. So they run him
To stand at bay until the whole pack gathers
And all together nip and slash and fasten   100
Till there is no more room for wounds. He groans,
Making a sound not human, but a sound
No stag could utter either, and the ridges
Are filled with that heart-breaking kind of moaning.
Actaeon goes to his knees, like a man praying,   105
Faces them all in silence, with his eyes
In mute appeal, having no arms to plead with,
To stretch to them for mercy. His companions,
The other hunting lads, urge on the pack

With shouts as they did always, and not knowing   110
What has become of him, they call *Actaeon!*
Actaeon! each one louder than the others,
As if they thought him miles away. He answers,
Hearing his name, by turning his head toward them,
And hears them growl and grumble at his absence,   115
Calling him lazy, missing the good show
Of quarry brought to bay. Absence, for certain,
He would prefer, but he is there; and surely
He would rather see and hear the dogs than feel them.
They circle him, dash in, and nip, and mangle   120
And lacerate and tear their prey, not master,
No master whom they know, only a deer.
And so he died, and so Diana's anger
Was satisfied at last.

              And gossip argued
All up and down the land, and every which way: 125
Some thought the goddess was too merciless
And others praised her; maidenhood, they claimed,
Deserved just such stern acts of reckoning,
And both sides found good reason for their judgment.

CHAPTER 5

Theater à la Mode:
Shakespeare and the Kinds of Drama

><

According to the English novelist Somerset Maugham, "There are three rules for writing the novel. Unfortunately, no one knows what they are." The joke exposes the ambivalence felt by writers and critics about the wish for a formula for fiction, whether narrative or dramatic. Although it would be comforting to have a set of rules for writing a successful play, this notion contradicts what writers know instinctively — that plays can't be written according to formula. Ever since Aristotle's attempt to describe the principles of tragedy sometime in the fourth century B.C., people have wanted to codify the rules for literary forms, disseminate those rules, and discourage deviation from them. Yet in practice dramatic modes are irregular and ever-changing. Literary history records an expansion of formal classifications, and even if such categories are not as complicated and various as Polonius thought ("tragical-comical-historical-pastoral"), they still tend to combine and overlap.

Practicing playwrights have usually been less concerned with the "laws" of form than some eighteenth-century critics and modern educators have, but it is nevertheless useful to know something about these literary kinds, especially their historical appeal and their affective powers. For the purposes of clarity and convenience, I will refer to drama as a *genre*, like other forms of literature such as novels or lyric poetry, and to the various subgenres of drama as *modes*. While a modern reader may find it helpful to be aware of what English spectators at the turn of the seventeenth century expected when they went to see a comedy or a tragedy, a prerequisite for such awareness is the recognition that the boundaries between the several dramatic forms were not clearly fixed.

In terms of his attraction to different modes, Shakespeare's career divides conveniently into two phases. In general, we may see the first ten-year period, from about 1590 to 1600, as devoted to comedies and histories, and the second decade, from about 1601 to 1611, as focused on tragedies and romances. The division is rough, however, for each decade contains major examples of the other modes. Early in his career Shakespeare wrote at least two tragedies, *Titus Andronicus* and *Romeo and Juliet,* and many of the history plays composed during this period take the form of tragedy. But for the most part Shakespeare spent his first ten years producing histories, or chronicle plays, and experimenting with various kinds of comedy, from the farcical and classically influenced *Comedy of Errors* to the fantastic *Midsummer Night's Dream* to romantic comedies such as *Much Ado about Nothing* and *As You Like It.*

The second decade is similarly varied. From about 1601 to 1607 Shakespeare wrote mainly the major tragedies, including *Hamlet, Othello, King Lear,* and *Macbeth;* then in the last four or five years of his career he turned to romance, or tragicomedy, creating magical plays such as *The Winter's Tale* and *The Tempest.* But this half exhibits major exceptions as well. In the midst of this tragic phase he also produced *All's Well That Ends Well* and *Measure for Measure,* two plays variously described as *dark comedies, tragicomedies,* and *problem plays,* but which are recognizably comic in shape and effect. And the play that no one seems to know how to categorize, *Troilus and Cressida,* was also composed about this time, perhaps in 1601 or 1602; some complete editions of Shakespeare place it among the tragedies, some with the comedies. To make matters even more complicated, there is the matter of collaboration: at the very end of his writing career, perhaps after he had left London for Stratford, Shakespeare and his younger colleague John Fletcher worked together on three plays, *Henry VIII, The Two Noble Kinsmen,* and the lost *Cardenio.* And recently some scholars have begun to think that Shakespeare may also have collaborated with other playwrights, most notably with Thomas Middleton on *Timon of Athens* (Wells and Taylor 501–02).

Shakespeare's dramatic structures faithfully represent the variety and complexity of the theatrical culture he inhabited: comedy and tragedy constitute the major kinds of drama, but there is considerable permutation in each, the boundaries between modes are not clear, and virtually all the subgenres interpenetrate and modify one another. All this is true about practice; it is not true about early modern theory. Twentieth-century ideas about dramatic form are considerably more subtle than those expressed in the sixteenth and seventeenth centuries. The First Folio divides Shakespeare's plays into three kinds — comedies, tragedies, and histories — and as the documents that follow this chapter indicate, contemporary descriptions about dramatic forms were for the most part rudimentary. The categories I have mentioned and will analyze below represent comparatively recent attempts at critical description: for example, *romance* did not exist as a dramatic classification in the Renaissance, although its characteristics and appeal were generally acknowledged. It is important to keep in mind that practice usually precedes theory; that is, certain forms of comedy and tragedy are associated with particular emotional and ideological effects, but they generate these effects because Shakespeare's own formal experiments created such possibilities.

Comedy

Comedy refers to a literary structure, be it drama or novel or film, that moves toward a happy ending and implies a positive understanding of human experience. Comedy is usually funny, although this is not a prerequisite. Dante called his great poem depicting the movement of the human soul toward a final union with God *The Divine Comedy*. Although there are moments of grim humor in the sections devoted to the punishment of sinners — the flatterers must live in excrement, for example, condemned to swim in what they used to sling — *The Divine Comedy* is not known for its jokes. But it is comic in form and in outlook. In most comedy the happy ending involves a marriage or at least some kind of union or reunion that resolves the conflict and brings the characters into a state of harmony. In *The Divine Comedy*, the marriage is between the human soul and God; in less elevated works, the final union is more carnal. Comedy moves from confusion to order, from ignorance to understanding, from law to liberty, from unhappiness to satisfaction, from separation to union, from barrenness to fertility, from singleness to marriage, from two to one.

This progression is easily discerned by comparing the opening and closing of *A Midsummer Night's Dream*. At the beginning, Duke Theseus is impatient at having to cool his passion and to wait for the day of his wedding to Hippolyta; Hermia is in love with Lysander but is ordered by her father and the Duke to marry Demetrius, who professes love for her; Helena loves Demetrius, who used to love her but now scorns her; Oberon and Titania, king and queen of the fairies, are engaged in a marital brawl that is disturbing the mortal world. In contrast, the end of the play celebrates three marriages and one remarriage. Although the promised joy may be mitigated somewhat, things are better at the end than they were at the beginning. After the festivities of the last act, it is vital that we recognize where the characters go as they leave the stage, and it is the same destination in all of Shakespeare's comedies.

They go off to bed. There may be a dinner first, or a dance of some kind, but these are more polite and social images of the kind of union that will ultimately take place when the hero and heroine are alone together. Love first, then marriage, then sexual union, then, implicitly, birth. At the end of Henry Fielding's *Tom Jones*, when the proper Squire Allworthy remarks that Tom will use his "best endeavours" to deserve Sophia, the vulgar Squire Western responds: " 'His best endeavours!' cries Western; 'that he will, I warrant un. —— Harkee, Allworthy, I'll bet thee five pounds to a crown we have a boy tomorrow nine months.' " Embedded within the proper congratulations is a joke about the wedding night and youthful virility and fertility. Sexual union is seen as the happy conclusion that will perpetuate the species. In *Much Ado about Nothing*, the confirmed bachelor Benedick justifies his unexpected attraction to Beatrice with the words, "the world must be peopled." The characters act on their intuition that the world is good, that life is worth living, that conflict will ultimately find a positive resolution.

Well, yes, one might say, but what about the jokes? The word *comedy* is more likely to conjure up a favorite sitcom or the Marx Brothers than Dante or Fielding, and such a response is entirely legitimate, since one of comedy's main attractions is the laughter that derives from wordplay, intricate plotting, and pies in the face. But the mirth we associate with comedy depends on our acquaintance with the conventions of the form, especially its customary ending. In other words, we laugh because we know that the characters are protected from serious harm, because we have the distance to enjoy the jokes, because nobody is going to be seriously injured on that banana peel. Modes of literature offer us images of life filtered through a certain kind of lens, and the closure of the comic fiction directs us to conclude that there is good reason to laugh at the world, that life leads finally to satisfaction and away from despair, that problems can be solved, that happiness is possible. It promotes the value of wit, especially in the service of genuine feeling; it sides with youth and passion over age and money; its principal effects are ironic pleasure and confirmation of the social order.

The complementary values just mentioned, wit and desire, provide a spectrum along which we may arrange the major examples of dramatic comedy. So different in emphasis are the various types that it might be more appropriate to talk about *comedies* than *comedy*. To name only the most obvious examples, there is farce, satire, slapstick, intrigue comedy, romantic comedy, tragicomedy, religious comedy, and comedy of manners. However earthy the plot and language, virtually all comedy has a religious dimension. The words we use to talk about the endings indicate as much, words such as *grace, faith, pardon, union,* and *love.* At the same time, however elevated and romantic, virtually all comedy has a ridiculous dimension. Sixteenth-century critics tended to emphasize the ridiculousness, as the passage from Sir Philip Sidney's *Defense of Poesy* (see p. 171) suggests. Characters behave foolishly, get themselves into embarrassing scrapes, and find themselves turned into asses — literally in *A Midsummer Night's Dream,* and figuratively in a multitude of other works.

Herein lies the paradox on which theatrical comedy, and especially Shakespearean comedy, depends. Critics may expatiate on harmony, joy, and perpetuation of the species, but people go to see these kinds of plays because they want to be made to laugh. In other words, although the comic ending affirms that men and women can find happiness and that the world is a comprehensible and benevolent place, this clarification occurs only in the last five minutes. For some two hours, the audience is asked to concentrate on and take pleasure in misunderstanding, confusion, envy, and foolishness. The emphasis of comedy is positive, but the human being is shown to be a small and silly creature. The comic dramatist, depending on the point of view that motivates and shapes the work, may elect to emphasize the reconciliation over the comic conflict. In an early play like *The Comedy of Errors* (1592–94), based directly on two plays by the Roman dramatist Plautus, Shakespeare spends most of his energy magnifying and exploiting the confusion generated by two sets of twins. Several years later, in another twin comedy, *Twelfth Night* (1601–02), the misunderstandings still evoke laughter and derision, but here the playwright complicates the tone by exploring the pleasures of romantic love and offering large doses of melancholy and music. No comedy is purely farcical or purely romantic, and Shakespeare is the master of the combined response. All his comedies are hybrids, complicated mixtures of farce and romance, sunshine and shadow, absurdity and profundity.

Nature seems to endorse amorous or procreative desires, conspiring to assist the characters in their fulfillment. In *A Midsummer Night's Dream*, for example, the fairies Oberon and Puck represent natural forces, or supernatural forces that control natural forces, and Oberon's natural impulse is to give the characters what they want, to arrange that Demetrius fall back in love with Helena. In this respect Oberon acts as a stand-in for the playwright, who guarantees that conflicts are resolved and desires gratified — usually, that is. Several Shakespearean comedies have problematic endings, in which the promised marriage is delayed or in some way compromised. In *Love's Labor's Lost*, for instance, a messenger enters amid the jollity of the final scene to announce the death of the Princess's father. Consequently, her wedding, along with several others that have seemed inevitable for most of the play, is postponed for a year, and Berowne, the main male character, is sent for that year to exercise his wit among the sick. This unconventional ending is uncharacteristic for such an early comedy. As Shakespeare continues to explore the tonal possibilities of comedy, the romantic unions come to seem less joyous and more inflected with irony and potential failure. Such irony tinges even the title of one of the problem comedies, *All's Well That Ends Well*, for the happy ending to which it refers amounts to a forced marriage between a persistent young woman and a personally unappealing young man who has declared repeatedly that he doesn't want her. In performances of *A Midsummer Night's Dream*, Demetrius's affectionate return to Helena is usually convincing; in stagings of *All's Well That Ends Well*, Bertram's final acceptance of *his* Helena is usually not.

The conventions of comedy, like those of all literary modes, are consistent with the customs of the society in which it is produced; the society of early modern England was patriarchal and authoritarian, inhospitable to disruption or disorder. Shakespeare's comedies, then, can be seen as instruments of social stability in their representation of the unshakable power of husbands, aristocrats, and other dominant cultural voices. It is true that in *A Midsummer Night's Dream* Shakespeare sides with Hermia in her desire to marry Lysander and thus rejects her father's proprietary claim that she should marry Demetrius, the man he chooses. Egeus's insistence on his right to dispose of his daughter as he wishes indicates, particularly in his use of pronouns, the conventional expectations surrounding arranged marriages:

> Scornful Lysander, true, he [Demetrius] hath my love;
> And what is mine, my love shall render him.
> And she is mine, and all my right of her
> I do estate unto Demetrius. (1.1.95–98)

In *Romeo and Juliet,* the parallel tragedy written at about the same time, Juliet's father at first mouths enlightened sentiments about needing his daughter's consent before he agrees to her marriage to Paris; but by the fourth act he echoes Egeus in his intemperate assertion of his fatherly right. Although both plays reject such paternal claims, endorsing the daughters' desires for companionate marriage (a wedding of two kindred souls), they reflect the cultural anxiety pervading early modern England, when notions of romantic love were beginning to challenge the norms of patriarchal authority in the matter of marriage.

Even though he sides with his young women, however, Shakespeare finally marries them to husbands whose superior power is assumed: the last scene of *A Midsummer Night's Dream* presents the exchange of one male authority figure for another. Although the other women, particularly Titania and Hippolyta, seek to assert their independence from their husbands, the play ends with their submission. In the wood near Athens where the main events take place, Oberon magically overrules his wife's desire that she be allowed to keep a little Indian boy as her page, and he takes revenge on her by mating her temporarily with the monstrously transformed Bottom. At the end of this episode Titania yields to Oberon and returns to the role of submissive wife. Likewise, Hippolyta seems to understand much better than Theseus what has happened to the lovers in the forest, "the story of the night," but after hesitating, she keeps quiet and lets her husband think what he likes. Viewed from a feminist perspective, *A Midsummer Night's Dream* becomes a story of female independence thwarted by male power, a depiction of a society in which women either fail to fulfill their desires or, if they do, are able to look no further for that satisfaction than another man.

This problem is especially acute in *The Taming of the Shrew.* For many years critics and audiences regarded Katherina as a miserable, unsocialized creature whose refusal of suitors and defiance of her father are signs of a maladjusted personality and an uncontrolled ego. Thus Petruchio's scheme of marrying her in a wild ceremony and depriving her of food and sleep until she learns to behave — "he kills her in her own humor," as one of the servants puts it — becomes an exercise in comic justice issuing in marriage and quiet life: ". . . amid this hurly I intend / That all is done in reverend care of her" (4.1.203–04). In a play full of disguises, role-playing, and transformations carried out in the name of love, Petruchio apparently transforms Kate from miserable shrew to gratified partner. But the same plot can be staged as an insensitive, even cruel exertion of male power, a sexist suppression of female desire in the interests of financial advantage and patriarchal norms. According to this more recent view, Kate's long, final speech about the need for wives to submit to their husbands is nothing more than "a ventriloquization of male superiority" (Boose 193) and the play less a boisterous comedy than an unpalatable document in the history of misogyny.

Which is it? And might this reading not pertain to other comic texts as well? *As You Like It* may be seen as a play in which the unparalleled wit of a Rosalind is squandered on the unworthy Orlando, or *The Merchant of Venice* as a kind of male fantasy in which Portia's dead father controls her choice of a husband by arranging the riddle of the caskets of gold, silver, and lead. What about *Measure for Measure,* in which the young novice Isabella spends much of the play defending her chastity against the sexually rapacious Angelo but finds herself in the last act claimed in marriage by the very Duke who has conspired to protect her? All these opposing interpretations constitute legitimate reactions to the conflicts of value and ideology out of which the plays are constructed. Each reading, positive or negative, festive or critical, depends on the reader's or the theatrical director's decision to emphasize certain actions and ideas at the expense of others. The ambiguity is inherent in the clashes of gender and generation that all literature represents. It is Shakespeare's extraordinary sensitivity to both sides of these questions that makes his plays almost infinitely amenable to such different responses.

Tragedy

A glance at the title page of a complete volume of Shakespeare reveals that comedies are usually given general titles: *The Comedy of Errors, Much Ado about Nothing, All's Well That Ends Well.* One explanation for this phenomenon, put forward by Northrop Frye in his *Anatomy of Criticism,* is that comedy tends to focus on the group or community. In *As You Like It,* for example, an audience takes satisfaction not only in the happiness of Rosalind and Orlando but also in the wedding of Celia and Oliver and in the restored authority of Duke Senior. The titles of the tragedies, on the other hand, indicate a more limited emphasis: *Hamlet, Prince of Denmark; Romeo and Juliet; Richard II; Othello, the Moor of Venice; Antony and Cleopatra.* In these dramas the audience is invited to witness the misfortunes of charismatic and powerful individuals. *Tragedy* refers to a literary structure that moves toward an unhappy ending and thus implies an unfavorable assessment of human experience. Death is the tragic counterpart to the marriage that concludes comedy. Not only does the hero or heroine die, but others do also, often at the hands of the tragic figure. Tragedy ends in annihilation, misery, separation, loss. It is a pedagogical cliché that order is invariably restored at the end of Shakespearean tragedy, but this gesture hardly compensates for the death of a Hamlet or the unspeakable suffering of a King Lear. The emphasis is on failure, waste, disappointment, and self-destruction. The form of tragedy that Shakespeare helped to shape was developed from a variety of sources: from ancient tragedy, primarily Roman rather than Greek, and from medieval and early Tudor English tragedy, which stressed the moral benefit to be derived from watching the horrifying experiences of fallen princes. Sidney's description (see p. 172) reflects contemporary thinking about the affective power of tragedy. In Shakespeare's particular treatment of the mode, the poignancy of the action derives from the dramatic irony: it is the tragic figure's talent that leads to destruction.

The tragic pattern is clearly visible in *Macbeth.* A heroic and patriotic nobleman, rewarded for extraordinary courage and service to his king, is made

Thane of Cawdor and granted the favor of a royal visit. By the end of the play this noble figure has become a lonely and fearful monster, guilty not only of murdering the king his kinsman but even of infanticide and the pollution of his kingdom. The audience last sees Macbeth as a head on a pole when Malcolm is crowned King of Scotland. Tragedy promotes the impression that hope is futile, that the heroic figure, no matter how magnificent, can never escape the traps that await anyone who inhabits our imperfect and even vicious world. Nature seems to conspire against humans rather than cooperate with them — the benevolent sprites of *A Midsummer Night's Dream* or the unnamed providential forces that assist the characters in *The Comedy of Errors* or *Much Ado about Nothing* become the witches who tempt Macbeth or the distant and inscrutable gods of *King Lear*.

Like comedy, Shakespearean tragedy depends on a paradox. Although the curve of the action is negative and completes itself with the death of the hero — the occasion, Aristotle says, for pity and fear (see p. 172) — an undeniable effect of this action is to create admiration for the tragic protagonist. It would be irresponsible of us to conclude that the tragic figure is merely a victim of unfair circumstances or a vicious environment: the hero bears responsibility for the misery that ensues. Macbeth, demonic prophecies notwithstanding, is a murderer. But it is a curious paradox that audiences admire him anyway. Tragedy is sometimes defined as a great person suffering greatly, and the heroic reaction of the tragic figure to extreme suffering commands immense respect and sympathy. Ironically, that heroism also serves to console the spectator: the world may be a wicked place, the deck may be stacked against us, but the tragic action demonstrates that the human creature is capable of extraordinary heroism and endurance.

Our admiration for an Antigone or a King Lear is a function not only of their courage, but also of their own consciousness of the cause of their suffering. Lear's mad confession to the blind Gloucester discloses that awareness — his sense of his tragic error — and makes for one of the most poignant moments in the play:

> ... They flatter'd me like a dog, and told me I had the white hairs in my beard ere the black ones were there. To say "ay" and "no" to every thing that I said! "Ay," and "no" too, was no good divinity. When the rain came to wet me once, and the wind to make me chatter, when the thunder would not peace at my bidding, there I found 'em, there I smelt 'em out. Go to, they are not men o' their words: they told me I was every thing. 'Tis a lie, I am not ague-proof. (4.6.96–105)

The old king admits to a blind man his own blindness and mortality. Having inhabited the untrustworthy realm of the court and believed the flattery of his wicked daughters, King Lear had regarded himself as different from ordinary men, immune to the infections of the world. Now he has come to recognize that he is only a man as other men are, that his saying something does not make it so, that the rain falls on him as it does on the beggar and the thief, that he is vulnerable, finally, to the fevers ("agues") that afflict us all. The experience of tragedy is the discovery of mortality, and this understanding deepens the tragic paradox visible in the experience of the hero: the ability to recognize one's weakness constitutes an enormous strength.

So the tragic playwright, like the writer of comedy, may encourage in the audience a range of possible responses. The emphasis may fall on the horrors of the human situation, or on the hero's inspiring reaction to those horrors. Just as comic characters may be simultaneously foolish and delightful, tragic figures may be both monstrous and admirable. And just as comedy is both ridiculous and reassuring, tragedy is dispiriting and uplifting at the same time.

Attention to the tragic protagonist should not lead us to neglect the political implications of tragedy. Recent critics particularly urge that we redirect our attention to the local and ideological resonances that plays such as *Hamlet* and *Macbeth* must have had in England at the turn of the seventeenth century. For contemporary audiences, tragedy was inevitably political, a representation of the actions of monarchs and a study — however guarded — of the problem of good government. Many of the crucial issues of Shakespeare's day were represented in the stories he elected to dramatize in his tragic phase between 1599 and 1608: succession and regicide (*Hamlet* and *Macbeth*), political division and monarchical irresponsibility (*King Lear*), pride and absolutism (*Julius Caesar* and *Coriolanus*), financial folly (*Timon of Athens*), political conspiracy (*Julius Caesar* and *Macbeth*), the conflict of personal desire and political responsibility (*Antony and Cleopatra*). Such topically relevant issues have frequently been acknowledged, with critics arguing variously that the tragedies represented either barely veiled critiques of contemporary political practices (*Coriolanus*) or endorsements of contemporary orthodoxy (*Macbeth*).

Responses to *Macbeth* pointedly illustrate the course of recent political criticism. The play has long been regarded as a fictional defense of Jacobean ideology, especially given the notoriety of the Gunpowder Plot, an attempt to assassinate the king on a royal visit to open Parliament in November of 1605. At that time, the King's Men were performing frequently at court, James's preference for short plays was well known, and the Stuarts' legendary lineal connection to Banquo was a familiar tenet of royal mythology. But such an interpretation assumes authorial intention, and many poststructuralist critics have shifted from a focus on a playwright and his hero to a culturally founded understanding of dramatic writing. Materialist critics contend that the term *tragedy,* in the traditional sense, is an "honorific" means of mystifying Shakespeare's plays and promoting an old-fashioned conception of moral action and human freedom that ignores the ideological implications of all texts. Instead, these critics assert, plays like *Macbeth* should be read "dissidently," "against the grain," as exposures — whether intentional or not is incidental — of the apparatus of power in the Jacobean state. One of the best-known exponents of the critical school known as cultural materialism, Alan Sinfield, offers a passionate statement of this view:

It is often said that *Macbeth* is about "evil," but we might draw a more careful distinction: between the violence the state considers legitimate and that which it does not. Macbeth, we may agree, is a dreadful murderer when he kills Duncan. But when he kills Macdonwald — "a rebel" (1.2.10) — he has Duncan's approval.

... Violence is good, in this view, when it is in the service of the prevailing dispositions of power; when it disrupts them, it is evil. A claim to a monopoly of legitimate violence is fundamental in the development of the modern state; when that claim is successful, most citizens learn to regard state violence as qualitatively different from other violence, and perhaps they don't think of state violence as violence at all (consider the actions of police, army, and judiciary as opposed to those of pickets, protesters, criminals, and terrorists). *Macbeth* focuses major strategies by which the state asserted its claim at one conjuncture. (95)

The focus of political criticism has also been redirected. Sinfield and other critics, particularly feminist writers such as Janet Adelman and Lynda Boose, read the tragedies as exposures of misogynist and racist ideology. *Macbeth* and *Coriolanus* may be seen as critiques of the savagery and repression that constituted early modern constructions of masculinity, *Othello* and *Antony and Cleopatra* as documents of the tendency of Western societies to distance and finally to destroy what they perceive as threats from blacks, women, and other such manifestations of the "other."

However we read the tragedies, as the stories of great individuals or critiques of social practice, two matters need clearing up — or at least bringing up, since they've proved resistant to repeated efforts to clarify and put them in perspective. The first is the doctrine of the *tragic flaw*, the second the effect known as *catharsis*, and both are part of the critical tradition descending from Aristotle's discussion of tragedy in the *Poetics*. As numerous scholars have pointed out, the notion of a flaw actually represents a mistranslation of the Greek *hamartia*, a term more properly understood as an error in action rather than as a fatal weakness of character. To think of the tragic hero as afflicted with a "fatal flaw" is to simplify and misunderstand the complex problem of the tragic protagonist and the society with which he or she is in conflict. (In fact, the very simplicity of the idea helps to account for its popularity.) To say that all tragic figures are flawed to a greater or lesser extent is not to make much progress in distinguishing them from other dramatic characters in tragedy and comedy, or in life for that matter. Defining the tragic figure mainly in terms of a flaw makes it too easy for us to pigeonhole the experience of a complicated character and thus insulates us from complicity in that character's responsibility or guilt. Once again, the appropriate word is *paradox*, a radical form of irony. Tragic drama presents its audience with a spectacle in which heroic men and women are destroyed by their own capable hands, victims of the very traits that set them apart from the rest of us.

Hamlet is frequently described as flawed by an inability to make up his mind, but the term *procrastination* does not do justice to the experience that *Hamlet* represents. The Prince of Denmark is a seeker of truth, a subtle thinker who wants to know the facts and then to act rightly on the basis of what he knows. The play represents the collision between the hero's admirable aim and the traps and obstacles that the world places in his way. Hamlet's hesitation may derive from a laudable moral repugnance at undertaking the role of the avenging son, and in any case it seems right that he should proceed cautiously. But his idealism carries a tragically high price — the death of Polonius, the suffering and suicide of Ophelia, and the entrapment of the hero in the very world he has set out to oppose. Nor does the term *ambition* capture the complexity of tragic experience explored in *Macbeth*, although the relative simplicity and emotional directness of the Scottish play have led thousands of students to approach it in that way. Ambition is only one facet of Macbeth's persona, and it becomes comprehensible only when seen in relation to his other dominant characteristics, particularly his superhuman courage and his irrepressible moral sensitivity. That Shakespeare is not concerned chiefly with ambition is indicated by the placement of Duncan's murder: it occurs very early, at the beginning of the second act. The audience is invited to concentrate instead on the *con-sequences* of killing the king, on those horrible feelings and events that result from, or, as the etymology suggests, "follow with," the act of murder.

The tragic flaw is a problem because it is misleading; the trouble with catharsis is that it is nebulous. According to Aristotle, tragedy "effects through pity and fear the purgation of these emotions." Things seem clear enough until we come to that last phrase, "the purgation of these emotions." Most audiences have no trouble feeling pity for the experience of a character like King Lear, and the spectacle of tragic waste and misery is a fearsome thing. But commentators on the *Poetics* have debated at length the question of purgation. A modern authority on the treatise, Stephen Halliwell, believes that Aristotle proposed the idea of catharsis as a defense of the theater, a counterargument to the Platonic distrust of poetry and drama. Plato feared that the theatrical experience threatened the audience, and implicitly society at large, by stimulating and releasing in the spectator dangerous feelings that ought to be kept under control. Aristotle, on the other hand, saw tragedy as a channel for containing such emotions.

According to Halliwell, catharsis should be understood "as a powerful emotional experience which not only gives our natural feelings of pity and fear full play, but does so in a way which conduces to their rightful functioning as part of our understanding of, and response to, events in the human world" (90). Such an emotional experience entails the spectator's recognition that no one is exempt from the suffering represented in tragedy. In the Aristotelian view, "the heart of tragedy" resides "in the poetic demonstration of ways in which suffering is entangled in even the finest strivings of human action" (Halliwell 91–92), and the normal response to such a demonstration is pity and fear. This conception of catharsis returns us, then, to the tragic paradox, in which the hero's gifts are also the cause of his or her fall. Both the idea of *hamartia* and the problem of catharsis are still much discussed in analysis of tragedy, probably too much so. It is worth pointing out that a philosopher's reflections on the emotional effect of Greek tragedy may be of limited relevance to a sixteenth-century English audience's experience of Shakespeare's efforts in that form, and also to our own.

The inevitable tendency to invoke Aristotelian theory probably reflects our desire to comprehend and define as precisely as possible the effect of tragedy, and probably we should resist that impulse. Such definitions are rarely satisfactory. Elizabethan literary critics conceived of tragedy in didactic terms, seeing it as a warning against the dangers of tyranny, usurpation, and political unrest. But Shakespeare, following the lead of his immediate predecessor Christopher Marlowe, extended the possibilities of the form far beyond those narrow limits. Most significantly, he complicated the psychological dimension of the central character and the audience's sense of relation to that character. Shakespeare encourages a simultaneous engagement and detachment that make every tragedy different from every other, every performance of *Hamlet* or *Macbeth* different from every other, and every spectator's response different from every other. Each performance impresses each spectator with varying degrees of sympathy, judgment, identification, distance, pity, and fear. Rather than seeking to make Shakespeare's practice conform to an ancient theory, we should devote our energies to clarifying and articulating our own mixed reactions.

History

Shakespeare's history plays probably offer the greatest challenge to the modern reader and spectator because they are less familiar than comedy and tragedy. It may help us to know that the chronicle play or history was also less familiar to Shakespeare and his audiences than comedy and tragedy because it was being invented at the very moment that Shakespeare began working in the form. The great classical tragedies with which the Renaissance was familiar tended to focus on the experience of a heroic figure, not a series of historical events. The more influential model for Shakespeare's histories was the English political-morality play, in which the subject was tyranny or insurrection and the emphasis given to the health of the body politic; such plays included John Bale's *King Johan* (c. 1530) and Thomas Sackville and Thomas Norton's *Gorboduc* (c. 1562). Thus Shakespeare's history plays were to some extent dramatic experiments, narrative plays whose dramatic kind and emotional impact, positive or negative, depended somewhat on the historical episode being staged. And even when the requisite moral response was unambiguous, the play itself was almost always a hybrid, a combination of comic and tragic effects. To a great extent, Shakespeare was making it up as he went along.

Richard III is a good indicator of this formal indeterminacy. Technically, the play is a tragedy: it is so advertised on the title page of the First Quarto and in the Folio (see p. 176). And it is tragic, particularly in the medieval sense, portraying as it does a fall from a high position brought about by the tragic figure's own errors or crimes. To many members of a Tudor audience, however, the ending of *Richard III* would have been an occasion for rejoicing: the deformed tyrant is defeated at the battle of Bosworth Field by the earl of Richmond, the future Henry VII and grandfather of Queen Elizabeth. As the conqueror puts it, "The day is ours, the bloody dog is dead" (5.5.2). The play's effect is further complicated by the fact that Richard's murderous schemes for attaining the crown are drawn from the bag of tricks usually associated with comedy, and Shakespeare's clever dramatic structure seduces the audience into sharing Richard's confidences and participating in his plots. At the same time, the deeds that constitute the plot are appalling: for all the verve and glee with which he carries out his schemes, Richard is a criminal. The play's final effect is mixed. Morally and intellectually, spectators are led to applaud the victory of Richmond and the punishment of Richard; theatrically, they lament the death of Richard, against whose histrionic talent Richmond hasn't a chance.

This mixture of comic and tragic stories and of perceptions about those stories also characterizes the group of plays known as the Great (or Second) Tetralogy, which includes *Richard II; Henry IV, Part 1; Henry IV, Part 2;* and *Henry V.* Modern critics see these plays as a group, and some refer to them as "The Henriad." While no one can prove that Shakespeare initially conceived of them as a cycle, it seems clear that by the time he wrote *Henry IV, Part 2*, he had begun to perceive the shape of an epic story beginning with Bullingbrook's usurpation of the throne in *Richard II* and ending with his son's victory at the battle of Agincourt. This cycle comprises several potentially tragic and comic actions. The fate of Richard II is tragic in the loose sense of a fall from a high place, but it qualifies in a more sophisticated sense of the term as well, in that Richard's faith in his divinely sanctioned privilege is what leads him to undo himself. Moreover, the epiphany he experiences in the prison cell just before his assassination adds a heroic dimension to a character who may until this point have seemed a fool. Similarly, the difficulty of distinguishing naiveté from heroism appears with particular force in the portrayal of Harry Percy — Hotspur — the rival of the Prince of Wales in *Henry IV, Part 1.* Hotspur's absolute commitment to honor leads him to act recklessly in challenging the king but also to misread the significance of his diminished forces. Like the tragic figures of whom he is an early version, the young rebel enacts a story of wasted talent.

The clearest case of squandered ability is that of Sir John Falstaff, whose experience strikes audiences as alternately comic and tragic. In *Henry IV, Part 1*, Falstaff seems to be the irresistible comic figure who can't be kept down or shaken off. Descended from the Roman stock character known as the *miles gloriosus* (the braggart soldier), Falstaff is the play's clown, the childish drunkard blessed with divine immunity. At the end of the battle of Shrewsbury, Prince Hal stands over the inert and apparently deceased figures of Hotspur and Falstaff, but as soon as Hal exits, Falstaff rises to declare his unreadiness to die. In *Henry IV, Part 2*, Falstaff exhibits many of the same conventionally comic traits, but his ending is prototragic. Although Shakespeare postpones his death until *Henry V*, where the Hostess describes it in a memorable passage, Falstaff truly is finished at the end of *Part 2* when the Prince banishes him. The old fool is vanquished largely by excessive faith in his own wit, charm, and verbal skill.

The entire tetralogy may be regarded as an enormous comedy weighted with intense tragic insights. Looked at from one perspective, the cycle presents the success story of the Prince of Wales, who expiates his father's crime, leads his country to victory at Agincourt, and, in the archetypal comic conclusion, marries the princess of France. But this positive interpretation requires that a great deal be suppressed — the human cost of Bullingbrook's usurpation, particularly the death of Richard and the ensuing civil war; Prince John's lying to the rebels at Gaultree Forest, one of many instances of verbal deception; Hal's apparently heartless rejection of Falstaff; the self-serving motives with which the church promotes and justifies Henry's invasion of France; and the slaughter of the French prisoners. After the joyous spectacle that concludes *Henry V,* the audience hears an epilogue in which these harmonies are contradicted by a glimpse into the near future. Speaking of Henry as the "star of England," the Chorus summarizes and prophesies:

> Fortune made his sword;
> By which the world's best garden he achieved,
> And of it left his son imperial lord.
> Henry the Sixt, in infant bands crown'd King
> Of France and England, did this king succeed;
> Whose state so many had the managing,
> That they lost France, and made his England bleed.   (Epilogue 6–12)

This tension between achievement and failure, promise and disappointment, although it influences our responses to all four plays, is especially keen in *Henry V,* where interpretive incompatibility is built into our experience of the play. Norman Rabkin, in a brilliant essay called "Rabbits, Ducks, and *Henry V,*" argues that the play is like an inkblot: we can see either a rabbit or a duck, but never both at the same time (33–62). At one moment Henry V appears to be the model of a Christian king whose victory and marriage are grounds for celebration and approval. At the same time he seems the model of a Machiavellian self-server who banishes his former friends, unjustifiably invades France, breaks his word to his own men, and ignominiously slaughters the French prisoners. History is difficult to read.

One of the most beguiling scenes in *Henry IV, Part 2,* is the meeting of Falstaff and Justice Shallow in the latter's orchard in Gloucestershire, where the two old men reflect on their younger days and lament the passing of time and the loss of many of their old chums. If spectators are touched by the ancient Justice Shallow's memories of his hell-raising days as a law student, they may be shocked when, as the old man leaves the stage, Falstaff confides in them:

> I do see the bottom of Justice Shallow. Lord, Lord, how subject we old
> men are to this vice of lying! This same starv'd justice hath done nothing
> but prate to me of the wildness of his youth, and the feats he hath done

about Turnbull Street, and every third word a lie.... And now is this Vice's dagger become a squire, and talks as familiarly of John a' Gaunt as if he had been sworn brother to him, and I'll be sworn 'a ne'er saw him but once in the Tilt-yard, and then he burst his head for crowding among the marshal's men. I saw it, and told John a' Gaunt he beat his own name, for you might have thrust him and all his apparel into an eel-skin.   (3.2.302–07; 319–26)

Shakespeare uses the reminiscence and the commentary on it to introduce doubts about the truth of memory and thus about the reliability of history, the very form in which he himself is working and that the audience is watching. All that has amused and touched us, according to Falstaff, has been a fiction, but that qualifier, "according to Falstaff," is a crucial part of the problem. For after ridiculing Justice Shallow for name-dropping about John of Gaunt, Falstaff drops the name of John of Gaunt. Whose version is accurate? And, implicitly, whose version of the story of the House of Lancaster is reliable?

It depends, of course, on who is telling the story. The Great Tetralogy, compared to the First, exhibits an increased consciousness of the mediated and conditional nature of all historical writing, and this axiom has exerted a strong influence on recent critics. The parallel phrases now used to describe this perception are "the textuality of history" and "the historicity of texts." The "textuality of history" suggests that history can be represented only in texts, that we know what happened in the fourteenth and fifteenth centuries only by means of written records, and that such verbal documents are subject to the limitations and complexity of language. Likewise, the "historicity of texts" asserts that all written language (whether plays or letters or textbooks) is inextricably rooted in its own time and culture, and that comprehension of any historical writing requires an awareness of the milieu that produced it. The emergence of these ideas has significantly affected critical response to Shakespeare's history plays. In the first half of the twentieth century, the prevailing view, expressed most emphatically by E. M. W. Tillyard in his *Shakespeare's History Plays,* was that the history plays reflected an ordered conception of the universe to which virtually everyone in the culture subscribed. Shakespeare was an orthodox writer, and that was as it should be. Recent critics, among them Stephen Greenblatt and other subscribers to the school of criticism known as new historicism, or cultural poetics, have dissented, arguing that Shakespeare's plays did not merely reflect the hierarchical and oppressive views of his place and time, but that they actually helped to produce and sustain the dominant political theory. In other words, these critics see the plays not merely as effects of ideology but as creators of it.

There are modern and postmodern variations on all of these cultural readings. Some believe that the histories, like the later tragedies, were intentionally subversive of Tudor orthodoxy; others, that they were unconsciously so. Greenblatt and other new historicists hold that the histories served the Crown as an outlet for subversive doctrine, as a container of rebellious impulses that might have erupted in the streets had they not been released and defused within the confines of the public theaters. It is indisputable that the Tudor and

Stuart regimes were aware of — and wary of — the power of historical theater to influence political feeling. As I discussed in Chapter 2, in February 1601 the Lord Chamberlain's Men were paid by supporters of the earl of Essex to stage a performance of Shakespeare's *Richard II,* the play in which a strong and popular leader deposes an increasingly unpopular and ineffectual monarch. The rebellion failed, a member of the company was summoned to explain its presentation of the play (see excerpt on p. 71), and Elizabeth herself was apparently conscious of the performance and its significance, as her comments to William Lambarde indicate (see p. 178). What all this suggests is that history plays are no less complex than comedies and tragedies. The theater has political power, but Shakespeare's histories reveal the difficulty of attempting to determine and control the nature of that power.

Romance

At the end of his career Shakespeare experimented with a new dramatic mode that we call romance. His efforts in this form include *Pericles, Cymbeline, The Winter's Tale,* and *The Tempest,* as well as the two collaborations written at the very end of his career with John Fletcher, *The Two Noble Kinsmen* and probably *Cardenio.* Never one to be bound by the Roman models to which some of his contemporaries were faithful, Shakespeare was by this time uncommonly adventurous in combining kinds and adapting into drama the various tales and narratives that appealed to him. Many of his contemporaries were adventurous too, for by about 1608 the London stages offered audiences a range of choice: historical tragedy, domestic tragedy, imitations of classical tragedy, romantic comedy, city comedy, satire, prodigal-son plays, apprentice-makes-good stories, chronicle plays, and tragicomedy. Francis Beaumont and John Fletcher, writing under the influence of Continental models, were gaining attention for their development of English tragicomedy in plays such as *Philaster* and *A King and No King.* Shakespeare's last plays most resemble this kind of tragicomedy, which, as Fletcher's description makes clear (see p. 178), threatens its audience with disaster or death and abruptly changes gears so that the action comes to a happy ending.

The romance form is difficult to define, particularly because it has appeared and reappeared repeatedly in the history of literature. I do not wish to suggest that romance — or any of the modes I have discussed — is a transhistorical category that works the same across all cultures and all periods. But there is something familiar about romance, as Howard Felperin points out: "To the extent that all literary experience involves a journey into another world inherently removed from present time and place, all literature is fundamentally romantic" (*Shakespearean Romance* 7). Romance seems to exhibit many of the same properties in its various manifestations, whether in the mode of Greek romance, from which much Renaissance literature derives; or in medieval quest romance, such as Sir Thomas Malory's *Morte d'Arthur;* in Edmund Spenser's epic poem *The Faerie Queene;* in its later appearance among the nineteenth-century poets we know as the Romantics; and in modern cinematic versions, such as the Western or the space epic. A touchstone for the formal and tonal properties we are concerned with is George Lucas's *Star Wars*, with its otherworldly locations, youthful hero, displaced princess, battles between the agents of good and evil, and supernatural Force. The most productive approach to Shakespearean romance is to offer a series of descriptions, none comprehensive but each contributing a partial explanation of the effect or shape of the form.

As a distinctive kind of comedy, romance arrives at a happy ending by an unusually perilous route. As our sense of the term implies, the action usually involves amorous desire and fulfillment, but the essential characteristic of fictional romance is an adventure story. Etymologically the word derives from the same root that gives us both the French and German words for "novel," *roman*. The main characters must endure a series of hazards and trials that lead ultimately to success and reward. The form is given to extremes, for the ending is not only happy but joyous, even revelatory, and the progression to that ending is much more arduous than in traditional comedy. In other words, the fundamentally comic shape of the action is darkly colored by tragic concerns and perceptions: the marriage or reunion that ends the play is preceded in the middle by some form of catastrophe, either death or some similarly grave loss.

These tonal oppositions of inexpressible despair and joy are matched by other extremes. *Pericles*, for example, opens with a riddle that the hero must solve for King Antiochus; the answer reveals the king's incest with his daughter. A wide geographical range is employed as well. Pericles travels throughout the Mediterranean; *Cymbeline* takes place in ancient Britain, ancient Rome, and the wilds of Wales; and *The Tempest* is set on a magical island. Often temporal limits are ignored: *The Winter's Tale* covers a period of sixteen years. At the conclusion of the hero's trials, magic or the supernatural contributes to the ending, often creating a sense of miracle. The vaguely providential force that, in the earlier comedies, seems to safeguard the characters and bring about a happy resolution is here specifically identified with divine protection, and in several of the plays this immortal force is theatrically incarnated, as in Jupiter's appearance in a dream at the end of *Cymbeline* or Diana's in *Pericles*. Such instances of theophany, or the appearance of a god or goddess, attest to the religious affinities of Shakespearean romance.

The cardinal feature of the form, the key to its emotional power, is the gap between the desperate middle and the joyful ending. Characters in these plays are able to recover what seemed irretrievably lost, what they themselves have foolishly attempted to destroy: penitent husbands find themselves reunited with wives they wished dead; lost children are restored to their parents; impossible wishes are granted. It has often been pointed out that the *Odyssey* is the first romance, an adventure story that is also a love story, and one that delays the pleasure of Ulysses' homecoming for twenty years by taking him all over the known world (not to mention a visit to the underworld). And it is this wandering that makes the poem; that's what it's about. So with Shakespeare's romances. Although we look forward to the endings, the playwright spends most of his time not ending the play and then, when he finally does so, surprising us. So crucial is this incongruity that we might say that Shakespeare makes his romances *about* endings, playing self-consciously on the audience's desire for a happy outcome. These are fantasy plays that stimulate, frustrate, and fulfill our fantasies of resolution, but above all they force us to examine and evaluate our need for satisfactory closure. At the end of *Cymbeline*, the sleeping hero dreams that Jupiter descends from above and explains to his family why their son has had to endure such misery: "Whom best I love, I cross; to make my gift, / The more delay'd, delighted" (5.4.101–02). The god insists that waiting for fulfillment intensifies the emotion, that the more difficult the trial, the more satisfying the victory.

But Jupiter appears in a character's dream, distanced from the audience and even from the reality of the play-world. In other words, the deity's appearance is a form of illusion occurring within a play that is itself an illusion. This dramatic tactic confirms the principle that the choice of a mode implies particular meanings about the world and the human experience of it. By turning at the end of his career to stories of fantasy and magic, Shakespeare has committed himself not only to the power of the imaginary, but also to the value of fiction in general. This turn to romance is especially revealing because the tragedies seem obsessed with the perils and deceits of illusion. The apparitions of the deceptive witches in *Macbeth*, the fatal trickery of Iago's performance in *Othello*, or the lies of the elder daughters in *King Lear* — all these betray Shakespeare's mistrust of theatricality and perhaps even doubt about his own profession. As Anne Righter puts it in discussing the "Tomorrow and tomorrow and tomorrow" speech, "The final attitude of Macbeth, the passionate reduction of all human endeavour to the meaningless posturing of a player on a darkening stage, is scarcely flattering to the theatre. Such an image expresses not only the hollowness of life, but also the degradation and stupidity of the actor's profession" (169). Shakespeare's late interest in romance suggests a reversal in his thinking; his professional doubts, if not dismissed, appear to have been at least allayed.

Thus in the last plays the instances of spectacle tend to be affirmative rather than threatening, a point best demonstrated in the powerful last scene of *The Winter's Tale*. Hermione, dead, or apparently dead, for sixteen years, has been memorialized in a statue, and as her penitent husband, the one responsible for her death, stands before it, the statue comes to life. This spectacular moment could be terrifying: as Paulina puts it, ". . . you'll think / (Which I protest against) I am assisted / By wicked powers" (5.3.89–91). But instead of a demonic show, Paulina presents her audiences, both onstage and in the theater, with what amounts to a miracle. The appropriate response is spiritual wonder at an act of grace. As Paulina also says, "It is requir'd / You do awake your faith" (5.3.94–95). A statue, a work of art, an imitation of life, suddenly becomes "real," a miracle that occurs in a play that is itself an imitation of life, a fiction in which imaginary persons come to life for the pleasure of a credulous audience. Shakespeare prizes the indistinguishability of the illusory and the actual. The artificiality of all experience, with Providence as the artist, the divine playwright, is the great theme of Shakespeare's last phase. Here it would be fitting to cite Prospero's famous "Revels" speech from the fourth act of *The Tempest* about the unreality of the whole world; instead, I shall quote a much more contemporary instance of the same perception, from Cormac McCarthy's novel *The Crossing* (1994): "For this world also which seems to us to sing of stone and flower and blood is not a thing at all but is a tale. And all in it is a tale and each tale the sum of all lesser tales and yet these also are the self-same tale and contain as well all else within them" (143).

Mixed Modes

A great many of Shakespeare's plays transgress the formal boundaries described in this chapter and are therefore difficult to classify. In certain comedies, particularly those written after his initial efforts at farcical and romantic comedy, the ironies can become so bitter and the obstacles to joyful closure so formidable that the work may seem nearer to tragedy than to its comic siblings. *The Merchant of Venice* is probably the most illustrative example of the high cost of comic resolution. The lovers' gathering at Belmont in act 5, musical and joyous though it may be, is overshadowed by their intolerable treatment of Shylock in the trial scene (4.1). The movement toward assimilation that normally unites the cast in the last moments is not strong enough to include Shylock, who is stripped of his wealth, his daughter, and his religion and who leaves the stage for the last time in act 4. Although the merchant Antonio is present for the festivities in the last act, he has no partner and must go home alone. *Twelfth Night* closes with a similar if less extreme case of rejection, when Malvolio refuses the Countess's offer of reconciliation and storms off the stage vowing revenge. A few moments later, another Antonio, clearly infatuated with his friend Sebastian, is left alone as the pairs of lovers exit together. Virtually all comedy rejects or neglects someone — a father who won't agree to a marriage, or a malcontent family member like Don John in *Much Ado about Nothing* — but most of the time the audience sanctions this exclusion of the uncooperative individual in the interests of community. Such characters do appear in the early plays, but as his comedies become more tonally complicated, Shakespeare contrives to give such people a greater claim on our emotions, to make the rejection more disturbing, and even to endanger the expected comic festivity.

Likewise in tragedy the audience's need to sympathize with the protagonist is often thwarted or made more difficult by an emphasis on the character's weaknesses. Historically, the critical reception of *Othello*, for example, reveals that some readers find the protagonist so hasty and foolish in his suspicions of Desdemona's fidelity that they feel only contempt, a response expressed in one of the early critiques of the play, Thomas Rymer's *Short View of Tragedy* (see p. 179). When such foolishness is heightened by a director or the actor playing Othello, sympathetic engagement or tragic pity and fear may be pushed aside by scornful laughter. Similarly, in *Antony and Cleopatra,* the Queen of Egypt can be played as a dishonest and manipulative opportunist. Just as comic joy is subject to being compromised or diminished, the potential for antiheroic mockery always lurks beneath the surface of the tragedies. Shakespeare encourages such doubts more readily in some plays than in others, and no matter how subtle the ironic suggestions may be, directors can take those cues and adjust the emotional tone, thus promoting a dramatic experience that Shakespeare himself might not have recognized. Such is the ambiguous nature of human behavior and the vehicles created to depict it.

It should be clear by now that each of Shakespeare's modes is plastic, subject to reshaping by the playwright and reconsideration by critical history, and that almost none of the plays fits neatly into a box that we can label comedy or tragedy. *Twelfth Night,* a play in which everyone wants to get married, ends with a song that does not ignore the miseries of marriage: "But when I came, alas, to wive, / With hey ho, the wind and the rain." And the King's Men apparently finished their performances of tragedy with a rousing jig, as was the custom in the early modern playhouses. It may be difficult for us to comprehend a theatrical experience in which *Hamlet* is followed by a jolly dance performed by some of the players who have just expired in the final scene. But Elizabethan audiences were evidently used to such contrarieties, and Shakespeare exploited rather than suppressed them. His own subtle and even contradictory understanding of human experience prompted him to reconstruct and complicate the dramatic forms he inherited, to push the formal boundaries. This remaking of his medium to suit his meaning is probably the most powerful evidence of Shakespeare's artistic originality.

In fact, great playwrights have regularly strained against conventional limits, reconceiving forms in accord with their expressive needs and exploiting the interrelation of dramatic modes. Anton Chekhov wrote *The Cherry Orchard* as a comedy, but Konstantin Stanislavsky, the original director, produced it as a tragedy. Both labels seem apt. Our contemporary playwright Tom Stoppard was alert to the fragility of dramatic modes when he produced an adaptation called *Dogg's Hamlet* that includes almost all Shakespeare's action, takes fifteen minutes to perform, and has the audience rolling in the aisles.

→ SIR PHILIP SIDNEY

From *The Defense of Poesy* *c. 1581*

Sir Philip Sidney's remarks on comedy and tragedy offer one of the fullest analytical descriptions of the state of the two modes in the 1580s. The influence of classical models is apparent. Also notable is Sidney's devotion to the didactic function of comedy and tragedy, particularly their attention to folly and tyranny, respectively, and their power to urge audiences away from engaging in such behavior. The difference between the single tonality suggested in these excerpts and the multivocality of Shakespearean comedy and tragedy arises partly from the rapid development of English drama in the twenty years after the *Defense* was composed.

COMEDY

No, perchance it is the comic, whom naughty play-makers and stage-keepers have justly made odious. To the arguments of abuse I will answer after. Only thus much now is to be said, that the comedy is an imitation of the common errors of our life, which he representeth in the most ridiculous and scornful sort that may be, so as it is impossible that any beholder can be content to be such a one. Now, as in geometry the oblique must be known as well as the right, and in arithmetic the odd as well as the even, so in the actions of our life who seeth not the filthiness of evil wanteth a great foil to perceive the beauty of virtue. This doth the comedy handle so in our private and domestical matters, as with hearing it we get as it were an experience, what is to be looked for of a niggardly Demea, of a crafty Davus, of a flattering Gnatho, of a vainglorious Thraso [conventional characters in Roman comedy]; and not only to know what effects are to be expected, but to know who be such, by the signifying badge given them by the comedian. And little reason hath any man to say that men learn evil by seeing it so set out; since, as I said before, there is no man living but, by the force truth hath in nature, no sooner seeth these men play their parts, but wisheth them in *pistrinum* [flour mill, workhouse]; although perchance the sack of his own faults lie so behind his back that he seeth not himself dance the same measure; whereto yet nothing can more open his eyes than to see his own actions contemptibly set forth.

TRAGEDY

So that the right use of comedy will (I think) by nobody be blamed; and much less of the high and excellent tragedy, that openeth the greatest wounds, and showeth forth the ulcers that are covered with tissue; that maketh kings fear to be tyrants, and tyrants manifest their tyrannical humors; that with stirring the affects of admiration and commiseration teacheth the uncertainty of this world, and upon how weak foundations gilden roofs are builded; that maketh us know,

> Qui sceptra saevus duro imperio regit,
> Timet timentes, metus in auctorem redit.[1]

But how much it can move, Plutarch yieldeth a notable testimony of the abominable tyrant Alexander Phereaus, from whose eyes a tragedy, well made and represented, drew abundance of tears, who without all pity had murdered infinite numbers, and some of his own blood, so as he that was not ashamed to make matters for tragedies yet could not resist the sweet violence of a tragedy. And if it wrought no further good in him, it was that he, in despite of himself, withdrew himself from hearkening to that which might mollify his hardened heart. But it is not the tragedy they do mislike; for it were too absurd to cast out so excellent a representation of whatsoever is most worthy to be learned.

---

[1] Seneca, *Oedipus*, 705–06: "The savage tyrant who sways his scepter with a heavy hand fears the subjects that fear him, and fear returns upon its creator."

→ ARISTOTLE

From *Poetics*

fourth century B.C.
Translated by Richard McKeon

Although Aristotle's theory of tragedy was not well known in sixteenth-century England, his philosophical views had entered the culture indirectly through the ideas of humanist commentators. The analysis of tragic drama, excerpted here from a modern translation, has come to be extremely influential in modern treatments of Shakespearean and other forms of tragedy.

Let us proceed now to the discussion of Tragedy; before doing so, however, we must gather up the definition resulting from what has been said. A tragedy, then, is the imitation of an action that is serious and also, as having magnitude, complete in itself; in language with pleasurable accessories, each kind brought in separately in the parts of the work; in a dramatic, not in a narrative form; with incidents arousing pity and fear, wherewith to accomplish its catharsis of such emotions. Here by "language with pleasurable accessories" I mean that with rhythm and harmony or song superadded; and by "the kinds separately" I mean that some portions are worked out with verse only, and others in turn with song.

I. As they act the stories, it follows that in the first place the Spectacle (or stage-appearance of the actors) must be some part of the whole; and in the second Melody and Diction, these two being the means of their imitation. Here by "Diction" I mean merely this, the composition of the verses; and by "Melody," what is too completely understood to require explanation. But further: the subject represented also is an action; and the action involves agents, who must necessarily have their distinctive qualities both of character and thought, since it is from these that we ascribe certain qualities to their actions. There are in the natural order of things, therefore, two causes, Thought and Character, of their actions, and consequently of their success or failure in their lives. Now the action (that which was done) is represented in the play by the Fable or Plot. The Fable, in our present sense of the term, is simply this, the combination of the incidents, or things done in the story; whereas Character is what makes us ascribe certain moral qualities to the agents; and Thought is shown in all they say when proving a particular point or, it may be, enunciating a general truth. There are six parts consequently of every tragedy, as a whole (that is) of such or such quality, viz. a Fable or Plot, Characters, Diction, Thought, Spectacle, and Melody; two of them arising from the means, one from the manner, and three from the objects of the dramatic imitation; and there is nothing else besides these six. Of these, its formative elements, then, not a few of the dramatists have made due use, as every play, one may say, admits of Spectacle, Character, Fable, Diction, Melody, and Thought.

II. The most important of the six is the combination of the incidents of the story. Tragedy is essentially an imitation not of persons but of action and life, of happiness and misery. All human happiness or misery takes the form of action; the end for which we live is a certain kind of activity, not a quality. Character gives us qualities, but it is in our actions — what we do — that we are happy or the reverse. In a play accordingly they do not act in order to portray the Characters; they include the Characters for the sake of the action. So that it is the action in it, i.e., its Fable or Plot, that is the end and purpose of the tragedy; and the end is everywhere the chief thing. Besides this, a tragedy is impossible without action, but there may be one without Character. . . . The first essential, the life and soul, so to speak, of Tragedy is the Plot; and . . . the Characters come second — compare the parallel in painting, where the most beautiful colors laid on without order will not give one the same pleasure as a simple black-and-white sketch of a portrait. We maintain that Tragedy is primarily an imitation of action, and that it is mainly for the sake of the action that it imitates the personal agents. Third comes the element of Thought, i.e., the power of saying whatever can be said, or what is appropriate to the occasion. This is what, in the speeches in Tragedy, falls under the arts of Politics and Rhetoric; for the older poets make their personages discourse like statesmen, and the modern like rhetoricians.

One must not confuse it with Character. Character in a play is that which reveals the moral purpose of the agents, i.e., the sort of thing they seek or avoid,
where that is not obvious — hence there is no room for Character in a speech
on a purely indifferent subject. Thought, on the other hand, is shown in all they
say when proving or disproving some particular point, or enunciating some universal proposition. Fourth among the literary elements is the Diction of the personages, i.e., as before explained, the expression of their thoughts in words,
which is practically the same thing with verse as with prose. As for the two remaining parts, the Melody is the greatest of the pleasurable accessories of
Tragedy. The Spectacle, though an attraction, is the least artistic of all the parts,
and has least to do with the art of poetry. The tragic effect is quite possible without a public performance and actors; and besides, the getting-up of the Spectacle is more a matter for the costumer than the poet.

Having thus distinguished the parts, let us now consider the proper construction of the Fable or Plot, as that is at once the first and the most important thing in Tragedy. We have laid it down that a tragedy is an imitation of an
action that is complete in itself, as a whole of some magnitude; for a whole
may be of no magnitude to speak of. Now a whole is that which has beginning, middle, and end. A beginning is that which is not itself necessarily after
anything else, and which has naturally something else after it; an end is that
which is naturally after something itself, either as its necessary or usual conse-
quent, and with nothing else after it; and a middle, that which is by nature after one thing and has also another after it. A well-constructed Plot, therefore,
cannot either begin or end at any point one likes; beginning and end in it must
be of the forms just described. Again: to be beautiful, a living creature, and
every whole made up of parts, must not only present a certain order in its
arrangement of parts, but also be of a certain definite magnitude. Beauty is a
matter of size and order, and therefore impossible either (1) in a very minute
creature, since our perception becomes indistinct as it approaches instantane-
ity; or (2) in a creature of vast size — one, say, 1,000 miles long — as in that
case, instead of the object being seen all at once, the unity and wholeness of it
is lost to the beholder. Just in the same way, then, as a beautiful whole made
up of parts, or a beautiful living creature, must be of some size, but a size to be
taken in by the eye, so a story or Plot must be of some length, but of a length
to be taken in by the memory. . . .

Tragedy, however, is an imitation not only of a complete action, but also of
incidents arousing pity and fear. Such incidents have the very greatest effect
on the mind when they occur unexpectedly and at the same time in consequence of one another; there is more of the marvelous in them then than if
they happened of themselves or by mere chance. Even matters of chance seem
most marvelous if there is an appearance of design as it were in them; as for
instance the statue of Mitys at Argos killed the author of Mitys' death by
falling down on him when a looker-on at a public spectacle; for incidents like
that we think to be not without a meaning. A Plot, therefore, of this sort is
necessarily finer than others.

. . .

Plots are either simple or complex, since the actions they represent are naturally of this twofold description. The action, proceeding in the way defined, as one continuous whole, I call simple, when the change in the hero's fortunes takes place without Peripety or Discovery; and complex, when it involves one or the other, or both. These should each of them arise out of the structure of the Plot itself, so as to be the consequence, necessary or probable, of the antecedents. There is a great difference between a thing happening *propter hoc* and *post hoc* ["because of this" and "after this"].

A Peripety is the change of the kind described from one state of things within the play to its opposite, and that too in the way we are saying, in the probable or necessary sequence of events; as it is for instance in *Oedipus:* here the opposite state of things is produced by the Messenger, who, coming to gladden Oedipus and to remove his fears as to his mother, reveals the secret of his birth [*Oedipus the King* 911–1085]. And in *Lynceus* [by Theodectes]: just as he is being led off for execution, with Danaus at his side to put him to death, the incidents preceding this bring it about that he is saved and Danaus put to death. A Discovery is, as the very word implies, a change from ignorance to knowledge, and thus to either love or hate, in the personages marked for good or evil fortune. The finest form of Discovery is one attended by Peripeties, like that which goes with the Discovery in *Oedipus.* There are no doubt other forms of it; what we have said may happen in a way in reference to inanimate things, even things of a very casual kind; and it is also possible to discover whether someone has done or not done something. But the form most directly connected with the Plot and the action of the piece is the first-mentioned. This, with a Peripety, will arouse either pity or fear — actions of that nature being what Tragedy is assumed to represent; and it will also serve to bring about the happy or unhappy ending. The Discovery, then, being of persons, it may be that of one party only to the other, the latter being already known; or both the parties may have to discover themselves. Iphigenia, for instance, was discovered to Orestes by sending the letter [*Iphigenia in Tauris* 727ff.]; and another Discovery was required to reveal him to Iphigenia.

Two parts of the Plot, then, Peripety and Discovery, are on matters of this sort. A third part is Suffering; which we may define as an action of a destructive or painful nature, such as murders on the stage, tortures, woundings, and the like. The other two have been already explained. . . .

The next points after what we have said above will be these: (1) What is the poet to aim at, and what is he to avoid, in constructing his Plots? and (2) What are the conditions on which the tragic effect depends?

We assume that, for the finest form of Tragedy, the Plot must be not simple but complex; and further, that it must imitate actions arousing fear and pity, since that is the distinctive function of this kind of imitation. It follows, therefore, that there are three forms of Plot to be avoided. (1) A good man must not be seen passing from happiness to misery, or (2) a bad man from misery to happiness. The first situation is not fear-inspiring or piteous, but simply odious to us. The second is the most untragic that can be; it has no one of the requisites of Tragedy; it does not appeal either to the human feeling in us, or to our pity, or to our fears. Nor, on the other hand, should (3) an extremely bad man be seen falling from happiness into misery. Such a story may arouse the human feeling in us, but it will not move us to either pity or fear; pity is occasioned by undeserved misfortune, and fear by that of one like ourselves; so that there will be nothing either piteous or fear-inspiring in the situation. There remains, then, the intermediate kind of personage, a man not preeminently virtuous and just, whose misfortune, however, is brought upon him not by vice and depravity but by some error of judgment, of the number of those in the enjoyment of great reputation and prosperity — e.g., Oedipus, Thyestes, and the men of note of similar families. The perfect Plot, accordingly, must have a single, and not (as some tell us) a double issue; the change in the hero's fortunes must be not from misery to happiness, but on the contrary from happiness to misery; and the cause of it must lie not in any depravity, but in some great error on his part; the man himself being either such as we have described, or better, not worse, than that. . . .

The tragic fear and pity may be aroused by the Spectacle; but they may also be aroused by the very structure and incidents of the play — which is the better way and shows the better poet. The Plot in fact should be so framed that, even without seeing the things take place, he who simply hears the account of them shall be filled with horror and pity at the incidents — which is just the effect that the mere recital of the story in *Oedipus* would have on one. To produce this same effect by means of the Spectacle is less artistic, and requires extraneous aid. Those, however, who make use of the Spectacle to put before us that which is merely monstrous and not productive of fear, are wholly out of touch with Tragedy; not every kind of pleasure should be required of a tragedy, but only its own proper pleasure.

→ **Title Page of *Richard III***   *1597* ⤏

First Quarto

The title page pictured here (slightly reduced) indicates the problem of classifying early modern plays. What modern scholars call a history play was described to prospective buyers as a "tragedy." Early modern distinctions among dramatic modes were considerably less rigid than our own. One of the earliest of Shakespeare's plays to see print, *Richard III* was also one of the most popular; it was published seven times between 1597 and 1623.

THE TRAGEDY OF
King Richard the third.

Containing,
His treacherous Plots against his brother Clarence:
the pittiefull murther of his iunocent nephewes:
his tyrannicall vsurpation: with the whole course
of his detested life, and most deserued death.

As it hath beene lately Acted by the
Right honourable the Lord Chamber-
laine his seruants.

AT LONDON
Printed by Valentine Sims, for Andrew Wise,
dwelling in Paules Chuch-yard, at the
Signe of the Angell.
1597.

→ WILLIAM LAMBARDE

From His Notes of a Conversation with Queen Elizabeth I about *Richard II* 1601

William Lambarde, Queen Elizabeth's keeper of the records in the tower, recorded notes on his conversation with the queen in August 1601. The reference to Shakespeare's play concerns the earl of Essex's rebellion against Elizabeth, in preparation for which some of his supporters commissioned a performance of *Richard II.* The desired effect of such a performance would have been to figure Essex as the capable Bullingbrook and Elizabeth as the unfit Richard.

Her Majestie fell upon the reign of King Richard II, saying, "I am Richard II. Know ye not that?"

w. l.: "Such a wicked imagination was determined and attempted by a most unkind Gent [leman] the most adorned creature that ever your Majestie made."

HER MAJESTIE: "He that will forget God, will also forget his benefactor; this tragedy was played 40tie times in open streets and houses."

→ JOHN FLETCHER

From His Preface to *The Faithful Shepherdess* 1608

Shakespeare's occasional collaborator and successor as principal dramatist of the King's Men, John Fletcher helped to popularize the new Continental form of tragicomedy in England. This promotional description, from his prefatory remarks ("To the Reader") to his play *The Faithful Shepherdess* (1608), exhibits the influence of the Italian dramatist Giovanni Battista Guarini, whose tragicomedy *Il Pastor Fido* (The Faithful Shepherd) had received considerable attention. Along with one of his other collaborators, Francis Beaumont, Fletcher may have helped to shape the last phase of Shakespeare's career by developing the new form.

A tragicomedy is not so called in respect of mirth and killing, but in respect it wants deaths, which is enough to make it no tragedy, yet brings some near it, which is enough to make it no comedy: which must be a representation of familiar people, with such kind of trouble as no life be questioned, so that a God is as lawful in this as in a tragedy, and mean [lowly] people as in a comedy.

→ THOMAS RYMER

From *A Short View of Tragedy* 1693

Thomas Rymer's *A Short View of Tragedy* offers a contemptuous dismissal of *Othello* and typifies a frequent neoclassical reaction to Shakespeare's innovations in the tragic mode. Although the nineteenth-century essayist Thomas Babington Macaulay referred to Rymer as "the worst critic that ever lived," his narrow views of *Othello* have often been repeated, if more delicately, in modern criticism of the play.

THE FABLE

Othello, a blackamoor captain, by talking of his prowess and feats of war, makes Desdemona, a senator's daughter, to be in love with him, and to be married to him without her parents' knowledge. And having preferred Cassio to be his lieutenant (a place which his ensign, Iago, sued for), Iago in revenge works the Moor into a jealousy that Cassio cuckolds him, which he effects by stealing and conveying a certain handkerchief which had, at the wedding, been by the Moor presented to his bride. Hereupon, Othello and Iago plot the deaths of Desdemona and Cassio; Othello murders her, and soon after is convinced of her innocence. And as he is about to be carried to prison, in order to be punished for the murder, he kills himself.

Whatever rubs or difficulty may stick on the bark, the moral, sure, of this fable is very instructive.

1. First, this may be a caution to all maidens of quality how, without their parents' consent, they run away with blackamoors. . . .

Secondly, this may be a warning to all good wives, that they look well to their linen.

Thirdly, this may be a lesson to husbands, that before their jealousy be tragical, the proofs may be mathematical.

CHAPTER 6

"To What End Are All These Words?":
Shakespeare's Dramatic Language

―――――――――――――――――――― ❭❬ ――――――――――――――――――――

One major assumption informs this chapter: that Shakespeare's language is a primary source of our pleasure in his plays, not an obstacle to appreciation, not something we must overcome in order to understand the stories. In other words, there is no such thing as in other words. Shakespeare in other words is not Shakespeare. There is no denying the appeal of the tales he dramatized, but as Chapter 4 indicated, Shakespeare rarely invented them, preferring instead to appropriate stories that he read or biographies of historical figures or plots of plays he had seen and turn them into theatrical vehicles for his company. His characters have captured and held the imaginations of audiences over three centuries, but these persons are what they are because of what they say. The unparalleled success of Shakespeare's stories and characters depends on the communicative power of Shakespeare's language, and this chapter will suggest some ways of making his language more available to the twentieth-century reader. Once we become alert to the potential power of Shakespeare's words, especially to the sensuousness of their sounds and patterns, then we have access to pleasures and meanings that take us to the heart of his dramatic enterprise.

This chapter, then, constitutes an effort to alleviate a modern reader's difficulties with the language of a Renaissance playwright, but such an attempt at clarification cannot account for the distinctive brilliance of Shakespeare's poetry and prose. An introduction to such problems as pronoun usage, fluid syntax, wordplay, and verse forms in the sixteenth and seventeenth centuries leaves a number of essential topics unexplored. The most important of these is probably figurative language. Modern readers are immediately struck by the density and richness of Shakespeare's dramatic verse, and a primary source of that impression is the abundance and power of the images and metaphors in which characters express their thoughts. The properties we value in expository prose — simplicity, brevity, "naturalness" — are irrelevant to Shakespeare. We read and listen to his verse precisely because of its artificiality, its poetic appeals to the ear and to the mind's eye. Figurative language delights the senses and the intelligence by expressing one idea in terms of another, and in the hands of the greatest poets, the imagery employed for such expression is richly connotative, creating a network of pictures and ideas that resonates with other images, ideas, and themes throughout the poem or play.

Near the beginning of *Macbeth,* just before the murder of King Duncan, Banquo remarks to his son on the late hour, the dark night, and the fatigue that overwhelms him.

> There's husbandry in heaven,
> Their candles are all out. Take thee that too. [*Gives him his belt and dagger.*]
> A heavy summons lies like lead upon me,
> And yet I would not sleep.   (2.1.4–7)

The sky (heaven) is described as an economical household in which all sources of light (the stars and moon) have been extinguished. Some powerful force (like lead) calls the speaker to sleep (a heavy summons), and yet he resists. The ideas could have been expressed much more plainly, but the power of the lines rests in their resonance. The nouns — "husbandry," "candles," "summons," "lead" — are evocative in themselves, but in the context of the action they become even more charged with meaning. "Husbandry" connotes household management or government, which Macbeth is about to disrupt, and we have just heard Lady Macbeth ridicule her "husband" for cowardice or unmanliness. In handing the dagger to his son, Banquo foreshadows the hallucinated dagger that Macbeth imagines in his soliloquy a few lines later, as well as the actual dagger that he carries away from the murder. At the end of this scene, a ringing bell "invites" or summons Macbeth to perform the murder; in act 3 Banquo faces the even heavier summons of death, brought by the murderers Macbeth has engaged. The heaviness of lead evokes a burden of foreboding that marks all these early scenes. In her subsequent madness, Lady Macbeth, fearing the dark, carries a candle, and darkness in the moral sense — evil — is the principal subject of the play.

This brief sketch barely suggests the imaginative associations of a typical passage of figurative language. It represents what this chapter will not do, and it is included to indicate the kind of analysis that readers must learn to do for themselves. An increased sensitivity to poetic resonance should be the goal of anyone approaching Shakespeare's plays, but no matter how adept we become, still greater sensitivity is always possible. Subsequent readings always generate new imaginative connections. Shakespeare's verbal power is an inexhaustible subject; finally it is a mystery. The magic of his language, its irresistible attraction, is a result of an artistic imagination speaking to the imagination of the audience, and figurative language is the medium for that communication. As we learn from *A Midsummer Night's Dream,* images, imagination, and magic are all of a piece.

Early Modern English

The modern reader unacquainted with sixteenth- and seventeenth-century English will encounter certain technical difficulties with Shakespeare's language, quite apart from the writer's distinctive poetic and rhetorical effects. One such obstacle is provided by verbs with inflected endings, such as "hath" for the modern "has," "doth" for "does," "goeth" for "goes," and similar early modern forms that can immediately brand the text as old-fashioned and alien. It may be some comfort to discover that a few of these forms were beginning to sound old-fashioned at the time that Shakespeare was employing them, and they were gradually being displaced by more modern usage. We should keep in mind, moreover, that he frequently mixes the older endings with the modern "has," "does," and "goes," relying at times on the archaic style to achieve formality or intensity or a particular rhythmic goal but avoiding any consistent pattern.

The most familiar point of confusion among the older forms is what might be called the pronoun problem, or the frequent appearance of "thou," "thee," "thy," "thine," and "ye," words that serve for many to typify the strangeness of early modern speech. Here patterns of usage can be discerned, because certain of these pronouns, more so than the verbs, carry traces of meaning that Shakespeare frequently exploits. We cannot hope to recover the Renaissance listener's ear for such differences, a trained sensitivity that had become second nature, but awareness of the broad categories of usage can help us recognize the potential significance of a shift from one form to another. Sometimes, of course, these changes are not meaningful. For certain speakers or groups of speakers, pronoun usage was a matter of personal taste.

Where we employ "you" for all references to the second person, the Renaissance speaker had a choice between "you" and "thou." (It simplifies matters to know that "ye" and "thee" are merely the objective cases of "you" and "thou" — the equivalent of "me" in relation to the nominative "I" — and thus the same rules apply as for "you" and "thou.") "You" is the standard second-person pronoun in English, but other languages retain a distinction between different uses of "you," such as *tu* and *vous* in French, or *tu* and *usted* in Spanish, and familiarity with the different functions of these words can help with Renaissance usage. To speak very broadly, "you" was normally used in the plural; in certain circumstances it was used in the singular, for example, in speaking to a social superior or a parent, thus connoting respect or formality. "Thou," on the other hand, implied familiarity and was used for speaking to social inferiors, children, or loved ones.

Although Shakespeare does not usually employ these pronouns in any consistent pattern, he sometimes exploits their connotations for dramatic effect. For example, a deliberate shift from "you" to "thou" functions as a signal. In the first meeting between Petruchio and Katherina in *The Taming of the Shrew*, Petruchio passes back and forth between "you" and "thou" as he shifts between the polite and the personal. Katherina, however, resisting his overtures throughout the contest, attempts to keep him at a distance by consistently addressing him as "you" (2.1). The only exception occurs at the end of the scene when Katherina, on hearing Petruchio announce to her father that "upon Sunday is [their] wedding-day," responds with "I'll see thee hang'd on Sunday first." As this exchange suggests, the superiority implied by the speaker who employs "thou" makes it especially useful for insults. Old Queen Margaret in *Richard III* repeatedly uses the more familiar "thou" to lash out at her enemies, as in her curse on Richard: "Thou elvish-mark'd, abortive, rooting hog! / . . . / Thou slander of thy heavy mother's womb! / Thou loathed issue of thy father's loins!" (1.3.227-31).

Familiarity need not connote disrespect, however; it can also imply intimacy, as when lovers address each other as "thou." When Romeo and Juliet first meet at the Capulet party, for example, she properly addresses the attractive stranger as "you," whereas the more impetuous Romeo quickly shifts into the more familiar form: "Thus from my lips, by thine, my sin is purg'd [*Kissing her.*]" (1.5.107). Before their next meeting, as Juliet stands at her window meditating on her feelings, she has already adopted the more personal mode: "O Romeo, Romeo, wherefore art thou Romeo?" (2.2.33).

The other circumstance in which "thou" is always appropriate is the direct address to God or to divine powers generally, as when Henry V utters a prayer of thanks on learning of the small number of English dead at the battle of Agincourt: ". . . O God, thy arm was here; / And not to us, but to thy arm alone, / Ascribe we all!" (4.8.106–08). Or, similarly, Edmund's devotion to his own private deity in the second scene of *King Lear:* "Thou, Nature, art my goddess, to thy law / My services are bound" (1.2.1–2). As I have indicated, the numerous subtleties of such uses are no longer understood by most modern English speakers, but a feeling for the major distinctions will immeasurably enrich our responses to the social and personal dynamics of Shakespeare's characters and their dialogue.

All of these examples indicate that the English language available to Shakespeare was undergoing a period of transition from older, medieval forms to the patterns and diction more like those that we use. In fact, this was a period of rapid linguistic expansion, the result of numerous historical events and pressures. The most notable was the widespread use of the printing press — invented on the Continent in the first half of the fifteenth century and first used in England by William Caxton in 1474 — which made written language much more widely available in the sixteenth century than it had been in the fifteenth. Along with, and in great part due to, this mechanical aid came a corresponding increase in the number of readers, as education became more common among young men, particularly those residing in cities and towns. (That literacy was growing increasingly common is indicated by the characters Shakespeare creates: those who cannot read, such as Capulet's servant in the second scene of *Romeo and Juliet,* are treated as comic butts.) In short, more books and more people to read them help to account for the extraordinary number of changes in the English language in the years between 1500 and 1600. And in this dynamic period the language moved from a state that Chaucer would hardly have found strange to one that in many ways resembles our own.

Shakespeare's vocabulary can be a stumbling block, especially for readers. In the theater the speaking actor frequently relies on tone, semantic drive, narrative context, and body language to communicate the sense of utterly unfamiliar terms and phrases, but on the page such words become more noticeable and confusing. Among some scholars at the time, English was thought to be lacking in the expressive possibilities of a rich language such as Latin, and so writers at the end of the sixteenth century regularly invented, borrowed, or altered words to suit their narrative and expository needs. As knowledge increased in both the arts and sciences, so did the apparatus required to communicate that knowledge. The Saxon-Germanic foundations of English vocabulary were supplemented by an immense number of borrowings from Latin, some of them direct appropriations and others indirect derivations through French, a legacy of the Norman invasion led by William the Conqueror in 1066.

Shakespeare's own vocabulary seems to have been exceptionally large — about 29,000 words, nearly twice that of the average American college student — which attests to his acquaintance with a far wider range of specific topics and terms than the modern reader usually commands. Even more troublesome than those terms that we could know if our experience were broad enough are the many words that we probably could not, such as those that have dropped from common use, like "bisson" (blind), or those that the playwright seems to have created from Latin roots (or to have taken up shortly after their invention) but that did not catch on, such as "conspectuities" (eyesight or vision) or "unplausive" (doubtful or disapproving). Especially confusing are those words that have shifted meaning over the intervening centuries, such as "proper" (handsome), "nice" (squeamish or delicate), "silly" (innocent), or "cousin" (kinsman, that is, not necessarily the child of an aunt or uncle). In confronting these changes resulting from the vagaries of linguistic fashion, however, we should also remember that many Shakespearean words familiar to us would have been strange to Shakespeare's audience because they were the products of his invention or unique usage: "assassination," "bump" (in the sense of swelling or protuberance), and "dwindle."

Words and their meanings present fewer difficulties, however, than do the many sentences in which the words seem to be set down in an unfamiliar order. This is because the most significant difference between early modern English and our own is that over the past four centuries we have tended to standardize the positions into which the words are placed. Nowadays, as a rule the subject appears first, then the verb, and then the direct object or complement, with various modifiers and other subordinate elements distributed where they won't get in the way and won't disrupt what is felt to be the logical order. Even in the middle of the sixteenth century, grammarians attacked the convolutions of Latin syntax and called for "natural" phrasing in the composition of English prose (see p. 202). From Thomas Wilson and Francis Bacon in the sixteenth century to George Orwell and E. B. White in the twentieth, prominent advocates for simplicity and clarity have shaped our concept of normal English syntax. Bacon believed that to devote too much attention to style was to neglect the actual object of expression and instead "fall in love with a picture."

But Shakespeare, as an artist, was in the business of creating stage pictures out of poetry and therefore was influenced by considerations more numerous and varied than mere simplicity: iambic pentameter, particular rhythmic effects, a need for emphasis, principles of characterization (young women speak differently from old men, servants from kings), and larger aural questions of pace and variety. Fluidity is the rule in the Shakespearean sentence, and so we encounter an immense number of syntactic possibilities. Direct objects may open the sentence when we would normally expect a subject, as in Hamlet's complaint to his mother: ". . . Sense sure you have, / Else could you not have motion" (3.4.71–72). Prepositional phrases or modifying clauses sometimes intrude in positions that strike us as abnormal or may even violate what we have come to know as rules. At a crucial moment in *Hamlet*, for example, the Ghost speaks a sentence that may reflect Shakespeare's training in Latin but that sounds to our ears like a stunning dangling modifier:

> Sleeping within my orchard,
> My custom always of the afternoon,
> Upon my secure hour thy uncle stole,
> With juice of cursed hebona in a vial,
> And in the porches of my ears did pour
> The leprous distillment.   (1.5.59–64)

In this crucial sentence three introductory phrases delay the arrival of the subject, which (grammatically) should be "I" but is in fact "thy uncle." This error embodies the initial problem of the play: Claudius replaces Old Hamlet. Moreover, in a small but effective way the suspensions that begin the sentence heighten suspense about the identity of the criminal and the means of death. Virtually every scene is enriched by such manipulations of syntax, and as Shakespeare becomes more mature and playful, the variety of his syntactic arrangements increases remarkably. In the early plays, lines tend to be end-stopped, that is, the length of phrases and clauses is governed by, or at least corresponds to, the length of the poetic line.

> Now out of doubt Antipholus is mad,
> Else would he never so demean himself.
> A ring he hath of mine worth forty ducats,
> And for the same he promis'd me a chain:
> Both one and other he denies me now.   (*The Comedy of Errors* 4.3.81–85)

By the end of Shakespeare's career, enjambment is the rule: the tyranny of the poetic line has been vanquished by the claims of the sentence.

> Give me my robe, put on my crown, I have
> Immortal longings in me. Now no more
> The juice of Egypt's grape shall moist this lip.
> Yare, yare, good Iras; quick. Methinks I hear
> Antony call; I see him rouse himself
> To praise my noble act.   (*Antony and Cleopatra* 5.2.280–85)

But we have now moved beyond the conditions of Renaissance discursive models into the realm of style or, as Shakespeare's contemporaries would have known it, rhetoric.

Rhetoric

Apart from such technical problems, Shakespeare's language is puzzling to the modern reader because, generally speaking, the twentieth century takes a very different attitude toward verbal expression than did the sixteenth. Modes of dramatic or poetic speech that appealed to the Renaissance taste for abundance and decoration may strike us as inflated, elaborate, or excessively ornamented. Characters in modern plays seem to speak more "naturally" than their Shakespearean counterparts, but modern forms of theatrical language are no more real than those spoken by the characters in *Hamlet*. Both styles of speech are arranged and artificial; the differences arise from their authors' dependence on different conventions. The practices of sixteenth-century dramatic language were developed and refined by playwrights who were committed to the value of eloquence and thoroughly grounded in the study of rhetoric, for which Richard Reynolds (see p. 204) provides an eloquent statement.

In the 1570s Shakespeare probably attended the King's New School, the local grammar school in Stratford-upon-Avon, where the system of primary education was devoted to the study of Latin. English literature as a separate discipline for study and appreciation did not become a feature of British education until the end of the nineteenth century. In fact, well into the second half of the sixteenth century, many poets and scholars considered the English language an unworthy medium for the production of literature and hardly an appropriate subject for study. Chaucer was acknowledged as the brilliant exception, but Latin was still the preferred language for artistic or philosophical expression. The monarch and court were often entertained with dramatic performances in Latin; many churchmen and scholars objected to the translation of the Bible into the vernacular; the principal models for poetry or drama or even philosophical or historical writing — for any kind of serious discourse, that is — were Roman or Greek, or occasionally their Italian or French derivatives.

Shakespeare and his schoolmates were immersed in Latin grammar and literature, as the grammar-school curriculum described in Chapter 4 attests. Each student would have been required to translate, memorize, recite, and — most relevant for our understanding of Shakespeare's creativity — imitate the works he read. In learning to compose verses and speeches, that is, in the equivalent of present-day composition courses, the young scholars would have written in Latin. The method of double translation designed to increase their proficiency is described in the numerous handbooks for teachers published in the Renaissance by such pedagogues as Roger Ascham and John Brinsley. These pedagogues instruct the master to begin by reading aloud from a poetic passage that the students have never heard before, preferably some verses of Ovid. The pupil translates the passage read aloud from Latin into English, and then reverses the process, rendering the English version back into Latin as near to the original as possible (see Ascham's instructions, p. 205).

By means of such drills, students not only became familiar with the conventional patterns into which words were arranged but also became sensitive to the effects of those arrangements. The Romans themselves had begun the process of analyzing and organizing the stylistic methods of their great writers. In elaborate treatises devoted to the principles of composition, writers such as Cicero and Quintilian identified, explained, and illustrated numerous verbal patterns such as metaphor, apostrophe, paradox, and a multitude of others. Known as figures of speech, schemes, or tropes (verbal "turns"), these forms of expression were associated specifically with particular narrative situations, emotional states, or literary effects. These classical theorists and cataloguers inspired their Renaissance counterparts to produce rhetorical handbooks for those who wished to write in English. George Puttenham's *The Art of English Poesy* and John Hoskyns's *Directions for Speech and Style,* among many other such guides, converted classical examples into their English equivalents and supplied an abundance of native examples (see pp. 209 and 207). The educational system that inculcated these forms of rhetoric was not limited to slavish translation, however. As students advanced, they were eventually given poetic or dramatic situations taken from the classical authors and asked to amplify the episode or invent language appropriate to the scene. And in some cases, notably those of Shakespeare and other brilliant Elizabethans such as Sir Philip Sidney, Edmund Spenser, John Donne, and Ben Jonson, imitation led to creation, reproduction to original artistic production.

The systematized forms of rhetoric inculcated in the classroom and outlined in these handbooks were so familiar to the educated Elizabethan that it was easy for a playwright to get a laugh by simply referring to them. Grumio in *The Taming of the Shrew* predicts that Petruchio will dazzle Katherina with his verbal skills, or "rope-tricks," Grumio's own blunder for rhetorics, or "rhet-tricks": "She may perhaps call him half a score knaves or so. Why, that's nothing; and he begin once, he'll rail in his rope-tricks. I'll tell you what, sir, and she stand him but a little, he will throw a figure in her face, and so disfigure her with it, that she shall have no more eyes to see withal than a cat" (1.2.110–15). The apparently uneducated Grumio may not know "rope-tricks" from "rhet-tricks" or rhetorics, but even he employs a classically sanctioned figure of speech in playing on the words "figure" and "disfigure." Polonius, the old counselor in *Hamlet,* is exceedingly vain about his rhetorical skills, which leads the Queen to complain "More matter with less art." *Love's Labor's Lost,* one of Shakespeare's earliest comedies, vigorously mocks the pedantic rigidity associated with Tudor systems of rhetoric. Many of its jokes escape most of us because the educational system that fostered them no longer exists. (Readers five hundred years from now will probably be similarly puzzled by references in our literature to "grinds," "the thesis paragraph," "physics for poets," and other staples of the American high-school or college experience.) It is vital that we try to appreciate the delight in ornament and pleasure in pattern that characterize Renaissance literature. As C. S. Lewis puts it,

> Rhetoric is the greatest barrier between us and our ancestors. . . . Nearly all our older poetry was written and read by men to whom the distinction between poetry and rhetoric, in its modern form, would have been meaningless. The "beauties" which they chiefly regarded in every composition were those which we either dislike or simply do not notice. This change of taste makes an invisible wall between us and them. (61)

In order to break down this wall, we will do well to think of rhetoric as a species of verbal play. As such, it was an indispensable tool for a Renaissance playwright whose first aim was to amuse his audience.

Wordplay

We cannot hope to recover the automatic acquaintance with most forms of rhetoric that a sixteenth-century playgoer of average education would have had; the names and functions of the many tropes and figures have become the province of specialists. But we must be aware of how meaningful such patterns were to the age that produced Shakespeare, and more important, we must use our knowledge of the existence of those systems to understand the Renaissance delight in language, its taste for copiousness or elaboration, and its pleasure in verbal games. The touchstone for such matters is Shakespeare's — and his culture's — fondness for wordplay.

In act 2, scene 3, of *Much Ado about Nothing*, Beatrice enters seeking Benedick, who has just been tricked into believing that she is in love with him. When she delivers her message, "Against my will I am sent to bid you come in to dinner," and leaves the stage after a moment of additional backchat, Benedick turns to the audience to offer a reading of the invitation: " 'Against my will I am sent to bid you come in to dinner' — there's a double meaning in that." In this case Benedick is mistaken: Beatrice means what she says and no more. But in a larger sense he is right, if we consider that Beatrice has yet to acknowledge her attraction to Benedick and that she has been sent to provoke Benedick by the very pranksters who fooled him. Benedick's triumphant discovery of a double meaning is especially ironic because in almost any other case he would have been correct. Double meanings, the kind found most obviously in puns and other forms of wordplay, pervade Shakespeare's work; and one source of their abundance is that Shakespeare is an eloquent spokesman for his age's perception of the ambivalence of all human experience.

Samuel Johnson reflected an eighteenth-century bias toward the rational and the solemn when he criticized Shakespeare's fondness for the pun, complaining that "a quibble [a pun], poor and barren as it is, gave him such delight, that he was content to purchase it, by the sacrifice of reason, propriety and truth. A quibble was to him the fatal Cleopatra for which he lost the world, and was content to lose it" (qtd. in *The Works of Samuel Johnson* 7:74).

But for most writers of the Renaissance, especially Shakespeare, wordplay carried no such moral charge. Preachers as well as playwrights eagerly embraced its temptations, taking advantage of double meanings in order to amuse their audiences and cultivate an awareness of the delights and the dangers of human speech. The prominence of the pun demonstrates that words, like the human actions they describe, are subject to multiple interpretations.

The most obvious form of wordplay is the homonym, in which a single sound calls forth more than one meaning. Pistol, the cowardly soldier in *Henry V*, resolves to quit the French campaign and return home to a life of crime: "To England will I steal, and there I'll steal" (5.1.87). A similar case is Hamlet's retort to Claudius's complaint that his "son" appears sullen, that "the clouds still hang on" him. The Prince replies, "Not so my lord, I am too much in the sun" (1.2.67). Hamlet is suffering under the light of public scrutiny, unnaturally made to be the son of two fathers, and oppressed by his role as the son of a murdered father. But human speech abounds with many looser forms of the pun, to which the classical rhetoricians gave a variety of names: *paronomasia, agnominatio, antanaclasis, syllepsis.* The anonymous Roman author of the *Rhetorica ad Herennium* defines *paronomasia* as "a figure in which, by means of a modification of sound or change of letters, a close resemblance to a given verb or noun is produced, so that similar words express dissimilar things." A Shakespearean instance of this variation is Falstaff's line to Prince Hal, "were it not here apparent that thou art heir apparent." Modern terms for the pun are more familiar but no less various: a quibble, a *double entendre,* an equivocation, a play on words. A useful way to describe its operation is as an exercise in substitution, a figure in which one meaning displaces another. Alternatively, it may be seen as a competition for dominance among two or more legitimate meanings. In all these cases, the principle in which wordplay is grounded is that the pun exposes differences among similar phenomena, or, conversely, reveals likeness in difference.

Shakespeare's plays exhibit many different kinds of puns — characters employ them consciously and unconsciously, for example — and they serve multiple functions. Wordplay often provides humor when a secondary meaning is released unexpectedly. It may reveal character, as in *Richard III*, when Richard of Gloucester employs double meanings to promote his double-dealings in quest of the English crown. Richard is a witty punster, but his quibbles are often sinister rather than comic. In fact, the automatic association of laughter with the pun is a modern phenomenon, one of the barriers that C. S. Lewis notes between the sensibilities of the sixteenth century and those of the twentieth. For Shakespeare and his contemporaries, wordplay could be a tool for seriously exploring the discrepancy between surface and substance.

The noncomic pun (as well as the humorous one) performs at least two important general functions. First, it supplies the audience with a kind of intellectual pleasure, allowing it to move nimbly back and forth among various meanings of a single term. Baldassare Castiglione comments on the way that such puns "inspire wonder" or admiration rather than humor, as the listener admires the speaker's "ingenuity" and appreciates the "richness" of the speaker's verbal ability (see the excerpt from *The Book of the Courtier* on p. 215). Many of Shakespeare's speakers evoke just this kind of intellectual admiration. In *Romeo and Juliet,* for example, a tragedy loaded with double meanings, comic and serious, a particularly complicated series of puns breaks forth when the Nurse enters with bad news (Tybalt's death) and Juliet fears for Romeo:

> Hath Romeo slain himself? Say thou but *ay,*
> And that bare vowel *I* shall poison more
> Than the death-darting *eye* of cockatrice [mythical monster].
> *I* am not *I,* if there be such an *ay,*
> Or those *eyes* shut, that makes thee answer *ay.*
> If he be slain, say *ay,* or if not, no.
> Brief sounds determine my weal or woe.   (3.2.45–51)

The wordplay here serves numerous functions, some already mentioned: it suggests passionate confusion, of course, and thus reveals character. The passage is also "one of Shakespeare's first attempts to reveal a profound disturbance of mind by the use of quibbles" (Mahood 70). But more than this it exercises the listener's intelligence, creating new senses out of a single syllable and leading the listener repeatedly to adjust and reinterpret the aural world. This pleasure is analogous to the larger intellectual and emotional exercise that the play as a whole promotes, as it pushes the audience back and forth between the interpretive poles of hope and judgment, sympathy and despair.

The other primary function of the pun is to open a window onto the main ideas of a play, capturing in individual words the conflicts and complex meanings of its characters' experience. In *Henry IV, Part 1,* for example, Falstaff's incessant punning establishes a contest among more and less legitimate meanings of the same sound, just as the play itself dramatizes a contest for the crown, a struggle that arises from Bullingbrook's doubtful legitimacy. At the battle of Shrewsbury that ends the play, the disguised kings sent onto the battlefield to confuse the enemy function as visual puns: they look alike, indeed they all look like King Henry, but they don't mean the same thing. So it is with double meanings in those comedies based on the confusion of twins, *The Comedy of Errors* and *Twelfth Night.* In Viola and Sebastian, an identical outward appearance conceals two very different persons, just as a homonym permits two distinct meanings. By exploiting such confusing resemblances, Shakespeare stimulates his audience's sense of the richness of the world and reveals the perils of drawing premature and certain conclusions about almost anything.

The impact of the serious pun is especially apparent in *Macbeth.* It is not merely that the text is rife with wordplay, although it is: gild/guilt, surcease/success, success (as in *victory/that which follows*), peerless (as in *unparalleled/alone*), consequence (as in *what follows/importance*), done (as in *performed/finished*), and done/Duncan (done-kin)/Dunsinane/Donalbain/ "dunnest smoke of hell." Equally significant is that the action of the play depends on the trickiness of words. Having placed his faith in the witches' prophecies, Macbeth finds that he has erroneously believed "th' equivocation of the fiend / That lies like truth" (5.5.42–43). He is vanquished, finally, by a pun. "None of woman born / Shall harm Macbeth," say the witches, and so he thinks himself immune. But Macduff, his conqueror, was "untimely ripped" from his mother's womb, delivered in Caesarean fashion. Ambiguity can be deadly: "Double, double, toil and trouble."

The Forms of Dramatic Language

If the intervening centuries have altered our attitude toward wordplay, they have also changed the conventions of dramatic speech: characters in modern plays rarely speak in verse. Thus a brief survey of Shakespearean forms of speech will yield a common set of terms so that we may proceed to notice how the forms of language function. These patterns divide, to begin with, into two: prose and poetry. Further subdivisions may be made, particularly in Shakespeare's poetry, but the dominant form is unrhymed iambic pentameter, or blank verse. I shall give considerable attention to the kinds of Shakespearean poetry, including blank verse, but for the sake of convenience I begin with prose.

The easiest definition of prose is that it is everything that isn't poetry — the newspaper, political orations, psychology textbooks, this chapter you are reading now. The problem with such a definition is that it requires you to know what poetry is so that prose can be distinguished from it. At this point the easiest maneuver is to examine the physical appearance of the lines as they are printed in the book: in so doing we can usually tell the difference between poetry and prose because prose goes all the way to the end of the page, whereas poetry doesn't. This distinction works a little better, although there are still gray areas where it can be hard to differentiate. English prose, our ordinary language, often arranges itself into rhythmic patterns, and sometimes these can become so regular that the sounds of the prose resemble the rhythms of poetry. Some public speakers, the occasional Southern senator or preachers in some African American churches, can develop their prose utterances into an elaborately patterned and highly musical performance. Although the concentration and intensity of poetic language give it an affective power not found in most prose, a good speaker can make prose utterances as potent as poetry. One of the most memorable passages in *Hamlet* is the Prince's eloquent "What a piece of work is a man" (2.2.303–08). Unlike the play's verse soliloquies, this speech depends not on the poetic alternation of syllables but instead draws its rhythmic power from patterns of verbal repetition. Some of Shakespeare's prose is extremely poetic, and some of his poetry is decidedly prosaic. Even experts disagree on whether to print certain passages as poetry or prose. But usually we can distinguish between the two, and as will become clear, it matters that we do so.

In *A Midsummer Night's Dream* a group of workers — "rude mechanicals," as they are called by one of the fairies — prepares a play to be performed at the

wedding celebration of Duke Theseus and his bride, Hippolyta. These ama-
teur actors, as they cast and begin to rehearse their play — which is itself written in an old-fashioned, singsong style of poetry — speak in prose, as when
Bottom the weaver proposes a solution to the problem of frightening the
ladies in the audience with a lion on stage: "Nay; you must name his name, and
half his face must be seen through the lion's neck, and he himself must speak
through, saying thus, or to the same defect: 'Ladies,' or 'Fair ladies, I would
wish you,' or 'I would request you,' or 'I would entreat you, not to fear, not to
tremble' " (3.1.36–41).

It used to be said, with some regularity, that Shakespeare used prose mainly
to establish social class. This is undeniably one of its functions in the opening
scene of *Julius Caesar*, where the laborers have taken to the streets of Rome on
a holiday, and in the mechanicals' scenes of *A Midsummer Night's Dream*. Bottom and company speak in prose, the least formal and least "elevated" kind of
dramatic speech available, not only because they are the lowest members of society depicted in the play, but also because they function as "clowns." In other
words, the identification of prose with the lower social and economic classes
inadequately represents the variety of Shakespeare's practice. Among the aristocracy prose may also indicate informality, as when Theseus and the young
lovers comment to each other, in prose, on the progress of the mechanicals'
performance. High-born characters often speak in prose: over half of *As You
Like It* is written in prose, and Rosalind, the banished Duke's daughter, is one
of its most gifted speakers. Prose is especially arresting when it marks a departure from the usual form of blank verse. In the first encounter between
Olivia and the disguised Viola in *Twelfth Night* (1.5), for example, Shakespeare
signifies Olivia's growing infatuation with Viola/Cesario by causing her to
shift from the casual prose she has been using to the verse that the attractive
young page speaks. Thus one of the most important characteristics of prose is
that it is not poetry.

In the tragedies particularly, prose can measure a collapse of some kind, as
when a character who has spoken grand and controlled verse is reduced to disordered prose. In the fourth act of *Othello*, the hero exhibits just such a change
of register when he falls under the spell of Iago's insinuations about his wife's
faithlessness.

> OTHELLO: What hath he said?
> IAGO: Faith, that he did — I know not what he did.
> OTHELLO: What? what?
> IAGO: Lie —
> OTHELLO: With her?
> IAGO: With her? On her; what you will.
> OTHELLO: Lie with her? lie on her? We say lie on her, when they belie her. Lie
> with her! 'Zounds, that's fulsome! Handkerchief —confessions — handker-
> chief! To confess, and be hang'd for his labor —first to be hang'd, and then
> to confess. I tremble at it.   (4.1.31–39)

Even such a short passage as this one displays not only the sudden shift from
verse to prose — the three utterances preceding Othello's long speech make

up one complete line of iambic pentameter — but also the disintegration of logical structure within a prose passage, as Othello moves toward incomprehensibility. Such a strategic deployment of prose attests to Shakespeare's acute ear for dramatic variety. Early in his career he recognizes and takes advantage of the tonal effects produced by an alternation between two forms of speech. Even though an audience may not immediately or consciously register the distinction between a speech in prose and a speech in poetry, it is subconsciously affected by their relative degrees of structure, and such aural differences help to establish and maintain a mood or tone that supports the dramatist's larger purpose.

Early in his career Shakespeare rarely wrote in prose. *Richard III*, for example, an early play of some thirty-five hundred lines, contains only about fifty lines of prose, or less than 2 percent. *Hamlet*, on the other hand, a play of slightly greater length and of similar gravity, but written in the middle of his career, contains about nine hundred lines of prose, or almost 30 percent. (See the chart on p. 218.) This difference indicates that as he developed artistically and increased his command of his dramatic tools, Shakespeare became considerably more flexible. About five years after *Richard III*, in *Henry IV, Part 1*, Shakespeare exploited with great subtlety the different effects obtainable from poetry and prose. Prose is the language of the everyday, the standard form of speech in the tavern at Eastcheap. The most gifted speaker of prose in this play is Sir John Falstaff, whose influence over the young prince — a dubious influence in the opinion of the court — is signaled most obviously in the way Prince Hal mimics the old rascal's linguistic forms. Throughout the first half of the play, except for the one verse soliloquy declaring his intention to surrender the pleasures of Eastcheap, spoken at the end of act 1, scene 2 ("I know you all"), the Prince speaks only prose in the tavern or in the company of Falstaff and his drinking companions; at the end of act 3, however, in Eastcheap and in the presence of the ne'er-do-wells he has hitherto addressed only in prose, the Prince shifts into verse. (It is worth noting that at this point Falstaff also adopts verse, parodying the Prince's new style.) Hal's commitment to the more formal voice audibly establishes his assumption of royal responsibility; when he "throw[s] off" the "loose behavior" of the first three acts, he also throws off the loose and informal patterns of prose. And members of an oral culture like Shakespeare's would probably have been more sensitive than we are to such a change.

The patterns of poetry on which Shakespeare depends vary from the rigorously structured to the flexibly organized, but the single feature that they all have in common, the quality that distinguishes poetry from prose, is music. One source of this poetic music is rhyme — and I speak here primarily of end rhyme, the repetition of sounds, a combination of vowels and consonants, at the end of two verse lines. Shakespeare does not employ an abundance of rhymed verse, although he does so from time to time, especially at the beginning of his career. As he matures poetically, he relies on rhyme to create certain specific effects: perhaps to heighten the emotional effect of a passage, occasionally to poke fun at the speaker, and most often to close off a scene, to indicate with a rhymed couplet that the episode is over. Helena, Lysander, and Hermia speak rhymed verse in the first act of *A Midsummer Night's Dream;* the following is an excerpt from Helena's first soliloquy:

> How happy some o'er other some can be!
> Through Athens I am thought as fair as she.
> But what of that? Demetrius thinks not so;
> He will not know what all but he do know;
> And as he errs, doting on Hermia's eyes,
> So I, admiring of his qualities.
> Things base and vile, holding no quantity,
> Love can transpose to form and dignity.   (1.1.226–33)

Rhyme enhances the music already created by the rhythm of the passage, but its singsong effect also introduces a delicately critical comment on the baffled Helena's perception of her misery. This excerpt exposes a feature of Renaissance language often puzzling to modern ears, that pronunciation was apparently as unfixed as syntax: here "eyes" rhymes with "qualities," although we cannot be sure whether "eyes" is pronounced *ees*, whether "qualities" concludes with a long *i* sound, or whether the sound might have been something in between. The resort to rhyme often pays ironic benefits, even in the tragedies: the tidy closure of Hamlet's second soliloquy, ". . . the play's the thing, / Wherein I'll catch the conscience of the King," seems so self-assured and definitive as to undercut and cast doubt on the prince's sudden confidence.

In the soliloquy just quoted, Helena speaks rhymed iambic pentameter, but other kinds of rhymed poetry often arrest the ear. Consider Oberon's chant as he applies a magic lotion to Titania's eyes:

> What thou seest when thou dost wake,
> Do it for thy true-love take;
> Love and languish for his sake.
> Be it ounce [lynx], or cat, or bear,
> Pard [leopard], or boar with bristled hair,
> In thy eye that shall appear
> When thou wak'st, it is thy dear:
> Wake when some vile thing is near.   (2.2.27–34)

This is tetrameter, lines with four beats, and the effect of combining such short lines and end rhymes sounds simple but is in fact complex. The combination creates something like an incantation (Oberon is, after all, casting a spell on Titania) and thus implies a magical mood; but violating as it does the five-beat pattern established in Oberon's normal pentameters, these short verse lines can be heard as jaunty or even humorous music for what is arguably one of the cruelest actions in the play.

The use of rhymed poetry decreases as Shakespeare matures artistically. *A Midsummer Night's Dream* is exceptional in that 45 percent of its lines are written in rhymed verse, a higher percentage than for any other play in the canon. We may attribute this to at least two probable causes: first, to the unreal, artificial, dreamlike quality for which Shakespeare is striving, and second, to the fact that one of the main subjects of *A Midsummer Night's Dream* is poetry itself — verse as a product of the imagination. Therefore, Shakespeare fits his method to his meaning.

The primary means by which Shakespeare creates musical effects is not rhyme but rhythm, the ordered repetition of syllables in verse lines. And by far the most significant poetic structure he employs is poetry that does not rhyme, more specifically, unrhymed iambic pentameter, or blank verse. The blank verse line is decasyllabic, composed of ten syllables; put another way, there are five iambic units per line. An iamb is simply a unit of sound with two beats, the first unstressed and the second stressed: da-DA. Multiply that by five and you have a line of iambic pentameter, or *penta*-meter. But what is the value of devoting time to identifying kinds of verse and differentiating iambic pentameter from trochaic trimeter? Actors do not deliver the lines in this exaggerated fashion; if they did, the result would be ludicrous and the audience would be heading for the exits. So how does it help to know about this kind of verse? And when we do know about it, what have we got? In the first place, the naming of parts is an instructive exercise. To know the components of a machine is to come closer to an understanding of how it works. Next, not to be too mystical about it, the rhythms of the verse affect us even though we may not be conscious of their effect. The five units of iambic pentameter give the line a basic structure, much like the time signature of a piece of music. We may not know that *Stars and Stripes Forever* is in four/four time, but if it were not played that way we would certainly hear the difference.

According to Sir Philip Sidney in *The Defense of Poesy* — and linguists have confirmed the perception — blank verse is particularly well suited to the natural rhythms of English speech, and so it serves as a useful medium for Shakespeare's drama. It was relatively new when Shakespeare took it up. Although the rhymed ten-syllable line had been the primary English poetic form since Chaucer's time, the earl of Surrey created blank verse when he gave up rhyme for his translations from Virgil's *Aeneid* (c. 1540), and indeed Shakespeare's appropriation of it accounts in large part for the dominance of blank verse during the last three hundred and fifty years of English poetry. Most of Shakespeare's most memorable poetic creations — "To be or not to be," "Tomorrow and tomorrow and tomorrow," "The quality of mercy is not strained," "Now is the winter of our discontent" — draw their power from the poet's skillful manipulation of the pentameter line.

Here is Titania, speaking in blank verse, when she refuses to surrender the Indian boy to Oberon:

> The fairy land buys not the child of me.
> His mother was a vot'ress of my order,
> And in the spiced Indian air, by night,
> Full often hath she gossip'd by my side,
> And sat with me on Neptune's yellow sands,
> Marking th'embarked traders on the flood;
> When we have laugh'd to see the sails conceive
> And grow big-bellied with the wanton wind;

Which she, with pretty and with swimming gait,
Following (her womb then rich with my young squire)
Would imitate, and sail upon the land
To fetch me trifles, and return again,
As from a voyage, rich with merchandise.
But she, being mortal, of that boy did die,
And for her sake do I rear up her boy;
And for her sake I will not part with him.   (2.1.122–37)

Although the listener does not hear "The FAIR-y LAND buys NOT the CHILD of ME," the five-beat structure works on the ear nonetheless. The smooth musicality of the meter, the regular repetition of unstressed and stressed sounds, combines with other forms of repetition (words, phrases, consonants, and vowels) to create a mood of intense emotion, even awe. The lyrical regularity of the iambic pattern entrances the listener into sympathy with the speaker, and as the speech draws to its close, Shakespeare intensifies that sense of enchantment by an even more subtle manipulation of the rhythm. The multisyllabic words that have been integrated into the poetic line ("imitate," "merchandise") are abandoned in the last two lines in favor of monosyllables that reinforce the incantatory tone. Everywhere in the canon such subtle variations help to shape the mood and meaning of a speaker's words.

Such bending or breaking of the iambic pattern is a crucial Shakespearean poetic strategy. Depending on the requirements of the speech or character or situation, iambic pentameter may be fiercely regular or it may be scarcely regular at all. And irregularity can make a huge dramatic difference. Consider this single line from *Julius Caesar,* one of the most famous lines in all of Shakespeare: "Friends, Romans, countrymen, lend me your ears!" If the line were entirely regular, we would hear it as

   Friends, Rŏmăns, cóuntrў̆mén, leńd mĕ yŏur eárs!

But it is irregular. Antony begins with a stressed syllable, overturning the established iambic pattern just at the moment that he takes control of the political events in the play. But he does not merely reverse the stress of the normal iamb. Instead, he follows that initial stress ("Friends") with another stress ("Ro-") that then restores the regular pattern of unstressed-stressed (da-DA). The reestablished pattern is quickly broken again by the force of the imperative "lend," part of an inversion ("lend me") inserted into the middle of the line. In scanning it, therefore, we hear it as follows:

   Friéhds, Rómăns, cóuntrў̆mén, leńd mĕ yŏur eárs!

Other patterns are audible as well. For example, the line accelerates: it begins with a monosyllable and then stops, continues with a word of two syllables and then stops, proceeds with a noun of three syllables (all of these nouns being similar to one another in meaning) and then stops, and finally provides the listener with the momentary release of "lend me your ears," a phrase of four words to complete the pattern of increasing syllables. The iambic pattern is retained, but only barely, and with competing patterns grafted onto it. A struggle between the rhythmic form of the verse and the semantic claims of the sentence creates an aural tension within the line, and this is a struggle for authority not unlike the competition for power occurring at this moment between Brutus and Antony. Such variation of the blank verse pattern to make meaning occurs everywhere in Shakespeare — in Hamlet's self-lacerations ("O, what a rogue and peasant slave am I!"); in Richard III's furious confrontation with a realm he seeks to master ("And I — like one lost in a thorny wood, / That rents the thorns, and is rent with the thorns"); in Cleopatra's suicide speech ("Give me my robe, put on my crown"). The more alert we are to such aural effects, the better we understand Shakespeare's talent.

A Midsummer Night's Dream offers an excellent opportunity for judging the variety and sophistication of Shakespeare's dramatic poetry because the playwright has built into the dramatic structure a foiling device, an example of bad poetry. The play-within-the-play, the Pyramus and Thisbe episode, sets off and calls attention to the excellence and beauty of his own creation; this is one of the early and simple instances in which Shakespeare attempts such a contrast. Moreover, this bad poetry is funny. The play-within-the-play mocks the style of drama that Shakespeare must have seen in his youth and that was still popular with certain audiences even during the years when *Twelfth Night* and *Hamlet* were being written. Most especially it mocks the bald and primitive style of verse that some of Shakespeare's predecessors composed. This is Pyramus's discovery of Thisbe's bloody mantle:

> But stay! O spite!
> But mark, poor knight,
> What dreadful dole is here!
> Eyes, do you see?
> How can it be?
> O dainty duck! O dear!
> Thy mantle good,
> What! stain'd with blood?
> Approach, ye Furies fell!
> O Fates, come, come,
> Cut thread and thrum,
> Quail, crush, conclude, and quell! (5.1.276–87)

This doggerel is not too far removed from the following passage from Thomas Preston's *Cambyses*, written in the form known as *fourteeners* (referring to the number of syllables per line) about twenty-five years before *A Midsummer Night's Dream*. This is the king's death speech:

> Who but I in such a wise his deaths wound could have got?
> As I on horse back up did leap, my sword from scabbard shot,
> And ran me thus into the side, as you right well may see —
> A marvels chance unfortunate that in this wise should be!
> I feel myself a dying now, of life bereft am I,
> And Death hath caught me with his dart, for want of blood I spy.
> Thus gasping heer on ground I lye; for nothing I doe care;
> A just reward for my misdeeds my death doth plaine declare.

This comparison is pertinent because Shakespeare seems to have had *Cambyses* in mind as he composed his comedy. Preston's play is titled *A Lamentable Tragedy, Mixed Full of Pleasant Mirth, Containing the Life of Cambyses, King of Persia*, which may be a source of the description of the Pyramus and Thisbe play as "tragical mirth."

A still more instructive poetic comparison emerges when we juxtapose the verse Bottom speaks as the dying Pyramus with a passage that Oberon delivers to Puck in act 2:

> Thou rememb'rest
> Since once I sat upon a promontory,
> And heard a mermaid on a dolphin's back
> Uttering such dulcet and harmonious breath
> That the rude sea grew civil at her song,
> And certain stars shot madly from their spheres,
> To hear the sea-maid's music? (2.1.148–54)

Some of the most prominent features of Bottom's doggerel are present, especially internal rhyme and insistent alliteration, but their effect here is very different. Bottom's short lines make the rhyme come so rapidly that its effect is comic rather than magical or tragic; Oberon's unrhymed pentameters are spacious and majestic. The figurative language in Oberon's remembrance is specific and palpable; in Bottom's lament it is trite. Most listeners will immediately recognize that Oberon's verse is fresh and powerful, whereas Bottom's is ludicrous. Having sensed the differences, we should make it our business to learn how to articulate them.

Language as Theme

These several verbal forms and patterns serve as tools, affective instruments designed to move the audience, to give pleasure, to engage, to amuse, to excite. Having established what these tools are, we must forget them, temporarily at least, and begin to consider how they work. Shakespeare's early plays give us an unusually candid look at how he causes these instruments to function. Around 1592 or 1593, Shakespeare seems to have experienced an epiphany, discovering more or less suddenly the almost limitless power of language. Our knowledge of dates is sketchy here, but we can still make a reasonable guess about which plays came at this time, and in works such as *Love's Labor's Lost* and *Richard III* particularly, we observe a sudden explosion of rhetorical ability, a sense of exuberance, of power at what words can do. The astonishing language of these plays has something of *The Sorcerer's Apprentice* about it, as if a young magician had suddenly come upon the secret of his magical powers and had begun to see how far he could push them. Moreover, it is at this same time that Shakespeare begins to explore the implications of the word *play*. He begins to think seriously about the dramatic text as a representation of reality: as he explores the relationship between life and the stage, between the world and the word, the idea of the theater becomes a major theme in his work. Shakespeare the dramatist begins playfully to examine the implications of his play, and Shakespeare the poet asks the same questions of language. Probably the most fruitful text for studying this topic is *Richard III.*

Usurper, hunchback, infanticidal psychopath — Richard is also a master of language. We are both repelled and attracted by him, complementary responses that he provokes chiefly on the basis of what he says. In his case at least, words speak louder than actions. At no point in the text is he shown killing anyone; others carry out his mischief for him, and they do so because Richard tells them or asks them or promises them something to do it. Richard gets what he wants with words, and his gift for language is almost unparalleled, as the very first lines of the play attest. Shakespeare's introduction of his heroic villain is characteristically original. The playwright is faithful to the demands of Tudor politics: because Richard was ultimately defeated at Bosworth by the earl of Richmond, who became Henry VII and grandfather of Shakespeare's queen, Elizabeth I, the Tudor dynasty had an investment in demonizing Richard. Shakespeare does not attempt to mitigate or to disguise Richard's wickedness. But, predictably, he does the unpredictable: he makes his villain a wit, a jokester, an actor. And Richard is such a memorable villain because his words are unforgettable.

Here is Richard III's notorious opening soliloquy:

Now is the winter of our discontent
Made glorious summer by this son of York;
And all the clouds that low'r'd upon our house
In the deep bosom of the ocean buried.
Now are our brows bound with victorious wreaths,
Our bruised arms hung up for monuments,
Our stern alarums chang'd to merry meetings,
Our dreadful marches to delightful measures.
Grim-visag'd War hath smooth'd his wrinkled front,
And now, in stead of mounting barbed steeds
To fright the souls of fearful adversaries,
He capers nimbly in a lady's chamber
To the lascivious pleasing of a lute.
But I, that am not shap'd for sportive tricks,
Nor made to court an amorous looking-glass;
I, that am rudely stamp'd, and want love's majesty
To strut before a wanton ambling nymph;
I, that am curtail'd of this fair proportion,
Cheated of feature by dissembling nature,
Deform'd, unfinish'd, sent before my time
Into this breathing world, scarce half made up,
And that so lamely and unfashionable
That dogs bark at me as I halt by them —
Why, I, in this weak piping time of peace,
Have no delight to pass away the time,
Unless to see my shadow in the sun

And descant on mine own deformity.
And therefore, since I cannot prove a lover
To entertain these fair well-spoken days,
I am determined to prove a villain
And hate the idle pleasures of these days.   (1.1.1–31)

The rhetorical fireworks in this passage are calculated to win the audience over to Richard, to exhibit his self-conscious wit, his pleasure in patterns, and his taste for performance. The speech begins with sweeping contrasts: war becomes peace, clouds are swept away by sunshine, chaos is converted into order, Lancaster yields to York, winter becomes summer. Each of the first two pairs of lines expresses one of these antitheses, and then Shakespeare begins to compress, shifting back and forth between war and peace within the same line. But all these oppositions merely serve as prologue to the larger contrast that informs the speech (and indeed the play as a whole), the conflict between Richard and everyone else. The soliloquy is typical of Richard's language because it illustrates the audacity and pride with which he aims his eloquence at his adversaries. He shows off his verbal ingenuity to the audience in the first scene; in the second scene he tells Lady Anne that he has killed her husband and her father-in-law, and then he woos her in marriage anyway; when the young prince of York asks for Richard's dagger the villainous uncle replies "with all my heart"; and Richard informs Queen Elizabeth that he intends to marry her daughter (his niece) and make her his queen. Most of the principal conflicts in *Richard III* are dramatized in rhetorical terms. And, forced to take sides, we choose Richard, at least at first. He talks us into it.

One way he does so is with beguiling sounds and images. His first line contains a metaphor ("winter of our discontent"), his second a pun ("son of York"), his third a quadruple internal rhyme ("clouds ... low'r'd ... our house"), and so we might proceed throughout the speech, noting particularly Richard's enthusiasm for seductive sounds. We hear the insistent repetition of consonants, "Unless to see my shadow in the sun" (alliteration, with assonance); the repetition of vowels, "Now are our brows bound" (assonance, with alliteration); the repetition of a word at the beginning of successive lines (anaphora); rhythmically and semantically balanced phrases, "dreadful marches to delightful measures" (isocolon); and other showy aural effects. This passion for patterns, for elaborate rhetorical arrangements, is shared with Richard by other characters in the play, notably his three main female adversaries, Lady Anne, old Queen Margaret, and Queen Elizabeth, and makes itself felt in virtually every scene. The point, of course, is that the great enthusiast for rhetoric is Shakespeare. The young playwright, like each of his characters, seeks to hold audiences by the skillful manipulation of words.

In suggesting that Richard is a kind of actor, we should remember that the Greek word for actor is *hypokrites*, our "hypocrite," one who pretends to be what one is not. We might also say that Richard is a kind of playwright, an artist, with a plot to gain the Crown, a script written to put himself on the throne, and a sensibility that causes him to think in theatrical terms: "Plots have I laid, inductions dangerous" (1.1.33). We might even see Richard as something of a critic, offering rave reviews of his own performance, as when he turns to the audience immediately after Lady Anne has yielded to him: "Was ever woman in this humor woo'd? / Was ever woman in this humor won?" (1.2.27–28).

The point of these metaphors, of course, is that Shakespeare depicts Richard as a creature of prodigious — if perverted — imagination, and in this respect Richard's most important descendant is Iago in *Othello*. In seeking, for whatever complicated set of reasons, to destroy his friend and superior officer, Iago imagines a scenario in which Othello will play the role of the wronged husband and brutally punish his faithful wife. It is Iago's talent for language and fiction — or lies — that permits him to realize those imagined circumstances. Iago takes the same attitude toward words that he takes toward other people: they are merely instruments, vehicles that he uses on the road to vengeance. An audience's moral revulsion at Iago's plot is overpowered, at least occasionally, by its admiration for his wicked creativity and his skillful use of words. And yet for all the linguistic verve and imaginative talent of a Richard or an Iago, these gifted speakers are finally guilty of betraying the word, of using language dishonestly. In Shakespeare's book this is a very serious offense. Words are the medium of the imagination, and the imagination is Shakespeare's means of livelihood. The perils of imagination as registered by the perversion of language is one of Shakespeare's abiding themes.

But the complement is also true. Creatively arranged words repeatedly bear witness to the positive uses of the imagination. In *Much Ado about Nothing,* the witty lies that Don Pedro and friends invent for tricking Beatrice and Benedick into falling in love with each other exhibit the benefits of imaginative invention. Similarly, in many of the other comedies, the disguises adopted by the heroines — Rosalind in *As You Like It,* Viola in *Twelfth Night* — serve as visual emblems of a verbal performance that leads to marriage and harmony. The great tragedies also are often said to be studies in the duality of language. Macbeth, as I have indicated, is finally betrayed by a kind of pun when he mistakenly interprets the witches' prophecies about his being vulnerable only to one "not born of woman." And yet the same play insists that if words can destroy, they can also enrich. Macbeth delivers some of the most stirring and memorable speeches in all of literature. Iago's lies and plots are illusions that demonstrate the deadly power of words; and yet those lies and illusions make up the dramatic fiction of *Othello* that — as a theatrical creation — demonstrates the opposite, the positive and living power of language. Language — its beauties, its power, its inadequacies, its dangers, its pleasures — is never far from the center of Shakespeare's thinking. Paradoxically for modern readers, as soon as we become comfortable enough with the technical properties of Shakespeare's language to forget them, to concentrate on what the playwright is talking about, we find that much of the time he is talking about language itself, and we are never allowed to forget it.

➔ THOMAS WILSON

From *The Art of Rhetoric*   *1553*
Of Composition

Thomas Wilson (1525?–1581) was one of the many humanist educators who sought to apply the rhetorical principles of classical oratory to the writing of English. In this section of *The Art of Rhetoric,* he considers the appropriate ways of "composing," or putting words together in proper order (from the Latin *com,* "with," and *pos,* "put"). Note particularly Wilson's simile designed to suggest that, in the sentence as in society, man should naturally come before woman.

When we have learned usual and accustomable words to set forth our meaning, we ought to join them together in apt order, that the ear may delight in hearing the harmony. I know some Englishmen that in this point have such a gift in the English as few in Latin have the like, and therefore delight the wise and learned so much with their pleasant composition, that many rejoice when they may hear such, and think much learning is got when they may talk with them. Composition, therefore, is an apt joining together of words in such order that neither the ear shall espy [observe] any jar, nor yet any man shall be dulled with overlong drawing out of a sentence, nor yet much confounded with mingling of clauses, such as are needless, being heaped together without reason and used without number. For by such means the hearers will be forced to forget full oft what was said first, before the sentence be half ended, or else be blinded with confounding of many things together.

Some again will be so short, and in such wise curtail their sentences, that they had need to make a commentary immediately of their meaning, or else the most that hear them shall be forced to keep counsel.

Some will speak oracles that a man cannot tell which way to take them; some will be so fine and so poetical withal, that to their seeming there shall not stand one hair amiss, and yet everybody else shall think them meeter [more appropriate] for a lady's chamber than for an earnest matter in any open assembly.

Some will rove so much, and babble so far without order, that a man would think they had a great love to hear themselves speak.

Some repeat one word so often that if such words could be eaten and chopped in so oft as they are uttered out, they would choke the widest throat in all England. As thus: "If a man knew what a man's life were, no man for any man's sake would kill any man, but one man would rather help another man, considering man is born for man to help man and not to hate man." What man would not be choked, if he chopped all these men at once into his mouth and never drunk after it? Some use overmuch repetition of some one letter, as "Pitiful poverty prayeth for a penny, but puffed presumption passeth not a point, pampering his paunch with pestilent pleasure, procuring his passport to post it to hell-pit, there to be punished with pains perpetual." Some will so set their words that they must be fain to gape after every word spoken, ending one word with a vowel and beginning the next with another, which undoubtedly maketh the talk to some most unpleasant. As thus: "Equity assuredly every injury avoideth."

Some will set the cart before the horse, as thus: "My mother and my father are both at home," even as though the goodman of the house did wear no breeches, or that the gray mare were the better horse. And what though it often so happeneth (God wot [knows] the more pity), yet in speaking at the least let us keep a natural order and set the man before the woman for manners' sake. Another coming home in haste after a long journey saith to his man: "Come hither, sir knave, help me off with my boots and my spurs." I pray you, sir, give him leave first to pluck off your spurs ere he meddle with your boots, or else your man is like to have a mad plucking. Who is so foolish as to say the "council and the king," but rather the "king and his council," the "father and the son," and not contrary. And so likewise in all others, as they are in degree first, evermore to set them foremost. The wise, therefore, talking of divers [several] worthy men together, will first name the worthiest and keep a decent order in reporting of their tale.

Some end their sentences all alike, making their talk rather to appear rhymed meter than to seem plain speech, the which as it much delighteth being measurably used, so it much offendeth when no mean is regarded. I heard a preacher delighting much in this kind of composition, who used so often to end his sentence with words like unto that which went before, that in my judgment there was not a dozen sentences in his whole sermon but they ended all in rhyme for the most part. Some not best disposed wished the preacher a lute, that with his rhymed sermon he might use some pleasant melody, and so the people might take pleasure divers ways and dance if they list [like]. Certes [Surely] there is a mean, and no reason to use any one thing at all times, seeing nothing delighteth — be it never so good — that is always used.

Quintilian [Roman rhetorician] likeneth the colors of rhetoric to a man's eyesight. "And now," quoth he, "I would not have all the body to be full of eyes, or nothing but eyes, for then the other parts should want their due place and proportion." Some overthwartly [perversely] set their words, placing some one a mile from his fellows, not contented with a plain and easy composition, but seek to set words they cannot tell how; and therefore one not liking to be called, and by print published, "Doctor of Physic," would needs be named of "Physic Doctor," wherein appeared a wonderful composition (as he thought), strange undoubtedly, but whether wise or no, let the learned sit in judgment upon that matter. Another. "As I rose in the morning," quoth one, "I met a cart full of stones empty." Belike the man was fasting when the cart was full, and yet we see that through strange composition this sentence appeareth dark.

Some will tell one thing twenty times, now in, now out, and when a man would think they had almost ended, they are ready to begin again as fresh as ever they were. Such vain repetitions declare both want of wit and lack of learning. Some are so homely in all their doings, and so gross for their invention, that they use altogether one manner of trade and seek no variety to eschew tediousness.

Some burden their talk with needless copy [*copia,* too many words] and will seem plentiful when they should be short. Another is so curious and so fine of his tongue that he cannot tell in all the world what to speak. Every sentence seemeth common, and every word generally used is thought to be foolish in his wise judgment. Some use so many interpositions both in their talk and in their writing, that they make their sayings as dark as hell.

Thus when faults be known, they may be avoided, and virtue the sooner may take place, when vice is foreseen and eschewed as evil.

➔ RICHARD REYNOLDS

From *The Foundation of Rhetoric* 1563

Another of the humanist educators devoted to the adaptation of classical techniques for sixteenth-century use, Reynolds is here especially interested in the historical importance of eloquence, or the art of speaking well, which the study of rhetoric is designed to promote.

These two singular gifts of nature [Logic and Rhetoric] are absolute and perfect in few [people]: for many there be, which are exquisite and profound in argument, by art to reason and discuss of any question or proposition propounded, who by nature are disabled and smally adorned to speak eloquently, in whom nevertheless more abundant knowledge doth sometimes remain than in the other, if the cause shall be in controversy joined, and examined to try a manifest truth. But to whom nature hath given such ability, and absolute excellency, as that they can both copiously dilate any matter or sentence, by pleasantness and sweetness of their witty and ingenious oration to draw unto them the hearts of a multitude, to pluck down and extirpate affections and perturbations of people, to move pity and compassion, to speak before princes and rulers and to persuade them in good causes and enterprises, to animate and incense them to Godly affairs and business, to alter the counsel of kings, by their wisdom and eloquence, to a better state, and also to be exquisite in the other, is a thing of all most noble and excellent. The eloquence of Demosthenes, Isocrates, Tisias, Gorgias, Eschines, were a great bulwark and stay to Athens and all Greece. Rome also by the like virtue of eloquence, in famous and wise orators [was] upheld: the wise and eloquent orations of Tully against Catiline, the grave and sententious orations of Cato in the Senate, have been only the mean [the only means] to uphold the mighty state of

Rome in his [its] strength and ancient fame and glory. Also the chronicles of ancient time do show unto us, the state of Rome could by no means have grown so marvelous mighty, but that God had indued the whole line of Caesars with singular virtues, with abundant knowledge and singular eloquence.

→ ROGER ASCHAM

From *The Schoolmaster*   1570

Scholar of Latin and Greek and tutor to Queen Elizabeth, Roger Ascham (1515–1568) was one of the most learned men of his day. His posthumously published *Schoolmaster* is designed to instruct the teacher in educating students effectively. The excerpt printed here offers advice on the proper means of teaching Latin, particularly the system of double translation from Latin into English and then back into Latin.

After the child hath learned perfectly the eight parts of speech, let him then learn the right joining together of substantives [words or phrases serving as nouns] with adjectives, the noun with the verb, the relative with the antecedent. And in learning further his syntaxes, by mine advice, he shall not use the common order in common schools, for making of Latins: whereby, the child commonly learneth, first, an evil choice of words (and right choice of words, saith Caesar, is the foundation of eloquence); then, a wrong placing of words; and lastly, an ill framing of the sentence, with a perverse judgment, both of words and sentences. These faults, taking once root in youth, be never or hardly plucked away in age. Moreover, there is no one thing that hath more either dulled the wits, or taken away the will of children from learning, than the care they have to satisfy their masters, in making of Latins.

For the scholar is commonly beat for the making, when the master were more worthy to be beat for the mending, or rather marring of the same, the master many times being as ignorant as the child, what to say properly and fitly to the matter. . . .

There is a way, touched in the first book of Cicero, *De Oratore*, which, wisely brought into schools, truly taught, and constantly used, would not only take wholly away this butcherly [brutal] fear in making of Latins, but would also, with ease and pleasure, and in short time, as I know by good experience, work a true choice and placing of words, a right ordering of sentences, an easy understanding of the tongue, a readiness to speak, a faculty to write, a true judgment, both of his own and other men's doings, what tongue so ever he doth use.

The way is this. After the three Concordances learned, as I touched before, let the master read unto him the *Epistles* of Cicero, gathered together and chosen out by Sturmius [German scholar (1507–1589), editor of Cicero], for the capacity of children.

First, let him teach the child, cheerfully and plainly, the cause and matter of the letter; then, let him construe it into English, so often as the child may easily carry away the understanding of it; lastly, parse it over perfectly. This done thus, let the child by and by both construe and parse it over again, so that it may appear that the child doubteth in [is uncertain in] nothing that his master taught him before. After this, the child must take a paper book, and sitting in some place where no man shall prompt him, by himself, let him translate into English his former lesson. Then showing it to his master, let the master take from him his Latin book, and pausing an hour, at the least, then let the child translate his own English into Latin again, in another paper book. When the child bringeth it, turned into Latin, the master must compare it with Tully's [Cicero's] book, and lay them both together: and where the child doth well, either in choosing, or true placing of Tully's words, let the master praise him, and say, "Here you do well." For I assure you, there is no such whetstone, to sharpen a good wit and encourage a will to learning, as is praise.

But if the child miss, either in forgetting a word, or in changing a good with a worse, or misordering the sentence, I would not have the master either frown or chide with him, if the child have done his diligence, and used no truantship therein. For I know by good experience that a child shall take more profit of two faults, gently warned of, than of four things, rightly hit. For then, the master shall have good occasion to say unto him: "Tully would have used such a word, not this; Tully would have placed this word here, not there; would have used this case, this number, this person, this degree, this gender; he would have used this mood, this tense, this simple, rather than this compound; this adverb here, not there; he would have ended the sentence with this verb, not with that noun or participle, etc."

In these few lines, I have wrapped up the most tedious part of grammar, and also the ground of almost all the rules, that are so busily taught by the master, and so hardly learned by the scholar, in all common schools: which after this sort, the master shall teach without all error, and the scholar shall learn without great pain, the master being led by so sure a guide, and the scholar being brought into so plain and easy a way. And therefore, we do not contemn [scorn] rules, but we gladly teach rules, and teach them, more plainly, sensibly, and orderly than they be commonly taught in common schools. For when the master shall compare Tully's book with his scholar's translation, let the master, at the first, lead and teach his scholar to join the rules of his grammar book with the examples of his present lesson, until the scholar by himself be able to fetch out of his grammar every rule, for every example, so as the grammar book be ever in the scholar's hand and also used of him as a dictionary, for every present use. This is a lively and perfect way of teaching of rules: where the common way, used in common schools, to read the grammar alone by itself, is tedious for the master, hard for the scholar, cold and uncomfortable for them both.

Let your scholar be never afraid to ask you any doubt, but use discreetly the best allurements you can, to encourage him to the same, lest his overmuch hearing of you drive him to seek some misorderly shift: as, to seek to be helped by some other book, or to be prompted by some other scholar, and so go about to beguile you much, and himself more.

With this way, of good understanding the matter, plain construing, diligent parsing, daily translating, cheerful admonishing, and heedful amending of faults, never leaving behind just praise for well doing, I would have the scholar brought up withal, till he had read and translated over the first book of *Epistles* chosen out by Sturmius, with a good piece of a comedy of Terence also.

→ JOHN HOSKYNS

From *Directions for Speech and Style*   *c. 1599*

Scholar, lawyer, and member of Parliament, John Hoskyns (1566–1638) sought to instruct young men in the proper modes of writing by providing examples from Sir Philip Sidney's *Arcadia,* a long pastoral romance first published in 1590. Although Hoskyns's book of rhetorical instruction was not printed until much later in the seventeenth century, it circulated in manuscript during his lifetime. Here he advises the aspiring writer on the functions and value of metaphor.

FOR VARYING

A METAPHOR, or TRANSLATION, is the friendly and neighborly borrowing of one word to express a thing with more light and better note, though not so directly and properly as the natural name of the thing meant would signify. As, *feigned sighs:* the nearest to feigning is teaching an imitation of truth by art and endeavor; therefore Sir Philip Sidney would not say *unfeigned sighs,* but *untaught sighs. Desirous:* now desire is a kind of thirst, and not much different from thirst is hunger, and therefore for *swords desirous of blood* he saith *hungry of blood;* where you may note three degrees of metaphors in the understanding: first that the fitness of bloodshed in a weapon usurps the name *desirous,* which is proper to a living creature, and then that it proceedeth to *thirst,* and then to *hunger.* The rule of a metaphor is that it be not too bold nor too far-fetched. And though all metaphors go beyond the signification of things, yet are they requisite to match the compassing sweetness of men's minds, that are not content to fix themselves upon one thing but they must wander into the confines; like the eye, that cannot choose but view the whole knot when it beholds but one flower in a garden of purpose; or like an archer that, knowing his bow will overcast or carry too short, takes an aim on this side or beyond his mark.

Besides, a metaphor is pleasant because it enricheth our knowledge with two things at once, with the truth and with similitude; as this: *heads disinherited of their natural seigniories* [territories], whereby we understand both beheading and the government of the head over the body as the heir hath over the lordship which he inheriteth. Of the same matter in another place: *to di-*

vorce the fair marriage of the head and the body, where besides the cutting off the head we understand the conjunction of head and body to resemble marriage. The like in *concealing love,* uttered by these words: *to keep love close prisoner;* and in number of places in your book, which are all noted with this letter, *M,* in the margent; *there came along the streets a whole fleet of coaches,* for *a great number.*

An ALLEGORY is the continual following of a metaphor (which before I defined to be the translation of one word) and proportionable through the sentence, or through many sentences; as,

> Philoclea was so environed with sweet rivers of virtue as that she could neither be battered nor undermined,

where Philoclea is expressed by the similitude of a castle, her nature (defense) by the natural fortification of a river about a castle, and the metaphor continues in the tempting her by force or craft, expressed by battering and undermining. Another:

> But when that wish had once his ensign in his mind, then followed whole squadrons of longing, that so it might be a main battle of mislikings and repinings against their creation.

Ensigns, squadrons, main battle — metaphors still derived from the same thing [as] at first, war.

As I said before that a metaphor might be too bold or too far-fetched, so I now remember that it may be too base; as, *the tempest of judgment had broken the main-mast of his will, a goodly audience of sheep, shoulders of friendship,* and suchlike too base; as in that speech, *fritter of fraud and seething-pot of iniquity,* and they that say *a red herring is a shoeing-horn to a pot of ale.* But they that speak of a scornful thing speak grossly. Therefore, to delight generally, take those terms from ingenious and several professions; from ingenious arts to please the learned, and from several arts to please the learned of all sorts; as from the meteors, planets, and beasts in natural philosophy, from the stars, spheres, and their motions in astronomy, from the better part of husbandry, from the politic government of cities, from navigation, from military profession, from physic; but not out of the depth of these mysteries. But ever (unless your purpose be to disgrace) let the word be taken from a thing of equal or greater dignity, as, speaking of virtue, *the sky of perfect virtue ever clouded with sorrow,* where he thought it unfit to stoop to any metaphor lower than heaven. You may assure yourself of this observation, and all the rest, if you but compare those places in your book noted with this note, *M;* and in truth it is the best flower, growing most plentifully, in all Arcadia.

An emblem, an allegory, a similitude, a fable, and a poet's tale differ thus: an EMBLEM is but the one part of the similitude, the other part (viz., the application) expressed indifferently and jointly in one sentence, with words some proper to the one part, some to the other; a SIMILITUDE hath two sentences, of several proper terms compared; a FABLE is a similitude acted by fiction in beasts;

a POET'S TALE, for the most part, by gods and men. In the former example, plant a castle compassed with rivers and let the word be, *Nec obsidione nec cuniculis* (neither by siege nor undermining): that is an emblem, the proper terms of the one part. Lay it as it is in Sir Philip S[idney]: *Philoclea's virtue*, the proper terms of the one part; *environed, rivers, battered, undermined,* the terms of the other part; all these terms in one sentence and it is an allegory. Let it be this:

> There was a lamb in a castle, and an elephant and a fox besieged it. The elephant would have assailed the castle, but he would not swim over the river. The fox would make a hole in the earth to get under it, but he feared the river would have sunk in upon him and drowned him.

Then is it a fable. Let Spenser tell you such a tale of a Faery Queen, and Ovid of Diana, and then it is a poet's tale. But utter it thus in one sentence:

> Even as a castle compassed about with rivers cannot be battered or undermined,

and this in another:

> Philoclea, defended round about with virtuous resolutions, could neither be forced nor surprised by deceit,

then it is a similitude in his own nature — which is the ground of all emblems, allegories, fables, and fictions.

→ GEORGE PUTTENHAM

From *The Art of English Poesy* 1589

One of the most thorough of sixteenth-century guidebooks, George Puttenham's *The Art of English Poesy* (published anonymously) is a treasury not only of rhetorical instruction but also of information about Elizabethan education and society in general. It is divided into three books, the first on the importance and the proper kinds of poetry, the second on metrical models, and the third on the definition and function of rhetorical tropes. Included here are Puttenham's introductory remarks on the value of poetic ornament found at the beginning of Book 3 and two sections from Book 3, Chapter 19: the first contains a discussion and illustration of some rhetorical figures; the second is his explanation of "the rebound," a central figure in sixteenth-century wordplay.

BOOK 3, CHAPTER 1

Of Ornament Poetical

As no doubt the good proportion of any thing doth greatly adorn and commend it, and right [just] so our late remembered proportions do to our vulgar poesy: so is there yet requisite to the perfection of this art another manner of exornation [ornamentation], which resteth in the fashioning of our maker's language and style to such purpose as it may delight and allure as well the mind as the ear of the hearers with a certain novelty and strange manner of conveyance, disguising it no little from the ordinary and accustomed; nevertheless making it nothing the more unseemly or misbecoming, but rather decenter and more agreeable to any civil ear and understanding. And as we see in these great Madames of honor, be they for personage or otherwise never so comely and beautiful, yet if they want their courtly habiliments or at leastwise such other apparel as custom and civility have ordained to cover their naked bodies, would be half ashamed or greatly out of countenance to be seen in that sort, and perchance do then think themselves more amiable in every man's eye, when they be in their richest attire, suppose of silks or tissues and costly embroideries, than when they go in cloth or in any other plain and simple apparel. Even so cannot our vulgar poesy show itself either gallant or gorgeous if any limb be left naked and bare and not clad in his kindly clothes and colors, such as may convey them somewhat out of sight, that is, from the common course of ordinary speech and capacity of the vulgar judgment, and yet being artificially handled must needs yield it much more beauty and commendation. This ornament we speak of is given to it by figures and figurative speeches, which be the flowers, as it were, and colors that a poet setteth upon his language of art, as the embroiderer doth his stone and pearl, or passements of gold upon the stuff of a princely garment, or as the excellent painter bestoweth the rich Orient colors upon his table of portrait: so nevertheless as if the same colors in our art of poesy (as well as in those other mechanical arts) be not well tempered, or not well laid, or be used in excess, or never so little disordered or misplaced, they not only give it no manner of grace at all but rather do disfigure the stuff and spill the whole workmanship, taking away all beauty and good liking from it, no less than if the crimson taint, which should be laid upon a lady's lips, or right in the center of her cheeks, should by some oversight or mishap be applied to her forehead or chin, it would make (you would say) but a very ridiculous beauty, wherefore the chief praise and cunning of our poet is in the discreet using of his figures, as the skillful painter's is in the good conveyance of his colors and shadowing traits of his pencil, with a delectable variety, by all measure and just proportion, and in places most aptly to be bestowed.

BOOK 3, CHAPTER 19

Of Figures Sententious, Otherwise Called Rhetorical

Now if our presupposal be true, that the poet is of all other the most ancient orator, as he that by good and pleasant persuasions first reduced the wild and beastly people into public societies and civility of life, insinuating unto them, under fictions with sweet and colored speeches, many wholesome lessons and doctrines, then no doubt there is nothing so fit for him, as to be furnished with all the figures that be rhetorical, and such as do most beautify language with eloquence and sententiousness. Therefore, since we have already allowed to our maker his auricular figures, and also his sensible, by which all the words and clauses of his meters are made as well tunable to the ear, as stirring to the mind, we are now by order to bestow upon him those other figures which may execute both offices, and all at once to beautify and give sense and sententiousness to the whole language at large. So as if we should entreat our maker to play also the orator, and whether it be to plead, or to praise, or to advise, that in all three cases he may utter, and also persuade both copiously and vehemently.

And your figures rhetorical, besides their remembered ordinary virtues, that is, sententiousness, and copious amplification, or enlargement of language, do also contain a certain sweet and melodious manner of speech, in which respect they may, after a sort, be said auricular: because the ear is no less ravished with their current tune, than the mind is with their sententiousness. For the ear is properly but an instrument of conveyance for the mind, to apprehend the sense by the sound. And our speech is made melodious or harmonical, not only by strained tunes, as those of music, but also by choice of smooth words: and thus, or thus, marshaling them in their comeliest construction and order, and as well by sometimes sparing, sometimes spending them more or less liberally, and carrying or transporting of them farther off or nearer, setting them with sundry relations, and variable forms, in the ministry and use of words, do breed no little alteration in man. For to say truly, what else is man but his mind? which, whosoever have skill to compass, and make yielding and flexible, what may not he command the body to perform? He therefore that hath vanquished the mind of man hath made the greatest and most glorious conquest. But the mind is not assailable unless it be by sensible [of the senses] approaches, whereof the audible is of greatest force for instruction or discipline: the visible, for apprehension of exterior knowledges, as the philosopher saith. Therefore the well tuning of your words and clauses to the delight of the ear, maketh your information no less plausible to the mind than to the ear: no, though you filled them with never so much sense and sententiousness. Then also must the whole tale (if it tend to persuasion) bear his just and reasonable measure, being rather with the largest than with the scarcest. For like as one or two drops of water pierce not the flint stone, but many and often droppings do, so cannot a few words (be they never so pithy or sententious) in all cases and to all manner of minds, make so deep an impression, as a more multitude of words to the purpose discreetly and without superfluity uttered: the mind being no less vanquished with large load of speech, than the limbs are with heavy burden. Sweetness of speech, sentence, and amplification are therefore necessary to an excellent orator and poet; he may in no wise be spared from any of them.

And first of all others your figure that worketh by iteration or repetition of one word or clause doth much alter and affect the ear and also the mind of the hearer, and therefore is counted a very brave figure both with the poets and rhetoricians, and this repetition may be in seven sorts.

ANAPHORA, or the Figure of Report. Repetition in the first degree we call the figure of *report,* according to the Greek original, and is when we make one word begin and, as they are wont to say, lead the dance to many verses in suit [in sequence], as thus:

> *To think on death it is a misery,*
> *To think on life it is a vanity:*
> *To think on the world, verily it is*
> *To think that here man hath no perfect bliss.*

And this written by Sir Walter Raleigh of his greatest mistress in most excellent verses:

> *In vain, mine eyes, in vain you waste your tears,*
> *In vain, my sighs, the smokes of my despairs,*
> *In vain you search th' earth and heavens above,*
> *In vain you seek, for fortune keeps my love.*

Or as the buffoon in our interlude called *Lusty London* said very knavishly and like himself:

> *Many a fair lass in London town,*
> *Many a bawdy basket borne up and down,*
> *Many a broker in a threadbare gown,*
> *Many a bankrupt scarce worth a crown,*
> > *In London.*

ANTISTROPHE, or the Counterturn.   You have another sort of repetition quite contrary to the former, when you make one word finish many verses in suit, and that which is harder, to finish many clauses in the midst of your verses or ditty (for to make them finish the verse in our vulgar [tongue] it should hinder the rhyme) and because I do find few of our English makers use this figure, I have set you down two little ditties which ourselves in our younger years played upon the *antistrophe*, for so is the figure's name in Greek: one upon the mutable love of a lady, another upon the meritorious love of Christ our Savior, thus:

> *Her lowly looks, that gave life to my love,*
> *With spiteful speech, curstness, and cruelty:*
> *She killed my love, let her rigor remove,*
> *Her cheerful lights and speeches of pity*
> *Revive my love. Anon with great disdain*
> *She shuns my love, and after by a train [trap]*
> *She seeks my love and saith she loves me most.*
> *But seeing her love so lightly won and lost,*
> *I longed not for her love for well I thought:*
> *Firm is the love, if it be as it ought.*

The second, upon the merits of Christ's passion toward mankind, thus:

> *Our Christ, the son of God, chief author of all good,*
> *Was he, by his allmight, that first created man,*
> *And with the costly price of his most precious blood,*
> *He that redeemed man, and by his instance won*
> *Grace in the sight of God, his only father dear,*
> *And reconciled man, and to make man his peer*

Made himself very man. Brief to conclude the case,
This Christ, both God and man, he all and only is:
The man brings man to God and to all heaven's bliss.

The Greeks call this figure *antistrophe*, the Latins *conversio*, I, following the original, call him the *counterturn*, because he turns counter in the midst of every meter.

SYMPLOCHE, *or the Figure of Reply.* Take me the two former figures and put them into one, and it is that which the Greeks call *symploche*, the Latins *complexio*, or *conduplicatio*, and is a manner of repetition, when one and the self [same] word doth begin and end many verses in suit and so wraps up both the former figures in one, as he that sportingly complained of his untrusty mistress, thus:

Who made me shent [disgraced] for her love's sake?
  Mine own mistress.
Who would not seem my part to take?
  Mine own mistress.
What made me first so well content?
  Her courtesy.
What makes me now so sore repent?
  Her cruelty.

The Greeks name this figure *symploche*, the Latins *complexio*, perchance for that he seems to hold in and to wrap up the verses by reduplication, so as nothing can fall out. I had rather call him the figure of reply.

ANADIPLOSIS, *or the Redouble.* You have another sort of repetition, when with the word by which you finish your verse, you begin the next verse with the same, as thus:

Comfort it is for man to have a wife,
Wife, chaste, and wise, and lowly all her life.

Or thus:

Your beauty was the cause of my first love,
Love while I live, that I may sore repent.

The Greeks call this figure *anadiplosis*, I call him the *redouble* as the original bears.

EPANALEPSIS, *or the Echo Sound, Otherwise the Slow Return.* You have another sort of repetition, when you make one word both begin and end your verse, which therefore I call the *slow return*, otherwise the *echo sound*, as thus:

Much must he be beloved, that loveth much,
Fear many must he needs, whom many fear.

Unless I called him the *echo sound,* I could not tell what name to give him, unless it were the *slow return.*

EPIZEUXIS, the Underlay, or Cuckoo Spell. You have another sort of repetition, when in one verse or clause of a verse, you iterate one word without any intermission, as thus:

It was Maryne, Maryne that wrought mine woe.

And this bemoaning the departure of a dear friend.

The chiefest staff of mine assured stay,
With no small grief, is gone, is gone away.

And that of Sir Walter Raleigh's very sweet:

With wisdom's eyes had but blind fortune seen,
Then had my love, my love for ever been.

The Greeks call him *epizeuxis,* the Latins *subjunctio,* we may call him the *underlay;* me thinks if we regard his manner of iteration, and would depart from the original, we might very properly, in our vulgar and for pleasure call him the cuckoo spell, for right as the cuckoo repeats his lay, which is but one manner of note, and doth not insert any other tune betwixt, and sometimes for haste stammers out two or three of them one immediately after another, as *cuck, cuck, cuckoo,* so doth the figure *epizeuxis* in the former verses, *Maryne, Maryne,* without any intermission at all.

PLOCHE, or the Doubler. Yet have you one sort of repetition, which we call the *doubler,* and is as the next before, a speedy iteration of one word, but with some little intermission by inserting one or two words between, as in a most excellent ditty written by Sir Walter Raleigh these two closing verses:

Yet when I saw my self to you was true,
I loved my self, because my self loved you.

And this spoken in common proverb.

An ape will be an ape, by kind as they say,
Though that you clad him all in purple array.

Or as we once sported upon a fellow's name who was called *Woodcock,* and for an ill part he had played entreated favor by his friend.

I pray you entreat no more for the man,
Woodcock will be a woodcock [fool] do what you can.

Now also be there many other sorts of repetition if a man would use them, but are nothing commendable, and therefore are not observed in good poesy, as a vulgar rhymer who doubled one word in the end of every verse, thus:

adieu, adieu,
my face, my face.

And another that did the like in the beginning of his verse, thus:

To love him and love him, as sinners should do.

These repetitions be not figurative but fantastical, for a figure is ever used to a purpose, either of beauty or of efficacy: and these last recited be to no purpose, for neither can you say that it urges affection, nor that it beautifieth or enforceth the sense, nor hath any other subtlety in it, and therefore is a very foolish impertinency of speech and not a figure. . . .

ANTANACLASIS, *or the Rebound.*   You have another figure which by his nature we may call the *rebound,* alluding to the tennis ball which being smitten with the racket rebounds back again, and where the last figure before played with two words somewhat like, this playeth with one word written all alike but carrying divers senses, as thus:

The maid that soon married is, soon marred is.

Or thus better because *married* and *marred* be different in one letter:

To pray for you ever I cannot refuse,
To pray [prey] upon you I should you much abuse.

Or as we once sported upon a country fellow who came to run for the best game, and was by his occupation a dyer and had very big swelling legs:

He is but course [coarse] to run a course,
Whose shanks are bigger than his thigh:
Yet is his luck a little worse,
That often dyes before he dye.

Where you see this word *course* and *dye,* used in divers senses, one giving the *rebound* upon the other.

→ BALDASSARE CASTIGLIONE

From *The Book of the Courtier*   *1528*

The Book of the Courtier, written in Italian at the beginning of the sixteenth century and translated into English by Sir Thomas Hoby (pub. 1560), became one of the most influential books in early modern Europe. Purporting to record the conversations of a group of aristocrats, it promotes the humanist values of learning, civility, gracefulness, wit, and the dignity of man. This passage (in a modern translation) explores the pleasures of wordplay and, by implication, the power relations associated with the skillful use of puns.

The discussion continuing, Bernardo said:
   "You have now heard all I have to say about those jokes which rely on a continuous narration; so now we should talk of those which consist in a single remark, and whose sharp wit is concentrated in a brief sentence or word. And

just as with the first kind of amusing anecdote one must, when telling the story or indulging in mimicry, avoid resembling clowns and parasites and those who make others laugh by their own foolishness, so in these terse comments the courtier should guard against appearing malicious or spiteful, or repeating witticisms and quips merely to tease and wound. Because such men often have their whole body deservedly chastised for the sins of their tongue.

"Now, of the spontaneous jokes that consist in a brief remark, those which arise from some ambiguity are the most effective, although they do not always arouse mirth, since they are more usually praised for their ingenuity than for their humor. For example, a few days ago our Annibale Paleotto was talking to someone who was recommending him a tutor to teach his sons grammar and who, after commending the teacher for his learning, when he came to the question of his salary said that as well as money he wanted to have a room furnished for living and sleeping, because he lacked a bed. Annibale immediately retorted: 'Then how can he be learned, if he hasn't read?'[1] You see how well he exploited the ambiguous meaning of *non aver letto*. But since these puns are very subtle, in that someone employs words in a sense quite different from what is given them by everyone else, it appears that, as I have said, they inspire wonder more often than laughter, except when they are accompanied by something more. The kind of witticism that customarily arouses laughter occurs when we expect to hear one thing and the one who is talking says something different, and this is called the 'unexpected retort'; and if there is also some double meaning, then the witticism becomes extremely rich, as happened the other day when there was a discussion about making a fine brick floor for the Duchess's room, and after a lot had been said you, Gian Cristoforo, remarked: 'If we could get the Bishop of Potenza and lay him flat it would suit the purpose well, since he is the biggest born fool I ever saw.' Everyone laughed out loud, for you made a pun by splitting the word *mattonato* into two; and then in addition your saying that a bishop should be laid flat and used for the floor of a room was a totally unexpected notion, and so the joke was very pointed and very funny.[2]

"However, there are many different kinds of pun; and so one must be cautious in their use, hunting carefully for the right words, and avoiding those that cause the joke to fall flat and seem too labored, or, as we have said, that are too wounding. For example, once when several companions met at the house of one of their friends, who happened to be blind, after the host had asked them to stay for dinner, they all left except one, who remarked: 'Well, I'll stay, since I see you've got an empty place.' And he pointed his finger at the man's empty socket. This of course is too cruel and discourteous, for it wounded the blind man's feelings to no purpose and without provocation; moreover, the jibe could have been at the expense of all those who are blind, and sweeping insults of this kind give no pleasure, because they appear to be premeditated. Of this sort was the remark made to a man who had lost his nose, namely: 'Where, then, do you rest your spectacles?' or 'How do you smell the roses every year?'

---

[1] The pun is on *letto*, which means either "bed" or "read."
[2] *Matto nato* means a "born fool" and *mattonato* a "brick floor."

"Among other witticisms, however, those are very elegant which depend on turning someone's own sarcastic remarks against him, using the very same words as he does, and hoisting him with his own petard. For example, there was the litigant who, in the presence of the judge, was asked by his adversary: 'What are you barking for?' And he retorted: 'Because I see a thief.' The same kind of joke was when Galeotto Marzi was on his way through Siena and stopped in the street to ask the way to the inn; and when a Sienese noticed how corpulent he was, he laughed and said: 'Others bring their baggage along behind but this fellow carries his in front.' And Galeotto retorted: 'That's what you have to do in a land of robbers.'

"There is another kind still, which we call playing on words, and this relies on changing a word by adding or taking away a letter or a syllable, as when someone said: 'You must be more experienced in the literature of the *latrines* [Latins] than of the Greeks.' And to you, madam [Emilia Pia], a letter was addressed: 'To signora Emilia impia' [unholy, cruel].

"It is also amusing to quote a verse or two, putting it to a use other than what the author intended, or some other common saying, perhaps to the same purpose, but with a word altered. Thus a gentleman who had an ugly and shrewish wife, being asked how he was, replied: 'Just you imagine, seeing that *Furiarum maxima iuxta me cubat.*'[3]

"And Girolamo Donato, when in company with many other gentlemen he was making the Stations in Rome during Lent, encountered a group of beautiful Roman ladies; and when one of the gentlemen said: '*Quot colum stellas, tot habet tua Roma puellas,*' he immediately added: '*Pascua quotque haedos, tot habet tua Roma cinaedos,*'[4] pointing out a group of young men who were coming from the other direction.

"Then there is the way in which Marc'Antonio dalla Torre spoke to the Bishop of Padua. For there was a nunnery in Padua in charge of a cleric who was thought to be extremely devout and learned, and who used to go the familiar rounds of the convent, often hearing the nuns' confessions. And then five of the mothers, and there were no more than as many again, became pregnant, and the father was seized by the Bishop after he had tried unsuccessfully to run away. He immediately confessed that because of the temptation of the devil he had got those five nuns pregnant, and consequently my Lord Bishop was resolved to chastise him very severely. However, the culprit was a very learned man and so he had very many friends, all of whom made efforts to help him; and along with the others Marc'Antonio also went to the Bishop to plead with him to be lenient. After they had been very insistent, recommending the culprit and pleading in extenuation the easy opportunities he had been given, the frailty of human nature, and various other factors, the Bishop said at length: 'I will do nothing for him, because I have to render my account to God.' They still insisted, however; and then the Bishop added: 'What shall I

---

[3] This is a play on Virgil's "*Furiarum maxima iuxta accubat*" (*Aeneid* VI, 605–06), meaning "Lying nearby the greatest of the Furies . . . ," to give the sense "The greatest of the Furies sleeps with me."
[4] The line from Ovid's *Ars Amatoria* (*Art of Love*) running "Your Rome has as many girls as the sky has stars" is answered by: "Your Rome has as many homosexuals as the meadows have kids."

answer when on the Day of Judgment the Almighty says to me: *"Redde rationem villicationis tuae?"'* To which Marc'Antonio swiftly replied: 'My Lord, in the words of the Evangelist: *Domine, quinque talenta tradidisti mihi; ecce alia quinque superlucratus sum.'*[5] At this the Bishop could not stop from laughing and he greatly mitigated both his anger and the punishment he had designed for the wrongdoer."

[5] Namely, God will say: "Give an account of your stewardship" (Luke 16.2), and the bishop should answer: "Lord, you delivered five talents to me: see, I have gained over and above them five more" (Matthew 25.20).

Chart of the Relative Proportions of Poetry and Prose in Shakespeare's Plays

This table, reprinted from *The Complete Pelican Shakespeare*, edited by Alfred Harbage, indicates the relative amounts of poetry and prose in Shakespeare's plays, along with the names of the characters with the longest parts in each play, and other information.

	Total Lines	% Blank	% Rhyme	% Prose	Scenes	Casts Men	Casts Women	Songs	Longest roles (with count for those over 500 lines)
COMEDIES									
Errors	1756	65.8	21.5	12.7	11	11	5		Antipholus S., Adriana, Dromio S.
Shrew	2584	72.5	5.8	21.7	12	19	4	2	Petruchio (549), Tranio, Katherina
T.G.V.	2199	68.7	5.8	25.5	19	13	3	1	Proteus, Valentine, Julia
Dream	2106	35.4	45.5	19.1	7	15	6	2	Theseus, Helena, Bottom
L.L.L.	2667	21.8	43.1	35.1	9	13	5	2	Berowne (591), Navarre, Princess
Merchant	2564	73.5	5.5	21.0	19	16	3	1	Portia (565), Shylock, Bassanio
A.Y.L.	2636	35.2	10.3	54.5	22	17	4	5	Rosalind (668), Orlando, Touchstone
Much Ado	2549	25.3	3.0	71.7	17	14	4	2	Benedick, Leonato, Don Pedro
Twelfth Night	2423	31.4	7.3	61.3	18	11	3	4	Toby, Viola, Feste
Merry Wives	2598	9.6	3.8	86.6	21	16	4	1	Falstaff, Mrs. Page, Mr. Ford
All's Well	2760	43.6	10.3	46.1	23	8	6		Helena, Parolles, King
Measure	2671	59.0	3.4	37.6	15	17	5	1	Vincentio (820), Isabella, Lucio
HISTORIES									
1 Henry VI	2676	88.0	11.9	0.1	19	39	3		Talbot, Joan, York
2 Henry VI	3062	82.1	3.2	14.7	18	43	4		York, Margaret, Henry
3 Henry VI	2902	95.5	4.4	0.1	22	40	3		Warwick, Edward, Richard
Richard III	3602	93.8	4.4	1.8	23	40	5		Richard (1124), Buckingham, Elizabeth

(continued)

	Total Lines	% Blank	% Rhyme	% Prose	Scenes	Casts		Songs	Longest roles (with count for those over 500 lines)
						Men	Women		
John	2560	94.9	5.1	0.0	15	18	4		Faulconbridge (520), John, Constance
Richard II	2755	80.9	19.1	0.0	18	26	5		Richard (753), Bullingbrook, York
1 Henry IV	2954	54.3	2.7	43.0	17	32	3		Falstaff (585), Hotspur (545), Hal (535)
2 Henry IV	3182	48.7	2.6	48.7	17	39	5		Falstaff (593), Hal, Henry
Henry V	3176	57.2	3.2	39.6	20	39	4	1	Henry (1025), Fluellen, Canterbury
Henry VIII	2804	95.1	2.6	2.3	16	36	4	1	Henry, Wolsey, Katherine
TRAGEDIES									
Titus	2521	93.2	5.2	1.6	13	21	3		Titus (687), Aaron, Marcus
Romeo	2964	71.0	16.6	12.4	21	21	4	1	Romeo (591), Juliet (509), Laurence
Caesar	2453	92.5	1.3	6.2	13	36	2		Brutus (701), Cassius, Antony
Hamlet	3776	66.3	5.7	28.0	20	25	2	3	Hamlet (1422), Claudius (540), Polonius
Troilus	3326	63.0	6.1	30.9	18	24	4	1	Troilus, Ulysses, Pandarus
Othello	3228	78.4	3.1	18.5	15	14	3	3	Iago (1097), Othello (860), Desdemona
Lear	3195	69.9	5.3	24.8	22	22	3	4	Lear (697), Edgar, Kent
Macbeth	2113	80.3	12.1	7.6	26	25	7		Macbeth (681), Lady Macbeth, Malcolm
Timon	2281	66.4	7.0	26.6	17	27	2		Timon (795), Apemantus, Flavius
Antony	3019	90.5	1.3	8.2	36	30	4	1	Antony (766), Cleopatra (622), Caesar
Coriolanus	3294	77.4	0.8	21.8	27	29	4		Coriolanus (809), Menenius, Volumnia
ROMANCES									
Pericles	2322	59.7	22.4	17.9	22	22	7		Pericles (592), Marina, Simonides
Cymbeline	3266	79.9	6.3	13.8	23	24	3	2	Imogen (522), Posthumus, Iachimo
Winter's Tale	2946	71.5	3.1	25.4	14	15	6	6	Leontes (648), Paulina, Autolycus
Tempest	2026	71.4	7.5	21.1	9	15	4	7	Prospero (603), Ariel, Caliban

CHAPTER 7

Town and Country:
Life in Shakespeare's England

———————————————— >‹ ————————————————

Several scenes in the first two acts of *Henry IV, Part 1* are given over to a robbery. The Prince and his companion Ned Poins are expected to participate but instead play a trick on Falstaff by failing to join in the heist and then robbing him of the loot. The robbery itself is preceded by a short scene (2.1) set at the inn where the travelers who will be robbed have been spending the night and are now preparing to get on the road. Although it does little to advance the action and so is often cut in performance, the episode explores in a socially specific context the problems of loyalty and betrayal that are central to the play's political concerns: King Henry is accused of having stolen the crown. A more unusual function of the scene, however, is as a window onto the daily life of working people in sixteenth-century England. Devoted as it is not to kings but to laborers and criminals, the inn scene provides a useful introduction to the topics to be considered in this chapter — daily life (both urban and rural) in Shakespeare's England, the occupations of the populace, the geography of the London in which Shakespeare lived and worked, clothing, diet, travel, recreation, money, and other such features of Elizabethan culture. These are vast subjects, impossible to cover adequately. But my purpose is not to construct a social history of Tudor and Stuart England. Rather, it is to offer some perspectives on the material world that informs Shakespeare's work and to familiarize the modern reader with some early modern cultural contexts.

The time is early morning, before dawn. The place is the yard, or loading area, of an inn on the road to London, probably in the town of Rochester. (This is the equivalent of a truck stop between the eastern coastal towns and the metropolis.) In the first half of the scene, the two characters who share the stage are carriers, men who are transporting goods from the country to be sold in the city. One carries turkeys in a large basket, while another transports bacon and ginger. The second carrier is taking his provisions to Charing Cross, the area that in Shakespeare's time was a small village between the City of London and the royal palaces of Whitehall and Westminster.

These workers begin their day very early, at about two in the morning, although the first carrier, making a guess based on the position of the constellations in the sky, fears that it is already four o'clock and that he is running late. They are trying to get on the road but receive no assistance from the new ostler, the keeper of the horses at the inn. The old one, recently dead, was much more helpful: ". . . This house is turn'd upside down since Robin ostler died. . . . What, ostler! A plague on thee! hast thou never an eye in thy head? Canst not hear?" (2.1.10–11, 27–28). They complain not only about the service but also about the provisions at the inn. The fodder for the animals is moldy and makes them sick, and the carriers themselves fare no better. Because the management at the inn won't provide chamber pots, the guests have to urinate in the fireplace, a practice that the travelers believe breeds the fleas that have infested the house. The carriers are anxious about crime, too. When Gadshill enters and asks to borrow a lantern to find his horse, the carriers scornfully refuse, apparently knowing a thief when they see one. Thus they remain tight-lipped about their route or schedule:

> GADSHILL: Sirrah carrier, what time do you mean to come to London?
> SECOND CARRIER: Time enough to go to bed with a candle, I warrant thee.   (2.1.41–44)

The remainder of the scene depicts a private conversation between Gadshill and the Chamberlain, an attendant at the inn, who is on the take: the Chamberlain is acting as informant for Gadshill and his band of thieves, identifying the guests who are carrying large sums of money and thus setting up the highway robbery to come. Gadshill is the name both of the highwayman and of the spot where Falstaff's robbery will take place. To Shakespeare's contemporaries, the term was synonymous with danger to travelers.

Travel was a strenuous and potentially dangerous business in sixteenth-century England, as Shakespeare himself would have been aware from his frequent journeys on horseback between Stratford and London. The roads connecting the capital with the rest of the kingdom were fairly primitive, designed for pedestrians or single riders; coaches were seldom used outside London at this period. Whether on foot or on horseback, travelers were dependent on the inn for rest and refreshment and vulnerable to the numerous uncertainties that still afflict those who take to the road: miserable weather, unreliable roads, bad food, poor service, and highway robbery (whether literal or figurative). An excerpt from William Harrison's *Description of England* (see p. 238) outlines some of those perils in terms that are particularly germane to Shakespeare's portrait of the inn at Rochester. As Harrison's description indicates, the travelers coming down the hill in act 2, scene 2, of *Henry IV, Part 1*, could not have been completely surprised to hear the shouts of Falstaff and his cronies. To any traveler, a safe arrival in London must have been a relief.

London

To a first-time visitor from the country, arrival in London must have been an overwhelming experience. At the end of the sixteenth century, it had reached a population of about two hundred thousand. *London,* however, is a problematic term. Strictly speaking, the City of London was a relatively small area bounded on three sides by ancient walls, dating from Roman times, and by the Thames River on the fourth side. At various points along the walls were gates (such as Moorgate and Newgate) that allowed access into the City itself from outlying villages and fields. By the sixteenth century the walls no longer served a defensive function. Rather, they helped to define the central commercial, residential, and judicial district, which contained the Tower of London (built on a fortress begun in Roman times), St. Paul's Cathedral (although not the same building that stands on the site now), the guildhalls of tradesmen and merchants, the Inns of Court housing the lawyers, the offices of the municipal government, Sir Thomas Gresham's Royal Exchange (the newest public building in Elizabethan London), and the principal markets and shopping streets. The metropolitan area was considerably larger, however, and the City as it exists today has assimilated and still retains the names of places such as Charing Cross, Covent Garden, and Islington that in Shakespeare's day were villages or suburban areas only loosely connected to the City of London. In the early seventeenth century, for example, Hyde Park and St. James's Park, two of the green areas that today offer relief from the crowds and concrete of modern London, were forests in which King James hunted deer.

St. Paul's Cathedral was the social center of the City. It was not located in the geographical middle of town, however, but closer to the western wall and thus to Westminster, toward which London was expanding. St. Paul's was not only a house of worship, but also a popular place for meeting friends, making deals, hearing gossip, hiring help, finding employment, picking pockets, leaving messages, and buying books. As a site for various kinds of social interaction, the nave of St. Paul's appears frequently in the drama and prose of Shakespeare's contemporaries, particularly in the London comedies of Ben Jonson. Although Falstaff reports that he contracted for the services of Bardolph in the aisle of Paul's, such a reference is rare for Shakespeare because he doesn't write about contemporary London in the ways that playwrights such as Jonson and Thomas Dekker and Thomas Middleton do. Since the Middle Ages the impropriety of such commerce in the main church had made the city fathers anxious, and sporadic efforts were made to control or relocate it. But convenience and tradition triumphed over law. Most of the urban traffic would have been on foot, as people went about their daily business of buying and selling, carrying water, visiting friends, feeding themselves, and seeking various kinds of entertainment. Those who had to travel from one end of town to the other might have taken one of the water taxis on the Thames, a popular and rapid system of transportation mentioned by a Swiss visitor, Thomas Platter, in his record of his travels (see p. 241). Although coaches were becoming an increasingly frequent form of urban transportation, they were available only to aristocrats and wealthy merchants. For most Londoners, the area around St. Paul's served as a natural and traditional meeting place.

The business districts of the City of London were divided loosely according to merchandise or service, with the divisions to some extent grounded in the practical requirements of the business. To buy fresh fish, for example, the householder or housewife went to Bridge Street, near Billingsgate, a gate or pier on the banks of the Thames where the fish could be easily unloaded from skiffs, small boats that transferred to shore the catch from larger seagoing ships. But dried fish were sold elsewhere, a couple of blocks away in Thames Street. Such places as Shoe Lane or Poultry proclaim their function, and some of these streets and alleys survive even in modern London. Yet it is worth noting that as early as Shakespeare's day fowl were no longer sold in Poultry, having been displaced by other marketable goods. As John Stow records in his *Survey of London* (1598), commercial London was a dynamic place, with shops and services changing locations as the metropolis grew and neighborhoods changed (see p. 239).

One determinant of the geography of commercial London was the influence of the twelve great guilds: Mercers (dealers in expensive cloth), Grocers, Drapers (makers of or dealers in lesser fabrics), Fishmongers, Goldsmiths, Skinners, Merchant-Tailors, Haberdashers, Salters (makers of or dealers in salt), Ironmongers, Vintners, and Clothworkers. Their codes for supply, marketing, and training gave each group a kind of unity and spirit that helped to foster concentration in a particular location. This grouping by district was not absolute, as Stow's description indicates, and larger and less specialized markets had grown up in some of the wider thoroughfares such as Cheapside — one Elizabethan map illustrates temporary stalls placed in the center of the street — and on London Bridge itself. The merchants and tradesmen were a significant part of the newly prosperous urban class in Elizabethan London, and to some degree their economic prosperity was stimulated and protected by Elizabeth's and the City Aldermen's (or Elder-men's) political policy. The enforcement of church rules about meatless days, for example — Fridays, certain holidays, and Lent, that period of abstinence extending from late winter through Easter — was motivated as much by economics as by religion. As Harrison's *Description* records, the statutes served to protect the thriving fishing industry and all its attendant trades, such as river-carriers, wholesale and retail fishmongers, and shipbuilders (see p. 240).

A London merchant owned or leased the building in which his shop was located. The ground floor served as the place of business, with goods displayed indoors and perhaps outdoors on tables under an awning made of light wood. The merchant and his family lived behind and above the shop, together with his servants and apprentices. If the house were large enough, lodgers might be taken in: Shakespeare seems to have rented a room in the Cripplegate area from a French family, the Mountjoys, who were tire-makers (creators of ladies' headdresses). (See the map on p. 34.) Some merchants' houses even had gardens behind them. This combination of business and residence led to the crowding, bustle, and noise for which London was famous to visitors from the country and abroad. Most of the streets were narrow and seemed even narrower because the upper stories of the houses overhung the ground floor. This invasion of public air space gave the householder more square footage than he had paid for, but it also shut out sunlight from the street.

Most of the streets were intended for pedestrian traffic, although horses and carts and even small herds of animals used them as well. Horse-drawn coaches, which were becoming more common as the city prospered, were probably confined to the larger thoroughfares and to the main roads leading out of town. Certain intersections had conduits, or fountainlike spigots, from which water was collected by water-carriers — Ben Jonson depicts a colorful example of such a figure in his play *Every Man in his Humour* — and delivered in large wooden containers to customers throughout the city. Many streets had a gutter or channel in the center down which wastewater and sometimes sewage ran into ditches and then into the Thames.

On the margins of the City, however, there was more room, both for building and for recreational spaces. Along the river were impressive mansions — palaces, in some cases — built by great families as town houses and known by the familial names: Essex House, Arundel House, Somerset House. (Some of the later buildings that replaced these mansions have retained their names: Somerset House, for example, rebuilt in 1776 on the site of the original Tudor building and then renovated in the 1980s to contain the Courtauld collection of paintings, is located on the corner of the Strand and Waterloo Bridge, looking across the river to the present site of the National Theatre.) Occupying the northern (City) side of the Thames and extending from the western walls toward Westminster, these great houses were set back from the river, surrounded by grounds planted with trees and gardens, and fitted with private docks or piers for convenient access to transportation. To the north of the City was Moorfields, an open area planted as a kind of park and used for archery and other outdoor pastimes. And just to the north of Moorfields along Bishopsgate Street was the area known as Shoreditch, the site of two important early playhouses: the Theatre, built in 1576, and the Curtain, erected a year or two later.

On the western edge of the City of London were the Inns of Court, the buildings and grounds that served as home for the legal profession. The Inns were multifunctional, serving as graduate school, dormitory, library, dining hall, office building, social club, site of plays and revels, and legal center. Beyond the Inns lay the route to Westminster, the home of the monarch, the court, and Parliament: naturally regular traffic flowed between the palaces of Westminster and Whitehall, on the one hand, and the City of London on the other. When Shakespeare's *King Henry IV* laments that his son, the Prince of Wales, is wasting his time in "barren pleasures" and "rude society," he is objecting to Hal's drinking in one of the taverns a couple of miles down the road at Eastcheap, in the center of London proper. This movement between town and court along the Strand led to major commercial and residential development, notably the construction of the Cockpit theater in Drury Lane in 1616;

such growth would make this area the center of London life in the eighteenth century. But in Shakespeare's day it was semirural. Along the way was a garden once associated with a disbanded convent, the "convent garden" (or Covent Garden); the Church of St. Martin in the Fields, now facing the crowds of Trafalgar Square, was located in actual fields; and St. Martin's Lane was a small passage leading from the Thames to the countryside north of the suburbs. The quickest route between Westminster and London was the river. The monarchs had royal barges to transport themselves and important courtiers and visitors, while for ordinary citizens, the boatmen mentioned in Platter's account stood ready to take them upstream ("Westward Ho!"), downstream ("Eastward Ho!"), or across the river, perhaps to the Bankside to see a play.

London Bridge in the sixteenth century was much more than just a means of crossing the Thames, although, except for boats, it was the only way across. Like the medieval bridge across the Arno River that still survives in Florence, London Bridge was a virtual neighborhood in itself, the site of shops, houses, and street life. Above the archway leading onto the bridge the authorities mounted the decapitated heads of traitors and left them there to rot, as a warning against treason. John Stow in his *Survey of London* recounts the history of London Bridge and then describes its appearance in 1598:

> To conclude of this bridge over the said river of Thames, I affirm, as in other my descriptions, that it is a work very rare, having with the draw-bridge twenty arches made of squared stone, of height sixty feet, and in breadth thirty feet, distant from one another twenty feet, compact and joined together with vaults and cellars; upon both sides be houses built, so that it seemeth rather a continual street than a bridge; for the fortifying whereof against the incessant assaults of the river, it hath overseers and officers, viz., wardens, as aforesaid, and others.   (25–26)

London Bridge was vital in connecting the capital with the countryside and agricultural riches of the southern counties; indeed, it offered virtually the only practical land access to the southeastern quadrant of England. (See the extract from Lupold von Wedel's *Journey through England and Scotland*, p. 241).

The Suburbs

More immediately London Bridge connected the urban center with one of its liveliest and most notorious suburbs. The borough of Southwark and the Bankside contained prisons (the Clink), hospitals, taverns (the Tabard Inn, where Chaucer's pilgrims begin their journey), playhouses and other centers of entertainment such as gambling houses, brothels ("the stews"), and the arena for bearbaiting, the Bear Garden. This neighborhood, one of the several outlying districts known as the "Liberties" because they were beyond the jurisdiction of the City authorities until 1608, served as a haven for criminals, drifters (known as "masterless men"), the unemployed, the ill (particularly lepers), prostitutes, and others with a dubious relation to the law. In Queen Elizabeth's time, the Liberties on the Bankside were legally answerable to the bishop of Winchester, but in practice the "government" of all these areas — including some former monastic sites within the City itself — was negligible. The Liberties were useful to the City authorities as semidetached ghettos for crime and disease. Steven Mullaney has described the topographical and cultural ambiguities of such suburbs in early modern London.

> Whatever could not be contained within the strict bounds of the community found its place here, making the Liberties the preserve of the anomalous, the unclean, the polluted, and the sacred. Like the French *banlieux*, London's Liberties were places of exile, yet the banishment enacted in them was of a more ambivalent order. What was lodged outside the city was excluded, yet retained; denied a place within the community, yet not merely exiled. The licentious, dangerous, unclean, or polluted was cast out of the city, but was then maintained as such and even placed on public display. (22)

Although some urban historians consider Mullaney's claims overstated, it is nonetheless true that the Liberties functioned as a safety zone for the socially marginal.

Before Henry VIII abolished the Roman Catholic religious houses in the 1530s, Southwark had contained a number of abbeys and priories, as well as the homes of some powerful men, religious and secular. The dissolution of the abbeys increased the instability of the borough, but it had always been a rough neighborhood, as Stow indicates by his description of the long-standing parliamentary act regulating the operation of the brothels (see p. 242). He also mentions periodic efforts to close the brothels and clean up the neighborhood. "In the year 1546, the 37th [year in the reign] of Henry VIII, this row of stews in Southwark was put down by the king's commandment, which was proclaimed by sound of trumpet, no more to be privileged, and used as a common brothel, but the inhabitants of the same to keep good and honest rule as in other places of this realm, etc." But these attempts were of limited success and duration, and the records of the time indicate awareness and official toleration of what amounted to London's red-light district. (Thomas Nashe's *Christ's Tears over Jerusalem* registers outrage at the immorality of the London brothels; see p. 242.) It is worth emphasizing that the theaters that produced some of the greatest works of the English stage, the Rose and the Globe, were identified geographically (and, by some, morally) with prostitution, criminality, and excessive "liberty." (See the map of sixteenth-century theaters on p. 58.)

The Countryside

My description of London and its suburbs has concentrated on the arts we associate with civilization and urban life — architecture, commerce, government, theater, and various forms of petty crime, or con-artistry. It is axiomatic that to shift to the countryside takes us closer to nature, but this division between town and country is not as sharp as it might at first appear. While admiring the natural glories of the English countryside, with its pastures, farming lands, great forests, and wild coastline, we must remember that the bounty and to some extent the beauty of these lands have for centuries depended on the agricultural arts. Rural life, in other words, was also highly organized, arranged into patterns calculated through centuries of experience to take advantage of climate, soil, and the cycles of marketable crops. Careful management of land was essential to the survival of the individual family as well as the collective national family.

In the second act of *A Midsummer Night's Dream*, Titania deplores the consequences of her quarrel with Oberon: discord in the fairy realm results in horrible weather in the mortal world. The winds and rain have been so fierce that

> The ox hath therefore stretch'd his yoke in vain,
> The ploughman lost his sweat, and the green corn
> Hath rotted ere his youth attain'd a beard.
> The fold stands empty in the drowned field,
> And crows are fatted with the murrion flock. (2.1.93–97)

As a possible source for this description, scholars look to the summer of 1593, a year or two before *A Midsummer Night's Dream* was probably written, in which abnormal weather ruined crops and brought hardship to much of the English economy. But whether or not the lines refer to a particular summer, they speak to the direct connection between bad weather and economic disaster. In Titania's description, the rains have inundated the fields, undoing the work of the oxen, who would have pulled the farmer's plow and thus prepared the ground for the planting of seed. All this water has destroyed the crops on the stalk: the "green corn" that has been ruined is the young, unripe grain, probably wheat or barley (not the grain that North Americans call corn). The sheep, unable to graze the sodden pastures, are dying from the disease of sheep and cattle known as murrain, the only beneficiaries being the scavenger birds. Titania goes on to complain that the seasons have become indistinguishable from one another and to lament the effect on humankind. Even so brief a passage illustrates the correspondence between the seasonal cycles and human needs, which has come to seem less immediate to us thanks to the conveniences of modern life.

In *Henry IV, Part 2*, when the Hostess reflects sentimentally on her acquaintance with Falstaff, "I have known thee these twenty-nine years, come peasecod-time" (2.4.382–83), she indicates the way that certain times of the year were naturally and familiarly associated with the growth of certain foods. Fruit became available in the spring and early summer and continued through the fall, berries and other early varieties giving way to cherries, apples, and other orchard fruits; vegetables were likewise restricted according to season. A notable exception to this rule was grain, particularly winter wheat and rye, which could be sown from August through November and then harvested in the winter months. Domestic animals were born in the spring and slaughtered in the autumn and winter to supply food in the barren months of January,

February, and March; very little of the meat was eaten fresh, but was dried or smoked for later use. (There was, however, conspicuous consumption of meat and game by members of the nobility and, aping them, the wealthy citizens of the town.) As with meat, certain fruits, nuts, and vegetables were preserved and stored for use during the winter (importing exotic or unseasonal produce from warmer climates was practiced only by the most privileged). Sugar was a rare and precious commodity. Winter weather could also make the roads impassable and therefore hamper the transportation of meat and other provisions from the countryside to the city. The government's ban on meat during Lent and on holidays may have remained in force as long as it did not only for reasons of religious doctrine and for encouragement of the fishing industry, but also for practical reasons. In other words, it may have been a realistic response to the limited availability of meat. Awareness of such a correspondence between season and supply offers a revealing context for the numerous seasonal episodes and references that we find in Shakespeare's plays.

Our response to the sheepshearing festival in *The Winter's Tale*, for example, depends on our awareness of the festivity that resulted from the sense of abundance and fulfillment. (The time of the scene in the play is uncertain: the shearing of sheep usually took place in July, but this party seems later than that. Whatever the date, the emphasis on reward for labor and fulfillment after privation is unmistakable.) After months of shortage and expectation, the country people have shorn the sheep, collected and sold the wool, and are now spending the profits on edible treats and other pleasures. As Shakespeare's young shepherd makes his way to the market to purchase supplies for the festival, he counts his money and consults his list:

> Let me see: every 'leven wether tods [eleven sheep make one tod, or twenty-eight pounds of wool], every tod yields pound and odd shilling; fifteen hundred shorn, what comes the wool to? . . . I cannot do't without compters [counters, or metal disks for doing arithmetic]. Let me see: what am I to buy for our sheep-shearing feast? Three pound of sugar, five pounds of currants, rice — what will this sister of mine do with rice? But my father hath made her mistress of the feast, and she lays it on. She hath made me four and twenty nosegays for the shearers. . . . I must have saffron to color the warden [winter pear] pies; mace; dates, none — that's out of my note; nutmegs, seven; a race [root] or two of ginger, but that I may beg; four pounds of pruins, and as many of raisins o' th' sun. (4.3.32–49)

With each tod worth a little over a pound sterling, the profits amount to some 140 pounds. When we consider that the average wage for a laborer was perhaps seven pounds a year, it becomes clear that this is a very prosperous year for the Clown and his family. And even for those whose profits were not so high, the end of work gave way to a festive atmosphere and such luxuries and delights as holiday foods, flowers, singing, dancing, and buying from peddlers, the rural equivalent of shopping.

The Bohemian festival represented in *The Winter's Tale* may or may not be a historically accurate portrayal of English country life at the beginning of the seventeenth century, but it helps to introduce the values and routines of the rural existence that Shakespeare must have been exposed to while growing up in a small town in Warwickshire. Elizabethan towns and villages differed from one another according to their location and the natural resources associated with their geographical situation. The sheep farming in an inland area such as the Cotswolds, for example, would have produced villages that looked quite different from those in the coal mining districts of the northeastern coast. But certain features were probably common to most of them, such as those structures necessary to the conduct of community life: a parish church (with graveyard), a tavern or inn, a manor house and surrounding park for the local commanding gentry, a municipal hall of some kind, a village green for meeting neighbors, a mill for grinding wheat, a partly open marketplace, perhaps a schoolhouse, and common land for grazing. Since Stratford-upon-Avon was a market town, its population would have grown on market days, creating trade in secondary goods and services (meals, beer, entertainment) as well as primary products such as food and clothing. In addition to the regular markets held in such towns, special bazaars and fairs sprang up throughout the country, the largest of them devoted to the sale of items beyond daily needs. In effect these fairs were wholesale markets offering grain in large quantities, animals, and other kinds of agricultural "stock." The setting for Ben Jonson's *Bartholomew Fair* is just such a mart in the London suburb of Smithfield, and a quick look at that play reveals that the fairgoers hardly limit their activities to the buying and selling of necessities.

Rural Life

Whatever the commercial emphasis of a given village or town, some kind of farming would have occupied virtually every country family. Most of the villagers would have been tenant farmers, a term that requires some explanation. English agriculture, like the English language, the English church, and virtually everything else at the end of the sixteenth century, was in a state of flux. The medieval feudal system, in which most of the populace worked land owned by the lord of the manor for the primary benefit of that lord, had more or less dissolved by Shakespeare's day, but it had not yet developed into the private system of the family farm with which we are familiar. Some of the citizens in country towns had become extremely successful, and many towns saw the building of large new houses by those country farmers and merchants who, through entrepreneurial skill or good luck, had managed to take advantage of bountiful harvests or the strength of the emerging economy. (See the extract from Gervase Markham's *The English Husbandman,* p. 244.) Despite the private successes of certain families in every town, most of the land in a given parish legally was still owned by the lord of the manor, who received rent for its use, sometimes in cash and sometimes in goods. But practically speaking, this property was held in common and managed by the citizens who worked it.

Rural communities by the end of the sixteenth century had devised a fairly complicated system for the productive use of the common land. Some of the property, often that bordering a river, was designated as meadowland and reserved for grazing sheep and cattle — livestock, unlike crops, could be moved in the event of a flood. The brushy areas, or thickets, near the forests were not especially desirable, but they served their purpose. According to R. E. Prothero,

> These wastes and woods supplied many village wants. They provided heather and fern for thatching, or bedding for the cattle, or light fuel for brewing or baking; they fed the swine with beech-mast or acorns; in winter their trimmings and loppings helped to keep the half-starved stock alive; they furnished bushes to stop gaps as well as wood for movable fences, hop poles, and implements of husbandry. ("Agriculture and Gardening" 1:351)

As for the arable (or farmable) land, the most important principle in the system of management was rotation, and usually the available farmland was divided into three sections: one-third given over to rye or wheat, the principal grains cultivated for the making of bread; one-third to lesser grains such as barley, oats, and beans, some of which went for human consumption but most for silage; and one-third to lying fallow, so as to prevent depletion of the soil's nutrients.

Each villager was given a six-acre portion in each of these three areas, for a total of eighteen acres, only twelve of which he would use in any one year. Each six-acre assignment was not in one plot, but was made up of smaller portions, scattered through the field and demarcated by small strips of grass. This crazy-quilt arrangement ensured a fair distribution of the choicest land among all the tenants. Each farmer was thus responsible for and benefited from his own plots of this land, although certain functions, such as guarding the seeded land against birds, were performed by a villager assigned to the task and paid by the group. I have radically simplified the description of this system of agriculture; as economic historians have demonstrated, there were exceptions and variations in every village (see Coleman 31–34). Even those towns in which the use of land was most democratically organized contained private fields or pastures enclosed for the cultivation of domestic animals by a few well-to-do yeomen, or freeholders. Many areas in the south of England had been virtually privatized for some time, with hedges and fences separating the available land into individual plots. The village model set forth here was less common in the northern counties, simply because the region was sparsely populated and the land less suited to producing grain. Some citizens of a town or village did not participate as tenants but worked as laborers or servants to those who did. And scattered throughout the country were a few freeholders who owned their land and employed several farmhands. In other words, the English agricultural economy was varied.

It was also undergoing momentous changes. From time to time the lord of a manor sought to raise rents and thus make the land more profitable, although the lord's long-standing affiliations with the community usually kept greed in check. The more serious threat was the sale of property to merchants or other newly prosperous men from London who wished to consolidate the lands into larger, more productive farms and whose distance could easily insulate them from local hardship and complaint. There was constant tension between private and public rights to the arable lands and pastures. Likewise, disputes arose over the opposing claims of shepherds and tillers, conflicts similar to those between ranchers and farmers in the settling of the American West.

Such problems are best represented by the disputes over enclosure that became more and more frequent and violent in the sixteenth and early seventeenth centuries. As the wool trade expanded, stimulated partly by foreign demand for English cloth, much of the land that had been used for growing grain was being converted to pastureland for sheep and thus was being fenced, or enclosed. One of the primary effects of this conversion was unemployment. Sheepherding was far less labor-intensive than farming, and many of those people associated with agriculture — not only farmers and their helpers but related laborers, such as millers — lost their means of supporting their families. (See the excerpt from Fynes Moryson's *Itinerary*, p. 246, which speaks to this problem.) According to D. C. Coleman, "What mattered was the extinction of common rights. . . . Sometimes it was the pasturing on the commons of large numbers of cattle or sheep, by bigger farmers, thus making life more difficult for the smaller husbandman; sometimes it was the loss of ancient rights in the woodlands — to cut underwood, to run pigs" (40). Who had the ultimate claim on the land around the village? The lord to whom it had been legally entrusted by the Crown centuries before, or the villagers who had used it for farming and pasture down through those centuries? When grain shortages occurred, as they often did in the late sixteenth and early seventeenth centuries, many people understandably laid the blame on the enclosers. In several cases these tensions erupted into angry protest, with villagers taking shovels and other tools and leveling the fences erected by the enclosers. Such uprisings — like an important one that occurred in the Midlands in 1607 — may be reflected in the class disputes of *Coriolanus*.

Countrywomen worked ceaselessly at what we might call "keeping house," except that the term encompasses far more than it does today. The *huswife* or housewife — a term in common use at this period — spent her days baking bread, making butter and cheese, minding the poultry, brewing beer, gathering wood for the fire, tending the household garden, cooking meals, spinning yarn, making cloth, sewing clothes, washing clothes, making candles, fashioning tools of various kinds, supervising any servants, and all the while keeping one eye on the children. Although some items could be purchased in shops in larger villages and at fairs, most household goods were homemade, and because the husband was usually working in the field, it was up to the wife to make and maintain her own equipment. (See the passage from Anthony Fitzherbert's *The Book of Husbandry*, p. 246.) Women also worked in the fields, especially at times of urgent need, such as harvest or planting season, and even children had regular duties in and outside the home, such as carrying messages, carding wool, scaring crows or other predators away from the crops, and caring for the younger children.

The Daily Routine

Whether in the city or the country, the English day began early, the rhythms of daily life influenced above all by the rising and setting of the sun. The northern longitude of England means that the summer days are very long, the winter days very short. Before daybreak, someone in the household had to rise and prepare the house for the business of the day. A successful merchant in London would have assigned the job to a servant living in the household. In less prosperous houses, a member of the family, perhaps an older child, performed this task. In winter it meant stoking or relighting the fires needed for warmth; in summer it meant at least readying the fire in the stove for the morning meal. In all seasons water was needed for morning face washing and other such preparations: in the country, it came from a well or river; in the city, from one of the public conduits or wells, although the wealthy could afford to have their water delivered. Breakfast consisted of bread and butter, and perhaps cheese or fruit, or maybe both. There was no coffee or tea in Shakespeare's England: ale or beer was the main beverage, taken at all hours of the day. By the time the sun came up people were ready for business, with the farmer already in the field and the shopkeeper opening his doors and displaying merchandise in front of the shop.

With such an early start to the day, lunch was welcome when it came, just at the noon hour. This was the principal meal, when meat was served, if it was available, and the family assembled for conversation and an hour away from labor. (See the excerpt from Harrison's *Description*, p. 248.) In the city, the workday usually ended around five or so; in the country, sundown determined the end of work. Closing time or quitting time was followed by a light supper and, in the winter, prayers and bed. There may have been time for reading, if the family could afford books, but since candles were expensive, as was firewood, going to bed early was not only healthy but also economical. In summer, of course, the hours before sunset (9 or 10 P.M. throughout most of England) allowed time for recreation: perhaps walking in the meadows outside the City walls or along the river away from the village; making music or dancing; playing games, both card games and physical sports such as tag or archery; drinking with friends at a tavern and perhaps smoking a pipe of tobacco (a recent import from the New World); and, of course, talking about who was walking and dancing and playing and drinking with whom.

Clothing

The state of English dress at this period is too broad and complex to be covered adequately in a paragraph or two, but no topic so effectively introduces the dynamic and unfixed nature of English culture at the end of the sixteenth century. Fashion statements are hardly new, and the subjects of Elizabeth I could not resist making them — about their newfound wealth and the jewels it could buy, about their savvy in locating an exotic fabric, about the sophistication of their tailor (whose latest pattern for trunk hose [breeches] attested to his eye for novelty and his Continental connections), about the number of different garments in which they could afford to appear. Thanks to increasing prosperity and exchange with Europe, English fashions were changing rapidly and becoming ever more elaborate and various, so much so that the winds of fashion became a favorite topic both for Puritan outrage and for dramatic satire around the turn of the seventeenth century. The wealthy spent immense sums of money on clothing: a fine outfit for a man or a woman, even without jewelry and other such embellishments, might cost fifty to sixty pounds or more, perhaps ten times the annual wages of a laborer. When we consider that some of the most notable dramatists of the day were paid five pounds or so for a new play, we get a sense of how expensive clothing could be and how it could serve as a badge of economic or social success. (See Harrison's *Description* on p. 249 for an eloquent complaint about sartorial extravagance in the sixteenth century.)

The major articles of clothing for prosperous, fashionable men were the following: leather shoes; knitted stockings, which gave greater definition to the leg than the sewn leggings they replaced; short trousers, called trunk hose, in various shapes (a popular style being the Spanish pumpkin-shaped breeches stuffed with wool or even with bran), which were worn over tight-fitting thigh leggings much like our spandex bicycle shorts; a codpiece, often ornamented, to connote masculinity; a doublet or jacket, with several pairs of detachable sleeves; a rich shirt of linen or silk, worn under the doublet but peeking out from it; a ruff made of stiff white lace to set off the face and head; perhaps an earring; and sometimes a hat made of velvet or other luxurious fabric and adorned with feathers and jewels. Prosperous, fashionable women wore high-heeled shoes and stockings; an elaborate dress or skirt in a choice of voluminous styles, all of them designed to minimize the size of the waist by augmenting the hips; to support the skirt, an elaborate underframe called a farthingale, made of bone or wood, or in the simplest form, a padded cylinder like a child's inner tube wrapped around the hips and known as a bum roll; a jacket augmented with shoulder pads and nipped in at the waist; sleeves, separate from the bodice, secured with lace, and often puffed out with batting or other stuffing; sometimes openwork or a piece of sheer gauze to display part of the breasts; a ruff, perhaps supplemented with starched gauze wings behind the head; and, for the head, jewels, a small hat, a cloth covering, or an elaborate hairstyle. Cosmetics were worn, mostly in red and white, to achieve contrast between lips, cheeks, and the rest of the face. The popularity of makeup became a frequent target of dramatic satire, as in Hamlet's remarks to Ophelia ("God hath given you one face, and you make yourselves another" [3.1.143–44]) and to the skull of Yorick ("Now get you to my lady's chamber, and tell her, let her paint an inch thick, to this favor she must come" [5.1.192–94]).

Because for centuries differences in dress had been a reliable register of the hierarchies of class and position, the blurring of these distinctions and the rapid changes in fashion were alarming to political authorities. The social order depended on knowing who belonged in what slot, and in an age when the complete attire of a gentleman was available to anyone with the cash to purchase or the wit to steal it, the complications of dress were seen as a threat to that social order. Consequently, Tudor authorities occasionally sought to enforce the codes regulating dress, known as sumptuary laws, that had been on the books for decades but were only intermittently observed. Legally, rich materials such as fur and silk were to be worn only by earls, dukes, and other members of the aristocracy; the amount of fabric allowed for a man's pants (the trunk hose) was restricted to a yard and three-quarters; servants' clothing, usually dyed blue to identify the wearer's position in service, was to be without ornament. But these statutes conflicted with social practices. In their wills, great men often left their clothing to favorite servants as a sentimental gesture; these servants soon began to discover (unsentimentally) that they could make a profit by selling this rich apparel. Sometimes they sold it to the acting companies who needed fabulous costumes for the portrayal of royalty. (Puritan opponents of the theater fixed their moral outrage on this technical violation of decorum.) Alternatively, some servants found that by wearing their deceased masters' suits themselves, they could pass for persons of rank in society. The hangman, too, was entitled to receive the clothing of those who were executed. For all these reasons, a thriving trade arose in used clothing. As merchants began to prosper, their social ambitions led them to emulate the apparel of the aristocracy. At the beginning of Elizabeth's reign, in 1559, the government got tough, intending to preserve these sartorial boundaries by punishing violators, but the crackdown was a failure. Other restrictive efforts followed, all of them unsuccessful, so finally in 1604 Parliament admitted the impossibility of legislating style and repealed the sumptuary laws.

Getting and Spending

Implicit in this discussion of food and clothing has been the fact that there was much more to buy in England in 1600 than there had been in 1500, owing partly to the growth of London as a commercial center, the development of trade with the Continent, and a substantial increase in population. In other words, a sophisticated cash economy had begun to emerge. Especially in the city, people had money in their purses. But what kind, and how much? The English used a wide range of coins (paper money was to come later) and gave these coins a variety of names, both formal and slang. Shakespeare refers casually to numerous units of currency, often exploiting them for wordplay: pounds, shillings, marks, angels, nobles, florins, crowns, half-crowns, groats, pence, ha'pennies. To the modern American ear, these words and the distinctions they signify are perplexing, although the modern analogues (bucks, two bits, nickels, and dimes) give no trouble. The terms may be unfamiliar even to

Britons who have grown up since 1971, when the monetary system in the U.K. was simplified to pounds and pence.

In Shakespeare's day, a pound was worth twenty shillings, each shilling worth twelve pence, thus 240 pence in the pound. A mark equaled two-thirds of a pound; an angel-noble (or angel or noble), ten shillings and sixpence; a crown, five shillings or a quarter of a pound; a half-crown, two-and-a-half shillings; and a florin, two shillings. New coins were introduced from time to time, but old ones remained in circulation. With a little explanation, most of these nouns make sense: for example, the angel, in circulation from the mid–fifteenth to the mid–seventeenth century, got its name from the image with which it was stamped, a picture of the archangel Michael defeating a dragon. Sometimes coins were identified by the name of the monarch in whose reign they were issued and whose picture they bore (e.g., a "James shilling" or an "Elizabeth groat"). Finally, a significant distinction between the early modern monetary system and our own is that coins were not merely tokens of value but valuable in themselves for the precious metals they contained. Thus, when Mercutio accuses Romeo of having given him "the slip," the joke turns on a pun for a counterfeit coin.

Early modern nomenclature, if unfamiliar, can at least be learned, but the system of prices and values represented is much more elusive. As I indicated in the Introduction, any attempt to translate sixteenth-century wages and costs into modern terms will be thwarted by such problems as inflation and the altered values of goods and services. We will do better to consider a few examples of what people earned and what they had to pay for certain goods (for many of these figures I have relied on William Ingram's *The Business of Playgoing* 36ff.). The first rule is that the pound was a substantial sum of money. An unskilled laborer earned perhaps five or six pence per day, which would amount to something like seven pounds per year. Around 1600 "hired men" in the theater, those actors who did not own a share of the company, were paid ten shillings per week, or about half a pound. But this rate cannot simply be multiplied into an annual income of twenty-five pounds, since playing times were seasonal and affected by variables such as the plague. Prices of consumable goods are similarly hard to interpret, since much food was raised and prepared at home. When one did buy a loaf of bread, it cost a penny, which was also the price of a portion of ale in a tavern. The principle of supply and demand — not to mention the difference between early modern and modern pricing — is apparent in the relative costs of a chicken (two pence) and a lemon (six pence). Given these figures, the fifty-pound price on a smart suit of clothing makes Harrison's satiric analysis easy to understand.

Admission to the playhouse cost a penny, and entrance to the gallery (that is, the right to a seat) cost another penny. When the play being staged was published, it could be purchased in quarto form from the booksellers near St. Paul's at the price of six pence. In 1623 the Folio collection of Shakespeare's works went on sale there: the price (unbound) was about one pound. As a shareholder in his theatrical company, Shakespeare earned substantially more than the standard five- or six-pound fee for a script by collecting a percentage of the profits from performances. In 1597 he bought New Place, the imposing house in Stratford to which he retired. Legal records show that he paid William Underhill sixty pounds in silver but do not indicate if this was the total purchase price. By the standards here described, Shakespeare had become a wealthy man in his first decade in show business.

That players were making money was a source of outrage to many religious moralists and social critics who railed against money wasted on theatergoing. In *Vertues Commonwealth: or The High-way to Honour*, Henry Crosse complained of the "many poor, pinched, needy creatures, that live off alms, and that have scarce neither cloth to their back nor food for the belly, yet will make hard shift [will do anything] but they will see a play, let wife and children beg, languish in penury, and all they can rape and rend is little enough to lay upon such vanity" (qtd. in Ingram 41). This is a more serious version of Trinculo's remark, in *The Tempest*, about English values: "When they will not give a doit to relieve a lame beggar, they will lay out ten to see a dead Indian" [2.2.31–33]. Such polemics as Crosse's remind us that many Englishmen were desperately poor and without skills or other means of improving their lot. Such official assistance as existed was sporadic and locally organized: the parish church, for example, was responsible for ministering to the poor in its neighborhood. London writers comment repeatedly on the problem of masterless men, ne'er-do-wells without family or work who support themselves by crime or begging and who thus threaten the social order. Poverty in the countryside was even more common, if perhaps less conspicuous. While some people subsisted in misery, some thrived by virtue of commercial ingenuity or hard work or the misuse of others. Philip Henslowe, often mentioned in these pages for the theatrical acumen he displayed in managing the Lord Admiral's Men, apparently made less money from his theaters than from his brothels and his moneylending.

In describing the culture in which Shakespeare moved, I have fixed my attention almost entirely on the occupations and preoccupations of merchants, farmers, housewives, and others near the middle of the social and economic scale, those who were neither aristocrats nor beggars. Shakespeare himself was born into the middle class and became through his success a member of what we would probably call the upper middle class. But Shakespeare's own upward mobility aside, the rise of the middle class is arguably the most important historical phenomenon in the late sixteenth century. As I indicated in Chapter 6 on Shakespeare's dramatic language, the age of Elizabeth was a period of linguistic transition, in which a discourse that we recognize as "modern" and more or less like our own emerged from the less familiar conventions of Middle and Old English. Similar instabilities and fluctuations characterize the economic and social spheres, as England moved from feudalism to precapitalism, from a medieval to a modern society. What we witness in England and in Europe generally at the end of the sixteenth century is, for better or worse, the emergence of the culture of success. Most of the features of English life that I have described, from the growth of London to the struggles over enclosure to the power of fashion, are a function of this familiar modern phenomenon. And so, we might add, is the career of the young man who left the small town to make his fortune in the city and returned at the end of that career a famous and wealthy playwright.

→ WILLIAM HARRISON

From *The Description of England*   *1587*
The Conditions of English Inns and Overnight Travel

Printed as a part of the second edition of Raphael Holinshed's *Chronicles of England, Scotland, and Ireland,* William Harrison's *Description* is an encyclopedic survey not only of topography and other physical features of England but also of its social and political structures and the manners and habits of its people.

If the traveler have a horse, his bed doth cost him nothing, but if he go on foot he is sure to pay a penny for the same; but whether he be horseman or footman, if his chamber be once appointed he may carry the key with him, as of his own house, so long as he lodgeth there. If he lose aught whilst he abideth in the inn, the host is bound by a general custom to restore the damage, so that there is no greater security anywhere for travelers than in the greatest inns of England. Their horses in like sort [manner] are walked, dressed, and looked unto by certain hostlers or hired servants, appointed at the charges of the goodman of the house, who in hope of extraordinary reward will deal very diligently, after outward appearance, in this their function and calling. Herein, nevertheless, are many of them blameworthy, in that they do not only deceive the beast oftentimes of his allowance by sundry means — except their owners look well to them — but also make such packs with slipper merchants [con men] which hunt after prey (for what place is sure from evil and wicked persons?) that many an honest man is spoiled of his goods as he traveleth to and fro, in which feat also the counsel of the tapsters or drawers of drink and chamberlains is not seldom behind or wanting. Certes [certainly] I believe not that chapman [merchant] or traveler in England is robbed by the way without the knowledge of some of them; for when he cometh into the inn, and alighteth from his horse, the hostler forthwith is very busy to take down his budget [leather pouch] or capcase [small traveling bag] in the yard from his saddle-bow, which he peiseth [weighs] slyly in his hand to feel the weight thereof: or if he miss of this pitch [trick], when the guest hath taken up his chamber, the chamberlain that looketh to the making of the beds will be sure to remove it from the place where the owner hath set it, as if it were to set it more conveniently somewhere else, whereby he getteth an inkling whether it be money or other short wares [less valuable things], and thereof giveth warning to such odd guests as haunt the house and are of his confederacy, to the utter undoing of many an honest yeoman as he journeyeth by the way. The tapster in like sort for his part doth mark his behavior and what plenty of money he draweth when he payeth the shot [bill] to the like end, so that it shall be a hard matter to escape all their subtle practices. Some think it a gay matter to commit their budgets at their coming to the goodman of the house: but thereby they oft betray themselves. For albeit their money be safe for the time that it is in his hands (for you shall not hear that a man is robbed in his inn), yet after their departure the host can make no warrantise [guarantee] of the same, since his protection extendeth no further than the gate of his own house, and there cannot be a surer token unto such as pry and watch for those booties, than to see any guest deliver his capcase in such manner.

→ JOHN STOW

From *Survey of London*   *1598*

The Location of Tradesmen in London

A dedicated historian and collector of manuscripts, John Stow (1525?–1605) produced several accounts of English political history, but his most important work is surely the *Survey*, one of the great records of the growth of a great city. He offers abundant detail about the physical appearance of the city — its walls, bridges, monuments, markets, and neighborhoods — and here identifies the locations of the various tradesmen in the London of the 1590s.

Men of trades and sellers of wares in this city have often times since changed their places, as they have found their best advantage. For whereas mercers [dealers in expensive cloth] and haberdashers used to keep their shops in West Cheap, of later time they held them on London Bridge, where partly they yet remain. The goldsmiths of Guthertons [Gutter] Lane and Old Exchange are now for the most part removed into the south side of West Cheap, the pepperers and grocers of Sopers Lane are now in Bucklesbury, and other places. The drapers of Lombard Street and of Cornhill are seated in Candlewick Street and Watheling Street; the skinners from St. Mary Pellipers, or at the Axe, into Budge Row and Walbrooke; the stockfishmongers [sellers of dried fish] in Thames Street; wet fishmongers in Knightriders Street and Bridge Street; the ironmongers, of Ironmongers Lane and Old Jewry, into Thames Street; the vintners from the Vinetree [Vintry] into divers places. But the brewers for the more part remain near to the friendly water of Thames; the butchers in Eastcheap and St. Nicholas Shambles; the hosiers [makers or sellers of stockings] of old time in Hosier Lane, near unto Smithfield, are since removed into Cordwainer Street, the upper part thereof by Bow Church, and last of all into Birchoveris [Birchin] Lane by Cornhill; the shoemakers and curriers of Cordwainer Street removed, the one to St. Martins le Grand, the other to London Wall near unto Moorgate; the founders [casters of metal] remain by themselves in Lothbury; cooks or pastlers [bakers] for the more part in Thames Street, the other dispersed into divers parts; poulterers of late removed out of the Poultry betwixt the stocks and great conduit in Cheap, into Grass Street and St. Nicholas Shambles; bowyers [bow makers], from Bowyers Row by Ludgate into divers places, and almost worn out with the fletchers [arrow makers]; Pater Noster bead-makers and text-writers are gone out of Pater Noster Row into Stationers [booksellers' area] of Pauls Churchyard; patten makers [makers of clogs or overshoes] of St. Margaret, Pattens Lane, clean worn out; laborers every workday are to be found in Cheap, about Sopers Lane end; horse coursers [dealers or brokers] and sellers of oxen, sheep, swine, and such like, remain in their old market of Smithfield, etc.

→ WILLIAM HARRISON

From *The Description of England*   *1587*

Restrictions against Eating Meat

Although eating meat was forbidden on certain feast days and during Lent, an inheritance of England's Roman Catholic past, the custom may owe its survival to reasons other than religious ones. William Harrison offers an economic explanation in this excerpt.

In this season wherein we live, there is no restraint of any meat, either for religion's sake or public order, in England, but it is lawful for every man to feed upon whatsoever he is able to purchase, except it be upon those days whereon eating of flesh is especially forbidden by the laws of the realm, which order is taken only to the end our numbers of cattle may be the better increased and that abundance of fish which the sea yieldeth more generally received. Beside this there is great consideration had in making of this law for the preservation of the navy and maintenance of convenient numbers of seafaring men, both which would otherwise greatly decay if some means were not found whereby they might be increased. But howsoever this case standeth, white meats, milk, butter, and cheese, which were never so dear as in my time, and wont to be accounted of as one of the chief stays throughout the Island, are now reputed as food appertinent only to the inferior sort, whilst such as are more wealthy, do feed upon the flesh of all kinds of cattle accustomed to be eaten, all sorts of fish taken upon our coasts and in our fresh rivers, and such diversity of wild and tame fowls as are either bred in our Island or brought over unto us from other countries of the main.

→ THOMAS PLATTER

From *Travels in England* 1599

The Thames River *Translated by Clara Williams*

Thomas Platter was a well-educated Swiss printer who traveled extensively and kept a detailed journal of his experiences. This brief excerpt records his impressions of the Thames.

It is customary to cross the water or travel up and down the town as at Lyons and elsewhere by attractive pleasure craft, for a number of tiny streets lead to the Thames from both ends of the town; the boatmen wait there in great crowds, each one eager to be the first to catch one, for all are free to choose the ship they find most attractive and pleasing, while every boatman has the privilege on arrival of placing his ship to best advantage for people to step into. . . .

→ LUPOLD VON WEDEL

From *Journey through England and Scotland* 1584–85

A Visit to the Bearbaiting Arena *Translated by Gottfried von Bulow*

Lupold von Wedel describes his journey across London Bridge and into Southwark, finishing with his report on the entertainment known as bearbaiting, in which a large dog was made to fight with a bear (often tied to a stake).

The Thames is crossed by a bridge, leading to another town on the other side of the water called Sedorck [Southwark]. This bridge is built of stone, 470 paces long, but its upper part has not the appearance of a bridge, being entirely set with fine houses filled with all kinds of wares, very nice to look at. . . .

On the 23rd we went across the bridge to the above-mentioned town. There is a round building three stories high, in which are kept about a hundred large English dogs, with separate wooden kennels for each of them. These dogs were made to fight singly with three bears, the second bear being larger than the first, and the third larger than the second. After this a horse was brought in and chased by the dogs, and at last a bull, who defended himself bravely. The next was that a number of men and women came forward from a separate compartment, dancing, conversing, and fighting with each other; also a man who threw some white bread among the crowd, that scrambled for it. Right over the middle of the place a rose was fixed, this rose being set on fire by a rocket: suddenly lots of apples and pears fell out of it down upon the people standing below. Whilst the people were scrambling for the apples, some rockets were made to fall down upon them out of the rose, which caused a great fright but amused the spectators. After this, rockets and other fireworks came flying out of all corners, and that was the end of the play.

→ JOHN STOW

From *Survey of London*   *1598*
Ordinances Concerning Brothels

One of the fascinating qualities of John Stow's *Survey* is his attention to the origins of the geographical area or the social practice he is describing. Here he records the list of royal ordinances concerning the operation of stewhouses, or brothels. Many of these houses were located, as Stow points out, in the same neighborhood as the Globe and the Rose playhouses. Philip Henslowe, the theatrical entrepreneur, owned brothels as well as theaters.

In a Parliament holden at Westminster, the 8th of Henry the Second [in the eighth year of the reign of Henry II], it was ordained by the commons, and confirmed by the king and lords, that divers constitutions forever should be kept within that lordship or franchise, according to the old customs that had been there used time out of mind. Amongst the which these following were some, viz.:

That no stewholder or his wife should let [prevent] or stay any single woman to go and come freely at all times when they listed.

No stewholder to keep any woman to board, but she to board abroad at her pleasure.

To take no more for the woman's chamber in the week than fourteen pence.

Not to keep open his doors upon the holy days.

Not to keep any single woman in his house on the holy days. . . .

No single woman to be kept against her will that would leave her sin.

No stewholder to receive any woman of religion, or any man's wife.

No single woman to take money to lie with any man, but she lie with him all night till the morrow.

No man to be drawn or enticed into any stewhouse.

The constables, bailiff, and others, every week to search every stewhouse.

No stewholder to keep any woman that hath the perilous infirmity of burning [disease], nor to sell bread, ale, flesh, fish, wood, coal, or any victuals, etc.

These and many more orders were to be observed upon great pain and punishment.

→ THOMAS NASHE

From *Christ's Tears over Jerusalem*   *1592*
The Brothels of Suburban London

Thomas Nashe (1567–1601) was a colorful figure in the London literary world. Playwright, satirist, pamphleteer, and writer of prose fiction, Nashe often indulged in a bitter and polemical assault on the manners and morals of the day. This passage, excerpted from the 1613 edition, specifically attacks the toleration of the brothels of suburban London.

London, what are thy suburbs but licensed stews? Can it be so many brothel-houses of salary sensuality and six-penny whoredom (the next door to the magistrate's) should be set up and maintained, if bribes did not bestir them? I accuse none, but certainly justice somewhere is corrupted. Whole hospitals of ten-times-a-day dishonested strumpets have we cloistered together. Night and day the entrance unto them is as free as to a tavern. Not one of them but hath a hundred retainers. Prentices and poor servants they encourage to rob their masters. Gentlemen's purses and pockets they will dive into and pick, even whiles they are dallying with them.

No Smithfield ruffianly swashbuckler will come off with such harsh hell-raking oaths as they. Every one of them is a gentlewoman, and either the wife of two husbands, or a bed-wedded bride before she was ten years old. The speech-shunning sores, and sight-irking botches of their unsatiate intemperance, they will unblushingly lay forth, and jestingly brag of, wherever they haunt. To church they never repair. Not in all their whole life would they hear of God, if it were not for their huge swearing and forswearing by him. . . .

Great cunning do they ascribe to their art, as the discerning (by the very countenance) a man that hath crowns in his purse; the fine closing in with the next justice or alderman's deputy of the ward; the winning love of neighbors round about, to repel violence, if haply their houses should be environed or any in them prove unruly (being pilled and polled [stripped, shaved, or fleeced] too unconscionably). They forecast [scout] for back doors to come in and out by undiscovered. Sliding windows also, and trap-boards in floors, to hide whores behind and under, with false counterfeit panes in walls, to be opened and shut like a wicket [gate]. Some one gentleman generally acquainted [having many friends], they give his admission unto sans fee, and free privilege thenceforward in their nunnery, to procure them frequentance. Awake your wits, grave authorized law-distributors, and show yourselves as insinuative subtle, in smoking this city-sodoming trade out of his starting-holes, as the professors of it are in underpropping it. . . .

Monstrous creatures are they; marvel is it fire from heaven consumes not London, as long as they are in it. A thousand parts better were it to have public stews than to let them keep private stews as they do. The world would count me the most licentiate loose strayer under heaven, if I should unrip but half so much of their venereal machiavellism [sexual deceitfulness] as I have looked into. We have not English words enough to unfold it. Positions and instructions have they to make their whores a hundred times more whorish and treacherous than their own wicked affects [inclinations] (resigned to the devil's disposing) can make them. Waters and receipts [drinks and recipes; medicines] have they to enable a man to the act after he is spent, dormative potions to procure deadly sleep, that when the hackney [hired woman] he hath paid for lies by him, he may have no power to deal with her, but she may steal from him, whiles he is in his deep memento [reverie or doze], and make her gain of three or four other [customers].

↯ GERVASE MARKHAM

From *The English Husbandman*   *1613*
Rural Domestic Architecture and Interior Design

A versatile man of letters who wrote plays and poetry and may have moved in the same circles as William Shakespeare, Gervase Markham (1568–1637) is best remembered today for his pamphlets and advice on country life. This passage from one such pamphlet offers a description of a design for a modest country house.

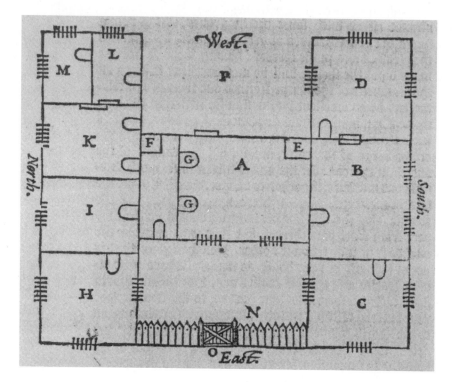

Here you behold the model of a plain country man's house, without plaster or imbosture [embellishment], because it is to be intended that it is as well to be built of stud and plaster, as of lime and stone; or if timber be not plentiful, it may be built of coarser wood, and covered with lime and hair; yet if a man would bestow cost in this model, the four inward corners of the hall would be convenient for four turrets, and the four gavel [gable] ends, being thrust out with bay windows might be formed in any curious manner: and where I place a gate and a plain pale [fence], might be either a terrace, or a gatehouse, of any fashion whatsoever; besides all those windows which I make plain, might be made bay windows, either with battlements or without: but the scope of my book tendeth only to the use of the honest husbandman and not to instruct men of dignity, who in architecture are able wonderfully to control me; therefore that the husbandman may know the use of this facsimile, he shall understand it by this which followeth.

A. Signifieth the great hall.
B. The dining parlor for entertainment of strangers.
C. An inward closet within the parlor for the mistress's use, for necessaries.
D. A stranger's lodging within the parlor.
E. A staircase into the rooms over the parlor.
F. A staircase into the goodman's rooms over the kitchen and buttery [room for storing provisions].
G. The screen in the hall.
H. An inward cellar within the buttery, which may serve for a larder.
I. The buttery.
K. The kitchen, in whose range may be placed a brewing lead [a vessel for brewing], and convenient ovens, the brewing vessels adjoining.
L. The dairy house for necessary business.
M. The milkhouse.
N. A fair sawn pale [well-cut fence] before the foremost court.
P. A place where a pump would be placed to serve the offices of the house.

This figure signifieth the doors of the house.

This figure signifieth the windows of the house.

This figure signifieth the chimneys of the house.

Now you shall further understand that on the south side of your house, you shall plant your garden and orchard, as well for the prospect thereof to all your best rooms, as also your house will be a defense against the northern coldness, whereby your fruits will much better prosper. You shall on the west side of your house, within your inward dairy and kitchen court, fence in a large base court, in the midst whereof would be a fair large pond, well stoned and graveled in the bottom, in which your cattle may drink, and horses when necessity shall urge be washed; for I do by no means allow washing of horses after instant labor. Near to this pond you shall build your dovecote, for pigeons delight much in the water; and you shall by no means make your dove-house too high, for pigeons cannot endure a high mount, but you shall build it moderately, clean, neat, and close, with water-pentises [penthouses, or overhangs] to keep away vermin. On the north side of your base court you shall build your stables, ox-house, cow-house, and swinecotes, the doors and windows opening all to the south. On the south side of the base court, you shall build your hay barns, corn barns, pullen-houses for hens, capons, ducks, and geese; your

French kiln, and malting floors, with such like necessaries: and over cross be-twixt both these sides you shall build your bound hovels [connected shacks], to carry your peas, of good and sufficient timber, under which you shall place when they are out of use your carts, wains, tumbrels [dung wagons], plows, harrows, and such like, together with plow-timber and axletrees [frames and axles], all which would very carefully be kept from wet, which of all things doth soonest rot and consume them. And thus much of the husbandman's house, and the necessaries thereto belonging.

→ FYNES MORYSON

From *An Itinerary* 1617
The Enclosure of Farmlands

Fynes Moryson's record of his travels throughout much of the world, including even the Middle East, offers a fascinating glimpse of different cultures seen through an English lens. The passage here makes brief reference to an increasingly serious prob-lem in rural England, the enclosure of farmlands for pasture. This economic issue may lie behind Shakespeare's portrayal of the starving crowd in *Coriolanus*.

England abounds with corn [wheat and other grains], which they may trans-port, when a quarter (in some places containing six, in others eight bushels) is sold for twenty shillings, or under; and this corn not only serves England, but also served the English army in the civil wars of Ireland, at which time they also exported great quantity thereof into foreign parts, and by God's mercy England scarce once in ten years needs supply of foreign corn, which want commonly proceeds of the covetousness of private men, exporting or hiding it. Yet I must confess, that daily this plenty of corn decreaseth, by reason that pri-vate men, finding greater commodity in feeding of sheep and cattle than in the plow, requiring the hands of many servants, can by no law be restrained from turning cornfields into enclosed pastures, especially since great men are the first to break these laws.

→ SIR ANTHONY FITZHERBERT

From *The Book of Husbandry* 1523
What Works a Wife Should Do

Sir Anthony Fitzherbert (1470–1538), justice of the court of common pleas, wrote an important summary of English law and a treatise on the rights of landlords and ten-ants. *The Book of Husbandry* is a practical manual designed to instruct farmers in the principles of agriculture.

First, in the morning when thou art waked and purpose to rise, lift up thy hand and bless thee and make a sign of the Holy Cross, *In nomine patris et filii et spiritus sancti. Amen.* In the name of the Father, the Son, and the Holy Ghost. And if thou say a *Pater Noster* [the Our Father], an *Ave* [the Hail Mary], and a *Credo* [the Creed], and remember thy Maker, thou shalt speed much the better. And when thou art up and ready, then first sweep thy house, dress up thy dishboard, and set all things in good order within thy house. Milk thy kie [kine, or cows], suckle thy calves, sile up [strain] thy milk, take up thy children and array them, and provide for thy husband's breakfast, dinner, supper, and for thy children and servants; and take thy part with them. And . . . ordain [set aside a portion of] corn [grain] and malt to the mill to bake and brew withal when need is. And mete [measure] it to the mill and from the mill, and see that thou have thy measure again besides the toll [charges] or else the miller dealeth not truly with thee, or else thy corn is not dry as it should be. Thou must make butter and cheese when thou may. Serve thy swine both morning and evening, and give thy pullen [poultry] meat [food] in the morning. And when time of year cometh, thou must take heed how thy hens, ducks, and geese do lay, and to gather up their eggs, and when they wax broody to set them there as no beasts, swine, nor other vermin hurt them. And thou must know that all whole-footed fowl will sit a month and all cloven-footed fowl will sit but three weeks except a peahen and such other great fowls as cranes, bustards [large birds], and such other. And when they have brought forth their birds to see that they be well kept from the gleyd [kites], crows, fully martes [foumarts, i.e., polecats], and other vermin.

And in the beginning of March, or a little before, is time for a wife to make her garden and to get as many good seeds and herbs as she can, and specially such as be good for the pot and for to eat. And as oft as need shall require, it must be weeded, for else the weed will overgrow the herbs. And also in March is time to sow flax and hemp, for I have heard old housewives say that better is March hurds than April flax, the reason appeareth [hurds are the tough part of flax; i.e., better to plant in March regardless of the product]. But how it should be sown, weeded, pulled, rippled [combed], watered, washed, dried, beaten, braked [crushed], tawed [softened], hackled [hacked], spun, wound, wrapped, and woven, it needed not for me to show, for they be wise enough. And thereof may they make sheets, boardcloths [tablecloths], towels, shirts, smocks, and such other necessaries. And therefore let thy distaff be always ready for a pastime that thou be not idle. . . .

It may fortune sometime that thou shalt have so many things to do that thou shalt not well know where is best to begin. Then take heed which thing should be the greatest loss if it were not done and in what space it would be done; and then think what is the greatest loss and there begin. . . .

It is a wife's occupation to winnow all manner of corns, to make malt [for brewing beer], wash and wring, to make hay, to shear corn, and in time of need to help her husband to fill the muck wain or dung cart, drive the plow,

to load hay, corn, and such other. Also to go or ride to the market to sell butter, cheese, milk, eggs, chickens, capons, hens, pigs, geese, and all manner of
corn. And also to buy all manner of necessary things belonging to a household, and to make a true reckoning and account to her husband what
she hath received and what she hath paid. And if the husband go to the market to buy or sell (as they oft do), he then to show his wife in like manner.
For if one of them should use [practice] to deceive the other, he deceiveth
himself, and he is not like to thrive, and therefore they must be true either
to other.

→ WILLIAM HARRISON

From *The Description of England* 1587
Dining Customs

William Harrison's record of English eating habits affords a specific picture of when
people took their meals. As with other customs, the time when people dined was to
some extent determined by the class to which they belonged.

With us the nobility, gentry, and students do ordinarily go to dinner at
eleven before noon, and to supper at five, or between five and six at afternoon.
The merchants dine and sup seldom before twelve at noon, and six at night,
especially in London. The husbandmen dine also at high noon, as they call it,
and sup at seven or eight; but out of the term in our universities the scholars
dine at ten. As for the poorest sort they generally dine and sup when they
may, so that to talk of their order of repast, it were but a needless matter. I
might here take occasion also to set down the variety used by antiquity in
their beginnings of their diets, wherein almost every nation had a several
[distinct] fashion, some beginning of custom (as we do in summer time) with
salads at supper, and some ending with lettuce, some making their entry with
eggs, and shutting up their tables with mulberries, as we do with fruit and
conceits [fancy trifles, sweets] of all sorts. Divers (as the old Romans) began
with a few crops [sprouts] of rue, as the Venetians did with the fish called
gobius; the Belgians with butter (or as we do yet also) with butter and eggs
upon fish days. But whereas we commonly begin with the most gross food,
and end with the most delicate, the Scot, thinking much [i.e., fearing] to
leave the best for his menial servants, maketh his entrance at the best, so that
he is sure thereby to leave the worst.

→ WILLIAM HARRISON

From *The Description of England* 1587

Fashion

Such detailed commentary on fashion is fascinating for the pictorial details it provides about what English men and women wore in sixteenth-century London. It is also instructive for its assault on sartorial folly and excess. Actors often came under attack for the impropriety of their costumes — as "vagabonds" they were not entitled to such splendor — and for the convention of cross-dressing.

The fantastical folly of our nation, even from the courtier to the carter, is such that no form of apparel liketh [pleases] us longer than the first garment is in the wearing, if it continue so long and be not laid aside, to receive some other trinket newly devised by the fickle-headed tailors, who covet to have several tricks in cutting, thereby to draw fond customers to more expense of money. For my part, I can tell better how to inveigh against this enormity than describe any certainty of our attire; since such is our mutability that today there is none to [nothing comparable to] the Spanish guise, tomorrow the French toys [trinkets] are most fine and delectable, ere long no such apparel as [i.e., except] that which is after the high Alman [German] fashion, by and by the Turkish manner is generally best liked of, otherwise the Morisco [Moorish] gowns, the Barbarian sleeves, the mandilion [a cape with sleeves] worn to Colley-Weston-ward, and the short French breeches make such a comely vesture that, except it were a dog in a doublet, you shall not see any so disguised as are my countrymen of England. And as these fashions are diverse, so likewise it is a world to see the costliness and the curiosity, the excess and the vanity, the pomp and the bravery [splendor], the change and the variety, and finally the fickleness and the folly, that is in all degrees, insomuch that nothing is more constant in England than inconstancy of attire. Oh, how much cost is bestowed nowadays upon our bodies, and how little upon our souls! How many suits of apparel hath the one, and how little furniture hath the other! How long time is asked in decking up of the first, and how little space left wherein to feed the latter! How curious [hard to satisfy], how nice [fastidious] also, are a number of men and women, and how hardly can the tailor please them in making it fit for their bodies! How many times must it be sent back again to him that made it! What chafing, what fretting, what reproachful language doth the poor workman bear away! And many times when he doth nothing to it at all, yet when it is brought home again, it is very fit and handsome; then must we put it on, then must the long seams of our hose be set by a plumb-line, then we puff, then we blow, and finally, sweat till we drop, that our clothes may stand well upon us.

I will say nothing of our heads, which sometimes are polled [cut short], sometimes curled, or suffered to grow at length like woman's locks, many times cut off above or under the ears round, as by [using] a wooden dish. Neither will I meddle with our variety of beards, of which some are shaven from the chin like those of Turks, not a few cut short like to the beard of Marquis Otto, some made round like a rubbing brush, other with a *pique de vant* [a short, pointed Vandyke beard] (oh, fine fashion!) or now and then suffered to grow long, the barbers being grown to be so cunning in this behalf as the tailors. And therefore, if a man have a lean and straight face, a Marquis Otto's cut will make it broad and large; if it be platterlike, a long slender beard will make it seem the narrower; if he be weasel-beaked, then much hair left on the cheeks will make the owner look big, like a bowdled [ruffled] hen, and so grim as a goose. . . . Many old men do wear no beards at all. Some lusty courtiers also and gentlemen of courage do wear either rings of gold, stones, or pearl in their ears, whereby they imagine the workmanship of God not to be a little amended. But herein they rather disgrace than adorn their persons, as by their niceness [luxuriousness] in apparel, for which I say most nations do not unjustly deride us, as also for that we do seem to imitate all nations round about us, wherein we be like to the *polypus* [octopus] or chameleon; and thereunto bestow most cost upon our asses, and much more than upon all the rest of our bodies, as women do likewise upon their heads and shoulders.

In women also it is most to be lamented that they do now far exceed the lightness [lasciviousness] of our men (who nevertheless are transformed from the cap even to the very shoe), and such staring attire as in time past was supposed meet for none but light hussies only, is now become an habit for chaste and sober matrons. What should I say of their doublets with pendant codpieces on the breast, full of jags and cuts, and sleeves of sundry colors? their galligaskins [loose breeches] to bear out their bums and make their attire to fit plum round (as they term it) about them? their farthingales and diversely colored nether stocks of silk, jersey, and such like, whereby their bodies are rather deformed than commended? I have met with some of these trulls [loose women] in London so disguised, that it hath passed my skill to discern whether they were men or women.

Thus it is now come to pass that women are become men and men transformed into monsters.

CHAPTER 8

Men and Women: Gender, Family, Society

⊰⊱

Statements about gender, family, and society in the sixteenth and seventeenth centuries must be qualified by considerations of economics, geography, class, and other such shaping factors. The Puritan cloth-seller and his wife who kept shop together in London should not be lumped together with the Catholic family living on a vast landed estate near the Scottish border nor with the widowed tenant farmer struggling to subsist on a small plot of land in the West country. Most of what we know about courtship, marital relations, child rearing, inheritance, and the organization of the early modern household derives from the families of property owners, a group that expanded dramatically between 1500 and 1600. As these prosperous people became more numerous and conspicuous, they tended to emulate the social and familial behaviors of the group just above them, the landed gentry descended from the ruling elites of the fourteenth and fifteenth centuries. Thus, some generalizations will apply to more than one distinct group, but we should keep in mind that early modern England comprised many social practices and experiences. In the pages that follow, the customs of distinct social and economic classes are frequently elided, and yet such inevitable distortions are the price of establishing historical difference, of explaining clearly how the lives of early modern men and women and their families do and do not resemble our own.

The Situation of Women

England was ruled by a brilliant and strong-willed woman in the second half of the sixteenth century, but the monarchy was not a career option for women. The normal occupation for women at the time was marriage and motherhood. This is not to say, however, that women did not work. On the contrary, the wife's job of running a household and rearing children was all-consuming, at least as demanding as, if not more so than, the corresponding duties of the husband. Upper-class women had servants to help with these tasks, while women of the lower social and economic strata did more of the actual labor themselves. But only a handful of very wealthy women were entirely at leisure. The comparative freedom of modern women to fulfill themselves in a variety of ways, with marriage and procreation as alternatives that may be embraced, postponed, combined with other professional pursuits, or rejected altogether, makes the limited options for women in early modern culture seem oppressive and unjust. While we deplore such restrictions, there is little point in what Stephen Booth calls "accusing the past of having been the past" (265). Instead, we must add to our disapproval an effort to appreciate the historical, economic, and philosophical causes of these constraints.

That women occupied a position subordinate to men in the early modern period is beyond dispute; that this was the "natural" state of affairs was almost beyond dispute. Although the idea is repugnant to modern sensibilities, most thinkers in the sixteenth century took it as axiomatic that men are superior to women. This is hardly the place to explore the ancient origins of gender hierarchies, but it is worth spending a moment to mention the cooperation of biology and philosophy in the creation of traditional roles for men and women. In primitive societies the greater physical strength of males led to a corresponding distribution of duties: the man killed the bear, the woman cooked it. Aristotle, much revered by humanist writers in early modern Europe, had offered a biological account of gender difference (see the passage on p. 275); and medieval theorists of the body developed and illustrated his ideas. According to the elemental theory, the human body was composed of four elements: air, fire, earth, and water. Of these, the first two were considered warm, dynamic, and therefore masculine; the latter pair were cold, moist, and feminine. Shakespeare's Cleopatra asserts her transcendence of her female body when, at her suicide — itself a Roman, masculine deed — she declares, "I am fire and air; my other elements / I give to baser life" (5.2.289–90).

From the ancient world through the Middle Ages and into the Renaissance, physical differences between men and women generated a hierarchy that came to be "naturalized" in early examples of social theory. Greater physical strength was linked with greater intellectual ability and more profound capacity for feeling. In the second act of *Twelfth Night*, Orsino lectures Viola (disguised as a male) on the inferiority of female affection:

> There is no woman's sides
> Can bide the beating of so strong a passion
> As love doth give my heart; no woman's heart
> So big, to hold so much; they lack retention.
> Alas, their love may be call'd appetite,
> No motion of the liver, but the palate . . .   (2.4.93–98)

Shakespeare, of course, is mocking Orsino's male ego, since his pupil is a woman who loves the Duke more profoundly and constantly than he loves the hard-hearted Olivia. But such constructions of male and female abilities and roles led to the orthodoxy of male dominance. In medieval and early modern Europe, these "scientific" justifications of female subordination were reinforced by Christian doctrine in both its Catholic and Protestant forms. The Pauline commitment to the husband as the head of the wife, as Christ is the head of the church, represents the standard viewpoint. Eve, having been created second, was thought to be further removed from God than Adam. Finally, the traditional association of woman with home and hearth was enforced by a fact of medical history: the absence of any reliable or consistently practiced form of contraception meant that women gave birth to children who had to be taken care of. And in order to ensure social stability, the traditional place of woman was developed by moralists and social theorists into an ideology of subordination and domestic responsibility.

Such physiological and ideological restrictions limited independence of action among women, but they did not suppress it entirely. There was at least some actual resistance to the social roles prescribed for women. One of the most notorious examples from the first decade of the seventeenth century was a London character named Mary Frith, also known as Moll Cutpurse, who wore men's clothes, carried a sword, and smoked a pipe. She attracted enough attention to become the subject of a play by Thomas Middleton and Thomas Dekker known as *The Roaring Girl,* which was performed at the Fortune theater with Moll herself in attendance. A few women even paraded through the streets of London wearing men's clothing, a practice that seriously disturbed King James and led to sermons against sartorial disorder. But such unconventionality was exceptional. It is telling that Mary Frith flourished in London, for cities have always tolerated greater freedom of behavior. Similarly, the more significant kind of female independence grew out of the mercantile culture of London. Married women became involved in their husbands' business enterprises by assisting in the shop and keeping accounts, and even though women could not legally own property by themselves, widows of shopkeepers and craftsmen sometimes assumed ownership and control of the business after the husband's death. A well-provided-for widow probably enjoyed the greatest freedom of any early modern woman. Moreover, a substantial number of English women seem to have entered the marketplace on their own, doing laundry, working in the cloth trade, or selling fruit or baked goods and other provisions. Ben Jonson's comedy, *Bartholomew Fair* (1614), presents an unforgettable entrepreneur in the person of Ursula the Pig Woman, who runs a kind of outdoor lunch counter specializing in pork and who also seems, as a kind of pimp, to sell human female flesh. At this point we verge on the kind of commerce represented by prostitutes and other social outcasts who populated the brothels, or *stews,* in Southwark. In *Pericles,* a late play, Shakespeare mordantly depicts the business practices of the brothel owners (male and female) and their kind, but those scenes also encourage sympathy for young women who, by various accidents, might have found themselves engaged in such a trade. (See the excerpt from Thomas Nashe's *Christ's Tears over Jerusalem,* p. 242.)

If ideology and law limited independence of action, they exerted less influence over freedom of thought. Education became increasingly available to the middle classes, an effect of the spread of Continental humanism, the arrival of a print-based culture, and the Protestant belief that individual Christians ought to be permitted and able to read the Bible in their own language. Such expanded opportunities did not effect an immediate change in literacy, however. Although statistics are sketchy and probably unreliable, it appears that less than 50 percent of males could read and write at the turn of the seventeenth century, and boys were schooled more frequently than girls. Still, the number of readers increased dramatically during the sixteenth century, and the widening pedagogical system began to produce greater numbers of literate and, in the highest reaches of society, extremely learned women. Some aristocratic women wrote verse, translated the Scriptures or classical literature, or produced philosophical treatises. Lady Mary Wroth, the niece of Sir Philip Sidney, wrote poetry — a sonnet sequence — and a long prose romance called *The Countess of Montgomery's Urania;* apparently she was the first English woman to produce either of these forms. Elizabeth Cary, viscountess of Falkland, composed a play, *The Tragedy of Mariam.* Although apparently not performed, it was the first published play by an Englishwoman (1613). Scholars have recently turned their attention to other *closet dramas,* plays composed not for public performance but for reading or private presentation, written by women of noble families. Many of these women acted as the literary patrons for male writers, notably Mary Herbert, the countess of Pembroke (Lady Mary Wroth's aunt), and Lucy Harington Russell, countess of Bedford.

The uncomfortable situation of educated women appears vividly in the case of Arbella Stuart (1575–1615), certainly one of the most learned and impressive women of her time. Child of a noble family and possessor of what some — herself included — considered a reasonable claim to the English throne, Stuart's aristocratic advantages make her atypical but nonetheless worthy of notice. Queen Elizabeth treated her properly but kept her under virtual house arrest, fearing her potential political strength; when her cousin James became king in 1603, he brought her to court but watched her closely. Stuart consoled herself by studying. She knew French, Italian, Latin, Greek, Hebrew, and perhaps Spanish; she was adept at music, dancing, embroidery, and other arts considered suitable for females; she also mastered skills usually reserved for males, such as hunting, hawking, and the keeping of accounts. She did not, however, regard these accomplishments as commensurate with her abilities and ambitions. In privately pursuing her monarchical claim by attempting to retrieve her ancestral properties and to arrange a canny political marriage, she was forced to maneuver at some distance from the actual center of power. Consequently, she produced a fascinating series of letters that, taken together, constitute a record of female independence and learning put to imaginative use. In the words of Barbara Lewalski, "her letters are noteworthy for their witty and ironic comments on Elizabethan and Jacobean court society; for their unconscious self-representation combined with highly conscious self-fashioning; and for their rhetorical strategies of self-defense, ranging from obfuscation to self-abasement to insistent self-justification. . . . In them, Arbella Stuart works out a rhetoric of concealment as a strategy for retaining some limited power of self-determination in a repressive milieu" (67).

The education of women stimulated a broader range of thought about gender roles, and such discourse in turn generated powerful cultural anxiety about potential disruption of the social order. In short, what we regard as progress was seen by some in the Renaissance as monstrous or dangerous, and a number of writers responded to such social changes with misogynistic polemics. One of the most frequent forms of abuse directed against educated women was the equation of eloquence and promiscuity: looseness of tongue came to symbolize looseness of body and spirit. Such conventional attacks on female speech were taken over from the Middle Ages, specifically from such church fathers as St. John Chrysostom, St. Jerome, and others, and then expanded to fit the circumstances of free-thinking women. In 1615 Joseph Swetnam published his *Arraignment of Lewd, Idle, Froward, and Unconstant Women*; it was reprinted nine times in twenty years. The word *froward* (forward or aggressive) appears repeatedly in contemporary antifeminist discourse: women are charged with being "unruly," "shrewish," "disorderly," and "monstrous." Some of Shakespeare's outspoken women endure mockery for using their tongues. Volumnia, the mother of Coriolanus, is accused of being "mankind," that is, masculine, for speaking incessantly and in an unladylike way, and Paulina in *The Winter's Tale* is called "a mankind witch," "a callet [scold] of boundless tongue," and "Dame Partlet [a clucking hen]" for daring to tell the king the truth. The attempt of women to rule over their husbands, when the opposite is the "natural" relation, is one of the frequent themes of the misogynist tradition, as is evident in John Taylor's versified form of the complaint:

> Ill fares the hapless family that shows
> A cock that's silent, and a Hen that crows.
> I know not which live more unnatural lives,
> Obedient husbands, or commanding wives.   (Qtd. in Underdown 118)

The abundance of such angry discourse suggests that the earliest hints of emancipation among women were producing a backlash among defenders of the status quo.

Patriarchy

Patriarchy has become a familiar term in recent critical discourse, and yet its familiarity, its status as a buzzword, can be an obstacle to a full understanding of its historical, economic, religious, and social implications. The origins of the concept are biblical, the etymological root being derived from the leaders of the twelve tribes of Israel described in the Pentateuch and closely associated with divine law. In the ancient world and down through the Middle Ages, the patriarch tended to be the leader of a clan or tribe or large group of kinfolk, sometimes the chief of all the people in a certain region or even the head of a nation. Sir Robert Filmer's historical treatise entitled *Patriarcha, or The Natural Power of Kings*, written in the middle of the seventeenth century, develops the analogy between the primitive tribe, the monarchical state, and the English family:

> . . . not only Adam, but the succeeding Patriarchs had, by right of fatherhood, royal authority over their children. . . . I see not then how the children of Adam, or of any man else, can be free from subjection to their parents. And this subordination of children is the only fountain of all regal authority, by the ordination of God himself.

However, with the emergence of the modern state — and England under Henry VIII and Elizabeth I is a good instance of this development — came the simultaneous rise of the smaller family. The consolidation of power in the monarch reduced the influence of the feudal families and the lords that headed them, and a concomitant effect of this shift from patron to sovereign was a dispersal of authority from a few powerful lords to the male partner of each conjugal unit. England in the sixteenth and seventeenth centuries is the site of origin for many modern notions about the structure and function of the family, particularly the role of the father, for out of these developments the nuclear family took its shape. (For a more extensive excerpt from *Patriarcha*, see p. 276.)

Authority in the early modern family rested finally with the father. Wives had authority over children and servants, but the principle that the woman was "the weaker vessel" and consequently dependent on the superior judgment and ability of her husband — a doctrine derived from St. Paul and his interpreters — gave the father uncontested rule over his wife and all members of the household. Writing in 1571, Edmund Tilney puts the doctrine in the mouths of two of his characters in a dialogue:

> Ye say well, Madam, quoth M. *Erasmus*. For in deede both divine, and humaine lawes, in our religion giveth the man absolute aucthoritie, over the woman in all places.
>
> And, quoth the Lady *Julia*, as I sayde before, reason doth confirme the same, the man being as he is, most apt for the soveraignetie being in governement, not onely skill, and experience to be required, but also capacity to comprehende, wisdome to understand, strength to execute, solicitude to prosecute, pacience to suffer, meanes to sustayne, and above all a great courage to accomplishe, all which are commonly in a man, but in a woman very rare. (*The Flower of Friendship* 134)

Wives, in other words, were to yield to their husbands. According to the *Homily of the State of Matrimony*, a widely disseminated sermon intended for delivery at the conclusion of the marriage service, "St. Paul expresseth it in this form of words: *Let women be subject to their husbands, as to the Lord; for the husband is the head of the woman, as Christ is the head of the Church* [Ephesians 5:22–23]. Here you understand that God hath commanded that ye should acknowledge the authority of the husband and refer to him the honor of obedience." As the language of this passage discloses, paternal dominion in the home was reinforced by the emphases and particularly the imagery of Elizabethan political and religious discourse. As God the Father was to all creation and the monarch to the state, so was the father to the household. (The complete homily is found on p. 278.) Some historians believe that the reason the homily was read so often is that masculine authority in the domestic sphere was increasingly under threat. According to Susan Amussen, "No one questioned women's subordination to their husbands — they just sometimes refused to give it" (210).

The Pauline insistence on female submission is grounded in the creation account recorded in Genesis 2 and 3, in which man is created first and then woman is formed from a rib taken from man. This passage, which develops the story of the serpent and the tree of knowledge, culminates in the punishment of Adam and Eve for the sin of disobedience: "Unto the woman he said, I will greatly increase thy sorrows, and thy conceptions. In sorrow shalt thou bring forth children, and thy desire *shall be subject* to thine husband, and he shall rule over thee" (Genesis 3:16, Geneva). Commentators in the sixteenth and seventeenth centuries, echoing the arguments of the medieval church fathers, made much of this hierarchical relation. William Gouge, author of a number of influential marriage manuals, asserted that the family was "a school wherein the first principles and grounds of government and subjection are to be learned . . . inferiors that cannot be subject in a family . . . will hardly be brought to yield such subjection as they ought in Church or Commonwealth" (qtd. in Amussen 200). (See p. 287 for Gouge's comparison between marriage and the social order.) The analogy between the marriage contract and the social contract, family and commonwealth, was useful to both political and domestic theorists because it was reversible. The challenges to the monarchy that became more frequent under the Stuarts and culminated in the English Civil Wars and the execution of King Charles (1649) meant that such commentary tended to be more abundant in the seventeenth century than in the sixteenth, when the doctrine of divinely given order was less open to question. Husbands, like monarchs, were expected to be conscious of their duty to their subjects and were exhorted not to behave tyrannically toward their wives, children, and servants.

Genesis contains another account of creation, however, one found in the first chapter and preceding the story of the rib. "Furthermore God said, Let us make man in our image according to our likeness, and let them rule over the fish of the sea, and over the fowl of the heaven, and over the beasts, and over all the earth, and over every thing that creepeth and moveth on the earth. Thus God created the man in his image: in the image of God created he him: he created them male and female" (1:26–27, Geneva). This alternative version of the creation of the race is consistent with the assertion appended to the story of the creation of woman out of man: "Therefore shall man leave his father and his mother, and shall cleave unto his wife: and they shall be one flesh" (Genesis 2:24). This emphasis on conjugal oneness is the source of a theme common to many writers on domestic ideology, the belief in mutuality and even equality. Throughout commentary on the relations of husbands and wives and the proper ordering of rights and responsibilities between them, the "natural" authority of the husband in the household is modified by an increasingly important Protestant religious doctrine: the principle of companionate marriage.

The basis for conjugal mutuality was the doctrine of spiritual equality among men and women, a belief that emerged in the humanist writings of the early sixteenth century and that, strangely enough, was derived also from St. Paul: "For all ye that are baptized into Christ, have put on Christ. There is neither Jew nor Grecian: there is neither bond nor free: there is neither male nor female: for ye are all one in Christ Jesus" (Galatians 3:27–28, Geneva). This text seems incompatible with the apostle's insistence, in the Letter to the Ephesians (5:22) and cited in the homily on marriage, on the natural subjection of wives to their husbands, and in fact this conflict between subjection and equality is replicated throughout the marriage manuals and domestic treatises. Many writers recommend that husband and wife ideally should bring to their marriage similarity in age, class, and economic status. But some commentators offer even bolder statements of the doctrine of equality that directly contradict the hegemony of the husband. For example, Tilney's *Flower of Friendship*, cited earlier on the topic of male superiority, also presents a statement of resistance to that argument based on the spiritual status of the wife and the strength of ancient example:

> There is another great mainteyner of the *Flower*, and that is the goodly grace of obedience. For reason it is that we obey our Husbandes. God commaundeth it, and we are bounde so to doe.
> I know not, quoth the Lady *Isabella*, what we are bound to do, but as meete is it, that the husband obey the wife, as the wife the husband, or at the least that there be no superioritie betwene them, as the auncient philosophers have defended. For women have soules as wel as men, they have wit as wel as men, and more apt for procreation of children than men. What reason is it then, that they shall be bound, whom nature hath made free? (133)

"For women have soules as wel as men" is a powerful — and irrefutable — claim, and yet in Tilney's fictional dialogue the young woman who makes this assertion is overruled. In fact, the statement of male superiority cited earlier is Lady Julia's refutation of her daughter's protofeminist claims. But the characters' dispute is especially useful in exposing the contradictions inherent in early modern thinking about gender and power. These conflicts seem particularly meaningful when we consider that Tilney's dialogue on female submission is dedicated "To the Noble and most Vertuous Princesse, Elizabeth, by the Grace of God, of England, Fraunce, and Irelande, Queene, defender of the Faith. Etc." and was published in London in 1568, at a point when the question of Elizabeth's marriageability was a topic of national concern.

The early humanists had developed the ideal of companionate marriage, and Puritan pressure on English thought magnified its importance. Reformed theology promoted not only the doctrine of Grace as given indiscriminately to men and women but also the supremacy of the individual conscience in matters of salvation; both of these principles served to elevate the status of women in relation to all mortal creatures, even their husbands. Moreover, the increasingly forceful emphasis among Puritan preachers on the Christian's freedom from the unjust control of secular authority, a tenet that would receive its strongest literary expression in the writings of John Milton, tended to complicate the traditional hierarchy, civilly sanctioned and enforced, between husband and wife. If, as radical Protestants believed, the individual soul was to be governed only by its perception of the divine will, then this principle posed a contradiction to the dominion of the spouse and cleared the way for the doctrine of companionate marriage. The same contradiction could be seen in the larger political arena. In other words, Milton's antiroyalism is perfectly consistent with his endorsement of divorce. While these generalizations are not meant to suggest anything as improbable as Miltonic feminism, it is nevertheless true that the Puritan devotion to conscience and individual salvation conflicted with the ideology of subjection that linked the family and the state in discussions of domestic and political order and obedience. The ideal of companionate marriage based on conjugal sympathy and even equality developed slowly throughout the seventeenth century and came to fruition in the eighteenth, but its origins can be heard resounding from the Reformed pulpit and Protestant pamphlets as early as Elizabeth's reign. Further, a version of it is both audible and visible in at least some of Shakespeare's comedies. Despite the traditions of masculine authority in the family, it seems quite clear at the end of *Much Ado about Nothing* that Benedick will not succeed in dominating Beatrice.

Primogeniture

In the second scene of *King Lear*, the illegitimate son of the Earl of Gloucester confides to the audience his conviction that he deserves to inherit his father's property and title because he is more capable than his legitimate older brother.

> Wherefore should I
> Stand in the plague of custom, and permit
> The curiosity of nations to deprive me,
> For that I am some twelve or fourteen moonshines
> Lag of a brother? (1.2.2–6)

Edmund's argument proceeds from his belief in his own strength. He considers himself smarter and more aggressive than Edgar, attributing these qualities to the passion that stimulated the liaison in which he was conceived. His contempt for the niceties of social convention expresses itself in his wordplay, his toying with the various forms of *bastard* and particularly his mockery of the word *legitimate*.

> Well then,
> Legitimate Edgar, I must have your land.

> Our father's love is to the bastard Edmund
> As to th' legitimate. Fine word, "legitimate."
> Well, my legitimate, if this letter speed
> And my invention thrive, Edmund the base
> Shall top th' legitimate.   (1.2.15–21)

Legitimate comes from the Latin for *law* (*lex, legis*), and Edmund's worrying of the word calls attention to its pertinence to the subject of the speech, the rights of heredity that customarily belong to the legally recognized eldest son. In seeking to substitute a biological or natural privilege — "Now, gods, stand up for bastards!" (1.2.22) — Edmund assails one of the foundations of English law, the convention of primogeniture. The passage from Sir Thomas Smith on page 288 provides a sixteenth-century justification of the practice.

Primogeniture (first-born) refers to the right of the eldest son to inherit the family property, and some of the early modern writers on politics and economics associate it specifically with the patriarchal transmission of governmental authority from tribal leaders down to contemporary rulers, whether of kingdoms or households. Taking hold as it did in the feudal practices of England in the Middle Ages, primogeniture was calculated to protect the property of large families, to keep estates from being dismantled or divided into a number of small and therefore weaker units. In the Renaissance the head of an important household was normally regarded as a caretaker of the family property, one to whom the ancestors had entrusted the health and prosperity of the family holdings. Thus the well-being of the group took precedence over that of any individual member, including the heir himself. Even when primogeniture worked as it was supposed to do, keeping estates from being broken up and land from being dispersed into smaller parcels, the price of the system could be ruinous for virtually all members of the family.

The eldest son, despite his apparent advantage, was in a sense trapped, having no real option but to await the death of his father so that he could succeed to guardianship of the estate. The younger children fared much worse, dependent as they were on the goodwill of their father to provide for them. In the case of daughters, this meant money for a dowry with which to attract a husband; in the case of younger sons, an education or a living, or at least the means to marry well. But sometimes goodwill was hindered by a lack of resources. Owing to financial hardships or entails (legal restrictions deriving from earlier wills that controlled the use of property or income), some apparently wealthy fathers were unable to provide for their younger children. A younger son was sometimes regarded as insurance against the death of the eldest son — Lawrence Stone compares such a boy to "a kind of walking sperm bank" — and many of these young men attended the university and became clergymen. But the problem was pervasive enough in England in the 1590s for Falstaff to joke about drafting the "younger sons of younger brothers," men who were at the bottom of the economic ladder and hadn't a shilling to give in the way of a bribe to escape military service.

The system of inheritance was complicated to start with and grew more so in the Renaissance. Even now English property laws are notoriously complex, one source being the movement from the feudal system, by which *land*-lords (the word needs defamiliarizing) held Crown properties in tenancy, to the modern system, by which a larger number of individuals own outright or hold in tenancy smaller units of land. (In England today, much of the land is still legally held by aristocratic estates rather than by the people who own houses or flats on that property.) The sixteenth century saw the beginnings of this shift, but it also introduced a host of other problems. The transformation of England's state religion from Catholicism to Protestantism, for example, led to the dissolution of religious houses such as monasteries and convents; one effect of this policy was a rise in the number of marriageable women, daughters who might have gone (cheaply) into convents but who now had to be provided for. Next, the significant increase in population between 1500 and 1600, with twice as many people occupying the same finite amount of land, created major economic and social dislocation. And the expansion of commerce produced cash that merchants and others wished to secure by investing in land. Shakespeare himself turned his London theatrical earnings into real estate investments in his hometown.

The social tensions inherent in the system of primogeniture find expression not only in diaries and court records but also in the theater of the period, where familial anxiety becomes the basis for dramatic conflict. In Thomas Middleton's *Your Five Gallants*, a character encounters a group of fashionable young men and greets them with, "Why so merry, gentlemen, are your fathers dead?" Such rivalry existed not only between fathers and children but also between widowed mothers and sons and among some siblings. One historian has suggested that the familial relationship least likely to suffer damage from the problems of inheritance was that between brother and sister, because the female's secondary legal status meant that property was not an issue. It was certainly an issue between brothers. At the beginning of *As You Like It*, Orlando bitterly complains of being misused by his elder brother, Oliver, and cheated of his small inheritance:

OLIVER: Know you where you are, sir?
ORLANDO: O, sir, very well; here in your orchard.
OLIVER: Know you before whom, sir?
ORLANDO: Ay, better than him I am before knows me. I know you are my
   eldest brother, and in the gentle condition of blood you should so
   know me. The courtesy of nations allows you my better, in that you are
   the first born, but the same tradition takes not away my blood, were
   there twenty brothers betwixt us. I have as much of my father in me
   as you. . . . (1.1.40–50)

This is different from Edmund's mockery of primogeniture. Orlando objects not to the system of inheritance ("the courtesy of nations") but to his brother's abuse of it in failing to honor their dead father's provision for Orlando. The drama of the period contains a sufficient number of such scenes and references to intimate that inheritance was becoming a widespread social concern. Indeed, on a national scale, the question of succession was of paramount importance at the turn of the seventeenth century, since Queen Elizabeth had no firstborn to inherit her throne. In the Shakespeare family, William, as the eldest son, was the beneficiary of primogeniture, inheriting in 1601 the Henley Street property, where his aunt Joan continued to live. We may remark in passing that he had a younger (legitimate) brother, also an actor, named Edmund.

Marriage and Money

Early modern matrimonial customs may seem cold-blooded, but it is important that we study them from a sixteenth-century point of view. Social historians such as Lawrence Stone and Ann Jennalie Cook have demonstrated that the ideas about romantic love and personal choice that govern our concepts of marriage are effects of social and attitudinal changes that took place in the eighteenth and nineteenth centuries. Stone urges that we "rid ourselves of three modern Western culture-bound preconceptions": (1) that marriage for love or personal attraction is morally superior to marriage for money or power, and that the categories are easily separable; (2) that authentic union must be underwritten by emotional attachment, or else the resulting marriage is the equivalent of commerce or prostitution; and (3) that personal autonomy or individual desire in the selection of a marriage partner should outweigh the claims of the family or the larger social group. As he argues, "Marriage among the property-owning classes in sixteenth-century England was, therefore, a collective decision of family and kin, not an individual one" (*Family* 85–87).

In the words of a sixteenth-century proverb, "More belongs to marriage than four bare legs in a bed." Marriage was part of a system of inheritance and economics so ingrained and pervasive that the emotional affections or physical desires of a man and woman diminished in importance. This was especially true among the upper classes, where the amount of property being inherited could be substantial, and where marriage was regarded as a convenient instrument for joining or ensuring peace between two powerful families, for consolidating land holdings, or for achieving other familial, financial, or even political ends. Once a marriage was agreed on, certain fiscal transactions took place. The bride's family promised to give to the married couple a *dowry* made up of property, valuables (silver and jewelry, for example), and cash. This was also called the bride's *portion*, and it was paid at the time of the wedding or soon after, occasionally in installments. If a young man could find a young woman whose family could afford a substantial dowry, then he could look forward to living comfortably. Moreover, his parents might be able to save some of their holdings to settle on their other children, perhaps their own daughters. The groom's family agreed to provide the couple with money to live on, to specify exactly what the groom would inherit at his father's death, and to guarantee a *dower* (the parallel term to dowry), the sum that the bride would inherit should the groom die before her. This money, also called the *jointure*, served as a kind of life insurance for the bride. In fact, it is useful to think of all of these settlements as a form of security, both for the couple being married and for the families sending them out into the world. The monetary arrangements I have described were designed to guarantee that the couple would live comfortably, and that if one partner should die the other would not be penniless or a drain on his or her family.

The complexities and permutations of this system were considerable, of course, but a few generalizations can be made about sixteenth- and seventeenth-century practices. It was better to have sons than daughters. Because primogeniture ensured that an estate was passed on intact from father to eldest son, that young man's prospects were very bright. His parents sought the daughter of a prominent or wealthy family whose dowry would be worthy of the inheritance he would receive. If his parents were dead, he presented himself to the family of an appropriate partner, as Petruchio does in *The Taming of the Shrew*. Indeed, consciousness of these economic and social customs makes such Shakespearean suitors as Petruchio and Claudio in *Much Ado about Nothing* look less like fortune hunters and more like prudent conservators of their familial legacy.

If the estate was extremely large, the father normally made financial arrangements for the daughters and younger sons; if it was extremely small, these younger children might be so disadvantaged that they would have to remain unmarried. For younger sons in particular, this was considered a reasonable option, for they could find ways of supporting themselves — by teaching, taking religious orders, or even going to sea. Daughters, though, could serve as a serious drain on a family's estate. The father would need to provide a dowry for each in order to get them married and out of his house, and women lacked the alternatives to marriage that young men had. Although daughters could be costly to provide for, an heiress could improve a family's fortune by attracting the son of a prominent landed family. This system of financial reciprocity meant that the upper classes tended to marry at a younger age than the middle and lower classes because the size of the estates involved was a primary consideration. Marriages might be arranged even in the infancy of the couple concerned and confirmed when the prospective bride and groom reached puberty. Our nearest contact with this system is the complex set of negotiations that still attend the wedding of a member of the royal family in Britain or Japan. Practically speaking, ending a marriage through divorce was not an option in the early modern period, although on those rare occasions when it did occur (for reasons of sexual impotence, for instance), great care was taken about the financial consequences.

These arrangements applied to the wealthiest and most prominent members of society, but the middle and even the lower classes, insofar as they could, emulated these contractual practices in order to protect their offspring and guarantee financial stability. Parents had authority over their children in matters of marriage, certainly until the young person reached adulthood and, in some cases, as long as the parents lived. The dowry system required that a young man or woman receive parental approval, and sometimes even then the marriage could not go forward until certain obstacles were removed: property might need to be sold or cash might need to be raised, a process that could take some time; a suitable house might have to be found for the couple; a groom might have to wait until the end of his apprenticeship. Conversely, a match proposed by parents might have to wait until the couple themselves could be made to agree to it. A Shakespearean version of this scenario is Capulet's trouble with his recalcitrant teenage daughter in the fourth act of *Romeo and Juliet*.

The primacy of money in the matrimonial process raises the question of attraction or "love." Although the emotions of the young couple were not the main consideration in courtship, they were not utterly irrelevant, and the evidence suggests that then, as now, parents wanted to accommodate a child's desires while doing what they thought best for the child's future happiness. The passage from George Whetstone's *Heptameron of Civil Discourses* (p. 289) indicates an awareness of the value of free choice. At the risk of overgeneralizing, we can say that the more money was at stake, the less personal affection counted in the business of courtship. Shakespeare's comedies often turn on the question of who will decide on a suitable marriage partner. In *A Midsummer Night's Dream*, when Egeus insists on his power to select his daughter's mate — "she is mine, and all my right of her / I do estate unto Demetrius" (1.1.97–98) — his diction, particularly the possessive pronouns and the verb *estate*, indicates the importance of property and his conception of his daughter as a possession. In *Much Ado about Nothing*, the young woman named Hero is an heiress who is a most eligible marriage partner, and when it appears that Don Pedro ("the Prince") will ask for her hand, her father appears ready to give her a choice: "I will acquaint my daughter withal, that she may be the better prepar'd for an answer" (1.2.21–22). It may be, however, that he is merely engaging in a formality, that he will instruct her to be prepared to accept. Two scenes later her cousin Beatrice exposes the potential conflict of will:

> ANTONIO [*to Hero*]: Well, niece, I trust you will be rul'd by your father.
> BEATRICE: Yes, faith, it is my cousin's duty to make cur'sy and say, "Father, as it please you." But yet for all that, cousin, let him be a handsome fellow, or else make another cur'sy and say, "Father, as it please me."
> (2.1.50–56)

In fact, Don Pedro acts as a go-between and asks for Hero's hand on behalf of Claudio, whose social rank (Count) satisfies her father and whose appearance satisfies her. Like most writers of comedy, Shakespeare usually sympathizes with the daughter. But in reality, as opposed to the reality portrayed on stage, the clash between a parent's wishes and those of a son or daughter was usually decided in favor of the parent.

Where huge fortunes were not in the balance — that is, among the vast majority of young people in England — personal autonomy carried greater weight. Other considerations increased in importance, matters such as age, companionship, emotional sympathy, and sexual attraction. Also, there was apparently more time for choice. While among the upper classes the need to make financial arrangements as early as possible meant that they tended to marry their children in their teens, many English people waited until their mid-twenties to marry. There are several reasons that explain this delay. In the early modern period, owing mainly to nutrition, children reached puberty somewhat later than they do now, perhaps a year or maybe even two or three years later, and this fact may have postponed slightly the physical urge to mate. But, as usual, the main causes were financial. A young man without family resources had to work for some time to afford the cost of marriage, which consisted at least of a dwelling for him and his bride and the establishment of a steady income to support her and the children who would follow. The effect of these circumstances was that most people put off getting married: in England in the sixteenth century, the average age for marriage was twenty-seven for men and twenty-four for women (see Laslett). In *Romeo and Juliet*, Shakespeare deliberately takes years off the age of the heroine in the sources (in one source she is seventeen, in another fifteen) for a variety of theatrical reasons, chiefly to magnify the drama of Juliet's progress from innocence to lovestruck girlhood to marriage to courageous suicide. But Romeo and Juliet should not be taken as typical candidates for marriage in sixteenth-century England. Although Shakespeare himself was eighteen on his wedding day, his wife was about twenty-six, and their surviving children, Susanna and Judith, did not marry until they were twenty-four and thirty-one.

Family Life

Most people got married, and most people had children, but family life in the Renaissance was different from our experience. Juliet's nurse, in her conversation with Juliet and Lady Capulet, offers a glimpse of one of the principal differences:

> But as I said,
> On Lammas-eve at night shall she be fourteen,
> That shall she, marry, I remember it well.
> 'Tis since the earthquake now aleven years,
> And she was wean'd — I never shall forget it —
> Of all the days of the year, upon that day;
> For I had then laid wormwood to my dug,
> Sitting in the sun under the dove-house wall.
> My lord and you were then at Mantua —
> Nay, I do bear a brain — but as I said,
> When it did taste the wormwood on the nipple
> Of my dug and felt it bitter, pretty fool,
> To see it teachy and fall out wi' th' dug!   (1.3.20–32)

This character is called Nurse because she has nursed Juliet as an infant, and here she describes how she weaned the toddler from her breast milk by applying a bitter substance to her nipple. Although *Romeo and Juliet* is set in Italy in an unspecified century, this scene at least reflects conventional practice in sixteenth-century England: most well-to-do mothers did not nurse their babies, but instead turned them over to a wet nurse who suckled them after having weaned her own children. Although resistance to the practice began to manifest itself in the medical discourse of the late sixteenth century, wet nursing was still the rule for those who could afford it.

Juliet's Nurse apparently lives in the Capulet household, but most English parents who could afford to do so gave up the child into the keeping and the household of the nurse, visiting it from time to time and then receiving it again into their home when the child was weaned. The choice of a proper nurse was important, as Gail Kern Paster, the most recent authority on the topic, points out.

> In hiring her services, parents leased exclusive rights to her lactating breasts and their milk. During the period of hire, the wet nurse was expected not to suckle another child and to maintain an adequate supply of milk. She was expected not to menstruate, not to become pregnant, and if she did, to notify her nurse-child's parents.   (199)

Paster goes on to add that "nurses' moral and ethical qualities mattered since these were believed to be transmitted through the milk" (200). Naturally these expectations put the nurse in an ambiguous position. Some nurses violated these strictures by nursing more than one child; likewise, some fathers disposed of a bastard child by giving it to a careless, overworked wet nurse who could be counted on to neglect it (Dolan 124–25). In other words, the marginality of the nurse's position could lead to exploitation, chicanery, and suspicion, especially given the cultural anxieties attending such matters as legitimacy and lineage. Contemporary records disclose accusations of baby switching, accidental and deliberate, and even of infanticide. To us the idea of wet nursing may seem heartless and even barbaric, but it continued in Britain until well into the nineteenth century.

Similarly alien to most of us is the practice of sending one's children away for education or apprenticeship. The most prominent members of the nobility engaged live-in tutors for their children as a substitute for formal schooling. Some villages had grammar schools for the sons of prosperous citizens, and some educated women ran *dame schools,* the equivalent of the modern preschool, in which a few very young local boys and girls were taught to read and write. But many parents who could afford to do so sent their sons away for education. Sons and daughters of the nobility and gentry were often placed in the houses of other aristocrats to serve as companions. In *Twelfth Night,* Olivia's lady-in-waiting, Maria, may represent such a practice, as may Beatrice in *Much Ado about Nothing,* who is Hero's cousin and who seems to be parentless. Less prosperous or prominent families often put their children in service or apprenticed the boys to artisans or tradesmen who taught them a skill.

Such patterns meant that many children actually lived with their parents for a relatively short period of time: in the case of wealthy children, from the time they returned from the wet nurse until they went away to school. Most children seem to have left home by their early teens, as apprenticeship or training for domestic service began around age fourteen. Evidence of these practices has led some historians to conclude that early modern family relations were characterized by a lack of affection, that mothers and fathers did not bind themselves emotionally to their children in the way that modern parents do. Childhood was brief — so the argument goes — and infant mortality high, so people sought to protect themselves from separation by means of emotional distance (Stone, *Family* 5). But such conclusions have recently been vigorously challenged. There is no question that the structure of the family was different from its modern counterpart, that the emphasis on parents and children bound closely into a separate unit did not fully develop until the eighteenth and nineteenth centuries. But ample evidence exists of parental attachment to children, such factors as wet nursing and early apprenticeship notwithstanding. For an especially poignant example, see Ben Jonson's poem "On My First Son," page 290.

One distinguishing trait of the early modern family was a relative absence of privacy in virtually all classes of society. Among the poor and the small property owners, interior space was at a minimum, and even large families lived in houses with a few rooms that were shared by all. The notion of a private chamber for each person is a much later development; in the Renaissance, it was not uncommon for all members of an immediate family to sleep in the same room, and for several children to occupy the same bed. In such circumstances, activities like sexual intercourse and relieving oneself in the chamber pot were performed with a minimum of privacy and perhaps none at all. At inns and other such public accommodations, travelers routinely shared beds with strangers, as the passage from a French manual on manners indicates (see p. 290). Enforced intimacy among family members was one of the factors that influenced early modern notions of community, and it is not too much to suggest that this absence of privacy helped to delay the emergence of "the individual" as a psychological category. Parents, siblings, other relatives, and even near neighbors were much more closely involved in one another's daily lives than is customary in our experience. Among the wealthy, too, the presence of servants diminished privacy, and personal servants often lived in virtually the same room as their masters. Finally, the architecture of large houses at the time — rooms connected to rooms rather than to a central corridor, making it necessary to go through others' rooms as one moved through the house — meant that the sense of personal space and separation from others was at a minimum. Adjustments were made to modify such openness, such as the use of curtained beds, but the notion of the personal and the private is largely a post-Enlightenment phenomenon.

The Renaissance offers exceptions to this paradigm of family life, the Virgin Queen being the most famous, but generally speaking the ideology of the family was inescapable. Elizabeth (at least publicly) considered herself married to her people, the head of a vast national family. Some people did not marry, such as younger sons who perhaps could not afford to set up housekeeping or daughters who found themselves without a dowry and thus unable to attract a suitor. But such nonparticipation in the experience of family life was considered not so much a choice as a misfortune. The practice of arranged marriage, especially in the upper classes, led some people (both male and female) to seek physical pleasure outside matrimony. During his marriage to Catherine of Aragon, Henry VIII had an illegitimate son, Henry Fitzroy, whom the king acknowledged and arranged to have reared on the margins of the court. The innumerable jokes about cuckolds in Renaissance dramatic texts, combined with the sermonizing against adultery, suggest that marital infidelity was a familiar and troublesome social problem.

Nor is sexual activity before marriage a twentieth-century invention. Even though adolescents reached puberty later than they do now, the relatively late age for getting married meant that young people's sexual urges had to be either postponed or satisfied illicitly. In some parts of the culture, especially among the rural poor, sexual intercourse for a betrothed couple and even their cohabitation were quietly tolerated. The Church of England recognized the validity of several kinds of "irregular" marriages. A couple who promised before witnesses to marry each other in the future and who then consummated the agreement sexually were considered legally wed, whether or not a church ceremony ever took place. This was called a marriage contract *per verba de futuro*. Likewise, a couple who declared to each other before witnesses a phrase such as "I hereby take you as my husband/wife" were considered married; their words constituted the contract. This was called a marriage contract *per verba de praesenti*. Such agreements, known variously as *spousals, handfasts,* and *precontracts,* play a minor role in many of Shakespeare's plays. In *Twelfth Night,* Olivia calls Sebastian her "husband" on the basis of a verbal agreement in the presence of a priest, but before a religious or legal ceremony has taken place. Spousals play a major role in *Measure for Measure,* where the making and breaking of marriage contracts is a source of conflict among four of the major and two of the minor characters. Of the randy Lucio, we learn that "Mistress Kate Keepdown was with child by him in the Duke's time; he promis'd her marriage. His child is a year and a quarter old . . ." (3.2.198–201).

Ecclesiastical regulations were frequently incompatible with civil law, which required a church ceremony, and the intricacy and variety of these matrimonial arrangements attest to the difficulty of aligning the legal system and the human heart, not to mention the libido. Questions of property and paternity attendant on these marriages were tried mostly in the ecclesiastical courts or, as they were more familiarly known for obvious reasons, the "bawdy courts," and they offer some helpful evidence on sexual mores in the period. But these records and the statistics they supply reflect only a fraction of the actual practice. We know that between 1550 and 1600 more than one in five brides — including Shakespeare's wife — were pregnant at the altar, that the actual ratio was almost certainly even higher, and that the frequency of premarital sexual activity was much higher than that (Stone, *Family* 610).

What about homosexuality in the Renaissance? This is a complex topic, embracing everything from King James's private affections to early modern medical theory to Shakespeare's sonnets. But recent critical studies of homosexuality have helped to shed some light on an issue that has often been misunderstood, repressed, or delicately ignored. One result of these recent investigations has been the recognition that "the homosexual" as a human category is fairly recent, and that the term *homosexuality* did not come into currency until the nineteenth century. As Bruce Smith, the author of the best book on this topic, notes, "No one in England during the sixteenth and seventeenth centuries would have thought of himself as 'gay' or 'homosexual' for the simple reason that those categories of self-definition did not exist" (11–12). The absence of a category or label does not imply, of course, that people did not engage in sexual activity with members of their own sex until the reign of Queen Victoria. From the beginnings of recorded time, from Sodom to Lesbos to Athens, men and women have done so. But ways of thinking about such sexual behavior have changed. Legally and religiously, homosexual acts were forbidden in Renaissance England (see the excerpt from Sir Edward Coke's *Institutes*, p. 291). But the language used to describe them — *buggery* and *sodomy* — was vague and also covered bestiality, child molestation, and certain heterosexual acts considered improper. It seems clear that homosexual acts were widely practiced in Renaissance England and that the legal penalty of death was exacted only in extreme cases, such as the rape of a child.

When homosexual desires and acts were discussed, they were condemned, notably by Puritan divines and writers, as part of the general depravity to which man's carnal nature was vulnerable. Mostly, however, they were not discussed. Still, it is clear that men had erotic feelings for other men and sometimes acted on them, and one of the primary sources for such information is the imaginative literature of the period. Even less is known about lesbian desire in the early modern period: it is not even acknowledged in most legal writing on sexual offenses, and since most imaginative literature was written by men, the subject is rarely addressed. In poetry and drama, male homosexual behavior was associated with the ancient tradition of friendship, which the Renaissance valued and which finds eloquent expression in Michel de Montaigne's essay "On Friendship." Military or naval service often generated a sense of comradeship that represents one aspect of this tradition: we might recall the devotion of the seafaring Antonio to the handsome young Sebastian in *Twelfth Night*. To many writers in Renaissance Europe, such affections appear to have been less culturally threatening than a corresponding obsession with women, a pursuit believed to make effeminate the men who fell victim to it. As for homosexual acts, the tension between prohibition and practice is puzzling. Again Bruce Smith is helpful:

> The one salient fact about homosexuality in early modern England, as in early modern Europe generally, is the disparity that separates the extreme punishments described by law and the apparent tolerance, even positive valuation, of homoerotic desire in the visual arts, in literature, and, I shall argue, in the political power structure. What are we to make of a culture that could consume popular prints of Apollo embracing Hyacinth and yet could order hanging for men who acted on the very feelings that inspire that embrace? (13–14)

Christopher Marlowe's *Edward II* depicts in its protagonist a king who suffers an amorous obsession for a beautiful young man. A significant number of

Shakespeare's sonnets are erotically charged with homosexual passion. But there is little profit in asking whether Shakespeare or Marlowe was "a homosexual." The point is that writers, like other people, did not define themselves in such terms.

The Social Structure

Even today commentators insist that to understand twentieth-century England it is necessary to admit the pervasiveness and depth of the class system, and the hierarchies that influence social practice in our time are a legacy of the distinct levels of status that obtained in the sixteenth and seventeenth centuries. Discrete and workable categories for the different groups that populated early modern England are difficult to establish, however. Lawrence Stone describes the problem as follows:

> If the historian is to reduce his evidence to intelligible order he is obliged to use abstract concepts and collective nouns. In discussing society he deals in groups labelled peasants, yeomen, gentry and aristocracy; or tenants and landlords, wage-labourers and capitalists; or lower class, middle class and upper class; or Court and Country; or bourgeois and feudal. Some of these categories, like titular aristocracy, are status groups; some, like capitalists, are economic classes with similar incomes derived from similar sources; some, like "Court," describe groups whose income, interests and geographical location are all temporarily based on a single institution. Every individual can be classified in many different ways, and the problem of how to choose the most meaningful categories is particularly difficult when dealing with mobile societies like that of seventeenth-century England. (*Causes* 33)

These subtleties notwithstanding, it is true that in the sixteenth and seventeenth centuries a man or woman was born into a family that inhabited one of several levels of society, and that people did not easily move from one class to another.

For purposes of outlining the social system in Shakespeare's England, we may divide the population into the following groups. Aristocracy: persons of noble birth who possessed large estates in the country but who also often took their place in London at court or in Parliament. Gentry, sometimes known as minor gentry: descendants of the aristocracy whose holdings were smaller but who still possessed considerable wealth, as well as persons who through commercial enterprise (such as ownership of a monopoly) had managed to amass property and prestige and thus were entitled to be called gentlemen. Citizens: mostly urban tradesmen or shopkeepers, who either made products for public consumption or sold them, e.g., leather goods, books, cloth, dairy products, wheels for carriages, and the like (this group would probably also include innkeepers). Yeomen: the rural equivalent of citizens, who owned (or in some cases had the use of) agricultural or grazing lands from which they made more than a subsistence wage — sometimes even handsome profits. Servants, laborers, or peasants: persons who owned little but made their living working for others, either on farms or in households (those who lived in the city tended to be better off financially than their rural counterparts). The indigent: beggars and others who, from geographical or social circumstances, injury, or personal temperament, found themselves unable to work. As the historian's reservations suggest, these groupings are inadequate. Where do we put lawyers, for example? A small professional class was emerging, but by 1600 it was not large enough to be reckoned significant. How to classify prostitutes? Or sailors? Or criminals? Finally, there were small, marginal categories such as "masterless men" or vagrants, some of them ex-soldiers, who moved from place to place picking up work as they could, stealing, or preying on the gullible. Among those who defied easy categorization, actors — "players" — were foremost. In fact, their dubious position necessitated that they put themselves under the nominal protection of an aristocratic patron.

Social conditioning tended to keep people in their places, and one aspect of the patriarchy that reinforced class boundaries was the paternalistic treatment of the lower classes by the upper. Theoretically, aristocrats took it as their duty to behave charitably and humanely toward those considered their social inferiors. As Derek Hirst has pointed out, most people did not seem to object to the class system per se, but rather to the injustices that it could breed. Even in food riots that occurred in the late sixteenth and early seventeenth centuries, the participants complained not so much about the wealth of their neighbors as about such abuses as grain hoarding or price gouging, about, in other words, the attempt to take unfair advantage (51). But social ordering was not merely traditional and psychological: laws existed to enforce social order, as a glance at royal proclamations from any five-year period between 1540 and 1640 will reveal (see pp. 293 and 295). Of such strictures, the sumptuary laws described in Chapter 7 are perhaps the most fascinating. In theory, a person's clothing revealed at a glance the social class to which he or she belonged: for example, only countesses and ladies above that rank could wear purple silk. But the regulatory statutes were frequently broken. Finally, the lack of easy geographical mobility helped to keep the population in place literally, for one could not simply decide to move from one part of the country to the other. An exception to this rule was London, which attracted a large number of industrious people hoping to make their fortunes, including William Shakespeare himself.

It is not surprising that the class system, despite its long history and the conditioning that helped to enforce it, was the source of tension and resentment. From the royal court to the alehouse, people objected to the behavior of others on grounds of status: either the adversary was called unworthy of the class represented, or the plaintiff thought himself equally important. Because, practically speaking, people were most immediately affected by local government, they had fairly direct means of redress against perceived injustices, and object they did. The records of local courts teem with complaints against others for what amount to violations of the social order. Public drunkenness, abusing the right to public land, quarreling, disputes about preferential seating in church — many of these common complaints involve issues of status and importance in the community, and the rhetoric in which these complaints were recorded attests to a colorful repertoire of class-based insults. "Henry Weavers claimed superiority when he told Mr. Miles Lynn, a parson, in 1613, that 'I am a better man than thou art, knave parson, a turd in thy teeth'" (qtd. in Amussen 212). Such class-connected language provides a useful context for Kent's contemptuous speech to Oswald in the second act of *King Lear*.

How fixed were these social structures? It is difficult to give an all-purpose answer, but to some extent the boundaries between classes became more permeable as the sixteenth century passed into the seventeenth. Apprenticeship was one means of social and economic ascent. A bright and industrious young man from a poor family or the younger son of a gentleman could apprentice himself to a craftsman and eventually set himself up in that trade. If the master had no children, the young man might inherit the business. The increasing availability of education also made for social and economic mobility. Once again the cardinal example is William Shakespeare, who parlayed his grammar school education into a career in the theater, a coat of arms for his family, and substantial real estate holdings in the town of his birth. For women the opportunities for social advancement were more limited, although some women were occasionally apprenticed in what were considered appropriate trades. In the city, where social lines were quicker to disintegrate, young women from humble backgrounds were able to better themselves economically (although less often socially) through advantageous marriages. Movement up the social and economic scale was not easy, but the history of the Tudor and Stuart period indicates that changes were occurring at large. As the yeomanry grew in number, as merchants began to exploit the possibilities of consumption, as the aristocracy began to lose its grip on real estate and similar financial resources, and as the population continued to increase, the rigid social boundaries were put under pressure and the familiar lines began to blur. The old feudal order that had dominated England until the end of the fifteenth century was gradually being supplanted by an early capitalist system that depended more heavily on individual ownership and allowed greater mobility largely on the basis of financial success.

Economically, England was heterogeneous. Racially, it was not. In the Middle Ages the Saxon tribes that had originally populated the island intermarried with the Europeans who immigrated there, beginning with the Romans and then with the Scandinavians. The Norman Conquest of 1066 produced an influx of the French who were eventually assimilated. The English nation in the sixteenth and seventeenth centuries, therefore, was largely made up of the descendants of Northern Europeans. Representatives of other races and nations were comparatively rare. The island's geographical isolation created a cultural insularity, and even xenophobia, unique in Europe. The Spanish and Portuguese had had commerce of various kinds with the African continent for hundreds of years, England for less than a century. Jews had been cast out of England in 1290, and while some Jews did manage to live and work in Shakespeare's London — the law was inconsistently enforced — the prohibition was not lifted until 1655, at the instigation of Oliver Cromwell.

Londoners (although probably not their country cousins) were occasionally exposed to visiting Africans and American natives. Their status as objects of curiosity is implicit in Trinculo's joke, in *The Tempest,* about what the English will pay to see "a dead Indian" (2.2.31–33). That foreigners were so regarded is indicative of the racial homogeneity of the culture as well as of the cultural anxieties strangers tended to generate. The reality of this prejudice appears in an edict issued by Elizabeth I in 1601, in which she is said "to be highly discontented to understand the great number of Negroes and blackamoors which (as she is informed) are carried into this realm . . ." and "hath given a special commandment that the said kind of people shall be with all speed avoided [expelled] and discharged out of this her majesty's realms" ("Licensing Casper van Senden," qtd. in Hughes and Larkin 3:221). (See the similar edict issued in July 1596, p. 296).

Shakespeare plays upon these anxieties in his depiction of such characters as Shylock the Jewish moneylender in *The Merchant of Venice,* Aaron the Moor in *Titus Andronicus,* and, most memorably, Othello. Other characters throughout the canon are described as "dark" or "tawny," but the terms probably refer to hair color and relatively dark Caucasian complexions rather than to African skin tones. The Dark Lady of the sonnets is usually thought to fall into this category, although Jonathan Crewe has teasingly wondered how our perceptions of Shakespeare might be changed if "instead of always genteelly speaking of Shakespeare's Dark Lady sonnets, we could bring ourselves to call them the Black Woman sonnets" (120). Was Shakespeare himself a racist? Strictly speaking, almost certainly. The culture that produced him had little acquaintance with and little sympathy for what modern cultural theorists have come to call the Other. And yet some of these theatrical representatives of Otherness, particularly Shylock and Othello, are portrayed with a high degree of sympathy. It appears that Shakespeare took theatrical advantage of his audience's cultural racism by presenting exotic figures who can behave barbarously and yet who command respect and sympathy, figures who, as Shylock points out, bleed when pricked and laugh when tickled.

Conclusion: The Body Politic

In the opening scene of *Coriolanus,* the aged and sage Menenius, a patrician member of the Roman establishment, gives an impromptu lecture, "The Fable of the Belly," to a group of hungry and rebellious plebeians in which he symbolically represents the proper functioning of society. The sources of the fable (in Plutarch and Sir Philip Sidney) would have been familiar to the educated auditors around 1607, and the rhetoric would have been familiar to all. The analogy between a well-ordered society and a healthy body was a commonplace in English social and political thought. The playwright's retelling of "The Fable of the Belly" represents a sophisticated and ambiguous move because one finds it difficult to decide whether Shakespeare is mocking or approving the old Roman's moral story about social order. And this difficulty is itself salutary in helping us to think about Shakespeare's ambiguous representation of the social, familial, and political structures that have served as the focus of this chapter. Clearly Shakespeare was no revolutionary. Far from challenging the systems with which he grew up, he exploited them, perhaps even reinforced them, for his own professional advantage. And yet neither was he a blind reactionary. Capable of seeing through the "robes and furred gowns" that King Lear deplores, those rich conventions that conceal inequity and corruption, Shakespeare asked his audience to think critically about the fundamental arbitrariness of the English — indeed, of any — social system. His questions are still relevant.

→ ARISTOTLE

From *Historia Animalium*

fourth century B.C.
Translated by Richard Cresswell

Although Aristotle's work was not as well known in early modern England as it is now, his thought had filtered into the culture through the writings of other ancient writers who had depended on his philosophical and scientific treatises. This passage, distinguishing between male and female characteristics in the animal kingdom, represents the ancient system of hierarchies on which Renaissance thinkers drew.

And in all animals in which there is a distinction of the sexes nature has given a similar disposition to the males and to the females. This is most conspicuous in man, and the larger animals, and in viviparous quadrupeds; for the disposition of the female is softer, and more tameable and submissive, and more ingenious; as the females of the Lacedemonian dog are more gentle than the males. . . .

The females of all animals are less violent in their passions than the males, except the female bear and pardalis [panther], for the female of these appears more courageous than the male. In other animals the females are more soft and insidious, less simple, more petulant, and more active in the care of their young. The disposition of the males is opposed to this; for they are more passionate and fierce, more straightforward, and less invidious. The vestiges of these dispositions exist, as we may say, in all, but are more conspicuous in those which have the strongest moral habits, and most of all in mankind; for the nature of the human subject is the most complete, so that these habits appear more conspicuous in mankind than in other animals.

Wherefore women are more compassionate and more readily made to weep, more jealous and querulous, more fond of railing, and more contentious. The female also is more subject to depression of spirits and despair than the male. She is also more shameless and false, more readily deceived, and more mindful of injury, more watchful, more idle, and on the whole less excitable than the male. On the contrary, the male is more ready to help, and, as it has been said, more brave than the female; and . . . if the sepia [cuttlefish] is struck with a trident, the male comes to help the female, but the female makes her escape if the male is struck.

→ SIR ROBERT FILMER

From *Patriarcha, or The Natural Power of Kings*   *c. 1630*

Sir Robert Filmer's treatise, although written after Shakespeare's death and not published until even later in the seventeenth century, provides an exceptionally detailed statement of early modern orthodoxy concerning familial, social, and political organization. This passage insists on the biblical origins of the analogy between fathers and kings.

It may seem absurd to maintain that kings now are the fathers of their people, since experience shows the contrary. It is true, all kings be not the natural parents of their subjects, yet they all either are or are to be reputed the next heirs to those first progenitors who were at first the natural parents of the whole people, and in their right succeed to the exercise of supreme jurisdiction; and such heirs are not only lords of their own children but also of their brethren and all others that were subject to their fathers. And therefore we find that God told Cain of his brother Abel, "His desires shall be subject unto thee, and thou shalt rule over him." Accordingly, when Jacob bought his brother's birthright, Isaac blessed him thus, "Be lord over thy brethren, and let the sons of thy mother bow before thee."

As long as the first fathers of families lived, the name of Patriarchs did aptly belong unto them; but after a few descents, when the true fatherhood itself was extinct and only the right of the father descended to the true heir, then the title of prince or king was more significant to express the power of him who succeeds only to the right of that fatherhood which his ancestors did naturally enjoy. By this means it comes to pass that many a child, by succeeding a king, hath the right of a father over many a gray-headed multitude, and hath the title of *Pater Patriae* [father of the fatherland].

It may be demanded what becomes of the right of fatherhood, in case the crown does escheat for want of an heir [in case there is no apparent successor to the throne]? Whether doth it not then devolve to the people? The answer is, it is but the negligence or ignorance of the people to lose the knowledge of the true heir. For an heir there always is. If Adam himself were still living, and now ready to die, it is certain that there is One Man, and but one in the world, who is next heir, although the knowledge who should be that one One Man be quite lost.

This ignorance of the people being admitted, it doth not by any means follow that for want of heirs the supreme power is devolved to the multitude and that they have power to rule and choose what rulers they please. No, the kingly power escheats in such cases to the prime and independent heads of families. For every kingdom is resolved into those parts whereof at first it was made. By the uniting of great families or petty kingdoms, we find the greater monarchies were at the first erected, and into such again as into their first matter many times they return again. And because the dependency [sequence] of ancient families is oft obscure or worn out of knowledge, therefore the wisdom of all or most princes have thought fit to adopt many times those for heads of families and princes of provinces whose merits, abilities, or fortunes have ennobled them or made them fit and capable of such regal favors. All such prime heads and fathers have power to consent in the uniting or conferring of their fatherly right of sovereign authority on whom they please. And he that is so elected claims not his power as a donative [gift] from the people, but as being substituted properly by God, from whom he receives his royal charter of an universal father, though testified by the ministry of the heads of the people.

If it please God, for the correction of the prince or punishment of the people, to suffer princes to be removed and others to be placed in their rooms, either by the factions of the nobility or rebellion of the people, in all such cases the judgment of God, who hath power to give and take away kingdoms, is most just. Yet the ministry of men who execute God's judgments without commission is sinful and damnable. God doth but use and turn men's unrighteous acts to the performance of his righteous decrees.

In all kingdoms or commonwealths in the world, whether the prince be the supreme father of the people or but the true heir of such a father, or whether he come to the crown by usurpation or by election of the nobles or of the people or by any other way whatsoever, or whether some few or a multitude govern the commonwealth — yet still the authority that is in any one, or in many, or in all these, is the only right and natural authority of a supreme father. There is and always shall be continued to the end of the world a natural right of a supreme father over every multitude, although by the secret will of God many at first do most unjustly obtain the exercise of it.

To confirm this natural right of regal power, we find in the decalogue [the Ten Commandments] that the law which enjoins obedience to kings is delivered in the terms of "Honor thy father," as if all power were originally in the father. If obedience to parents be immediately due by a natural law, and subjection to princes but by the mediation of an human ordinance, what reason is there that the laws of nature should give place to the laws of men, as we see the power of the father over his child gives place and is subordinate to the power of the magistrate?

If we compare the natural rights of a father with those of a king, we find them all one, without any difference at all, but only in the latitude or extent of them. As the father over one family, so the king as father over many families extends his care to preserve, feed, clothe, instruct, and defend the whole commonwealth. His war, his peace, his courts of justice, and all his acts of sovereignty tend only to preserve and distribute to every subordinate and inferior father and to their children their rights and privileges, so that all the duties of a king are summed up in an universal fatherly care of his people.

→ ## An Homily of the State of Matrimony   *1563*

This and other homilies, read from the pulpit during the Anglican Church service, were useful to Elizabeth's and James's government as instruments of political edification and social control. The *Homily of the State of Matrimony* constitutes the central Elizabethan statement on the duties of husbands and wives, the biblical mandate for these duties, and their implications for order in the state.

The word of almighty God doth testify and declare whence the original beginning of matrimony cometh and why it is ordained. It is instituted of God to the intent that man and woman should live lawfully in a perpetual friendly fellowship, to bring forth fruit, and to avoid fornication. By which means a good conscience might be preserved on both parties in bridling the corrupt inclinations of the flesh within the limits of honesty. For God hath straightly forbidden all whoredom and uncleanness and hath from time to time taken grievous punishments of [grievously punished] this inordinate lust, as all stories and ages hath declared. Furthermore, it is also ordained that the Church of God and his kingdom might by this kind of life be conserved and enlarged, not only in that God giveth children by his blessing, but also in that they be brought up by the parents godly in the knowledge of God's word, that this, the knowledge of God and true religion, might be delivered by succession from one to another, that finally many might enjoy that everlasting immortality.

Wherefore, forasmuch as matrimony serveth as well to avoid sin and offense as to increase the kingdom of God, you, as all other which enter that state, must acknowledge this benefit of God with pure and thankful minds, for that he hath so ruled your hearts that you follow not the example of the wicked world, who set their delight in filthiness of sin, where both of you stand in the fear of God and abhor all filthiness. For that is surely the singular gift of God, where the common example of the world declareth how the devil hath their hearts bound and entangled in divers snares so that they in their wiveless state run into open abominations without any grudge [remorse] of their conscience. Which sort of men that liveth so desperately and filthily, what damnation tarrieth for them? Saint Paul describeth it to them, saying: "Neither whoremongers, neither adulterers shall inherit the kingdom of God." This horrible judgment of God you be escaped through his mercy, if so be that you live inseparately [together] according to God's ordinance. But yet I would not have you careless, without watching. For the devil will assay to attempt all things to interrupt and hinder your hearts and godly purpose, if you will give him any entry. For he will either labor to break this godly knot once begun betwixt you, or else at the least he will labor to encumber it with divers griefs and displeasures.

And this is his principal craft, to work dissension of hearts of the one from the other, that whereas now there is pleasant and sweet love betwixt you, [he] will in the stead thereof bring in most bitter and unpleasant discord. And surely that same adversary of ours doth, as it were from above, assault man's nature and condition. For this folly is ever from our tender age grown up with us, to have a desire to rule, to think highly by our self, so that none thinketh it meet to give place to another. That wicked vice of stubborn will and self-love is more meet to break and dissever the love of heart than to preserve concord. Wherefore married persons must apply their minds in most earnest wise to concord, and must crave continually of God the help of his holy spirit so to rule their hearts and to knit their minds together that they be not dissevered by any division of discord.

This necessity of prayer must be oft in the occupying and using of married persons, that oft time the one should pray for the other lest hate and debate do arise betwixt them. And because few do consider this thing, but more few do perform it (I say to pray diligently) we see how wonderfully the devil deludeth and scorneth this state, how few matrimonies there be without chidings, brawlings, tauntings, repentings, bitter cursings, and fightings. Which things whosoever doth commit, they do not consider that it is the instigation of the ghostly enemy who taketh great delight therein. For else they would with all earnest endeavor strive against these mischiefs not only with prayer, but also with all possible diligence. Yea, they would not give place to the provocation of wrath, which stirreth them either to such rough and sharp words or stripes [blows], which is surely compassed by the devil, whose temptation, if it be followed, must needs begin and weave the web of all miseries and sorrows. For this is most certainly true, that of such beginnings must needs ensue the breach of true concord in heart, whereby all love must needs shortly be banished. Then cannot it be but a miserable thing to behold that yet they are of necessity compelled to live together which yet cannot be in quiet together. And this is most customably every where to be seen. But what is the cause thereof? Forsooth, because they will not consider the crafty trains of the devil and therefore giveth not themselves to pray to God that he would vouchsafe to repress his power. Moreover, they do not consider how they promote the purpose of the devil in that they follow the wrath of their hearts while they threat[en] one another, while they in their folly turn all upside down, while they will never give over their right as they esteem it, yea, while many times they will not give over the wrong part indeed. Learn thou, therefore, if thou desirest to be void of all these miseries, if thou desirest to live peaceably and comfortably in wedlock, how to make thy earnest prayer to God that he would govern both your hearts by his holy spirit to restrain the devil's power, whereby your concord may remain perpetually.

But to this prayer must be joined a singular diligence, whereof St. Peter giveth his precept, saying: "You husbands deal with your wives according to knowledge, giving honor to the wife, as unto the weaker vessel, and as unto them that are heirs also of the grace of life that your prayers be not hindered." This precept doth particularly pertain to the husband. For he ought to be the leader and author of love in cherishing and increasing concord, which then shall take place if he will use measurableness [temperance] and not tyranny, and if he yield some things to the woman. For the woman is a weak creature, not endued with like strength and constancy of mind. Therefore they be the sooner disquieted and they be the more prone to all weak affections and dispositions of mind more than men be, and lighter they be, and more vain in their fantasies and opinions. These things must be considered of the man, that he be not too stiff, so that he ought to wink at some things, and must gently expound all things, and to forbear.

Howbeit the common sort of men doth judge that such moderation should not become a man. For they say that it is a token of a womanish cowardness, and therefore they think that it is a man's part to fume in anger, to fight with fist and staff. Howbeit, howsoever they imagine, undoubtedly St. Peter doth better judge what should be seeming to a man and what he should most reasonably perform. For he saith reasoning should be used, and not fighting. Yea, he saith more, that the woman ought to have a certain honor attributed to her, that is to say, she must be spared and borne with, the rather for that she is the weaker vessel, of a frail heart, inconstant, and with a word soon stirred to wrath. And therefore, considering these her frailties, she is to be the rather spared. By this means, thou shalt not only nourish concord, but shalt have her heart in thy power and will. For honest natures will sooner be retained to do their duty rather by gentle words than by stripes. But he which will do all things with extremity and severity, and doth use always rigor in words and stripes, what will that avail in the conclusion? Verily nothing but that he thereby setteth forward the devil's work. He banisheth away concord, charity, and sweet amity, and bringeth in dissension, hatred, and irksomeness, the greatest griefs that can be in the mutual love and fellowship of man's life.

Beyond all this, it bringeth another evil therewith, for it is the destruction and interruption of prayer. For in the time that the mind is occupied with dissension and discord there can be no true prayer used. For the Lord's prayer hath not only a respect to particular persons, but to the whole universal, in the which we openly pronounce that we will forgive them which hath offended against us even as we ask forgiveness of our sins of God. Which thing, how can it be done rightly when their hearts be at dissension? How can they pray each for other when they be at hate betwixt themselves? Now, if the aid of prayer be taken away, by what means can they sustain themselves in any comfort? For they can not otherwise either resist the devil or yet have their hearts stayed in stable comfort in all perils and necessities, but by prayer. Thus all discommodities [disadvantages], as well worldly as ghostly [spiritual], follow this froward testiness and cumbrous [cumbersome] fierceness in manners, which be more meet for brute beasts than for reasonable creatures. St. Peter doth not allow these things, but the devil desireth them gladly. Wherefore take the more heed. And yet a man may be a man, although he doth not use such extremity, yea, though he should dissemble [ignore] some things in his wife's manners. And this is the part of a Christian man which both pleaseth God and serveth also in good use, to the comfort of their marriage state.

Now as concerning the wife's duty. What shall become her? Shall she abuse the gentleness and humanity of her husband and at her pleasure turn all things upside down? No surely, for that is far repugnant against God's commandment. For thus doth St. Peter preach to them: "You wives, be you in subjection to obey your own husband." To obey is another thing than to control or command, which yet they may do to their children and to their family. But as for their husbands, them must they obey and cease from commanding and perform subjection. For this surely doth nourish concord very much when the wife is ready at hand at her husband's commandment, when she will apply herself to his will, when she endeavoreth herself to seek his contentation [contentment] and to do him pleasure, when she will eschew all things that might offend him. For thus will most truly be verified the saying of the poet: "A good wife, by obeying her husband, shall bear the rule," so that he shall have a delight and a gladness the sooner at all times to return home to her. But on the contrary part, when the wives be stubborn, froward, and malapert [impudent], their husbands are compelled thereby to abhor and flee from their own houses, even as they should have battle with their enemies.

Howbeit, it can scantly [hardly] be but that some offenses shall sometime chance betwixt them, for no man doth live without fault, specially for that the woman is the more frail part. Therefore let them beware that they stand not in their faults and willfulness, but rather let them acknowledge their follies and say: "My husband, so it is that by my anger I was compelled to do this or that. Forgive it me, and hereafter I will take better heed." Thus ought women the more readily to do, the more they be ready to offend. And they shall not do this only to avoid strife and debate, but rather in the respect of the commandment of God as St. Paul expresseth it in this form of words: "Let women be subject to their husbands, as to the Lord; for the husband is the head of the woman, as Christ is the head of the Church." Here you understand that God hath commanded that ye should acknowledge the authority of the husband and refer to him the honor of obedience. And St. Peter saith in that same place afore rehearsed that "holy matrons did sometimes deck themselves, not with gold and silver, but in putting their whole hope in God" and in "obeying their husbands, as Sara obeyed Abraham, calling him Lord, whose daughters you be" (saith he) "if you follow her example." This sentence is very meet for women to print in their remembrance.

Truth it is, that they must specially feel the griefs and pains of their matrimony in that they relinquish the liberty of their own rule, in the pain of their travailing [labor of childbirth], in the bringing up of their children, in which offices they be in great perils and be grieved with great afflictions, which they might be without if they lived out of matrimony. But St. Peter saith that this is the chief ornament of holy matrons, in that they set their hope and trust in God, that is to say, in that they refused not from marriage for the business thereof, for the griefs and perils thereof, but committed all such adventures to God in most sure trust of help, after that they have called upon his aid. O woman, do thou the like, and so shalt thou be most excellently beautified before God and all his angels and saints, and thou needest not to seek further for doing any better works. For, obey thy husband, take regard of his requests, and give heed unto him to perceive what he requireth of thee, and so shalt thou honor God, and live peaceably in thy house. And beyond this, God shall follow thee with his benediction that all things shall well prosper both to thee and to thy husband, as the Psalm saith, "Blessed is the man which feareth God and walketh in his ways. Thou shalt have the fruit of thine own hands, happy shalt thou be, and well shall it go with thee. Thy wife shall be as a vine plentifully spreading about thy house. Thy children shall be as the young springs [shoots or sprigs] of the olives about the table. Lo, thus shall that man be blessed" (saith David) "that feareth the Lord."

This let the wife have ever in mind, the rather admonished thereto by the apparel of her head, whereby is signified that she is under covert [the protection] and obedience of her husband. And as that apparel is of nature so appointed to declare her subjection, so biddeth St. Paul that all other of her raiment should express both shamefastness and sobriety. For if it be not lawful for the woman to have her head bare, but to bear thereon the sign of her power [protector] wheresoever she goeth, more is it required that she declare the thing that is meant thereby. And therefore these ancient women of the old world called their husbands lords, and showed them reverence in obeying them.

But peradventure she will say that those men loved their wives indeed. I know that well enough and bear it well in mind. But when I do admonish you of your duties, then call not to consideration what their duties be. For when we ourselves do teach our children to obey us as their parents, or when we reform our servants and tell them that they should obey their masters, not only at the eye but as to the Lord, if they should tell us again our duties, we would not think it well done. For when we be admonished of our duties and faults, we ought not then to seek what other men's duties be. For though a man had a companion in his fault, yet should not he thereby be without his fault. But this must be only looked on, by what means thou mayest make thy self without blame. For Adam did lay the blame upon the woman and she turned it unto the serpent, but yet neither of them was thus excused. And therefore bring not such excuses to me at this time, but apply all thy diligence to hear thine obedience to thy husband. For when I take in hand to admonish thy husband to love thee and to cherish thee, yet will I not cease to set out the law that is appointed to the woman as well as I would require of the man what is written for his law. Go thou therefore about such things as becometh thee only and show thyself tractable to thy husband. Or rather, if thou wilt obey thy husband for God's precept, then allege such things as be in his duty to do, but perform thou diligently those things which the Lawmaker hath charged thee to do.

For thus is it most reasonable to obey God if thou wilt not suffer thyself to transgress his law. He that loveth his friend seemeth to do no great thing, but he that honoreth him that is hurtful and hateful to him, this man is worthy much commendation. Even so think thou, if thou canst suffer an extreme husband, thou shalt have a great reward therefore. But if thou lovest him only because he is gentle and courteous, what reward will God give thee therefore? Yet I speak not these things that I would wish the husbands to be sharp towards their wives. But I exhort the women that they would patiently bear the sharpness of their husbands. For, when either parts do their best to perform their duties the one to the other, then followeth thereon great profit to their neighbor for their example's sake. For when the woman is ready to suffer a sharp husband, and the man will not extremely entreat his stubborn and troublesome wife, then be all things in quiet as in a most sure haven.

Even thus was it done in old time that every one did their own duty and office and was not busy to require the duty of their neighbors. Consider, I pray thee, that Abraham tooketh him his brother's son; his wife did not blame him therefore. He commanded him to go with him a long journey; she did not gainsay it, but obeyed his precept. Again, after all those great miseries, labor, and pains of that journey, when Abraham was made as Lord over all, yet did he give place to Lot of his superiority, which matter Sara took so little to grief that she never once suffered her tongue to speak such words as the common manner of women is wont to do in these days when they see their husbands in such rooms to be made underlings and to be put under their youngers [younger men]. Then they upbraid them with cumbrous talk and call them fools, dastards, and cowards for so doing. But Sara was so far from speaking any such thing that it came never into her mind and thought so to say, but allowed the wisdom and will of her husband. Yea, beside all this, after the said Lot had thus his will and left to his uncle the lesser portion of land, he chanced to fall into extreme peril. Which chance, when it came to the knowledge of this said patriarch, he incontinently put all his men in harness and prepared himself with all his family and friends against the host of the Persians. In which case, Sara did not counsel him to the contrary, nor did say, as then might have been said, "My husband, whither goest thou so unadvisedly? Why runnest thou thus on head [ahead]? Why dost thou offer thyself to so great perils, and art thus ready to jeopard thine own life and to peril the lives of all thine, for such a man as hath done thee such wrong? At least way, if thou regardest not thy self, yet have compassion on me, which for thy love have forsaken my kindred and my country, and have the want both of my friends and kinfolks, and am thus come into so far countries with thee. Have pity on me, and make me not here a widow, to cast me to such cares and troubles." Thus might she have said. But Sara neither said nor thought such words, but she kept herself in silence in all things.

Furthermore, all that time when she was barren and took no pain as other women did by bringing forth fruit in his house, what did he? He complained not to his wife, but to almighty God. And consider how either of them did their duties as became them. For neither did he despise Sara because she was barren, nor never did cast it in her teeth. Consider again how Abraham expelled the handmaid out of his house when she required it. So that by this I may truly prove that the one was pleased and contented with the other in all things.

But yet set not your eyes only in this matter, but look further what was done before this, that Agar used her mistress despitefully, and that Abraham himself was somewhat provoked against her, which must needs be an intolerable matter, and a painful, to a freehearted woman and a chaste. Let not therefore the woman be too busy to call for the duty of her husband where she should be ready to perform her own, for that is not worthy any great commendation. And even so again let not the man only consider what [be]longeth to the woman and to stand so earnestly gazing thereon, for that is not his part or duty. But as I have said, let either parties be ready and willing to perform that which belongeth specially to themselves. For, if we be bound to hold out our left cheek to strangers which will smite us on the right cheek, how much more ought we to suffer an extreme and unkind husband?

But yet I mean not that a man should beat his wife. God forbid that, for that is the greatest shame that can be, not so much to her that is beaten, as to him that doth the deed. But, if by such fortune thou chancest upon such an husband, take it not too heavily, but suppose thou that thereby is laid up no small reward hereafter and in this lifetime no small commendation to thee if thou canst be quiet. But yet to you that be men, thus I speak. Let there be none so grievous fault to compel you to beat your wives. But what, say I, your wives? No, it is not to be borne with that an honest man should lay hands on his maidservant to beat her. Wherefore, if it be a great shame for a man to beat his bound servant, much more rebuke it is to lay violent hands upon his free-woman. And this thing may we well understand by the laws which the pay-nims [pagans] hath made, which doth discharge her any longer to dwell with such an husband, as unworthy to have any further company with her, that doth smite her. For it is an extreme point thus so vilely to entreat [treat] her like a slave that is fellow to thee of thy life and so enjoined unto thee beforetime in the necessary matters of thy living. And therefore a man may well liken such a man (if he may be called a man rather than a wild beast) to a killer of his father or his mother. And whereas we be commanded to forsake our father and mother for our wives' sake, and yet thereby do work them none injury but do fulfill the law of God, how can it not appear then to be a point of extreme madness to entreat her despitefully for whose sake God hath commanded thee to leave parents? Yea, who can suffer such despite? Who can worthily express the inconvenience that is, to see what weepings and wailings be made in the open streets when neighbors run together to the house of so unruly an husband as to a Bedlam man [madman] who goeth about to overturn all that he hath at home? Who would not think that it were better for such a man to wish the ground to open and to swallow him in than once ever after to be seen in the market?

But peradventure thou wilt object that the woman provoketh thee to this point. But consider thou again that the woman is a frail vessel and thou art therefore made the ruler and head over her, to bear the weakness of her in this her subjection. And therefore study thou to declare the honest commendation of thine authority, which thou canst no way better do than to forbear to utter [treat badly] her in her weakness and subjection. For even as the king appeareth so much the more noble, the more excellent and noble he maketh his officers and lieutenants, whom, if he should dishonor and despise the authority of their dignity, he should deprive himself of a great part of his own honor. Even so, if thou dost despise her that is set in the next room beside thee, thou dost much derogate and decay the excellency and virtue of thine own authority. Recount all these things in thy mind, and be gentle and quiet. Understand that God hath given thee children with her and are made a father and by such reason appease thyself.

Dost not thou see the husbandmen, what diligence they use to till that ground which once they have taken to farm, though it be never so full of faults? As for an example, though it be dry, though it bringeth forth weeds, though the soil cannot bear too much wet, yet he tilleth it and so winneth fruit thereof. Even in like manner, if thou wouldst use like diligence to instruct and order the mind of thy spouse, if thou wouldst diligently apply thyself to weed out by little and little the noisome weeds of uncomely manners out of her mind with wholesome precepts, it could not be but in time thou shouldst feel the pleasant fruit thereof to both your comforts.

Therefore, that this thing chance not so, perform this thing that I do here counsel thee. Whatsoever any displeasant matter riseth at home, if thy wife hath done aught amiss, comfort her and increase not the heaviness. For, though thou shouldst be grieved with never so many things, yet shalt thou find nothing more grievous than to want the benevolence of thy wife at home. What offense soever thou canst name, yet shalt thou find none more intolerable than to be at debate with thy wife. And for this cause most of all oughtst thou to have this love in reverence. And if reason moveth thee to bear any burden at any other men's hands, much more of thy wife's. For if she be poor, upbraid her not; if she be simple, taunt her not, but be the more courteous. For she is thy body and made one flesh with thee.

But thou peradventure wilt say that she is a wrathful woman, a drunkard, a beastly, without wit and reason. For this cause, bewail her the more. Chafe not in anger, but pray to almighty God. Let her be admonished and holpen [helped] with good counsel, and do thou thy best endeavor that she may be delivered of all these affections. But if thou shouldst beat her, thou shalt increase her evil affections, for frowardness [aggression] and sharpness is not amended with frowardness but with softness and gentleness. Furthermore, consider what reward thou shalt have at God's hand. For, where thou mightst beat her and yet for the respect of the fear of God thou wilt abstain and bear patiently her great offenses, the rather in respect of that law which forbiddeth that a man should cast out his wife, what fault soever she be cumbered with, thou shalt have a very great reward and before the receipt of that reward thou shalt feel many commodities, for by this means she shall be made the more obedient and thou for her sake shalt be made the more meek. It is written in a story of a certain strange philosopher which had a cursed wife [Socrates and Xanthippe], a froward, and a drunkard. When he was asked for what consideration he did so bear her evil manners, he made answer: "By this means" (said he) "I have at home a schoolmaster and an example how I should behave myself abroad. For I shall" (saith he) "be the more quiet with other, being thus daily exercised and taught in the forbearing of her." Surely it is a shame that paynims should be wiser than we, we I say, that be commanded to counterfeit angels or rather God himself through meekness. And for the love of virtue, this said philosopher Socrates would not expel his wife out of his house. Yea, some say that he did therefore marry his wife to learn this virtue by that occasion.

Wherefore, seeing many men be far behind the wisdom of this man, my counsel is that first and before all things that man do his best endeavor to get him a good wife, endued with all honesty and virtue. But if it so chance that he is deceived, that he hath chosen such a wife as is neither good nor tolerable, then let the husband follow this philosopher and let him instruct his wife in every condition and never lay these matters to sight. For the merchant man, except he first be at composition with his factor [agent] to use his interaffairs quietly, he will neither stir his ship to sail, nor yet will lay hands upon his merchandise. Even so let us do all things that we may have the fellowship of our wives, which is the factor of all our doings at home, in great quiet and rest. And by these means all things shall prosper quietly, and so shall we pass through the dangers of the troublous sea of this world. For this state of life will be more honorable and comfortable than our houses, than servants, than money, than lands and possessions, than all things that can be told [counted]. As all these, with sedition and discord, can never work us any comfort, so shall all things turn to our commodity and pleasure if we draw this yoke in one concord of heart and mind.

Whereupon do you best endeavor, that after this sort [in this way] you use your matrimony and so shall you be armed on every side. You have escaped the snares of the devil and the unlawful lusts of the flesh. You have the quietness of conscience by this institution of matrimony ordained by God. Therefore use oft prayer to him, that he would be present by you, that he would continue concord and charity betwixt you. Do the best you can of your parts to custom yourselves to softness and meekness, and bear well in worth such oversights as chance [happen]. And thus shall your conversation be most pleasant and comfortable. And although (which can no otherwise be) some adversities shall follow, and otherwhiles now one discommodity, now another, shall appear, yet in this common trouble and adversity, lift up both your hands unto heaven, call upon the help and assistance of God, the author of your marriage, and surely the promise of relief is at hand. For Christ affirmeth in his Gospel: "Where two or three be gathered together in my name, and be agreed, what matter soever they pray for, it shall be granted them of my heavenly father." Why therefore shouldst thou be afeared of the danger, where thou hast so ready a promise and so nigh an help? Furthermore, you must understand how necessary it is for Christian folk to bear Christ's cross, for else we shall never feel how comfortable God's help is unto us.

Therefore give thanks to God for his great benefit in that you have taken upon you this state of wedlock and pray you instantly that almighty God may luckily defend and maintain you therein, that neither you be overcomed with any temptation nor with any adversity. But before all things take good heed that you give no occasion to the devil to let and hinder your prayers by discord and dissension. For there is no stronger defense and stay in all our life than is prayer, in the which we may call for the help of God and obtain it, whereby we may win his blessing, his grace, his defense, and protection, so to continue therein to a better life to come. Which grant us he that died for us all, to whom be all honor and praise, for ever and ever. Amen.

→ WILLIAM GOUGE

From *Of Domestical Duties: Eight Treatises*   *1634*

William Gouge's work is a handbook on the theory and practice of Christian marriage, offering advice to husbands and wives, analysis of potential problems between spouses, and emphasis (derived from Puritan doctrine) on mutuality in spousal relationships. This excerpt from the third edition develops the familiar analogy between the marriage relationship and the social order.

COMMON-MUTUAL DUTIES BETWIXT MAN AND WIFE

Of the vices contrary to a joint care of governing the Family

The mind and practice of many, both husbands and wives, is contrary to this duty.

Many a husband because the wife's office is especially to abide at home will put off all government to the wife: leaving it to her not only to order the things in the house but also to bring in all needful things, to order and govern the children both young and old, yea even to provide for them also, to take in, to put out, to use all sorts of servants as pleaseth her. Yea, if servants shall be stubborn and stout against her, he will take no notice of it, nor endure to be told of it, much less afford her his assistance, but suffer her to be disgraced and despised. As for religious duties, he will no way meddle with them. Oh base-minded men, unworthy to be husbands and heads of wives! Shall your wives who were made to be a help to you have no help from you, no, not in those things which especially belong to your charge? Shall the weaker vessels bear all the burden? Assuredly as the man carrieth away the greatest reputation and honor when a family is well governed (though it be by the joint care and wisdom of his wife) so lieth he most open to the judgment of God, if the government thereof be neglected, and through the neglect thereof, children and servants grow impious: instance Eli, and David. For as in a Commonwealth the greatest honor of good government, victorious battles, happy peace, and prosperity, and the greatest dishonor and damage of the contrary, redoundeth to the King, so to the man who is chief governor in a family: for it is presupposed that all which do any good are instruments of the highest governor; if any evil or mischief fall out, that it is through his negligence.

On the other side, because the husband is the most principal, many wives think that the government of the family nothing at all appertains to them, and thereupon are careless of the good thereof and will not stir their least finger to order any thing aright: but if any thing be amiss lay all the blame on their husbands. Do not such pervert that main end for which God made them, even *to be an help?* Do they not carry themselves most unworthy of the place wherein God hath set them, namely, to be joint-governors with their husbands, and partakers of their dignities? As by their negligence they make themselves accessary to all the evil which falleth out in the family, so assuredly shall they have their part in those judgments which are executed on the head thereof.

Most contrary to the fore-named duty is the practice of such as are hindrances one to another in governing the family: as when wives are not only negligent themselves in coming to religious exercises, but keep back children and servants, and so are a great grief unto their religious husbands; or when they use any of the children or servants to be instruments of iniquity; or are themselves disquiet and troublesome in the house, like to her of whom Solomon speaketh in this proverb, "It is better to dwell in the corner of the house top, than with a contentious woman in a wide house."

Husbands also are oft an hindrance to that good government which their wives would help forward, when they scoff and scorn at that good counsel which their wives give them for that purpose; or when they will not suffer their wives to meddle with any thing at all, nor endure that they should find any fault, much less take in hand to redress any thing that is amiss. These and such like perverse dispositions are in husbands and wives, whereby it cometh to pass that they who were joined together to be a mutual help each to other prove heavy, yea, intolerable burdens.

➔ SIR THOMAS SMITH

From *De Republica Anglorum: The Manner of Government or Policy of the Realm of England*   *1583*
Of Children

Sir Thomas Smith (1513–1577) was an important Tudor legal scholar and theorist. His political treatise draws heavily on the traditions informing English law and social practice, many of which were inherited from the ancients. Here he explains and justifies the system of primogeniture as practiced in England in the sixteenth century.

The testator disposeth in his last will his moveable goods freely as he thinketh meet and convenient without controlment of wife or children. And our testaments for goods moveable be not subject to the ceremonies of the civil law, but made with all liberty and freedom. . . . Of lands as ye have understood before, there is difference: for when the owner dieth, his land descendeth only to his eldest son, all the rest both sons and daughters have nothing by the common law, but must serve their eldest brother if they will, or make what other shift they can to live: except that the father in life time do make some conveyance and estates of part of his land to their use, or else by devise, which word amongst our lawyers doth betoken a testament written, sealed, and delivered in the life time of the testator before witness: for without those ceremonies a bequest of lands is not available. But by the common law if he that dieth hath no sons but daughters, the land is equally divided among them, which portion is made by agreement or by lot. Although as I have said ordinarily and by the common law, the eldest son inheriteth all the lands, yet in some countries all the sons have equal portion, and that is called ganelkinde, and is in many places in Kent. In some places the youngest is sole heir: and in some places after an other fashion. But these being but particular customs of certain places and out of the rule of the common law, do little appertain to the disputation of the policy of the whole realm, and may be infinite. The common wealth is judged by that which is most ordinarily and commonly done through the whole realm.

→ GEORGE WHETSTONE

From *An Heptameron of Civil Discourses* 1582

Household Laws to Keep the Married in Love, Peace, and Amity

George Whetstone's treatment of the conditions necessary for satisfactory marriage (as "reported by Segnior Phyloxenus") examines the complementary claims of parents ("foresight") and children ("fancy") in the selection of a marriage partner. Such conflicts are obviously relevant to Shakespeare's plays in which betrothals are opposed by parents or by participants, notably *A Midsummer Night's Dream*, *Othello*, and *The Merry Wives of Windsor*.

The satisfaction of fancy is the source of joy in marriage. But there be many means to dam up the course of delight between the married, if the match be not made as well by foresight, as free choice.

The office of foresight is to prevent following [later] mischances and (advisedly) to consider if present ability will support a household, and (according to their calling) leave a portion to their posterity.

In this point, the experience of the parents is to be preferred before the rash imaginations of the son. For the aged married by proof know that in time many accidents of mischance will hinder the endeavors of the best husbands.

The office of foresight is likewise to consider of the equality in years, lest the one growing and the other declining in perfection, after a while repent, when remedy comes too late: the rose full blown seemeth fair for a time, but withereth much sooner than the tender bud.

It is the office of foresight to consider of the equality of bringing up, lest a diversity in manners between the married make a division of desires. For spaniels and curs hardly live together without snarling.

And it is the office of foresight to see that there be a consent in religion between the married, for if their love be not grafted in their souls, it is like[ly] their marriage will be infirmed with the defects of the body.

The office of free choice is the root or foundation of marriage, which consisteth only in the satisfaction of fancy. For where the fancy is not pleased, all the perfections of the world cannot force love, and where the fancy delighteth, many defects are perfected or tolerated among the married.

→ BEN JONSON

On My First Son

1603

Historians have established convincingly that relationships between parents and children were different in the early modern period than they are now. For example, the practices of sending infants out to nurse or of binding young boys as apprentices to a craftsman suggest a degree of emotional distance that we might find strange. Nevertheless, such practices do not signify an absence of emotional ties, as Ben Jonson's poetic lament for the death of his child will readily indicate.

Farewell, thou child of my right hand, and joy;
My sin was too much hope of thee, loved boy:
Seven years thou wert lent to me, and I thee pay,
Exacted by thy fate, on the just day.
O could I lose all father now! For why
Will man lament the state he should envy,
To have so soon 'scaped world's and flesh's rage,
And, if no other misery, yet age?
Rest in soft peace, and asked, say, "Here doth lie
Ben Jonson his best piece of poetry."
For whose sake henceforth all his vows be such
As what he loves may never like too much.

→ Excerpts from Conduct Books

1555–1774

These three passages from manuals of behavior describe proper bedroom conduct with regard to strangers. It was accepted practice for guests in inns to share rooms and even beds with one another.

From Of Good Manners and Proper Behavior *(1555) by Pierre Broë*

If you share a bed with another man, keep still.
Take care not to annoy him or expose yourself by abrupt movements.
And if he is asleep, see that you do not wake him.

From The Rules of Decency and Christian Manners
(1749 Edition) by Jean Baptiste de la Salle

You ought . . . neither to undress nor go to bed in the presence of any other person. Above all, unless you are married, you should not go to bed in the presence of anyone of the other sex.

It is still less permissible for people of different sexes to sleep in the same bed, unless they are very young children. . . .

If you are forced by unavoidable necessity to share a bed with another person of the same sex on a journey, it is not proper to lie so near him that you disturb or even touch him; and it is still less decent to put your legs between those of the other. . . .

It is also very improper and impolite to amuse yourself with talk and chatter. . . .

When you get up you should not leave the bed uncovered, nor put your nightcap on a chair or anywhere else where it can be seen.

From The Rules of Decency and Christian Manners
(1774 Edition) by Jean Baptiste de la Salle

It is a strange abuse to make two people of different sex sleep in the same room. And if necessity demands it, you should make sure that the beds are apart, and that modesty does not suffer in any way from this commingling. Only extreme indigence can excuse this practice. . . .

If you are forced to share a bed with a person of the same sex, which seldom happens, you should maintain a strict and vigilant modesty. . . .

When you have awakened and had sufficient time to rest, you should get out of bed with fitting modesty and never stay in bed holding conversations or concerning yourself with other matters . . . nothing more clearly indicates indolence and frivolity; the bed is intended for bodily rest and for nothing else.

→ SIR EDWARD COKE

From *The Third Part of the Institutes of the Laws of England* *1644*

Of Buggery or Sodomy

Sir Edward Coke (1552–1634) was chief justice of the King's Bench and crown prosecutor in the trials of the earl of Essex and the perpetrators of the Gunpowder Plot. His *Institutes* (published posthumously) outlines and explains the principal tenets of the English legal system; the following selection from the third edition sets forth the nature of the crime — "buggery," or sodomy — and gives the official view of the criminality of homosexual acts.

Buggery is a detestable and abominable sin, amongst Christians not to be named, committed by carnal knowledge against the ordinance of the Creator and order of nature, by mankind with mankind, or with brute beast, or by womankind with brute beast.

Bugeria is an Italian word, and signifies so much as is before described. *Paederastes* or *Paiderastes* is a Greek word, *Amator puerorum* [lover of boys], which is but a *Species* of Buggery: and it was complained of in Parliament, that the Lumbards had brought unto the Realm the shameful sin of Sodomy that is not to be named, as there it is said. Our ancient authors do conclude, that it deserveth death, *ultimum supplicium* [the final punishment], though they differ in the manner of punishment. *Britton* saith, that Sodomites and Miscreants shall be burnt: and so were the Sodomites by Almighty God. *Fleta* saith, *Pecorantes & Sodomitae in terra vivi confodiantur* [buggerers and sodomites should be buried alive]: and therewith agreeth the *Mirror, pur le grand abomination* [concerning the great abomination]; and in another place he saith, *Sodomitae est crime de Majestie vers le Roy celestre* [sodomy is a crime of *lese-majeste* against the King of Heaven]. But (to say it once for all) the judgment in all cases of felony is, that the person attainted be hanged by the neck until he or she be dead. But in ancient times in that case, the man was hanged and the woman was drowned, whereof we have seen examples in the reign of *R[ichard].*I. And this is the meaning of ancient Franchises granted *de Furca and Fossa,* of the Gallows and the Pit, for the hanging upon the one and drowning in the other: but *Fossa* is taken away, and *Furca* remains.

Cum masculo non commiscearis coitu foemineo, quia abominatio est. Cum omni pecore non coibis, nec maculaberis cum eo. Mulier non succumbet jumento, nec miscebitur ei, quia scelus est, etc. [Thou shalt not lie with mankind, as with womankind: it is abomination. Neither shalt thou lie with any beast to defile thyself therewith; neither shall any woman stand before a beast to lie down thereto: it is confusion, etc. (Leviticus 18:22–23, King James version).]

The Act of 25 *H[enry].8.[chapter 6]* hath adjudged it felony, and therefore the judgment for felony doth now belong to this offense, viz. to be hanged by the neck till he be dead. He that readeth the Preamble of this Act, shall find how necessary the reading of our ancient Authors is. The statute doth take away the benefit of Clergy from the Delinquent. But now let us peruse the words of the said description of Buggery.

Detestable and abominable.] These just attributes are found in the Act of 25 *H[enry].8.[chapter 6].*

Amongst Christians not to be named.] These words are in the usual Indictment of this offense, and are in effect in the Parliament Roll of 50 *E[dward].3. Ubi supra, nu. 58.*

By Carnal knowledge, etc.] The words of the Indictment be, *Contra ordinationem Creatoris and naturae ordinem, rem habuit veneream, dictumque puerum carnaliter cognovit, etc.* [against the ordinance of the Creator and the order of Nature, he had sexual intercourse and had carnal knowledge of the said boy]. So as there must be *penetratio,* that is, *res in re* [the thing in the thing], either with mankind or with beast, but the least penetration maketh it carnal knowledge. See the indictment of *Stafford,* which was drawn by great advice, for committing Buggery with a Boy; for which he was attainted and hanged.

The Sodomites came to this abomination by four means, viz. by pride, excess of diet, idleness, and contempt of the poor. *Otiosus nihil cogitat, nisi de ventre and venere* [the idle think of nothing but the belly and fornication]. Both the agent and consentient are felons: and this is consonant to the law of God, *Qui dormierit cum masculo coitu foemineo, uterque operatus est nefas, and morte moriatur* [If a man also lie with mankind, as he lieth with a woman, both of them have committed an abomination: they shall surely be put to death . . . (Leviticus 20:13, KJV)]. And this accordeth with the ancient Rule of law, *Agentes and consentientes pair poena plecentur* [the doers and those consenting to the doing alike deserve punishment].

Emissio seminis [ejaculation] maketh it not Buggery, but is an evidence in case of Buggery of penetration: and so in Rape the words be also *carnaliter cognovit* [had carnal knowledge], and therefore there must be penetration: and *emissio seminis* without penetration maketh no Rape. . . . If the party buggered be within [beneath] the age of discretion, it is no felony in him, but in the agent only. When any offense is felony either by the Common law, or by statute, all Accessories both before and after are incidentally included. So if any be present, abetting and aiding any to do the act, though the offense be personal and to be done by one only, as to commit Rape, not only he that doth the act is a principal, but also they that be present, abetting and aiding the misdoer, are principals also; which is a proof of the other case of Sodomy.

Or by woman.] This is within the Purvien [Purview] of this Act of 25 *H[enry].8.[chapter 6].* For the words be, *if any person, etc.* which extend as well to a woman as to a man, and therefore if she commit Buggery with a beast, she is a person that commits Buggery with a beast, to which end this word [*person*] was used. And the rather, for that somewhat before the making of this Act, a great Lady had committed Buggery with a Baboon, and conceived by it, etc.

There be four sins in holy Scripture called *Clamantia peccata*, crying sins, whereof this detestable sin is one, expressed in this *Distichon,*

Sunt vox clamorum, vox sanguinis, and Sodomorum,
Vox oppressorum, merces detenta laborum.

[They are the voice of shouts, the voice of blood, and of Sodomites, the voice of the oppressed, when punishment is withheld.]

→ QUEEN ELIZABETH I

List of Royal Proclamations   *1596–1601*

These titles of the proclamations issued by Elizabeth I in a five-year period provide a glimpse of some of the chief concerns of her government at the end of the sixteenth century. The proclamation is the early modern equivalent of the executive order and was used to control a wide range of economic, social, and political problems.

February 11, 1596	Enforcing Statutes against Vagabonds and Rogues
April 1596	Regulating Chester Wages
May 3, 1596	Ordering Punishment of Persons with Forged Credentials
May 29, 1596	Enforcing Statutes for Winding of Wool

July 31, 1596   Enforcing Orders for Marketing Grain; Prohibiting Unlicensed Manufacture or Sale of Starch

August 20, 1596   Ordering Peace Kept on Scottish Border

September 29, 1596   Licensing Collections for Marshalsea Prisoners

November 2, 1596   Enforcing Orders against Dearth; Ordering Hospitality Kept in Country, and Defenses Maintained

April 8, 1597   Regulating Chester Wages

July 6, 1597   Enforcing Statutes and Proclamations of Apparel

July 23, 1597   Dispensing Certain Persons from Statutes of Apparel

August 13, 1597   Ordering Peace Kept on Scottish Borders

September 15, 1597   Defending Lord Mayor from Slander; Ordering Grain to Markets

September 27, 1597   Granting Letters of Marque against Spanish Shipping

1597   Enforcing Statute for Making Caps

January 9, 1598   Ordering Deportation of Hanse Merchants [draft]

February 26, 1598   Enforcing Abstinence from Meat

May 20, 1598   Granting Monopoly for Starch

August 23, 1598   Enforcing Former Statutes, Proclamations, and Orders against Forestalling Grain

September 9, 1598   Placing London Vagabonds under Martial Law

February 8, 1599   Prohibiting Piracy against Allied Shipping

March 31, 1599   Declaring Reason for Sending Army into Ireland

January 14, 1600   Establishing Commission for Concealed Lands

January 14, 1600   Enforcing Statutes on Abstinence from Meat, Ale Houses, and Vagabonds

March 18, 1600   Enforcing Statutes against Export of Gold and Silver

March 28, 1600   Ordering Imprisonment of Persons Sowing Woad

June 2, 1600   Defending Lord Treasurer from Libels; Ordering Grain Hoarders Punished

December 21, 1600   Enforcing Statutes against Handguns

c. January 1601   Licensing Casper van Senden to Deport Negroes [draft]

c. 1600 (uncertain)   Authorizing Copper Coinage [draft]

January 9, 1601   Granting Patent for Customs on Silk, Lawn, Taffeta, etc.

February 7, 1601   Mitigating Statutes for Wool Cloth Manufacture

February 9, 1601   Announcing Arrest of Earl of Essex

February 15, 1601   Placing London Vagabonds under Martial Law

April 5, 1601   Offering Reward for Information on Libels against the Queen

July 3, 1601   Enforcing Statutes against Transporting English Coin to Ireland

November 28, 1601   Reforming Patent Abuses

→ QUEEN ELIZABETH I

Royal Proclamation against Vagabonds
and Unlawful Assemblies   *September 9, 1598*

Rogues and vagabonds constituted an intractable social evil in early modern London, at least in the eyes of the authorities. This royal proclamation represents one effort in an ongoing program to control vagrancy, begging, and crime.

BY THE QUEENE

The Queen's Majesty's proclamation for suppressing of
the multitudes of idle vagabonds, and for staying of all
unlawful assemblies, especially in and about the City
of London, and for orders to punish the same.

Forasmuch as it is seen that notwithstanding the good laws provided for the restraining of idle people and vagabonds, yet for want of due execution thereof by the justices of peace and other ministers authorized thereunto, there are in many parts of the realm and specially about the city of London and her majesty's court manifestly seen wandering in the common highways, to the annoyance of the common people both in their goods and lives, multitudes of able men, neither impotent nor lame, exacting money continually upon pretense of service in the wars without relief, whereas many of them never did serve, and yet such as have served, if they were maimed or lamed by service, are provided for in the countries by order of sundry good laws and statutes in that behalf made and provided: For reformation whereof her majesty straightly commandeth all justicers and officers to have better regard than heretofore they have had and to appoint upon certain days in the week monthly (for some convenient season) watches and privy searches in places needful, and thereby to attach and imprison such idle vagabonds, and to send the lame and maimed into the countries according to the said statutes; and doth further notify hereby to all her subjects that because the disorder of those vagrant persons is, through neglect of her ordinary officers of justice, grown to such unruliness and undutifulness, that there hath been of late divers routs and unlawful assemblies of rogues and vagabonds, coloring their wandering by the name of soldiers lately come from the wars, who, arming themselves with shot and other forbidden weapons, have not only committed robberies and murders upon her majesty's people in their travel from place to place, but also resisted and murdered divers constables and others that have come to the rescue. Her majesty therefore, being compelled to look with the eye of severity into these growing outrages, and being minded to provide for her good and dutiful subjects by cutting off in the beginning such lewd and notorious offenders, meaneth for that purpose to appoint a provost marshal with sufficient authority to apprehend all such as shall not be readily reformed and corrected by the ordinary officers of justice, and them without delay to execute upon the gallows by order of martial law. And these her majesty's commandments she willeth to be duly observed upon pain of her indignation. Given at her Majesty's Manor of Greenwich, the ninth day of September 1598, in the fortieth year of Her Highness' reign.

→ QUEEN ELIZABETH I

Edict Arranging for the Expulsion from England of Negroes and Blackamoors

July 18, 1596

Concerned about what she considered the excessive number of "blackamoors" in the realm, the queen licensed Casper van Senden, who had delivered to England eighty-nine prisoners held by the Spanish, to transport to Spain and Portugal the same number of black slaves living in England. The order is explained as repayment of a personal debt to van Senden, as well as in larger economic terms: these slaves were taking work away from Englishmen.

An open warrant to the Lord Mayor of London and to all vice-admirals, mayors, and other public officers whatsoever to whom it may appertain. Whereas Casper van Senden, a merchant of Lubeck, did by his labor and travel procure eighty-nine of her majesty's subjects that were detained prisoners in Spain and Portugal to be released, and brought them hither into this realm at his own cost and charges, for the which his expenses and declaration of his honest mind toward those prisoners he only desireth to have license to take up so much blackamoors here in this realm and to transport them into Spain and Portugal. Her majesty in regard of the charitable affection the suppliant hath showed, being a stranger [foreigner], to work the delivery of our countrymen that were there in great misery and thralldom and to bring them home to their native country, and that the same could not be done without great expense, and also considering the reasonableness of his requests to transport so many blackamoors from hence, doth think it a very good exchange, and that those kind of people may be well spared in this realm, being so populous and numbers of able persons, the subjects of the land and Christian people, that perish for want of service, whereby through their labor they might be maintained. They are therefore in their lordships' names required to aid and assist him to take up such blackamoors as he shall find within this realm with the consent of their masters, who we doubt not, considering her majesty's good pleasure to have those kind of people sent out of the land and the good deserving of the stranger toward her majesty's subjects, and that they shall do charitably and like Christians rather to be served by their own countrymen than with those kind of people, will yield those in their possession to him.

CHAPTER 9

Politics and Religion: Early Modern Ideologies

—✕—

Consideration of political and religious ideology and practice in the early modern period necessarily begins with Queen Elizabeth I, who ruled England for most of Shakespeare's lifetime. The foundation of Elizabeth's authority was laid a century before her prime, however, with the assumption of power by her grandfather, King Henry VII, who defeated Richard III at the battle of Bosworth Field in 1485. The first of the Tudor monarchs, Henry VII immediately and single-mindedly set about to consolidate power in the Crown so as to avoid the civil strife that had plagued the nation throughout most of the fifteenth century. His son, Henry VIII, followed his example by further strengthening the power of the monarchy, and that son's most celebrated daughter, Elizabeth I, perfected the strategy. (Her successor, James I, employed it less effectively thanks to his recklessly authoritarian style.) When Henry VIII took the throne in 1509 at the age of seventeen, one of his first public actions was to execute two councillors who had served his father loyally but angered the people. Elizabeth acted with similar determination when she was crowned in 1558, although the unsettled national mood — her half-sister, Mary, had brought England near to civil war during her brief reign by restoring Catholicism as the state religion — made her wary and deliberate. Throughout Elizabeth's forty-five-year reign she ruthlessly adhered to the principles of royal privilege and authority, managing both to check the influence of Parliament and to restrain the powerful noble families whose jostling for power had historically led to unrest and bloodshed. In terms of internal politics, the reign of Elizabeth was stable, if not entirely free of strife. And since the queen was de facto head of the Church of England as well as head of state, she managed to impose a similar balance in the religious sphere.

An Absolute Monarchy?

England was an absolutist state in Shakespeare's day and would remain so until the middle of the seventeenth century. The term *absolutist* requires some definition, however, for it was disagreement over the exact meaning of the word — how much power did the monarchy legitimately hold? — that, when magnified and backed with force, led to the Civil Wars of the 1640s. (The excerpt from Sir Thomas Smith's *De Republica Anglorum* on p. 320 addresses the problem of royal versus parliamentary authority.) At Runnymede in the thirteenth century, a group of powerful English nobles had forced King John to acknowledge in the *Magna Carta* that the supremacy of the monarch was conditional, thus creating the basis for what would become the "mixed constitution" of England, the system under which authority was held and exercised by the monarch, the House of Lords, and the House of Commons. Despite the faintly democratic sound of this arrangement, central political authority actually rested in the hands of a very few people. During the sixteenth and early seventeenth centuries the balance of power continually shifted among monarch and councillors and important members of the aristocracy. These fluctuations usually corresponded to the popularity and political savvy of the monarch. Elizabeth, an unfailing pragmatist, exhibited a genius for apparent consultation and compromise among disputing constituencies, a talent which paradoxically secured and increased her own power, whereas James I, who fancied himself a political theorist, loudly adopted a more dogmatic line about the unimpeachable sovereignty of the king and thus contributed ultimately to the diminution of that authority. (See the extended passage from James's speech to Parliament on p. 322.)

The absolute power of the monarch was limited to certain political areas, however, and sometimes limited even within those areas. Taxation — it will come as no surprise to the modern reader — was one of the most potentially volatile topics in early modern England, and in this sphere particularly the sovereign's power was dependent on the will of others, usually the most powerful members of the landed aristocracy who asserted themselves through Parliament. The expenses of running the government, and the means of covering those expenses, were considerably different in the sixteenth and seventeenth centuries than in modern times because government was a very different enterprise than it is now. To take the most immediate and costly examples, there were no standing military forces to support (although individual campaigns had to be funded from time to time), and comparatively few social services (the Poor Laws for the relief of the indigent were financed at the parish level). The costs of government arose mostly from the maintenance of the monarch and the accompanying expenses of the royal household, and though these budgets were not trivial, they amounted to a fraction of the expenditures associated with the modern state. The revenues needed to finance the royal establishment were obtained from two major sources: the profits from Crown lands, which were considerable, and the customs tax on imports (chiefly wine) and exports (chiefly wool), income that had benefited the monarch since the fourteenth century. Under normal circumstances, other forms of royal subsidy, which had to be approved by Parliament, were unnecessary. But normal circumstances were often disrupted by national and international problems in the second half of the sixteenth century, notably the high rate of inflation and the conflicts with Spain, and so the direct taxation of landowners and workers that was supposed to be exceptional became, as Elizabeth's reign progressed, more like the rule. Parliament jealously guarded its authority over taxation. It usually acceded to the requests of Elizabeth and her ministers, but after 1603, under the Stuarts, the royal demand for ever greater subsidies became an increasing source of friction between the kings and their Parliaments.

If England was an absolutist state and its people subject to the will of the monarch, then what was the role of Parliament? As the etymology of the word implies (from the French *parler*, to speak), the main function of Parliament was to discuss policy, not to make it. Officially it met to authorize taxation and to endorse important acts of state; frequent and fierce debate arose over whether its powers extended any further than this. The Crown retained the right to call the members into session, which it did mainly when it required money or official support for national or international policy. Toward the end of Elizabeth's reign Parliament was called frequently, to confront the various crises of the 1580s and 1590s, but "frequently" in this context means every few years, and not necessarily for long periods of time. As J. P. Kenyon points out, these various meetings "were all separate parliaments, and their sessions were brief; men still spoke of 'this parliament' or 'the parliaments,' not of 'Parliament' in general" (*Stuart England* 32).

Although the representational function of Parliament was often proclaimed, the assembly was hardly responsive to the people in the way that the modern legislative body has theoretically become. Wealthy landowners came to town to represent themselves, particularly to safeguard their economic interests; and even though the population of London had increased faster than the population of the nation as a whole, the makeup of Parliament was still heavily weighted toward the countryside. Sometimes members took it upon themselves to advise the monarch, as when one of Elizabeth's early parliaments urged her to marry and produce an heir. At one point in James's reign there was even serious debate over the relative sovereignty of king and Parliament when in 1610 the House of Commons declared that the English government ought to be described as consisting of "King in Parliament." But such instances of self-assertion were unusual, and from the Elizabethan era through the outbreak of the English Revolution, the monarchs tended to use Parliament when possible and otherwise to ignore or tolerate it. The concern that emerges from such Elizabethan and Jacobean plays as *Richard II* and *Coriolanus* over the proper origins and uses of political power attests to profound anxiety about the tension between popular and monarchical authority.

The day-to-day workings of government were carried out by executive officers and bureaucrats under the supervision of the monarch's principal ministers and councillors, who were also members of Parliament. As will become clear, Elizabethan and Jacobean government was a decentralized system, with most of the responsibility for decision making and judicial administration resting in the hands of magistrates and councils at the level of the town, the county, and the parish. Apart from religion — a very large exception, as we shall see — the main business of government was international, and the monarchs devoted a large portion of their time to international affairs. From 1558 when she took the throne, Queen Elizabeth regularly presented herself as a possible partner in marriage. Using the prospect of royal alliance as international leverage, she welcomed suitors (or their brokers) from Spain, France, Denmark, and other European states. King James played the same game with his children, Prince Henry, Princess Elizabeth, and then, unexpectedly, Prince Charles (after Henry's early death in 1612, at the age of eighteen). England was not immune to the turmoil that afflicted Europe in the second half of the sixteenth century: Spanish adventurism under Philip II, the religious strife that split the French nation between Catholics and Protestants and seriously affected the European balance of power, the vulnerable position of the Netherlands, the uncertain role of Scotland and its unpredictable Queen Mary Stuart, and papal opposition to the Anglican Church. Elizabeth remained constantly alert to this European instability, seeking to capitalize on opportunities and forestall perils. By the time of her death the configuration of power on the Continent had changed, and King James, conceiving of himself as pacifist and diplomat, devoted much energy to negotiating settlements with Spain and other former and prospective enemies.

Councillors

Foreign affairs and those national and local problems the Crown chose to address were conducted by the monarch with the assistance of a small group of influential advisers. The most powerful and trusted of these advisers comprised the Privy Council. In Elizabeth's circle the principal minister was Sir William Cecil, knighted in 1551 by her brother, Edward VI, and raised to the peerage as Baron Burghley by Elizabeth twenty years later. Serving the queen in various offices, including Secretary of State and Lord Treasurer, from her accession until his death in 1598, Burghley also groomed his son, Robert Cecil, to assist and follow him in office. Elizabeth's other chief ministers were colorful men as well. Sir Thomas Gresham was the financial genius who looked after economic affairs, borrowed money in Antwerp and other European financial centers, and built the Royal Exchange. Robert Dudley, earl of Leicester and Master of the Horse, was a particular favorite of Elizabeth, so much so that in the 1560s he was regularly mentioned as a likely husband for her. But Dudley presented two liabilities: first, the inconvenient fact that he was married already, and second, the scandal that ensued when, as his relations with the queen became more intimate, his wife was found dead, having apparently fallen to the bottom of a flight of stairs. Another major player, Francis Walsingham, was appointed principal secretary (one of two) in 1573, under the sponsorship of Burghley. Educated as was Burghley in the Protestant circles at Cambridge, Walsingham had fled the country in the 1550s in reaction to Mary Tudor's militant Catholicism; when he took his place in the Privy Council some fifteen years after his return, residual zeal made him probably the most radical of Elizabeth's advisers. Walsingham was also the genius behind the regime's sophisticated system of intelligence, the father, in short, of the early modern spy network. His web of informants and double agents paid its most handsome dividends in the entrapment of Mary, Queen of Scots, in a plot to assassinate Elizabeth. (This is not to say that Mary was innocent of conspiracy, but government moles certainly helped her along.) Further, Walsingham's men were present in a tavern at Deptford in 1593 when the playwright Christopher Marlowe was killed in a brawl, stabbed through the eye. There is evidence that Marlowe himself did some spying on the Continent, but whether his death was a political murder is still a matter of debate.

Robert Cecil, very short and very ambitious, provided continuity between Elizabeth's and James's reigns. Succeeding his father in 1596 as the queen's Secretary of State, he privately initiated and supervised the process by which the Scottish king assumed the English throne. This was a tricky business. The queen, aged and ill, resolutely refused (at least publicly) to name her successor, fearing that to do so would imperil her own security. James VI of Scotland was the most likely candidate, his claim resting on his descent from Margaret Tudor, the sister of Henry VIII and Elizabeth's aunt. So as early as March of 1601, two years before the old queen's death, Cecil entered into clandestine negotiations to arrange for James's succession when the time came, as the letter on page 325 indicates. For Cecil, a primary benefit of such an arrangement was that he could remain as Secretary of State; indeed, he prospered under the new king, who immediately made him Lord Cecil of Essendine and later earl of Salisbury and who endowed him with more and more political responsibility until Cecil's death in 1612. Another of James's chief officers was the philosopher and literary figure Francis Bacon, who served as Solicitor General, Attorney General, Lord Keeper, and Lord Chancellor, although his public career ended badly in 1621 when he was convicted, removed from office, and sentenced to prison for taking bribes.

If some of the most vivid figures in Elizabeth's time were her potential suitors, something similar might be said of the reign of King James. Although married (to Anne of Denmark) and the father of several children, James was famously susceptible to the attractions of good-looking young men, and so the Stuart court was adorned by the presence of such royal favorites as Robert Carr, earl of Somerset, and the last and most powerful, George Villiers, duke of Buckingham. (See James's letter to Buckingham on p. 326.) Undoubtedly these personal affections influenced James's domestic and international policies, but it is also important to remember that the Stuart regime was managed by a secretariat that was firmly Elizabethan in origin and disposition and that went about its business without too much concern for the king's most recent beau.

But description of those people who advised Elizabeth and James and who carried on the everyday business of government conveys an inadequate image of what the courts of the two monarchs were actually like. Elizabeth's father and grandfather had vastly increased the sophistication and glitter of the English court, attracting writers like Sir Thomas More and painters like Hans Holbein and making the royal households around London worthy of comparison with the more established European cultural centers. Elizabeth herself was intelligent and charismatic. She dominated the scene at court partly by mastering the arts of self-representation. Attending her until he lost favor and retired to his country home was the brilliant Sir Philip Sidney — courtier, sonneteer, fiction writer, soldier, and literary theorist. James I deliberately set about to make his court the

The "Ermine Portrait" of Elizabeth I.

envy of Europe, spending enormous sums on courtly entertainments, and to some extent he achieved that goal. But he also elicited ridicule for his practice of knighting multitudes of Scots who descended on London after his accession, and many of his subjects — see Sir John Harington's report on a famous courtly party on page 326 — were aware and critical of Jacobean extravagance.

The Monarchs

Elizabeth and James were symbolic figures, as the portraits reproduced here indicate. As Louis Adrian Montrose puts it in speaking of "The Queen," "here

Portrait of James I, by Paul van Somer.

I mean not the person of Elizabeth Tudor but rather the whole field of cultural meanings personified in her" ("Elizabethan Subject" 303). Montrose's distinction is important because it represents the emphasis of much recent interpretation, which has tended to favor the cultural over the personal. Mindful of royal symbolism, we may still find it fascinating to learn something about the two human beings who personify these meanings. If I have more to say about Elizabeth and her court than about James and his, it is because, speaking structurally or bureaucratically, much of what was true in 1590 was still true in 1610. And Shakespeare lived three times as long a subject of Elizabeth as he did of James.

The twentieth-century reputation of Queen Elizabeth offers a lesson in the extremes of historical evaluation. One school of thought, led by Sir John Neale, the author of a major biography published in 1934 that is still influential, has come near to canonizing Elizabeth. According to this view she was bright, independent, cautious, able to distinguish the essential from the temporary. She was also circumspect by nature and experience, her prudence deriving from an enormous sense of royal responsibility. She used apparent indecision strategically, to purchase time in order to gain advantage from delay. Her negotiation of a *via media*, or middle way, between Catholics and reformers was a brilliant act of diplomacy. The disappointments and crises of her reign — the execution of the Scottish queen, the military conflicts in France and the Netherlands, the fierce monetary inflation at the end of the century — all these were probably inevitable, not her fault. Predictably, such a hagiographic approach has generated its negative complement, to wit: the queen was capricious, bull-headed, vacillating, out of touch with reality. Her uncertainty was a function of monstrous personal vanity, which exaggerated her fear of making a mistake. Whatever the motives, her unwillingness to make decisions disabled any attempt at consistent policy. The religious accommodation was an unsatisfactory compromise that did not resolve conflict but merely postponed it. The disappointments and crises of her reign — diplomatic, military, and economic — were all her fault.

These two positions are interpretations, responses to evidence that may itself be interpretive, shaped by the conditions of its transmission. But whether historians emphasize the positive or negative valence, they are responding to the irreducible fact that Elizabeth was both brilliant and difficult. She spoke several languages (including French, Italian, and Spanish), translated Latin for pleasure, played the virginal (a forerunner of the piano), wrote verse, and impressed the diplomatic corps from other nations with her wit and force of personality. Having lived a virtual prisoner during the five-year reign of her sister Mary, she was wary and slow to commit herself to a course of action. For good or ill, she was a consummate politician.

No one ever described James I as brilliant. Despite his learning and his philosophical ambitions, it has become permissible and even customary to think of the first Stuart king as something of a fool. This extreme characterization is probably a result of the gap between his conception of his own talents and achievements and the judgment that history has rendered. His high opinion of his powers of intellect led him to compose political treatises, such as the *Basilikon Doron* of 1594 (see p. 328), a kind of political manual addressed to his son, in which he expatiated philosophically on the divine right of kings and its importance in a parliamentary monarchy. His diplomatic ambitions led him to seek glory in the wide and perilous theater of Continental politics. But it seems clear that such efforts constituted a kind of showboating, that in reality James was an indolent, self-satisfied man who preferred to spend the day hunting rather than wrangling over the quotidian details of political policy. While his tastes were extravagant, his gift for finances was practically nil. One of his contemporaries put it this way: "He was very liberal of what he had not in his own grip, and would rather part with £100 he never had in his keeping than one twenty-shilling piece within his own custody" (qtd. in Kenyon, *The Stuarts* 39–40). It is vital to remember that, as a Scot, James was a foreigner in England — in the seventeenth century the difference between the two cultures was immense. The king had great difficulty dealing with Parliament. He also hated crowds. According to J. P. Kenyon, quoting the Jacobean courtier Sir John Harington, "The demonstrativeness of the English people soon palled — 'The access of the people made him so impatient that he often dispersed them with frowns, that we may not say with curses,' and on being told that they only wanted to look upon his face he cried out in a tantrum, 'God's wounds! I will pull down my breeches and they shall also see my arse!'" (*The Stuarts* 42).

For all his faults, James had one virtue that redeems him: he loved the theater. As king of Scotland, he had summoned players from England to celebrate his marriage in 1589, and when he arrived in London to ascend the English throne in 1603 he became the patron of Shakespeare's company, renaming them the King's Men and inviting them frequently to perform at court. This devotion to the drama was part of James's larger taste for spectacle, which manifested itself in the lavish royal entertainment known as the court masque, an elaborate mixture of poetry, scenery, and dance (the last being the king's favorite part of the show). As a form, the masque was developed by Ben Jonson (the poet) and Inigo Jones (the designer) from the fairly modest courtly exercises performed during Elizabeth's time into an expensive and sophisticated celebration of Jacobean power, virtue, and royalty. Although professional actors were sometimes paid to swell the scene, the main performers were favorite courtiers and members of the royal family itself. In *The Masque of Queenes* of 1609, players may have taken the parts of the witches who open the show and are then banished, but the climax of the evening was the spectacular entry of Queen Anne and her attendants bejeweled and costumed as great ladies of history, from Cleopatra to Boadicea. We get a glimpse of what the court masque might have been like in *The Tempest*, in the masque of Ceres with which Prospero honors the espousal of Ferdinand and Miranda.

Queen Elizabeth also took pleasure in plays. Although the story that Shakespeare composed *The Merry Wives of Windsor* because the queen had been captivated by the character of Falstaff in the two *Henry IV* plays and wanted to see Falstaff in love is probably apocryphal, court records attest that she saw several of Shakespeare's plays performed at court by the Lord Chamberlain's Men. Her real passion, however, was the theater of politics. There she was the principal thespian, the star performer ever conscious of her effect on her courtly and popular audiences. It might be said that a gift for the histrionic was the source of her political genius and survival. Her pattern of vacillation and postponement, which frustrated her ministers and which modern historians have seen as a cornerstone of her policy, involved such theatrical strategies as poses and deception and a highly developed sense of timing. As she herself acknowledged in 1586, "We princes, I tell you, are set on stages, in sight and view of all the world" (qtd. in Levin 129).

The execution of Mary, Queen of Scots, in 1587 reveals the complicated interplay of histrionics and sincerity that characterized Elizabeth's style. When, thanks to Walsingham and his spies, Mary was convicted of involvement in the Babington conspiracy to murder Elizabeth and take the English throne, Elizabeth found herself in a serious dilemma. There was no precedent for trying a prince under English law, and so Elizabeth appointed a royal commission to investigate the charges. It pronounced Mary's guilt emphatically, whereupon Parliament formally demanded her execution and reacted angrily to the queen's unwillingness to proceed. Elizabeth wanted to be rid of her troublesome kinswoman but hesitated to take responsibility for killing a fellow monarch. She was also vexed by the potential impact on foreign relations: Scotland, France (Mary was the widow of King Francis II), and Spain (Mary was Catholic) could be expected to respond angrily, perhaps even militarily, to the execution of Mary. The queen procrastinated, arguing that Parliament would receive only "an answer answerless." Like Henry IV at the end of Shakespeare's *Richard II,* she appears to have hinted that she would welcome an unauthorized murder. Ultimately she signed Mary's death warrant but refused to release it so that it could be acted upon.

After more than eight weeks of torturous deliberation and uncertainty, Burghley and other cabinet ministers took action. Meeting in secret at Burghley's house on the third of February 1587, they agreed to send the warrant and execute Mary without the queen's knowledge. When the deed was done and word reached the capital, people celebrated by lighting bonfires, ringing bells, and feasting for a week. Before the execution, Elizabeth's irresolution seems to have been made up of both moral reservations and concern for appearances; after the fact, her actions imply a high degree of theatricality. She did not celebrate Mary's death. On the contrary, apparently distraught with grief, the queen dressed herself in mourning and commanded that a royal funeral be held publicly in the cathedral at Peterborough. She fulminated against the Privy Council and for a full month refused to see Burghley at all. William Davison, the secretary who had released the warrant without her permission, was committed to the Tower, kept there for a year and a half, and subjected to punishing fines. But these fines were later forgiven and Davison continued to receive his fees as secretary for the remainder of his life — a hint that these broad gestures were moves in a performance intended for audiences both domestic and international, and calculated to distance the queen from the execution.

Such a sense of performance was crucial to Elizabeth's success, as the accounts of various ambassadors and courtiers attest. In August 1588, just after the defeat of the Spanish Armada, but while the nation was still under threat of invasion from the duke of Parma, Elizabeth made a triumphant appearance among the English troops gathered at Tilbury. Disregarding the advice of those who feared for her safety, she arrayed herself in armor, rode boldly through the assembled militia, and inspiringly addressed the cheering men:

> I am come amongst you, as you see, at this time, not for my recreation and disport, but being resolved, in the midst and heat of the battle, to live or die amongst you all, to lay down for my God, and for my kingdom, and for my people, my honor and my blood, even in the dust. I know I have the body of a weak and feeble woman, but I have the heart and stomach of a king, and of a king of England too, and think foul scorn that Parma or Spain, or any prince of Europe should dare to invade the borders of my realm; to which, rather than any dishonor shall grow by me, I myself will take up arms, I myselve will be your general, judge, and rewarder of every one of your virtues in the field.   (Qtd. in Neale 302)

Although historians debate whether the words that have come down to us are actually those spoken at Tilbury, most accept the speech as genuine. She was described on this occasion by a contemporary as "full of princely resolution and more than feminine courage" and as having "passed like some Amazonian empress through all her army" (Neale 302). The costume, the speech, the audacity of her being there at all — these declare her acute sense of audience and her understanding of how to make the spectators adore her.

In the Tilbury speech, Elizabeth accentuates the positive, and such a stance was a familiar part of her style of government, at least as far as the public was concerned. Leaving ministers and lackeys to censure, to punish, to refuse, she dwelt on the affirmative themes of unity, forgiveness, and affection for her people, and doing so with graciousness and majesty, she thereby won their hearts. So apparent was this style in all her dealings, according to Sir John Harington, that she "convert[ed] her reign, through the perpetual love-tricks that passed between her and her people, into a kind of romance" (qtd. in Lockyer 210). The excerpt from Simon Forman's *Diary*, page 330, provides an astonishing example of this mode of thought. But what about more conventional amours? She employed the same "love-tricks" with the various suitors who, earlier in her reign, had come calling from the courts of Europe and the great houses of England. Apart from Robert Dudley, the most prominent suitors were the Austrian Archduke Charles, brother of the Holy Roman Emperor, and two Frenchmen, the duke of Anjou (who became King Henry III) and the duke of Alençon. Elizabeth seriously considered the first two candidates fairly early in her reign, in the 1560s and in 1571–72 respectively. She very nearly married Alençon in 1579, when she was forty-five, in what many considered a last attempt, at the end of her childbearing years, to settle the question of the succession. But doubt among her ministers was compounded by mounting opposition among the people, particularly those with Puritan leanings who feared Catholic encroachment, and so inertia won the day. Ultimately Queen Elizabeth rejected all suitors in favor of a corporate spouse, the

English people at large. William Shakespeare, connoisseur of the theatrical, and professional analyst of monarchy, living as he did in the capital in the last fifteen years of Elizabeth's reign and performing before her at court, must have observed and to some degree appreciated these tactics.

Elizabeth was entering her late sixties at the end of the 1590s, and by that time her willfulness, short temper, and habit of playing one courtier against another had created a fractious and risky atmosphere at court. Although Robert Cecil and other advisers continued to perform their duties with a mixture of genuine service and self-interest, a final favorite had captured the queen's eye. Attractive, courageous, reckless, perhaps even unbalanced, Robert Devereux, earl of Essex, had been a member of Elizabeth's court for over a decade, but his heroic performance at the siege of Cadiz against the Spanish in 1596 made him something of a national, as well as a royal, favorite. The unusual and uncertain nature of the relationship between a glamorous young courtier and a vain and aged female monarch has proved endlessly fascinating to historians, not to mention Italian composers (Gaetano Donizetti's opera of 1836, *Roberto Devereux*) or Hollywood scriptwriters (the 1939 film with Bette Davis and Errol Flynn, *The Private Lives of Elizabeth and Essex*). To what extent was their friendship amorous or sexual? We cannot say for sure. Given Elizabeth's fondness throughout her reign for attractive young men, one of the most intensely debated questions about her is whether the Virgin Queen actually preserved her virginity.

What we do know about the Essex affair is that it ended badly and to some degree poisoned the last years of the Elizabethan age. Essex actively encouraged not only the affections of his sovereign but also of the people. He attracted the loyalty of a group of young aristocrats in London, including Shakespeare's one-time patron, the earl of Southampton, and there was even cautious talk that Essex should be king. In 1598 Elizabeth sent Essex to Ireland to quell the rebels gathered under the earl of Tyrone. Disregarding the queen's explicit orders for managing the campaign, he failed in his mission, returned to England, and presented himself (unannounced) in the queen's bedchamber to justify his actions. Spooked by his popular appeal and swayed by his enemies, notably the Cecil faction, Elizabeth placed him under house arrest. Then, in 1601, Essex gambled and lost. Claiming mistreatment by the queen and slander by the Cecils, he mounted what was in effect a coup d'état, a march on London intended, Essex said, to correct the mistreatment he had suffered, and calculated, others said, to remove Elizabeth from the throne and replace her either with James VI of Scotland or with Essex himself. Essex had a few powerful supporters; as the excerpt on page 71 indicates, the day before his march on the palace, some of them sponsored the Lord Chamberlain's Men in a performance of Shakespeare's *Richard II*, the play in which a king is deposed. But the coup was poorly planned and immediately put down, and Essex was executed on a wintry morning in 1601. Elizabeth had not seen him since his wild return from Ireland.

The Church

Religion and politics were virtually inseparable in the sixteenth century, and the greatest danger facing Elizabeth on her accession in 1558 was the religious crisis. Mary Tudor, her half sister who had ruled England for the previous five years, had swiftly reversed the ecclesiastical reforms initiated by Henry VIII and Edward VI and reinstituted Catholicism as the state religion, thus bringing the nation close to civil war. Worse still to many minds was that Queen Mary had married Philip II of Spain. Hundreds of Protestant activists had fled the land for Holland, the German principalities, and the Calvinist enclave at Geneva, and among many who remained at home the resistance to a reconciliation with Rome was formidable. The conflict between the new regime and a number of intransigent Protestant bishops appointed by Henry and Edward led to the persecution of heretics under Mary — hence the queen's nickname "Bloody Mary." The most famous incident occurred at Oxford in October 1555 when Hugh Latimer and Nicholas Ridley were burned at the stake. (See John Foxe's account on p. 131.) Although these two clergymen were celebrities, most of those executed were lay people. These violent consequences of royal succession were still fresh in the English consciousness when Elizabeth was crowned in November of 1558, and people naturally wanted to know where the young queen stood on the issues of the mass, the administration of the sacraments, whether *The Book of Common Prayer* should be used (and which version?), priestly marriage, the former monastic properties, and other fiercely debated questions. Such disputes, with their potentially deadly outcomes, form the background for Shakespeare's obsession, in the English histories and tragedies such as *King Lear*, with "the division of the kingdom."

In negotiating a smooth transition back to Anglican practice, the young queen succeeded because she was a pragmatist. Her compromise, known as the Elizabethan Settlement, did not completely and permanently eliminate the animosity between Catholic and Protestant zealots, but its terms managed to accommodate most reasonable leaders of the opposing factions. Elizabeth from the beginning had sought to maintain what was called the *via media*, the middle way, wanting to preserve the more or less Catholic elements of ritual that had survived Henry's break with Rome, while at the same time adhering in most matters to the doctrines that had motivated the European reformers. At Mary's death, many influential Protestants returned from the Continent fired with the radical enthusiasm of John Calvin and his followers, and some of these men took seats in Parliament. One of the first problems was the need to agree on an acceptable version of *The Book of Common Prayer*. The radical reformers wanted the 1552 edition, which reflects a more vigorous anti-Catholic ideology. For example, it treats the Communion service not as transubstantiation, a sacrament in which the bread and wine are actually changed into the body and blood of Christ, but rather as a symbolic representation. Moreover, it includes a petition that God should deliver the Christian from "the Bishop of Rome and all his detestable enormities." Elizabeth and her advisers favored the earlier, more nearly Roman document, and so a compromise was reached in which the 1552 Protestant book was approved but with a series of major revisions tempering its reformist ideology. The appurtenances of Roman ritual were mostly discarded, and yet the priests of the Church of England were instructed to wear white surplices and special dress for the serving of Holy Communion. Neither hard-line Marian Catholics nor radical Protestants were pleased, but most everyone to the center of these two positions was able to live with the Elizabethan Settlement.

These religious controversies never disappeared; zealots on both sides repeatedly challenged Elizabeth's efforts to maintain the middle way. Catholicism was mostly kept in check, since Catholics were forbidden by the Act of Uniformity (1559) to practice their faith and in fact were obliged to attend the Anglican service every Sunday or be fined. But there was considerable pressure from the Continent. In 1570 Pius V issued a papal bull titled *Regnans in excelsis* excommunicating Elizabeth; his successor, Pope Gregory XIII, went so far as to encourage true Christians to assassinate the "Jezebel" who ruled England, offering to absolve them in advance. Missionary Jesuit priests sent secretly to England, treasonous plots on behalf of the Scottish queen, and war (or rumors of war) with Spain combined to foster stronger enforcement of anti-Catholic measures. For the most part, Elizabeth saw to it that private faith was not threatened: the law required attendance at the Anglican service, but the queen resolutely opposed legislation that would have made the taking of Communion compulsory. Governmental policy was aimed at suppressing Catholicism in its more public and evangelical forms. For example, anyone saying mass was subject to a huge monetary fine and a year in prison; similarly, those attempting to make converts were treated harshly. These statutes had some effect, but the government's most valuable instrument was the passage of time. Legitimate Catholic services could be conducted only by an ordained priest, and as the years went by such a figure became harder and harder to find. As one historian has pointed out, by the time of Elizabeth's death no more than a dozen or so Catholic priests survived from Mary's reign, and the authorities had strictly enforced the prohibition against Catholic immigration. Fewer priests meant fewer services and fewer Catholics; by the end of the sixteenth century England had outlasted the Roman peril (see Guy 300–01).

The more insidious threat to Elizabeth's desire for religious balance came from Protestant ideologues or, as they came to be called toward the end of the century, Puritans. Vigorous scholarly debate has arisen over the term *Puritan* because it has been employed too loosely, invoked to describe people who were philosophically and chronologically diverse, from violent anti-Catholics of the 1560s to Cromwellian anti-Royalists of the 1650s. (Jonas A. Barish, quoting the historian Christopher Hill to the effect that "the word Puritan . . . is an admirable refuge from clarity of thought," goes on to defend his use of the noun: "Nevertheless, the term has come to stand, with some justice, for a complex of attitudes best represented by those strictly designated as Puritans . . ." [82n].) I use it here to describe those members of the Church of England who, especially in the late years of Elizabeth's reign, sought to purify the English church of the residual evidence of Roman practice in the liturgy and ceremony of the Anglican service — the wearing of vestments, the adoration of the cross, kneeling, elaborate music. Under the influence of Calvin and his followers in Geneva, many Protestants had come to regard salvation as more personal and internal. The reformers thus sought to remake the hierarchical system of church government, returning greater authority to individual congregations. They urged a greater emphasis on preaching and, in certain quarters, "prophesying." The hatred of Elizabeth in the Catholic capitals of Europe gave strength to the cause of radical Protestantism in England, and the queen's own inner circle contained several advisers with Puritan sympathies, men trained at Cambridge who had absorbed elements of radical Genevan theology. (See p. 331 for an instance of Puritan polemics.)

Elizabeth herself, however, was uncompromisingly middle of the road. John Whitgift, professor of divinity at Cambridge who was appointed Archbishop of Canterbury in 1583, attempted in 1595 to supplant the Thirty-nine Articles that governed the Church of England with a more Calvinist set of principles; the sharp-eyed queen thwarted the attempt, however, instructing Cecil to inform Whitgift that "she mislikes much that any allowance hath been given by your Grace of any points to be disputed of predestination (being a matter tender and dangerous to weak, ignorant minds) and thereupon requireth your Grace to suspend them" (qtd. in Lockyer 202). By means of such vigilance Elizabeth managed to check the extremists in both camps. She commissioned Richard Hooker to write a philosophical defense of the Anglican Church and its system of church government. *The Laws of Ecclesiastical Polity,* printed in multiple volumes beginning in 1593, differentiated the English church from the radical Calvinist system of individually organized ecclesiastical units. As one distinguished historian puts it, Hooker "supplied a learned and reasoned basis for the theological position of the church of England, and commended the *via media,* not as a convenient halfway house between Rome and Geneva, but as the true, if reformed, descendant of the primitive church" (Davies 68). Elizabeth's commitment to the middle way gave the Protestant cause forty-five years to set down deep roots, and by the time James took the throne, the Church of England, its root system firmly in place, had flowered.

It was not without natural enemies, however. When statutes aimed at discouraging the practice and especially the spread of Catholicism were reenacted in 1604, and persecution, particularly of Jesuit priests, continued, the reaction took a violent course. In 1605 the Catholic opponents of James's religious policy attempted a fatal strike at the monarch, with a conspiracy known as the Gunpowder Plot. A group of dissidents, including Robert Catesby, a Jesuit priest named Father Henry Garnet, and the trigger man, Guy Fawkes, had rented space beneath the houses of Parliament (not the grand nineteenth-century structure as we know it, but its more modest predecessor), packed it with explosives, and planned to blow up the building on the occasion of the king's visit to open Parliament on November 5. The scheme was exposed at the last moment and the conspirators hanged, but the Gunpowder Plot was a national scandal that shattered James's image of himself as beloved leader and conciliator. Shakespeare was clearly affected by it. *Macbeth*, a play about a Scottish political assassination written for a Scottish king about 1606, seems to refer to Father Garnet and his notoriously ambiguous responses at his trial. After the murder of Duncan, the Porter imagines himself the keeper of the gates of Hell and welcomes such a devious speaker: "Faith, here's an equivocator, that could swear in both the scales against either scale, who committed treason enough for God's sake, yet could not equivocate to heaven" (2.3.8–11). Predictably, this terrorist act led to further suspicion and surveillance of Catholics.

But Puritans were discontented as well. James attempted to defang the fiercest of the radical reformers by convening and personally chairing a royal symposium on religious practice, the Hampton Court Conference of 1604, although he did not accede to most of their extreme Protestant demands. (It was this conference that led to the retranslation of the Bible published in 1611, the one we know as the King James Bible, or Authorized Version.) As I have indicated, a crux of religious contention at this stage of the English Reformation was church government. Among Puritans the Calvinist insistence on independence and local authority in church government carried over into secular politics, creating among many English people a protodemocratic and antiauthoritarian climate intolerable to King James. For his part, the king had begun to relish his authority as head of the Anglican Church, particularly after his relative insignificance in Scotland's radically reformed presbyterian structure. It is this linkage of hierarchy in church government with hierarchy in politics that marks one of James's most cherished principles, that expressed in his axiom "No bishop, no king." In other words, in James's view the religious principle of episcopacy, of authority vested in the bishop, also underwrote the structure of monarchy. Many Englishmen, especially some members of Parliament, passionately contested such ideology, and the conflict was never entirely resolved. In fact, failure to resolve it was one of the causes, some forty years later, of the English Revolution.

The Ideology of Order

In pressing the identification of religious with political sovereignty, King James hardly offered the world a new idea but instead adopted and exaggerated a familiar tenet of sixteenth-century thought. Because less than half the male population, and still less of the female, could read, books were expensive, and newspapers nonexistent, a primary source of intellectual and philosophical guidance was the Sunday sermon. The government saw to it that such a forum did not go to waste. Elizabeth and her ministers were ever conscious of their power to use the pulpit for political ends, and they did so by encouraging the clergy to promulgate an ideology of order and obedience. As the sixteenth century drew to its close and the practices of Protestantism began to take firm hold in the Anglican Church, the Sunday sermon became an increasingly dominant feature of the divine service — the more Puritan the congregation, the more central was preaching — and frequently the sermon became a vehicle for the promotion of political values acceptable and advantageous to the Elizabethan regime. In those parishes where the priest was not licensed to preach, other ways were devised of acquainting the public with official political doctrine. One such maneuver was the use of the homily, a formal exhortation read from the pulpit to promote the interests of the state: it served to link the spiritual and the political into an ideological program of order and fear.

One of the most significant, *An Homily against Disobedience and Willful Rebellion*, was issued in 1570 in answer to the Northern Rebellion, the uprising of the previous year in support of Mary, Queen of Scots. A brief paragraph expresses the tenor of the piece, with an extended excerpt reprinted on page 334.

> Thus do you see that neither heaven nor paradise could suffer any rebellion in them, neither be places for any rebels to remain in. Thus became rebellion, as you see, both the first and greatest, and the very root of all other sins, and the first and principal cause both of all worldly and bodily miseries — sorrows, diseases, sicknesses and deaths — and, which is infinitely worse than all these, as is said, the very cause of death and damnation eternal also.

The identification established here between political and religious disobedience, sedition and sin, is one of the defining characteristics of ideology in early modern England. To lose one's life in political conflict could be construed as honorable, even glorious — the cardinal example in Shakespeare is Hotspur in *Henry IV, Part 1* — but to lose one's soul is another matter. Thus the policy makers in Elizabeth's government saw to it that rebellion was associated with grave spiritual consequences. Moreover, they made the Bible a political instrument, particularly the Old Testament with its morally charged narratives of disobedience to an angry God and its record of a people for whom religion and government were one and the same.

The official commitment to order and obedience was intimately connected to the cultural doctrine that we know as the Great Chain of Being. This theory of cosmic organization, which came down to the Elizabethans from the religious and political thinkers of the Middle Ages, held that God had created the universe according to a system of hierarchies, that every living creature and even every inanimate object occupied its ordained place in an elaborate interlocking scheme, and that awareness of that scheme and one's place in it was a precondition for the peaceful and productive operation of society. Moreover, the elaborate specificity of the system meant that it produced a vast system of analogies. The sun was chief among heavenly bodies, the king chief among men, the lion among beasts, the rose among flowers, and so on. In the fifteenth century Sir John Fortescue had written a disquisition on natural law that insists upon the naturalness of hierarchical authority:

> In this order hot things are in harmony with cold, dry with moist, heavy with light, great with little, high with low. In this order angel is set over angel, rank upon rank in the kingdom of heaven; man is set over man,

beast over beast, bird over bird, and fish over fish, on the earth in the air and in the sea: so that there is no worm that crawls upon the ground, no bird that flies on high, no fish that swims in the depths, which the chain of this order does not bind in most harmonious concord. Hell alone, inhabited by none but sinners, asserts its claim to escape the embraces of this order. . . . God created as many different kinds of things as he did creatures, so that there is no creature which does not differ in some respect from all other creatures and by which it is in some respect superior or inferior to all the rest. So that from the highest angel down to the lowest of his kind there is absolutely not found an angel that has not a superior and inferior; nor from man down to the meanest worm is there any creature which is not in some respect superior to one creature and inferior to another. So that there is nothing which the bond of order does not embrace.   (Qtd. in Tillyard 26–27)

The utility of such a hierarchical philosophy for the governments of Elizabeth and James is obvious. As the doctrine made its way into English law, its effect was to criminalize extreme forms of ambition and social disruption.

Internal unrest that occurred despite this ideology, such as the Northern Rebellion of 1569 mentioned above, was suppressed by the raising of local militia on an as-needed basis. For other kinds of crime — theft, murder, treason, or other individual transgressions — justice was enforced by a system of freelance officers, local constables, justices of the peace, and a tough system of penalties. In some cases offenders were tortured with special instruments. Prisons were used chiefly as a holding tank while decisions were made about guilt or appropriate sentencing (except in the case of debtors, who were imprisoned at their own expense). Punishment was for the most part corporal, involving public whipping, dismemberment, and death. By law, stealing even a small sum of money, anything over two shillings, was considered a capital crime, although courts often intentionally undervalued goods in order to protect the petty thief from execution. In theory, the Elizabethan system of justice was severe; in fact, enforcement was hit or miss. From Hamlet's lament about "the law's delay" to the endless and inconclusive interrogation of Pompey in *Measure for Measure,* Shakespeare's plays repeatedly allude to the imperfections of human judicial systems.

Imperfect or not, the Elizabethan judicial system could function swiftly and fiercely. Executions were usually public and often celebratory. In 1579, as the queen seriously considered marriage to the French duke of Alençon, a Puritan gentleman named John Stubbs published a pamphlet titled "The Discovery of a Gaping Gulf whereinto England is like to be swallowed by another French marriage, if the Lord forbid not the banns by letting her Majesty see the sin and punishment thereof." Stubbs considered himself a patriot, a concerned citizen looking out for his monarch's safety. For this offense, he and his publisher were taken to the scaffold. Sir John Neale describes what happened there:

At the scaffold, each made a loyal speech to the people, Stubbs ending with a pun: "Pray for me," he begged, "now my calamity is at hand"; and when his right hand had been cut off, he took his hat from his head with his left, cried "God save the Queen!" and swooned. The publisher lifted his bloody stump; "I have left there a true Englishman's hand," he cried, and went away very stoutly and with great courage. A deep silence pervaded the multitude of spectators. (246)

Such public displays of royal power were not infrequent. In the first few years of James's reign, his government executed some seventy persons each year in London, a city of fewer than 250,000 occupants (see Wotton 25). That there were not more is a testimony to the orthodoxy of hierarchy and order.

Another proof of the pervasiveness of this doctrine is the absence of a police force or a standing army in England in the sixteenth and early seventeenth centuries. The most compelling explanation is financial: Elizabeth preferred not to tax her people in order to support a professional militia, and her foreign policy was not expansionist. But the nation did not escape foreign entanglements. Since her predecessor had lost the English foothold in France, the town of Calais, Elizabeth sought to regain control of it or another French port. More than once she dispatched money and soldiers to the Netherlands to aid the Dutch in their struggles with Spain. (In one of these campaigns, Sir Philip Sidney was wounded in the leg and consequently died.) The rebellious Irish repeatedly threatened English hegemony there, and the occupation was costly. Militarily, Elizabeth's tightfistedness was aided by geography: isolation helped to protect the populace from external threat. In *Richard II,* John of Gaunt figuratively refers to England as

> this little world,
> This precious stone set in the silver sea,
> Which serves it in the office of a wall,
> Or as a moat defensive to a house,
> Against the envy of less happier lands.   (2.1.45–49)

In other words, the island nation was spared the need for an army. Substantial sums were spent on naval operations, however, which not only provided defense but also promoted exploration and colonization. After the execution of Mary, Queen of Scots, Spain attempted to invade England, but the effort was thwarted by the superior artillery of the English ships and the brilliant seamanship of Sir Francis Drake, whose forces defeated the Spanish Armada in July 1588. Occasional conflicts continued to erupt during the remainder of Elizabeth's reign and into James's, but as the Stuart kings (both James and Charles) began to misuse and lose their authority, external conflict gave way to civil war.

Shakespeare's Theater and the Problem of Authority

Shakespeare provides a clear statement of the ideology of order, one that depends on many of the same images and analogies found in the major philosophical expositions of the idea. In the first act of *Troilus and Cressida,* as the

Greeks lament the length of the Trojan War and deplore Achilles' sulking in his tent, Ulysses delivers an extended speech in which he assigns responsibility for the impasse to the dissolution of authority and degree in his own camp.

Troy, yet upon his bases, had been down,
And the great Hector's [the Trojan champion's] sword had lack'd a
    master,
But for these instances:
The specialty of rule hath been neglected,
And look how many Grecian tents do stand
Hollow upon this plain, so many hollow factions.
When that the general is not like the hive
To whom the foragers shall all repair,
What honey is expected? Degree being vizarded [covered],
Th'unworthiest shows as fairly in the mask.
The heavens themselves, the planets, and this centre
Observe degree, priority, and place,
Insisture, course, proportion, season, form,
Office, and custom, in all line of order;
And therefore is the glorious planet Sol
In noble eminence enthron'd and spher'd
Amidst the other; whose med'cinable eye
Corrects the ill aspects of planets evil,
And posts like the commandment of a king,
Sans check, to good and bad. But when the planets
In evil mixture to disorder wander,
What plagues and what portents, what mutiny!
What raging of the sea, shaking of earth!
Commotion in the winds! frights, changes, horrors
Divert and crack, rend and deracinate [uproot]
The unity and married calm of states
Quite from their fixure! O, when degree is shak'd,
Which is the ladder of all high designs,
The enterprise is sick. How could communities,
Degrees in schools, and brotherhoods in cities,
Peaceful commerce from dividable shores,
The primogenity and due of birth,
Prerogative of age, crowns, sceptres, laurels,
But by degree stand in authentic place?
Take but degree away, untune that string,
And hark what discord follows. Each thing meets
In mere oppugnancy [complete opposition]: the bounded waters
Should lift their bosoms higher than the shores,
And make a sop of all this solid globe;
Strength should be lord of imbecility,
And the rude son should strike his father dead;
Force should be right, or rather, right and wrong
(Between whose endless jar justice resides)
Should lose their names, and so should justice too!
Then every thing include itself in power,

Power into will, will into appetite,
And appetite, an universal wolf
(So doubly seconded with will and power),
Must make perforce an universal prey,
And last eat up himself. Great Agamemnon,
This chaos, when degree is suffocate,
Follows the choking,
And this neglection of degree it is
That by a pace goes backwards with a purpose
It hath to climb. The general's disdain'd
By him one step below, he by the next,
That next by him beneath; so every step,
Exampled by the first pace that is sick
Of his superior, grows to an envious fever
Of pale and bloodless emulation [rivalry],
And 'tis this fever that keeps Troy on foot,
Not her own sinews. To end a tale of length,
Troy in our weakness stands, not in her strength.   (1.3.75–137)

The rhetoric Ulysses employs did not originate with Shakespeare. The imagery in particular — the beehive, the planetary system of concentric spheres, the ladder, the musical scale, the sun, the king, the boundaries of sea and shore, chaos, cannibalism, fever — derives from the same tradition that produced the standard contemporary works on the subject of political and divine order, such as Hooker's *Laws of Ecclesiastical Polity* and Sir Thomas Elyot's *The Book Named the Governor* (see p. 339). Ulysses' speech is a powerful denunciation of those who neglect degree and fail to observe the divinely inscribed system of hierarchies, but we should remember that it is the speech of a fictional character whose political ends and distaste for Achilles require that he take this stand and who can scarcely be heard over the grinding of his ax.

Is it also an expression of Shakespeare's own position? Many readers over the past four centuries have thought so. As I have suggested, Shakespeare has often been considered a willing spokesman for the orthodoxy of his age, a loyal monarchist with a hatred for disorder and a contempt for political rebellion and disobedience. E. M. W. Tillyard opens his chapter on "Order" in *The Elizabethan World Picture* by quoting Ulysses' speech and implying that it is an expression of Shakespeare's own personal views. According to this early critical orthodoxy, the history plays constitute a warning against political division and opportunism, and *King Lear* represents a passionate exposition of the danger of breaking what Sir John Fortescue over a century earlier had called the "bond of order."

Some recent students of the period have taken a contrary position. While acknowledging the average Elizabethan's familiarity with the Chain of Being, they dispute Tillyard's assertion that it was universally regarded as natural and divinely ordained. Rather, they consider the paradigm a political tool employed by the state, particularly through the pulpit, to legitimate existing political structures and justify unjustifiable social and economic conditions.

Some of these critics also credit Shakespeare (along with more outspoken dissenters of his age) with great intellectual liberty. Cultural materialists, most of them British followers of the Marxist cultural critic Raymond Williams, believe that Shakespeare's theater presented a deliberate threat to established authority in representing the means by which the government deployed its power and repressed opposing voices. Jonathan Dollimore, for example, sees *Measure for Measure* as sexually subversive, as sympathetic to the marginalized claims of deviant sexuality — specifically prostitution — and as a challenge to those forces of Jacobean authority that would attempt to regulate desire ("Transgression and Surveillance" 84).

Even more sophisticated readings of these political and theatrical conflicts are available. Certain American literary critics known as new historicists, influenced heavily by the French theorist Michel Foucault, insist that Shakespeare's theatrical enterprise was an unwitting instrument of state power, that it contributed paradoxically to the maintenance of the dominant political ideology. Stephen Greenblatt contends that the plays written for the public theater, especially Shakespeare's, generate subversive ideas about Elizabethan and Jacobean political authority but then reabsorb those subversive energies so that the critique of authority is contained within the theatrical system. His reading of the Great Tetralogy is characteristic: "the Henry plays confirm the Machiavellian hypothesis that princely power originates in force and fraud even as they draw their audience toward an acceptance of that power" (65). In other words, the theater functioned as a safety valve: it created and released a performed version of political dissidence while reinforcing the very powers that it challenged.

The Stage and Its Opponents

The view that the Crown tolerated the public theaters because they offered a sanitized form of resistance is made more plausible by the presence of a fierce antitheatricalism among the most extreme Puritan factions. The location of the public theaters, in the Liberties outside the walls of the City of London, was a result of opposition to the stage on the part of the City authorities, many of whom were themselves Puritans or were influenced by the heavy concentration of Puritans within their precincts. This compromise represents one instance of détente in a larger struggle between the monarch and the civic powers. Elizabeth and James not only put up with the acting companies but actually sponsored them and paid them to perform at court, and both monarchs' taste for "play" enraged the most fervent of the Protestant reformers.

Beginning in the 1570s and continuing into the seventeenth century, fierce attacks on the practices of the stage began to appear in print, a function of the professionalization of the theater, the construction of the permanent playhouses, and the increasing popularity of theatergoing among the people. Stephen Gosson published the vitriolic *Plays Confuted in Five Actions* in 1582, and though Gosson himself was not a Puritan, there is evidence that his polemic was commissioned by the City authorities. The following year Philip Stubbes, a Puritan zealot and furious opponent of the stage, produced a similar assault on the immorality of the theater called *The Anatomy of Abuses*, and it was subsequently reprinted (see p. 340). These antitheatrical arguments are grounded in the Protestant abhorrence of ceremony and spectacle, and related to the more general suspicion of representation of any sort. Stubbes makes much of the etymological connection between "actor" and "hypocrite," and a corollary argument deplores the erasure of social and class distinctions in stage performances. (Ulysses' speech on social order reflects this position: "Degree being vizarded, / Th'unworthiest shows as fairly in the mask" [*Troilus and Cressida*, 1.3.83–84].) His other major complaint involves cross-dressing, or men taking women's parts:

> Our Apparell was given us as a signe distinctive to discern betwixt sex and sex, and therfore one to weare the Apparel of another sex is to participate with the same, and to adulterate the veritie of his own kinde. Wherefore these Women may not improperly be called *Hermaphroditi*, that is, Monsters of bothe kindes, half women, half men. (Stubbes sig. F5v)

All of these contentions are linked by a distaste for transgression and fear that boundaries might be blurred.

Shakespeare himself survived these vehement assaults on his livelihood. He mostly avoided topical representation of contemporary controversy and so had little to say artistically about the Puritan detractors, unlike his colleague Ben Jonson, who in *The Alchemist* created a devastating portrait of two Puritan zealots, the wild-eyed Ananias and his elder and more sinister associate, Tribulation Wholesome. Shakespeare's treatments of the stage and of the imagination generally tend to be affirmative and oblique, displaced in the plays-within-plays in *Love's Labor's Lost*, *A Midsummer Night's Dream*, and *Hamlet*. But in one case he permitted himself a swipe at the antitheatrical faction. In *Twelfth Night*, Maria, describing the sober and hypocritical Malvolio, says that "sometimes he is a kind of puritan." Although she does not specifically identify him with a particular sect of religious reformers, Maria does glance disapprovingly at the self-righteousness and antifestivity characteristic of Protestant zeal. In the last moments of the play, tricked and humiliated by a comic scheme, Malvolio leaves the stage with a parting resolution: "I'll be reveng'd on the whole pack of you" (5.1.378). History made the line prophetic. Less than fifty years later Oliver Cromwell, leading the descendants of the Elizabethan Puritans, deposed and executed Charles I, abolished the monarchy, took control of the state, and closed the playhouses.

SIR THOMAS SMITH

From *De Republica Anglorum: The Manner of Government or Policy of the Realm of England* *1583*

Of Parliament and the Monarchy

Sir Thomas Smith's posthumously published work describes the respective functions of Parliament and the monarchy. Although Smith does not seem to acknowledge a potential conflict, the relationship between these two institutions became increasingly fractious after the death of Elizabeth I.

BOOK 2, CHAPTER I

Of the Parliament and the Authority Thereof

The most high and absolute power of the realm of England consisteth in the Parliament. For as in war where the King himself in person, the nobility, the rest of the gentility, and the yeomanry are, is the force and power of England; so in peace and consultation where the Prince is to give life, and the last and highest commandment, the barony for the nobility and higher, the knights, esquires, gentlemen and commons for the lower part of the commonwealth, the bishops for the clergy be present to advertise, consult, and show what is good and necessary for the commonwealth, and to consult together, and upon mature deliberation every bill or law being thrice read and disputed upon in either house, the other two parts first each a part, and after the Prince himself in presence of both the parties doth consent unto and alloweth. That is the Prince's and whole realm's deed: whereupon justly no man can complain, but must accommodate himself to find it good and obey it.

That which is done by this consent is called firm, stable, and *sanctum* [holy], and is taken for law. The Parliament abrogateth old laws, maketh new, giveth orders for things past, and for things hereafter to be followed, changeth rights and possessions of private men, legitimateth bastards, establisheth forms of religion, altereth weights and measures, giveth forms of succession to the crown, defineth of doubtful rights whereof is no law already made, appointeth subsidies, tails [a kind of tax], taxes, and impositions, giveth most free pardons and absolutions, restoreth in blood and name as the highest court, condemneth or absolveth them whom the Prince will put to that trial. And to be short, all that ever the people of Rome might do either in *Centuriatis comitiis* or *tributis* [Roman representative assemblies] the same may be done by the Parliament of England, which representeth and hath the power of the whole realm both the head and the body. For every Englishman is intended to be there present, either in person or by procuration and attorneys, of what preeminence, state, dignity, or quality soever he be, from the Prince (be he King or Queen) to the lowest person of England. And the consent of the Parliament is taken to be every man's consent.

BOOK 2, CHAPTER 3

Of the Monarch King or Queen of England

The Prince whom I now call (as I have often before) the Monarch of England, King or Queen, hath absolutely in his power the authority of war and peace, to defy what Prince it shall please him, and to bid him war, and again to reconcile himself and enter into league or truce with him at his pleasure or the advice only of his privy council. His privy council be chosen also at the Prince's pleasure out of the nobility or barony, and of the knights, and esquires, such and so many as he shall think good, who doth consult daily, or when need is of the weighty matters of the realm, to give therein to their Prince the best advice they can. The Prince doth participate to them all, or so many of them as he shall think good, such legations and messages as come from foreign Princes, such letters or occurrents [news] as be sent to himself or to his secretaries, and keepeth so many ambassades [messages] and letters sent unto him secret as he will, although these have a particular oath of a councillor touching faith and secrets administered unto them when they be first admitted into that company. So that herein the kingdom of England is far more absolute than either the dukedom of Venice is, or the kingdom of the Lacedemonians [Spartans] was. In war time, and in the field the Prince hath also absolute power, so that his word is a law, he may put to death, or to other bodily punishment, whom he shall think so to deserve, without process of law or form of judgment. This hath been sometime used within the realm before any open war in sudden insurrections and rebellions, but that not allowed of wise and grave men, who in that their judgment had consideration of the consequence and example, as much as of the present necessity, especially, when by any means the punishment might have been done by order of law. This absolute power is called martial law. . . .

To be short the Prince is the life, the head, and the authority of all things that be done in the realm of England. And to no Prince is done more honor and reverence than to the King and Queen of England, no man speaketh to the Prince nor serveth at the table but in adoration and kneeling; all persons of the realm be bareheaded before him: insomuch that in the chamber of presence where the cloth of estate is set, no man dare walk, yea though the Prince be not there, no man dare tarry there but bareheaded. This is understood of the subjects of the realm.

→ KING JAMES I

From *A Speech to the Lords and Commons of the Parliament at Whitehall* *March 21, 1610*

James's insistence on the monarch's supremacy to Parliament draws on the familiar imagery of divinity (kings as gods), paternity (kings as fathers), and biology (kings as heads of bodies). The timing of this speech is significant: some six years after James's assumption of the English throne, Parliament was becoming disillusioned with the king's authoritarian attitude and, as a result, increasingly recalcitrant.

The state of monarchy is the supremest thing upon earth. For kings are not only God's lieutenants upon earth, and sit upon God's throne, but even by God himself they are called gods. There be three principal similitudes that illustrates the state of monarchy. One taken out of the word of God, and the two other out of the grounds of policy and philosophy. In the Scriptures kings are called gods, and so their power after a certain relation compared to the divine power. Kings are also compared to fathers of families, for a king is truly *parens patriae*, the politic father of his people. And lastly, kings are compared to the head of this microcosm of the body of man.

Kings are justly called gods for that they exercise a manner or resemblance of divine power upon earth. For if you will consider the attributes to God, you shall see how they agree in the person of a king. God has power to create, or destroy, make, or unmake at his pleasure, to give life, or send death, to judge all, and to be judged nor accountable to none; to raise low things, and to make high things low at his pleasure, and to God are both soul and body due. And the like power have kings. They make and unmake their subjects; they have power of raising and casting down, of life and of death; judges over all their subjects, and in all cases, and yet accountable to none but God only. They have power to exalt low things and abase high things, and make of their subjects like men at the chess: a pawn to take a bishop or a knight, and to cry up or down any of their subjects, as they do their money. And to the king is due both the affection of the soul and the service of the body of his subjects. . . .

As for the father of a family, they had of old under the law of nature *patriam potestatem* [ancestral power], which was *potestatem vitae et necis* [power of life and death] over their children or family. I mean such fathers of families as were the lineal heirs of those families whereof kings did originally come, for kings had their first original from them who planted and spread themselves in colonies through the world. Now a father may dispose of his inheritance to his children at his pleasure: yea, even disinherit the eldest upon just occasions, and prefer the youngest, according to his liking; make them beggars or rich at his pleasure; restrain, or banish out of his presence, as he finds them give cause of offence, or restore them in favor again with the penitent sinner. So may the king deal with his subjects.

And lastly, as for the head of the natural body, the head has the power of directing all the members of the body to that use which the judgment in the head thinks most convenient. It may apply sharp cures, or cut off corrupt members, let blood in what proportion it thinks fit, and as the body may spare, but yet is all this power ordained by God *ad aedificationem, non ad destructionem* [for constructive, not destructive use]. For though God have power as well of destruction as of creation or maintenance, yet will it not agree with the wisdom of God to exercise his power in the destruction of nature and overturning the whole frame of things, since his creatures were made that his glory might thereby be the better expressed. So were he a foolish father that would disinherit or destroy his children without a cause, or leave off the careful education of them. And it were an idle head that would in place of physic so poison or phlebotomize [bleed] the body as might breed a dangerous distemper or destruction thereof.

But now in these our times we are to distinguish between the state of kings in their first original, and between the state of settled kings and monarchs that do at this time govern in civil kingdoms. For even as God, during the time of the Old Testament, spake by oracles and wrought by miracles, yet how soon it pleased him to settle a Church which was bought and redeemed by the blood of his only Son, Christ, then was there a cessation of both, he ever after governing his people and Church within the limits of his revealed will. So in the first original of kings, whereof some had their beginning by conquest, and some by election of the people, their wills at that time served for law. Yet how soon kingdoms began to be settled in civility and policy, then did kings set down their minds by laws, which are properly made by the king only, but at the rogation [formal request] of the people, the king's grant being obtained thereunto. And so the king became to be *lex loquens* [a speaking law], after a sort, binding himself by a double oath to the observation of the fundamental laws of his kingdom: tacitly, as by being a king; and so bound to protect as well the people as the laws of his kingdom, and expressly, by his oath at his coronation. So as every just king in a settled kingdom is bound to observe that paction [contract] made to his people by his laws, in framing his government agreeable thereunto, according to that paction which God made with Noah after the deluge: "Hereafter seed-time and harvest, cold and heat, summer and winter, and day and night shall not cease, so long as the earth remains." And therefore a king governing in a settled kingdom leaves to be a king, and degenerates into a tyrant, as soon as he leaves off to rule according to his laws. In which case the king's conscience may speak unto him as the poor widow said to Philip of Macedon: "Either govern according to your law, *aut ne rex sis* [or you are no king]." And though no Christian man ought to allow any rebellion of people against their prince, yet does God never leave kings unpunished when they transgress these limits. For in that same psalm where God says to kings *vos dii estis* [you are gods], he immediately thereafter concludes, "But ye shall die like men." The higher we are placed, the greater shall our fall be. *Ut casus sic dolor* [As the fall is, so is the grief]: the taller the trees be, the more in danger of the wind; and the tempest beats sorest upon the highest mountains. Therefore all kings that are not tyrants, or perjured, will be glad to bound themselves within the limits of their laws; and they that persuade them the contrary are vipers and pests, both against them and the commonwealth. For it is a great difference between a king's government in a settled state and what kings in their original power might do in *individuo vago* [as unrestrained individuals]. As for my part, I thank God I have ever given good proof that I never had intention to the contrary. And I am sure to go to my grave with that reputation and comfort, that never king was in all his time more careful to have his laws duly observed, and himself to govern thereafter, than I.

I conclude then this point touching the power of kings with this axiom of divinity: that as to dispute what God may do is blasphemy, but *quid vult deus* [what God wishes], that divines may lawfully and do ordinarily dispute and discuss, for to dispute *a posse ad esse* [from potential to actual] is both against logic and divinity, so is it sedition in subjects to dispute what a king may do in the height of his power. But just kings will ever be willing to declare what they will do, if they will not incur the curse of God. I will not be content that my power be disputed upon. But I shall ever be willing to make the reason appear of all my doings, and rule my actions according to my laws. . . .

But I would wish you to be careful to avoid three things in the matter of Grievances.

First, that you do not meddle with the main points of government. That is my craft: *tractent fabrilia fabri* [let craftsmen take care of their craft]; to meddle with that were to lesson me. I am now an old king, for six and thirty years have I governed in Scotland personally, and now have I accomplished my apprenticeship of seven years here; and seven years is a great time for a king's experience in government. Therefore there would not be too many Phormios to teach Hannibal. I must not be taught my office.

Secondly, I would not have you meddle with such ancient rights of mine, as I have received from my predecessors, possessing them *More Maiorum* [by the custom of our ancestors]: such things I would be sorry should be accounted for Grievances. All novelties are dangerous as well in a politic as in a natural body. And therefore I would be loath to be quarreled in my ancient rights and possessions. For that were to judge me unworthy of that which my predecessors had and left me.

And lastly, I pray you beware to exhibit for Grievance any thing that is established by a settled law, and whereunto (as you have already had a proof) you know I will never give a plausible answer. For it is an undutiful part in subjects to press their king, wherein they know beforehand he will refuse them. Now, if any law or statute be not convenient, let it be amended by Parliament, but in the mean time term it not a Grievance: for to be grieved with the law is to be grieved with the king, who is sworn to be the patron and maintainer thereof. But as all men are flesh, and may err in the execution of laws, so may you justly make a Grievance of any abuse of the law, distinguishing wisely between the faults of the person and the thing itself.

KING JAMES I

Secret Letter to Sir Robert Cecil   *c. 1602*

This is one of a series of private exchanges between James VI of Scotland (later James I of England) and Elizabeth's chief minister. Since the aging queen refused to name her successor, and since James's lineage gave him the most plausible claim, Cecil initiated a secret plan to insure James's succession to the English throne after the death of Elizabeth. Note the numerical code by which the various persons are denoted (Cecil is 10, Elizabeth is 24, James is 30). Another remarkable feature is the Scottish sound of James's spelling (here not modernized).

My dearest 10 [Sir Robert Cecil], I ame ashamed that I can as yett by no other meanes uitnesse my thankefulnes for youre daylie so honorable iudiciouse and painfull labouris for the furtherance of my greatest hoapes, then by baire inke and paper, and that youre trauellis of so great uorthe and inæstimable ualew shoulde be repayed uith so poore a recompence, but the best excuse is that these paperis are but uitnessis of that treasure of gratitude quhiche by youre goode desairtis is daylie noorished in my hairte.

I ame not a lytle encouraged by the letre of 24 [Queen Elizabeth] quhiche discoveris a great integritie in her affection, and plainnes in her dealing; quhom I oucht to thanke for her goode temper, ye may easilie guesse. I haue ansourid her in the best sorte I coulde, as by the coppie thairof ye will persaue, and that ye maye haue proofe that my confidence is fullie setlid upon you, I haue sent you the substance of tuo messages that Sir Antonie Shurley hath latelie sent me, uithout keeping up one iote thairof, quhose errouris appeare rather to proceide from ignorance then malice. Ye can not doe me a greatter seruice then to moue 24 [Queen Elizabeth] to continew this inuarde and privie forme of intelligence, quhairby I hoape ye shall in the ende proue a honest and happie minister.

To faithfull 8 [Mr. Edward Bruce] his lettir I remitte all particulairs, and speciallie my opinion hou ye shall behaue youre self in that maitter, quhiche, god knowis, is more greeuouse unto me then any temptation that satan by goddis permission coulde haue deuysed to haue aflicted me uith. But heir I ende, with the assurance of the continuance of my constant loue to my most faithfull 3 [Lord Henry Howard], assuring him that, as I ame infinitelie sorie for that defluxion fallin upon his eye, so uoulde I thinke ane hospitall a reuairde that uolde keepe no proportion, ather for a kings honoure to giue, or by him for so uell meriting seruices to be receaued. And thus, my dearest 10 [Sir Robert Cecil], I bidde both you and 3 [Lord Henry Howard] most hairtelie fair uell.

Your moste louing and assurid freind

30 [KING JAMES].

→ KING JAMES I

Letter to George Villiers, Duke of Buckingham   *c. December 1623*

Written less than two years before James's death, the letter expresses the profundity of the king's affection for his handsome young courtier. Buckingham was the most important in a long line of royal favorites.

I cannot content myself without sending you this present [letter], praying God that I may have a joyful and comfortable meeting with you and that we may make at this Christmas a new marriage ever to be kept hereafter; for, God so love me, as I desire only to live in this world for your sake, and that I had rather live banished in any part of the earth with you than live a sorrowful widow's life without you. And so God bless you, my sweet child and wife, and grant that you may ever be a comfort to your dear dad and husband.

→ SIR JOHN HARINGTON

Letter Describing the Revels at King James's Court   *1606*

Godson of Queen Elizabeth and a witty observer of court manners, Sir John Harington (1561–1612) describes the revels at James's court on the occasion of the visit of Queen Anne's brother, King Christian of Denmark. The excesses of the court noticed here were a subject of fierce satire in the period. Although Shakespeare usually avoids such concrete satire, the performance of his plays at court on similar evenings must have made him aware of this type of behavior.

One day, a great feast was held, and after dinner the representation of Solomon, his temple, and the coming of the Queen of Sheba was made, or (as I may better say) was meant to have been made, before their Majesties, by device of the Earl of Salisbury and others. — But, alas! as all earthly things do fail to poor mortals in enjoyment, so did prove our presentment hereof. The lady who did play the queen's part did carry most precious gifts to both their Majesties; but forgetting the steps arising to the canopy, overset her caskets into his Danish Majesty's lap and fell at his feet, though I rather think it was in his face. Much was the hurry and confusion; cloths and napkins were at hand, to make all clean. His Majesty then got up and would dance with the Queen of Sheba; but he fell down and humbled himself before her, and was carried to an inner chamber and laid on a bed of state; which was not a little defiled with the presents of the queen which had been bestowed on his garments; such as wine, cream, jelly, beverage, cakes, spices, and other good matters. The entertainment and show went forward, and most of the presenters went backward, or fell down, wine did so occupy their upper chambers. Now did appear, in rich dress, Hope, Faith, and Charity. Hope did assay to speak, but wine rendered her endeavors so feeble that she withdrew, and hope the king would excuse her brevity: Faith was then all alone, for I am certain she was not joined with good works, and left the court in a staggering condition. Charity came to the king's feet and seemed to cover the multitude of sins her sisters had committed; in some sort she made obeisance and brought gifts, but said she would return home again, as there was no gift which heaven had not already given his Majesty. She then returned to Hope and Faith, who were both sick and spewing in the lower hall. Next came Victory, in bright armor, and presented a rich sword to the king, who did not accept it, but put it by with his hand; and, by strange medley of versification, did endeavor to make suit to the king. But Victory did not triumph long, for after much lamentable utterance, she was led away like a silly captive and laid to sleep in the outer steps of the antechamber. Now did Peace make entry, and strive to get foremost to the king; but I grieve to tell how great wrath she did discover unto those of her attendants; and much contrary to her semblance, most rudely made war with her olive branch, and laid on the pates of those who did oppose her coming.

I have much marveled at these strange pageantries, and they do bring to my remembrance what passed of this sort in our queen's days; of which I was sometime an humble presenter and assistant, but I never did see such lack of good order, discretion, and sobriety, as I have now done. I have passed much time in seeing the royal sports of hunting and hawking, where the manners were such as made me devise the beasts were pursuing the sober creation, and not man in quest of exercise or food. I will now, in good sooth, declare to you, who will not blab, that the gunpowder fright [the Gunpowder Plot of 1605, a Catholic attempt to assassinate King James] is got out of all our heads, and we are going on, hereabouts, as if the devil was contriving every man should blow up himself by wild riot, excess, and devastation of time and temperance. The great ladies do go well-masked, and indeed it be the only show of their modesty, to conceal their countenance; but, alack, they meet with such countenance to uphold their strange doings that I marvel not at aught that happens. The lord of the mansion is overwhelmed in preparations at Theobalds, and doth marvelously please both kings, with good meat, good drink, and good speeches. I do often say (but not aloud) that the Danes have again conquered the Britons, for I see no man, or woman either, that can command himself or herself. I wish I was at home: — *O rus, quando te aspiciam?* [O fields, when will I see you?"] — And I will; before the Prince Vaudemont cometh.

I hear the uniting the kingdoms is now at hand; when the Parliament is held more will be done in this matter. Bacon is to manage all the affair, as who can better do these state jobs? My cousin, Lord Harington of Exton, doth much fatigue himself with the royal charge of the princess Elizabeth; and midst all the foolery of these times, hath much labor to preserve his own wisdom and sobriety. If you would wish to see how folly doth grow, come up quickly; otherwise, stay where you are, and meditate on the future mischiefs of those our posterity, who shall learn the good lessons and examples held forth in these days. I hope to see you at the Bath and see the gambols you can perform in the hot waters very speedily, and shall rest your assured friend in all quiet enjoyments and hearty good affections.

→ KING JAMES I

From *Basilikon Doron* 1594

Almost ten years before assuming the throne of England, James VI of Scotland wrote *Basilikon Doron,* an analysis of the proper practice of monarchy addressed to his infant son, Prince Henry. James also wrote treatises on witchcraft and on tobacco.

And therefore to return to my purpose anent the government of your subjects, by making and putting good laws to execution, I remit the making of them to your own discretion, as you shall find the necessity of new-rising corruptions to require them. For *ex malis moribus bonae leges natae sunt* [from evil customs are born good laws]; besides, that in this country, we have already more good laws than are well executed, and am only to insist in your form of government anent their execution. Only remember, that as parliaments have been ordained for making of laws, so you abuse not their institution, in holding them for any men's particulars. For as a parliament is the honorablest and highest judgment in the land (as being the king's head court) if it be well used, which is by making of good laws in it, so is it the injustest Judgment-seat that may be, being abused to men's particulars: irrevocable decreits [decrees] against particular parties being given therein under color of general laws, and ofttimes the estates [parliamentary body] not knowing themselves whom thereby they hurt. And therefore hold no parliaments, but for necessity of new laws, which would be but seldom: for few laws and well put in execution are best in a well-ruled commonweal. As for the matter of fore-faltures [forcing nobles to forfeit land or title], which also are done in parliament, it is not good tigging [meddling] with these things. But my advice is, you fore-fault none but for such odious crimes as may make them unworthy ever to be restored again; and for smaller offenses, you have other penalties sharp enough to be used against them.

And as for the execution of good laws, whereat I left, remember that among the differences that I put betwixt the forms of the government of a good king and an usurping tyrant, I show how a tyrant would enter like a saint while he found himself fast underfoot, and then would suffer his unruly affections to burst forth. Therefore be you contrary, at your first entry to your kingdom, to that *Quinquennium Neronis* [the first five years (benevolent ones) of Nero's reign], with his tender-hearted wish, *Vellem nescirem literas* ["I wish I had not learned to write," Nero's response to signing a death warrant], in giving the law full execution against all breakers thereof but exception. For since you come not to your reign *precariò* [by anyone's permission], nor by conquest, but by right and due descent, fear no uproars for doing of justice, since you may assure yourself, the most part of your people will ever naturally favor justice, providing always that you do it only for love to justice, and not for satisfying any particular passions of yours, under color thereof. Otherwise, how justly that ever the offender deserve it, you are guilty of murder before God. For you must consider that God ever looketh to your inward intention in all your actions.

And when you have by the severity of justice once settled your countries and made them know that you can strike, then may you thereafter all the days of your life mix justice with mercy, punishing or sparing, as you shall find the crime to have been willfully or rashly committed, and according to the by-past behavior of the committer. For if otherwise you kyth [make known] your clemency at the first, the offenses would soon come to such heaps, and the contempt of you grow so great, that when you would fall to punish, the number of them to be punished would exceed the innocent, and you would be troubled to resolve whom-at to begin: and against your nature would be compelled then to wrack [injure] many, whom the chastisement of few in the beginning might have preserved. But in this, my over-dear bought [costly] experience may serve you for a sufficient lesson. For I confess, where I thought (by being gracious at the beginning) to win all men's hearts to a loving and willing obedience, I by the contrary found the disorder of the country and the loss of my thanks to be all my reward.

But as this severe justice of yours upon all offenses would be but for a time (as I have already said), so is there some horrible crimes that you are bound in conscience never to forgive: such as witch-craft, willful murder, incest (especially within the degrees of consanguinity), sodomy, poisoning, and false coin. As for offenses against your own person and authority, since the fault concerneth yourself, I remit to your own choice to punish or pardon therein, as your heart serveth you, and according to the circumstances of the turn, and the quality of the committer.

Here would I also eke [add] another crime to be unpardonable, if I should not be thought partial: but the fatherly love I bear you will make me break the bounds of shame in opening it unto you. It is, then, the false and unreverent writing or speaking of malicious men against your parents and predecessors: you know the command in God's law, "Honor your Father and Mother." And consequently, since you are the lawful magistrate, suffer not both your princes and your parents to be dishonored by any; especially sith the example also toucheth yourself, in leaving thereby to your successors, the measure of that which they shall mete out again to you in your like behalf. I grant we have all our faults, which, privately betwixt you and God, should serve you for examples to meditate upon, and mend in your person; but should not be a matter of discourse to others whatsoever. And sith you are come of as honorable predecessors as any prince living, repress the insolence of such, as under pretense to tax a vice in the person, seek craftily to stain the race, and to steal the affection of the people from their posterity. For how can they love you, that hated them whom-of you are come? Wherefore destroy men innocent young sucking wolves and foxes, but for the hatred they bear to their race? And why will a colt of a courser of Naples give a greater price in a market than an ass-colt, but for love of the race? It is therefore a thing monstrous to see a man love the child and hate the parents: as on the other part, the infaming and making odious of the parents is the readiest way to bring the son in contempt. And for conclusion of this point, I may also allege my own experience: for besides the judgments of God, that with my eyes I have seen fall upon all them that were chief traitors to my parents, I may justly affirm I never found yet a constant biding by me in all my straits by any that were of perfect age in my parents' days, but only by such as constantly bode by them. I mean specially by them that served the queen my mother: for so that I discharge my conscience to you, my son, in revealing to you the truth, I care not what any traitor or treason-allower think of it.

And although the crime of oppression be not in this rank of unpardonable crimes, yet the overcommon use of it in this nation, as if it were a virtue, especially by the greatest rank of subjects in the land, requireth the king to be a sharp censurer thereof. Be diligent therefore to try and awful to beat down the horns of proud oppressors. Embrace the quarrel of the poor and distressed, as your own particular, thinking it your greatest honor to repress the oppressors. Care for the pleasure of none, neither spare you any pains in your own person, to see their wrongs redressed: and remember of the honorable style given to my grandfather of worthy memory, in being called *the poor man's King*. And as the most part of a king's office standeth in deciding that question of *meum* and *tuum* [mine and thine], among his subjects; so remember when you sit in judgment that the throne you sit on is God's, as Moses saith, and sway neither to the right hand nor to the left, either loving the rich, or pitying the poor. Justice should be blind and friendless: it is not there you should reward your friends or seek to cross your enemies.

→ SIMON FORMAN

From His *Diary*   *January 1597*

On a Dream about an Encounter with Queen Elizabeth

Simon Forman (1552–1611), astrologer and pseudophysician, here privately describes a dream about Queen Elizabeth. The language and details of the entry suggest the underside of the "romance" between queen and subjects that Elizabeth sought to maintain.

Dreamt that I was with the Queen, and that she was a little elderly woman in a coarse white petticoat all unready. She and I walked up and down through lanes and closes, talking and reasoning. At last we came over a great close where were many people, and there were two men at hard words. One of them was a weaver, a tall man with a reddish beard, distract of his wits. She talked to him and he spoke very merrily unto her, and at last did take her and kiss her. So I took her by the arm still, and then we went through a dirty lane. She had a long white smock very clean and fair, and it trailed in the dirt and her coat behind. I took her coat and did carry it up a good way, and then it hung too low before. I told her she should do me a favor to let me wait on her, and she said I should. Then said I, "I mean to wait *upon* you and not under you, that I might make this belly a little bigger to carry up this smock and coat out of the dirt." And so we talked merrily; then she began to lean upon me, when we were past the dirt and to be very familiar with me, and methought she began to love me. When we were alone, out of sight, methought she would have kissed me.

→ JOHN FIELD AND THOMAS WILCOX(?)

From *An Admonition to the Parliament* 1572

Attributed to John Field and Thomas Wilcox, this document is an early attack on the corruption of the Anglican Church. It captures the tenor of reformist ideology and serves as a guide to the direction of Puritan thought in the last decades of the sixteenth century.

May it therefore please your wisdoms to understand, we in England are so far off from having a church rightly reformed according to the prescript of God's word, that as yet we are not come to the outward face of the same. For to speak of that wherein all consent, and whereupon all writers accord: the outward marks whereby a true Christian church is known, are preaching of the word purely, ministering of the sacraments sincerely, and ecclesiastical discipline which consisteth in admonition and correction of faults severely. Touching the first, namely the ministry of the word, although it must be confessed that the substance of doctrine by many delivered is sound and good, yet herein it faileth, that neither the ministers thereof are according to God's word proved, elected, called, or ordained: nor the function in such sort so narrowly looked unto, as of right it ought and is of necessity required. For whereas in the old church a trial was had both of their ability to instruct and of their godly conversation also, now by the letters commendatory of some one man, noble or other, tag and rag, learned and unlearned, of the basest sort of the people (to the slander of the Gospel in the mouths of the adversaries) are freely received. In those days no idolatrous sacrificers or heathenish priests were appointed to be preachers of the Gospel: but we allow and like well of popish mass-mongers, men for all seasons, King Henry's priests, King Edward's priests, Queen Mary's priests, who of a truth (if God's word were precisely followed) should from the same be utterly removed. Then they taught others; now they must be instructed themselves, and therefore like young children they must learn catechisms. Then election was made by the common consent of the whole church: now every one picketh out for himself some notable good benefice, he obtaineth the next advowson [right of office] by money or by favor, and so thinketh himself to be sufficiently chosen. Then the congregation had authority to call ministers; instead thereof now they run, they ride, and by unlawful suit and buying, prevent other suitors also. Then no minister [was] placed in any congregation but by the consent of the people; now that authority is given into the hands of the bishop alone, who by his sole authority thrusteth upon them such as they many times as well for unhonest life, as also for lack of learning, may and do justly dislike. Then none [was] admitted to the ministry, but a place was void before hand to which he should be called; but now bishops (to whom the right of ordering ministers doth at no hand appertain) do make 60, 80, or a 100 at a clap, and send them abroad into the country like masterless men. Then after just trial and vocation they were admitted to their function, by laying on of the hands of the company of the eldership only; now there is (neither of these being looked unto) required an alb, a surplice, a vestment, a pastoral staff, beside that ridiculous, and (as they use it to their new creatures) blasphemous saying, "Receive the holy ghost." Then every pastor had his flock, and every flock his shepherd, or else shepherds; now they do not only run fisking [scampering] from place to place (a miserable disorder in God's church) but covetously join living to living, making shipwreck of their own consciences, and being but one shepherd (nay, would to God they were shepherds and not wolves) have many flocks. Then the ministers were preachers; now bare readers. And if any be so well disposed to preach in their own charges, they may not without my Lord's license. In those days known by voice, learning, and doctrine; now they must be discerned from other by popish and Antichristian apparel, as cap, gown, tippet, etc. Then, as God gave utterance they preached the word only; now they read homilies, articles, injunctions, etc. Then it was painful; now gainful. Then poor and ignominious; now rich and glorious. And therefore titles, livings, and offices by Antichrist devised are given to them, as Metropolitan, Archbishop, Lord's Grace, Lord Bishop, Suffragan, Dean, Archdeacon, Prelate of the Garter, Earl, County Palatine, Honor, High Commissioners, Justices of Peace and Quorum, etc. All which, together with their offices, as they are strange and unheard of in Christ's church, nay plainly in God's word forbidden, so are they utterly with speed out of the same to be removed. Then ministers were not tied to any form of prayers invented by man, but as the spirit moved them, so they poured forth hearty supplications to the Lord. Now they are bound of necessity to a prescript order of service and book of common prayer in which a great number of things contrary to God's word are contained, as baptism by women, private Communions, Jewish purifyings, observing of holy days, etc., patched (if not all together, yet the greatest piece) out of the Pope's portuis [manual]. Then feeding the flock diligently; now teaching quarterly. Then preaching in season and out of season; now once in a month is thought sufficient, if twice, it is judged a work of supererogation. Then nothing taught but God's word; now princes' pleasures, men's devices, popish ceremonies, and Antichristian rites in public pulpits defended. Then they sought them; now they seek theirs.

These, and a great many other abuses are in the ministry remaining, which unless they be removed and the truth brought in, not only God's justice shall be poured forth, but also God's church in this realm shall never be built. For if they which seem to be workmen are no workmen in deed, but in name, or else work not so diligently and in such order as the workmaster commandeth, it is not only unlikely that the building shall go forward, but altogether impossible that ever it shall be perfected. The way therefore to avoid these inconveniences and to reform these deformities is this: your wisdoms have to remove advowsons, patronages, impropriations, and bishops' authority, claiming to themselves thereby right to ordain ministers, and to bring in that old and true election, which was accustomed to be made by the congregation. You must displace those ignorant and unable ministers already placed, and in their rooms appoint such as both can and will by God's assistance feed the flock. You must pluck down and utterly overthrow without hope of restitution the Court of Faculties, from whence not only licenses to enjoy many benefices are obtained, as pluralities, trialities, totquots [licenses for multiple benefices], etc., but all things for the most part, as in the court of Rome are set on sale, licenses to marry, to eat flesh in times prohibited, to lie from benefices and charges, and a great number beside of such like abominations. Appoint to every congregation a learned and diligent preacher. Remove homilies, articles, injunctions, a prescript order of service made out of the mass book. Take away the lordship, the loitering, the pomp, the idleness, and livings of bishops, but yet employ them to such ends as they were in the old church appointed for. Let a lawful and a godly seignorie look that they preach, not quarterly or monthly, but continually: not for filthy lucre's sake, but of a ready mind. So God shall be glorified, your consciences discharged, and the flock of Christ (purchased with his own blood) edified.

Now to the second point, which concerneth ministration of sacraments. In the old time, the word was preached before they were ministered; now it is supposed to be sufficient if it be read. Then, they were ministered in public assemblies; now in private houses. Then by ministers only; now by midwives, and deacons, equally. But because in treating of both the sacraments together we should deal confusedly: we will therefore speak of them severally. And first for the Lord's Supper, or Holy Communion.

They had no introit, for Celestinus a pope brought it in about the year 430. But we have borrowed a piece of one out of the mass book. They read no fragments of the Epistle and Gospel; we use both. The Nicene Creed was not read in their Communion; we have it in ours. There was then accustomed to be an examination of the communicants, which now is neglected. Then they ministered the Sacrament with common and usual bread; now with wafer cakes, brought in by Pope Alexander, being in form, fashion, and substance like their god of the altar. They received it sitting; we kneeling, according to Honorius' decree. Then it was delivered generally, and indefinitely, "Take ye and eat ye"; we particularly, and singularly, "Take thou, and eat thou." They used no other words but such as Christ left; we borrow from papists, "The body of our Lord Jesus Christ which was given for thee, etc." They had no "Gloria in excelsis" in the ministry of the Sacrament then, for it was put to afterward; we have now. They took it with conscience; we with custom. They shut men by reason of their sins, from the Lord's Supper; we thrust them in their sin to the Lord's Supper. They ministered the Sacrament plainly; we pompously with singing, piping, surplice and cope wearing. They simply as they received it from the Lord; we, sinfully, mixed with man's inventions and devices. And as for Baptism, it was enough with them, if they had water, and the party to be baptised faith, and the minister to preach the word and minister the sacraments.

Now we must have surplices devised by Pope Adrian, interrogatories ministered to the infant, godfathers, and godmothers, . . . holy fonts invented by Pope Pius, crossing and such like pieces of popery, which the church of God in the apostles' times never knew (and therefore not to be used), nay (which we are sure of) were and are man's devices, brought in long after the purity of the primitive church. To redress these, your wisdoms have to remove (as before) ignorant ministers, take away private communions and baptisms, to enjoin deacons and midwives not to meddle in ministers' matters; if they do, to see them sharply punished. To join assistance of elders and other officers, that seeing men will not examine themselves, they may be examined, and brought to render a reason of their hope. That the statute against wafer cakes may more prevail than an injunction. That people be appointed to receive the Sacrament rather sitting, for avoiding of superstition, than kneeling, having in it the outward show of evil, from which we must abstain. . . . That both the Sacrament of the Lord's Supper and Baptism also may be ministered according to the ancient purity and simplicity. . . . And finally, that nothing be done in this or any other thing but that which you have the express warrant of God's word for.

→ From *An Homily against Disobedience and Willful Rebellion* 1570

One of the most influential of the homilies read from the pulpit during Anglican Church services, the *Homily against Disobedience* was a direct response to the Northern Rebellion of 1569. It represents the Crown's attempts to use the church as a means of social control by identifying political with religious ideology: political rebellion was not only illegal but also sinful, a cause for spiritual damnation.

Obedience is the principal virtue of all virtues, and indeed the very root of all virtues, and the cause of all felicity. But as all felicity and blessedness should have continued with the continuance of obedience, so with the breach of obedience and breaking in of rebellion, all vices and miseries did withal break in and overwhelm the world. The first author of which rebellion, the root of all vices and mother of all mischiefs, was Lucifer, first God's most excellent creature and most bounden subject, who, by rebelling against the majesty of God, of the brightest and most glorious angel is become the blackest and most foulest fiend and devil, and from the height of heaven is fallen into the pit and bottom of hell.

Here you may see the first author and founder of rebellion, and the reward thereof. Here you may see the grand captain and father of all rebels, who, persuading the following of his rebellion against God their creator and lord, unto our first parents, Adam and Eve, brought them in high displeasure with God, wrought their exile and banishment out of Paradise, a place of all pleasure and goodness, into this wretched earth and vale of all misery, procured unto them sorrows of their minds, mischiefs, sickness, diseases, death of their bodies, and, which is far more horrible than all worldly and bodily mischiefs, he had wrought thereby their eternal and everlasting death and damnation, had not God by the obedience of his son, Jesus Christ, repaired that which man by disobedience and rebellion had destroyed, and so of his mercy had pardoned and forgiven him. Of which all and singular the premises the Holy Scriptures do bear record in sundry places. Thus you do see that neither heaven nor paradise could suffer any rebellion in them, neither be places for any rebels to remain in. Thus became rebellion, as you see, both the first and greatest, and the very root of all other sins, and the first and principal cause both of all worldly and bodily miseries — sorrows, diseases, sicknesses, and deaths — and, which is infinitely worse than all these, as is said, the very cause of death and damnation eternal also. After this breach of obedience to God and rebellion against his majesty, all mischiefs and miseries breaking in therewith and overflowing the world, lest all things should come unto confusion and utter ruin, God forthwith, by laws given unto mankind, repaired again the rule and order of obedience thus by rebellion overthrown, and, besides the obedience due unto his Majesty, he not only ordained that in families and households the wife should be obedient unto her husband, the children unto their parents, the servants unto their masters, but also, when mankind increased and spread itself more largely over the world, he by his Holy Word did constitute and ordain in cities and countries several and special governors and rulers, unto whom the residue of his people should be obedient.

As in reading of the Holy Scriptures we shall find in very many and almost infinite places, as well of the Old Testament as of the New, that kings and princes, as well the evil as the good, do reign by God's ordinance, and that subjects are bound to obey them; that God doth give princes wisdom, great power, and authority; that God defendeth them against their enemies, and destroyeth their enemies horribly; that the anger and displeasure of the prince is as the roaring of a lion, and the very messenger of death; and that the subject that provoketh him to displeasure sinneth against his own soul; with many other things concerning both the authority of princes and the duty of subjects.

But here let us rehearse two special places out of the New Testament, which may stand in stead of all other. The first out of Saint Paul's Epistle to the Romans, and the thirteenth chapter, where he writeth thus unto all subjects: "Let every soul be subject unto the higher powers, for there is no power but of God, and the powers that be are ordained of God. Whosoever therefore resisteth the power, resisteth the ordinance of God. And they that resist, shall receive to themselves damnation. For princes are not to be feared for good works, but for evil. Wilt thou then be without fear of the power? Do well, so shalt thou have praise of the same, for he is the minister of God for thy wealth; but if thou do evil, fear. For he beareth not the sword for naught, for he is the minister of God to take vengeance upon him that doth evil. Wherefore you must be subject, not because of wrath only, but also for conscience sake. For, for this cause you pay also tribute, for they are God's ministers, serving for the same purpose. Give to every man therefore his duty; tribute, to whom tribute belongeth; custom, to whom custom is due; fear, to whom fear belongeth; honor, to whom you owe honor." Thus far are Saint Paul's words. The second place is in St. Peter's first Epistle, and the second chapter, whose words are these: "Submit yourselves unto all manner [i.e., kinds of] ordinance of man for the Lord's sake, whether it be unto the king, as unto the chief head, either unto rulers, as unto them that are sent of him for the punishment of evildoers, but for the cherishing of them that do well. For so is the will of God, that with well doing you may stop the mouths of ignorant and foolish men: as free, and not as having the liberty for a cloak of maliciousness, but even as the servants of God. Honor all men, love brotherly fellowship, fear God, honor the king. Servants, obey your masters with fear, not only if they be good and courteous, but also though they be froward." Thus far out of Saint Peter.

By these two places of the Holy Scriptures it is most evident that kings, queens, and other princes (for he speaketh of authority and power, be it in men or women) are ordained of God, are to be obeyed and honored of their subjects; that such subjects as are disobedient or rebellious against their princes disobey God and procure their own damnation, that the government of princes is a great blessing of God given for the commonwealth, specially of the good and godly; for the comfort and cherishing of whom God giveth and setteth up princes; and on the contrary part, to the fear and for the punishment of the evil and wicked. Finally that if servants ought to obey their masters, not only being gentle, but such as be froward, as well and much more ought subjects to be obedient, not only to their good and courteous but also to their sharp and rigorous princes. It cometh therefore neither of chance and fortune (as they term it) nor of the ambition of mortal men and women climbing up of their own accord to dominion, that there be kings, queens, princes, and other governors over men being their subjects; but all kings, queens, and other governors are specially appointed by the ordinance of God. And as God himself, being of an infinite majesty, power, and wisdom, ruleth and governeth all things in heaven and in earth, as the universal monarch and only king and emperor over all, as being only able to take and bear the charge of all: so hath he constituted, ordained, and set earthly princes over particular kingdoms and dominions in earth, both for the avoiding of all confusion, which else would be in the world if it should be without such governors, and for the great quiet and benefit of earthly men their subjects, and also that the princes themselves in authority, power, wisdom, providence, and righteousness in government of people and countries committed to their charge, should resemble his heavenly governance, as the majesty of heavenly things may by the baseness of earthly things be shadowed and resembled. And for that similitude that is between the heavenly monarchy and earthly kingdoms well governed, our savior Christ in sundry parables saith that the kingdom of heaven is resembled unto a man a king, and as the name of the king is very often attributed and given unto God in the Holy Scriptures, so doth God himself in the same Scriptures sometime vouchsafe to communicate his name with earthly princes, terming them gods: doubtless for that similitude of government which they have or should have not unlike unto God their king. Unto the which similitude of heavenly government, the nearer and nearer that an earthly prince doth come in his regiment, the greater blessing of God's mercy is he unto that country and people over whom he reigneth: and the further and further that an earthly prince doth swerve from the example of the heavenly government, the greater plague he is of God's wrath, and punishment by God's justice, unto that country and people over whom God for their sins hath placed such a prince and governor. For it is indeed evident both by the Scriptures and by daily experience, that the maintenance of all virtue and godliness, and consequently of the wealth and prosperity of a kingdom and people, doth stand and rest more in a wise and good prince on the one part, than in great multitudes of other men being subjects: and on the contrary part, the overthrow of all virtue and godliness, and consequently the decay and utter ruin of a realm and people doth grow and come more by an undiscreet and evil governor, than by many thousands of other men being subjects. Thus say the Holy Scriptures: "Well is thee, O thou land (saith the preacher) whose king is come of nobles, and whose princes eat in due season, for necessity, and not for lust." Again: "A wise and righteous king maketh his realm and people wealthy; and a good, merciful, and gracious prince is as a shadow in heat, as a defense in storms, as dew, as sweet showers, as fresh water springs in great droughts." Again, the Scriptures of undiscreet and evil princes speak thus: "Woe be to thee, O thou land whose king is but a child, and whose princes are early at their banquets." Again: "When the wicked do reign, then men go to ruin." And again: "A foolish prince destroyeth the people, and a covetous king undoeth his subjects." Thus speak the Scriptures; thus experience testifieth of good and evil princes.

What shall subjects do then? Shall they obey valiant, stout, wise, and good princes, and condemn, disobey, and rebel against children being their princes, or against undiscreet and evil governors? God forbid. For first, what a perilous thing were it to commit unto the subjects the judgment [as to] which prince is wise and godly, and his government good, and which is otherwise. As though the foot must judge of the head, an enterprise very heinous, and must needs breed rebellion. For who else be they that are most inclined to rebellion, but such haughty spirits? From whom springeth such foul ruin of realms? Is not rebellion the greatest of all mischiefs? And who are most ready to the greatest mischiefs, but the worst men? Rebels therefore the worst of all subjects are most ready to rebellion, as being the worst of all vices, and furthest from the duty of a good subject. As on the contrary part, the best subjects are most firm and constant in obedience, as in the special and peculiar virtue of good subjects. What an unworthy matter were it then to make the naughtiest subjects, and most inclined to rebellion and all evil, judges over their princes, over their government, and over their councillors, to determine which of them be good or tolerable, and which be evil and so intolerable that they must needs be removed by rebels, being ever ready as the naughtiest subjects, soonest to rebel against the best princes, specially if they be young in age, women in sex, or gentle and courteous in government, as trusting by their wicked boldness easily to overthrow their weakness and gentleness, or at the least so to fear the minds of such princes, that they may have impunity of their mischievous doings. But whereas indeed a rebel is worse than the worst prince, and rebellion worse than the worst government of the worst prince that hitherto hath been: both are rebels unmeet ministers, and rebellion an unfit and unwholesome medicine to reform any small lacks in a prince, or to cure any little griefs in government, such lewd remedies being far worse than any other maladies and disorders that can be in the body of a commonwealth. But whatsoever the prince be, or his government, it is evident that for the most part those princes whom some subjects do think to be very godly and under whose government they rejoice to live, some other subjects do take the same to be evil and ungodly and do wish for a change. If therefore all subjects that mislike of their prince should rebel, no realm should ever be without rebellion. It were more meet that rebels should hear the advice of wise men, and give place unto their judgment, and follow the example of obedient subjects, as reason is that they whose understanding is blinded with so evil an affection, should give place to them that be of sound judgment, and that the worse should give place to the better: and so might realms continue in long obedience, peace, and quietness. But what if the prince be undiscreet, and evil indeed, and it also evident to all men's eyes that he so is? I ask again, what if it be long of [a result of] the wickedness of the subjects, that the prince is undiscreet or evil? Shall the subjects both by their wickedness provoke God for their deserved punishment to give them an undiscreet or evil prince, and also rebel against him, and withal against God, who for the punishment of their sins did give them such a prince? Will you hear the Scriptures concerning this point? "God," say the Holy Scriptures, "maketh a wicked man to reign for the sins of the people." Again: "God giveth a prince in his anger (meaning an evil one) and taketh away a prince in his displeasure," meaning specially when he taketh away a good prince for the sins of the people, as in our memory he took away our good Josias, King Edward, in his young and good years for our wickedness. And contrarily the Scriptures do teach that God giveth wisdom unto princes, and maketh a wise and good king to reign over that people whom he loveth, and who loveth him.

Again: "If the people obey God, both they and their king shall prosper and be safe, else both shall perish," saith God by the mouth of Samuel.

Here you see, that God placeth as well evil princes as good, and for what cause he doth both. If we therefore will have a good prince, either to be given us, or to continue, now we have such a one, let us by our obedience to God and to our prince, move God thereunto. If we will have an evil prince (when God shall send such a one) taken away, and a good in his place, let us take away our wickedness which provoketh God to place such a one over us, and God will either displace him, or of an evil prince, make him a good prince. So that we first will change our evil into good. For will you hear the Scriptures? "The heart of the prince is in God's hand; which way soever it shall please him, he turneth it." Thus say the Scriptures, wherefore let us turn from our sins unto the Lord with all our hearts, and he will turn the heart of the prince unto our quiet and wealth. Else for subjects to deserve through their sins to have an evil prince, and then to rebel against him, were double and treble evil, by provoking God more to plague them. Nay let us either deserve to have a good prince, or let us patiently suffer and obey such as we deserve. And whether the prince be good or evil, let us according to the counsel of the Holy Scriptures pray for the prince, for his continuance and increase in goodness if he be good, and for his amendment if he be evil.

→ SIR THOMAS ELYOT

From *The Book Named the Governor*   *1531; rpt. 1553*

Sir Thomas Elyot (1490–1546) was one of the most learned and influential of the sixteenth-century English humanists, the intellectual heir of Sir Thomas More and Desiderius Erasmus. *The Book Named the Governor*, originally dedicated to Henry VIII, offers a clear statement of Tudor orthodoxy concerning the parallel between hierarchy in the social and the natural realms.

Moreover, take away order from all things, what should then remain? Certes, nothing finally, except some man would imagine eftsoons [soon afterward] Chaos, which of some is expounded a confused mixture.

Also where there is any lack of order, needs must be perpetual conflict. And in things subject to nature, nothing of himself only may be nourished, but when he hath destroyed that wherewith he doth participate by the order of his creation, he himself of necessity must then perish, whereof ensueth universal dissolution.

But now to prove by example of those things that be within the compass of man's knowledge, of what estimation order is, not only among men, but also with God, albeit his wisdom, bounty, and magnificence, can be with no tongue or pen sufficiently expressed. Hath not he set degrees and estates in all his glorious works?

First in his heavenly ministers whom, as the church affirmeth, he hath constituted to be in divers degrees, called hierarchies. Also Christ saith, by his evangelist, that in the house of his father (which is God) be many mansions.

But to treat of that which by natural understanding may be comprehended. Behold the four elements, whereof the body of man is compact, how they be set in their places, called spheres, higher or lower, according to the sovereignty of their natures: that is to say, the fire as the most pure element, having in it nothing that is corruptible, in his place is highest and above other elements. The air, which next to the fire, is most pure in substance, is in the second sphere or place. The water, which is somewhat consolidate and approacheth to corruption, is next unto the earth. The earth, which is of substance gross and ponderous, is set of all elements most lowest.

Behold also the order that God hath put generally in all his creatures, beginning at the most inferior or base, and ascending upward. He made not only herbs to garnish the earth, but also trees of a more eminent nature than herbs. And yet in the one and the other, be degrees of qualities, some pleasant to behold, some delicate or good in taste, other wholesome and medicinable, some commodious and necessary. Semblably in birds, beasts, and fishes, some be good for the sustenance of man; some bear things profitable to sundry uses; other be apt to occupation and labor; in divers is strength and fierceness only; in many is both strength and commodity; some other serve for pleasure; none of them hath all these qualities; few have the more part or many, specially beauty, strength, and profit. But where any is found that hath many of the said properties, he is more set by [valued] than all the other, and by that estimation the order of his place and degree evidently appeareth. So that every kind of trees, herbs, birds, beasts, and fishes, beside their diversity of forms, have (as who saith) a peculiar disposition, appropried [given, appropriated] unto them by God their creator. So that in every thing is order, and without order may be nothing stable or permanent. And it may not be called order, except it do contain in it degrees high and base, according to the merit or estimation of the thing that is ordered.

→ PHILIP STUBBES

From *The Anatomy of Abuses*   *1583*

One of the most vocal and intemperate of Puritan social and religious critics, Philip Stubbes (c. 1555–c. 1610) here attacks the immorality in and around the public playhouses. He typically associates actors with various forms of sexual and social crime and develops the argument that plays exemplify and encourage immoral behavior.

Do they not maintain bawdry, insinuate foolery, and renew and remembrance of heathen idolatry? Do they not induce whoredom and uncleanness and nay, are they not rather plain devourers of maidenly virginity and chastity? For proof whereof, but mark the flocking and running to theaters and curtains, daily and hourly, night and day, time and tide, to see plays and interludes, where such wanton gestures, such bawdy speeches, such laughing and fleering [ridiculing], such kissing and bussing, such clipping and culling, such winking and glancing of wanton eyes and the like is used, as is wonderful to behold. Then the godly pageants being done, every mate sorts to his mate, every one brings another homeward of their way very friendly, and in their secret conclaves (covertly) they play the Sodomites, or worse. And these be the fruits of plays and interludes, for the most part. And whereas, you say, there are good examples to be learned in them.

Truly, so there are. If you will learn falsehood, if you will learn cozenage; if you will learn to play the hypocrite; to cog, lie, and falsify; if you will learn to jest, laugh, and fleer, to grin, to nod, and mow [jest]; if you will learn to play the vice, to swear, tear, and blaspheme both heaven and earth. If you will learn to become a bawd, unclean, and to devirginate maids, to deflower honest wives; if you will learn to murder, slay, kill, pick, steal, rob, and rove; if you will learn to rebel against princes, to commit treasons, to consume treasures, to practice idleness, to sing and talk of bawdy love and venery; if you will learn to deride, scoff, mock, and flout, to flatter and smooth; if you will learn to play the whoremaster, the glutton, drunkard, or incestuous person; if you will learn to become proud, haughty, and arrogant; and finally, if you will learn to con- temn God and all his laws, to care neither for heaven nor hell, and to commit all kind of sin and mischief, you need to go to no other school, for all these good examples may you see painted before your eyes in interludes and plays. . . .

Therefore I beseech all players and founders of plays and interludes, in the bowels of Jesus Christ, as they tender the salvation of their souls, and others, to leave off that cursed kind of life and give themselves to such honest exer- cises and godly mysteries as God hath commanded them in his word to get their livings withal. For who will call him a wise man that playeth the part of a fool and a vice? Who can call him a Christian who playeth the part of a devil, the sworn enemy of Christ? Who can call him a just man that playeth the part of a dissembling hypocrite? And to be brief, who can call him a straight-dealing man, who playeth a cozener's trick? And so of all the rest. Away therefore with this so infamous an art, for go they never so brave [no matter how splendid they appear], yet are they counted and taken but for beggars. And is it not true? Live they not upon beggings of every one that comes? Are they not taken by the laws of the realm for rogues and vagabonds? I speak of such as travel the countries with plays and interludes, making an occupation of it, and ought to be punished, if they had their deserts.

Bibliography

The Bibliography is divided into two parts, "Works Cited" and "Suggestions for Further Reading." The first part contains all primary and secondary works quoted or discussed in the text or excerpted at the end of each chapter. Titles of primary texts have been modernized. The second part is an extremely selective list of materials that will be of use to the student wishing to know more about Shakespeare's art and culture. It is subdivided into six broad categories: "Miscellaneous Resources"; "Contexts: Intellectual, Social, Ideological"; "Shakespearean Performance"; "Text and Language"; "Dramatic Forms and Influences"; and "Critical and Theoretical Works." With one or two exceptions, a book or article that appears in "Works Cited" is not recorded again under "Suggestions for Further Reading." Thus, both lists should be consulted.

Works Cited

Amussen, Susan D. "Gender, Family, and the Social Order, 1560–1725." Fletcher and Stevenson 196–217.

Aristotle. *Historia Animalium.* Trans. Richard Cresswell. London, 1883.

——— . *The "Poetics."* See Halliwell.

Ascham, Roger. *The Schoolmaster.* London, 1570.

Barish, Jonas A. *The Antitheatrical Prejudice.* Berkeley: U of California P, 1981.

Barroll, J. Leeds. *Politics, Plague, and Shakespeare's Theater: The Stuart Years.* Ithaca: Cornell UP, 1991.

Bentley, Gerald Eades. *Shakespeare: A Biographical Handbook.* New Haven: Yale UP, 1961.

Blayney, Peter W. M. *The First Folio of Shakespeare.* Hanover, Md.: Folger Library Publications, 1991.

The Book of Common Prayer 1559. Ed. John E. Booty. Charlottesville: U of Virginia P for the Folger Shakespeare Library, 1976.

Boose, Lynda E. *"The Taming of the Shrew,* Good Husbandry, Enclosure." *Shakespeare Reread: The Texts in New Contexts.* Ed. Russ McDonald. Ithaca: Cornell UP, 1994. 193–225.

Booth, Stephen. *The Book Called "Holinshed's Chronicles": An Account of Its Inception, Purpose, Contributors, Contents, Publication, Revision, and Influence on William Shakespeare.* N.p.: The Book Club of California, 1968.

——. "The Function of Criticism at the Present Time and All Others." *Shakespeare Quarterly* 41 (1990): 262–68.

Bowers, Fredson. *Textual and Literary Criticism.* Cambridge: Cambridge UP, 1959.

Brooke, Arthur. *The Tragicall History of Romeus and Juliet.* London, 1562.

Bullough, Geoffrey. *Narrative and Dramatic Sources of Shakespeare.* 8 vols. London: Methuen, 1957–75.

Cary, Elizabeth. *The Tragedy of Mariam, the Fair Queen of Jewry.* London, 1613.

Castiglione, Baldassare. *The Book of the Courtier.* Trans. George Bull. Harmondsworth: Penguin, 1967.

Chambers, E. K. *William Shakespeare: A Study of Facts and Problems.* 2 vols. Oxford: Oxford UP, 1930.

Cinthio, Giovanni Battista Giraldi. *Gli Hecatommithi.* 1565. Bullough 7:239–52.

Coke, Sir Edward. *The Third Part of the Institutes of the Laws of England.* 3rd ed. London, 1644.

Coleman, D. C. *The Economy of England 1450–1750.* Cambridge: Cambridge UP, 1977.

Cook, Ann Jennalie. *Making a Match: Courtship in Shakespeare and His Society.* Princeton: Princeton UP, 1991.

Crewe, Jonathan. *Trials of Authorship: Anterior Forms and Poetic Reconstruction from Wyatt to Shakespeare.* Berkeley: U of California P, 1990.

Crosse, Henry. *Vertues Commonwealth: or The High-way to Honour.* London, 1603.

Culler, Jonathan, ed. *On Puns: The Foundation of Letters.* Oxford: Blackwell, 1988.

Dasent, John R., et al., eds. *Acts of the Privy Council of England, 1452–1628.* 32 vols. London, 1890–1907.

Davies, Godfrey. *The Early Stuarts, 1603–1660.* 2nd ed. Oxford: Oxford UP, 1959.

Dolan, Frances E. *Dangerous Familiars: Representations of Domestic Crime in England, 1550–1700.* Ithaca: Cornell UP, 1994.

Dollimore, Jonathan. "Transgression and Surveillance in *Measure for Measure.*" Dollimore and Sinfield 72–87.

Dollimore, Jonathan, and Alan Sinfield. *Political Shakespeare.* Ithaca: Cornell UP, 1985.

Elias, Norbert. *The Civilizing Process: The Development of Manners.* Trans. Edmund Jephcott. New York: Urizen, 1978.

Elizabeth I, queen of England. "Edict Arranging for the Expulsion from England of Negroes and Blackamoors." Dasent et al. 26:22.

——. "Proclamation Placing London Vagabonds under Martial Law." Hughes and Larkin 3:196–97.

——. "Open Warrant to the Lord Mayor of London." Dasent et al. 26:20.

Elyot, Sir Thomas. *The Book Named the Governor.* 2nd ed. London, 1553.

Evans, G. Blakemore, ed. *The Riverside Shakespeare.* Boston: Houghton, 1974.

Farmer, Richard. *An Essay on the Learning of Shakespeare.* Cambridge, 1767.

Felperin, Howard. *Shakespearean Romance.* Princeton: Princeton UP, 1972.

Field, John, and Thomas Wilcox (?). *An Admonition to the Parliament.* London, 1572.

Fielding, Henry. *Tom Jones.* Ed. George Sherburn. New York: Random, 1950.

Filmer, Sir Robert. *Patriarcha, or The Natural Power of Kings.* London, 1680. See also Sommerville 6–7.

Firth, C. H. "Ballads and Broadsides." Lee and Onions 2:511–38.

Fitzherbert, Sir Anthony. *The Book of Husbandry.* London, 1523.

Fletcher, Anthony, and John Stevenson. *Order and Disorder in Early Modern England.* Cambridge: Cambridge UP, 1985.

Fletcher, John. "To the Reader." *The Faithful Shepherdess*. London, c. 1609.

Forman, Simon. From his *Diary*. In *Simon Forman: Sex and Society in Shakespeare's Age*. Ed. A. L. Rowse. London: Weidenfeld and Nicolson, 1974.

Fortescue, Sir John. *Works*. Trans. Chichester Fortescue. Ed. Lord Clermont. London, 1869. 1:322. See Tillyard 26–27.

Foxe, John. *Acts and Monuments of These Latter and Perilous Days*. London, 1563.

Frere, W. H., and C. E. Douglas. *Puritan Manifestoes: A Study of the Origin of the Puritan Revolt*. 1907. Rpt. London: Church Historical Society, 1954.

Frisbee, George. *Edward de Vere, A Great Elizabethan*. London: Cecil Palmer, 1931.

Frye, Northrop. *Anatomy of Criticism*. Princeton: Princeton UP, 1957.

The Geneva Bible. A facsimile of the 1560 edition with an introduction by Lloyd E. Berry. Madison: U of Wisconsin P, 1969.

Gosson, Stephen. *Plays Confuted in Five Actions*. London, 1582.

Gouge, William. *Of Domestical Duties: Eight Treatises*. 2nd ed. London, 1626.

Greenblatt, Stephen. *Shakespearean Negotiations*. Oxford: Oxford UP, 1988.

Gurr, Andrew. *Playgoing in Shakespeare's London*. Cambridge: Cambridge UP, 1987.

——. *The Shakespearean Stage*. 3rd ed. Cambridge: Cambridge UP, 1992.

Guy, John. *Tudor England*. Oxford: Oxford UP, 1988.

Hall, Edward. *The Union of the Two Noble and Illustre Families of Lancaster and York*. 2nd ed. London, 1548.

Halliday, F. E. *A Shakespeare Companion*. Rev. ed. Harmondsworth: Penguin, 1964.

Halliwell, Stephen, ed. *The "Poetics" of Aristotle: Translation and Commentary*. Chapel Hill: U of North Carolina P, 1987.

Harbage, Alfred, ed. *The Complete Pelican Shakespeare*. Harmondsworth: Penguin, 1969.

Harington, Sir John. "To Secretary Barlow." July 1606. Letter 44 of *The Letters and Epigrams of Sir John Harington*. Ed. Norman Egbert McClure. Philadelphia: U of Pennsylvania P, 1930.

Harrison, G. B. *Introducing Shakespeare*. Rev. ed. Harmondsworth: Penguin, 1964.

Harrison, William. *The Description of England*. 2nd ed. London, 1587.

Henslowe, Philip. *Henslowe's Diary*. Ed. R. A. Foakes and R. T. Rickert. Cambridge: Cambridge UP, 1961.

Hinman, Charlton. *The Printing and Proofreading of the First Folio of Shakespeare*. Oxford: Oxford UP, 1966.

Hirst, Derek. *Authority and Conflict, 1603–1658*. Cambridge, Mass.: Harvard UP, 1985.

Holinshed, Raphael. *The Chronicles of England, Scotland, and Ireland*. 2nd ed. London, 1587.

An Homily against Disobedience and Willful Rebellion. London, 1570.

An Homily of the State of Matrimony. In *The Second Tome of Homilies*. London, 1563.

Hoskyns, John. *Directions for Speech and Style*. Ed. Hoyt H. Hudson. Princeton: Princeton UP, 1935.

Hughes, Paul L., and James F. Larkin. *Tudor Royal Proclamations*. 3 vols. New Haven: Yale UP, 1964–69.

Ingram, William. *The Business of Playing: The Beginnings of the Adult Professional Theater in Elizabethan London*. Ithaca: Cornell UP, 1992.

James I, king of England. *Basilikon Doron*. McIlwain 3–52.

——. "To George Villiers, Duke of Buckingham." December 1623(?). Letter 218 in *Letters of King James VI & I*. Ed. G. P. V. Akrigg. Berkeley: U of California P, 1984.

——. "A Speech to the Lords and Commons of the Parliament at Whitehall." March 21, 1610. McIlwain 306–25.

Johnson, Samuel. *The Works of Samuel Johnson.* Ed. Arthur Sherbo. New Haven: Yale UP, 1968. 7:74.

Jonson, Ben. "On His First Son." In *Works.* London, 1616.

Kenyon, J. P. *Stuart England.* Harmondsworth: Penguin, 1978.

———. *The Stuarts.* Rpt. London: Fontana, 1966.

Klein, Joan Larsen. *Daughters, Wives, and Widows: Writings by Men about Women and Marriage in England, 1500–1640.* Urbana: U of Illinois P, 1992.

Lanham, Richard. *A Handlist of Rhetorical Terms.* Berkeley: U of California P, 1968.

Laslett, Peter. *The World We Have Lost: England before the Industrial Age.* 3rd ed. New York: Scribner's, 1984.

Leary, Penn. *The Cryptographic Shakespeare: A Monograph Wherein the Poems and Plays Attributed to William Shakespeare are Proven to Contain the Enciphered Name of the Concealed Author, Francis Bacon.* Omaha, Neb.: Westchester, 1987.

Lee, Sidney, and C. T. Onions. *Shakespeare's England: An Account of the Life and Manners of His Age.* 2 vols. Oxford: Clarendon, 1916.

Lennox, Charlotte. *Shakespeare Illustrated: or the Novels and Histories on which the Plays are Founded.* London, 1753–54.

"A Letter to Rome . . ." [Ballad]. London, 1571(?).

Levin, Carole. *"The Heart and Stomach of a King": Elizabeth I and the Politics of Sex and Power.* Philadelphia: U of Pennsylvania P, 1994.

Lewalski, Barbara. *Writing Women in Jacobean England.* Cambridge, Mass.: Harvard UP, 1993.

Lewis, C. S. *English Literature in the Sixteenth Century.* Oxford: Clarendon, 1954.

Lockyer, Roger. *Tudor and Stuart Britain, 1471–1714.* New York: St. Martin's, 1964.

Mahood, M. M. *Shakespeare's Wordplay.* London: Routledge, 1957.

Markham, Gervase. *The English Husbandman.* London, 1613. Sigs. A4v–B1v.

Marlowe, Christopher. *Tamburlaine the Great.* London, 1590.

McCarthy, Cormac. *The Crossing.* New York: Knopf, 1994.

McIlwain, Charles Howard, ed. *The Political Works of James I.* Cambridge, Mass.: Harvard UP, 1918.

Meres, Francis. *Palladis Tamia: Wit's Treasury.* London, 1598. Chambers 2:193–95.

Middleton, Thomas. *Your Five Gallants.* London, 1608(?).

A Mirror for Magistrates. "Caius Julius Caesar." 1587 edition. Bullough 5:168–73.

Montaigne, Michel de. *The Complete Works of Montaigne: Essays, Travel Journals, Letters.* Trans. Donald M. Frame. Stanford: Stanford UP, 1958.

Montrose, Louis Adrian. "The Elizabethan Subject and the Spenserian Text." *Literary Theory/Renaissance Texts.* Ed. Patricia Parker and David Quint. Baltimore: Johns Hopkins UP, 1986.

———. " 'Shaping Fantasies': Figurations of Gender and Power in Elizabethan Culture." *Representations* 2 (1983): 61–94.

Moryson, Fynes. *An Itinerary.* London, 1617.

Moxon, Joseph. *Mechanic Exercises.* London, 1683.

Mullaney, Steven. *The Place of the Stage: License, Play, and Power in Renaissance England.* Chicago: U of Chicago P, 1988.

Nashe, Thomas. *Christ's Tears over Jerusalem.* Rev. ed. London, 1613.

Neale, John. *Elizabeth I.* Rpt. Harmondsworth: Penguin, 1990.

Ovid [Publius Ovidius Naso]. *The xv Books of P. Ovidius Naso, entitled Metamorphosis.* Trans. Arthur Golding. London, 1567.

———. *Metamorphoses.* Trans. Rolfe Humphries. Bloomington: Indiana UP, 1955.

Paster, Gail Kern. *The Body Embarrassed: Drama and the Disciplines of Shame in Early Modern England.* Ithaca: Cornell UP, 1993.

Platter, Thomas. *Travels in England.* Trans. Clare Williams. London: Jonathan Cape, 1937.

Plutarch. *The Lives of the Noble Grecians and Romans.* Trans. Thomas North. London, 1579.

Potter, Lois. "Reconstructing Shakespeare." *Times Literary Supplement* 7 Apr. 1995: 21.

Preston, Thomas. *A Lamentable Tragedy, Mixed Full of Pleasant Mirth, Containing the Life of Cambyses, King of Persia.* London, 1569(?).

Prothero, R. E. "Agriculture and Gardening." Lee and Onions 1:346–80.

Prynne, William. *Histriomastix: The Players' Scourge.* London, 1633.

Puttenham, George. *The Art of English Poesy.* London, 1589.

Rabkin, Norman. "Rabbits, Ducks, and *Henry V.*" *Shakespeare Quarterly* 28 (1977): 279–96. Rpt. in *Shakespeare and the Problem of Meaning.* Chicago: U of Chicago P, 1981.

Reynolds, Richard. *A Book Called the Foundation of Rhetoric.* London, 1563.

Rhetorica Ad Herennium. Qtd. in Lanham.

Righter [Barton], Anne. *Shakespeare and the Idea of the Play.* Harmondsworth: Penguin, 1961. Rpt. Westport: Greenwood, 1977.

Rymer, Thomas. *A Short View of Tragedy.* London, 1693.

Schoenbaum, Samuel. *Shakespeare: His Life, His Language, His Theater.* New York: Signet, 1990.

——. *William Shakespeare: A Compact Documentary Life.* Oxford: Oxford UP, 1977.

Shakespeare, William. *Mr. William Shakespeare's Comedies, Histories, & Tragedies.* F1. London, 1623.

——. *The Most Lamentable Roman Tragedy of Titus Andronicus.* Q1. London, 1594.

——. *The Riverside Shakespeare.* Ed. G. Blakemore Evans. Boston: Houghton Mifflin, 1974.

——. *The Tragedy of King Richard the Third.* Q1. London, 1597.

——. *The Tragical History of Hamlet, Prince of Denmark.* Q1. London, 1603.

——. *Mr. William Shakespeare, His True Chronicle History of the Life and Death of King Lear and His Three Daughters.* Q1. London, 1608.

Sidney, Sir Philip. *Astrophil and Stella.* London, 1598.

——. *The Defense of Poesy.* London, 1595.

Sinfield, Alan. *Faultlines: Cultural Materialism and the Politics of Dissident Reading.* Berkeley: U of California P, 1992.

Skura, Meredith. *Shakespeare the Actor and the Purposes of Playing.* Chicago: U of Chicago P, 1993.

Smith, Bruce. *Homosexual Desire in Shakespeare's England.* Chicago: U of Chicago P, 1991.

Smith, Sir Thomas. *De Republica Anglorum: The Manner of Government of England.* London, 1583.

Sommerville, Johann B., ed. *Patriarcha and Other Writings.* Cambridge: Cambridge UP, 1991.

Stone, Lawrence. *The Causes of the English Revolution, 1529–1642.* New York: Harper, 1972.

——. *The Family, Sex and Marriage in England, 1500–1800.* New York: Harper, 1977.

Stow, John. *A Survey of London.* London, 1598.

Strachey, Sir William. *A True Reportory of the Wreck and Redemption of Sir Thomas Gates.* Bullough 8:275–94.

Stubbes, Philip. *The Anatomy of Abuses.* London, 1583.

Swetnam, Joseph. *Arraignment of Lewd, Idle, Froward, and Unconstant Women.* London, 1615.

Taylor, Gary. Introduction. *Henry V.* By William Shakespeare. Oxford: Oxford UP, 1982.

Taylor, Gary, and Michael Warren, eds. *The Division of the Kingdoms: Shakespeare's Two Versions of "King Lear."* Oxford: Clarendon, 1983.

Tillyard, E. M. W. *The Elizabethan World Picture.* New York: Random House, n.d.

Tilney, Edmund. *The Flower of Friendship.* Ed. Valerie Wayne. Ithaca: Cornell UP, 1992.

"The True Form and Shape of a Monstrous Child." [Ballad]. London, 1565.

Underdown, David. "The Taming of the Scold: the Enforcement of Patriarchal Authority in Early Modern England." Fletcher and Stevenson 116–36.

Urkowitz, Steven. *Shakespeare's Revision of "King Lear."* Princeton: Princeton UP, 1980.

Ward, John. From his *Diary.* Chambers 2:249–50

Wedel, Lupold von. *Journey through England and Scotland Made by Lupold von Wedel in the years 1584 and 1585.* Ed. Gottfried von Bulow. *Transactions of the Royal Historical Society* ns 9 (1895): 228–30, 267.

Wells, Stanley, and Gary Taylor, with John Jowett and William Montgomery. *William Shakespeare: A Textual Companion.* Oxford: Clarendon, 1987.

Werstine, Paul. "Narratives about Printed Shakespeare Texts: 'Foul Papers' and 'Bad Quartos.'" *Shakespeare Quarterly* 41 (1990): 65–86.

Whetstone, George. *An Heptameron of Civil Discourses.* London, 1582.

Wilde, Oscar. *The Importance of Being Earnest.* In *Plays.* Harmondsworth: Penguin, 1954.

Wilson, Thomas. *The Art of Rhetoric.* London, 1553.

Wotton, David, ed. *Democracy and Divine Right.* Harmondsworth: Penguin, 1986.

Wright, George T. *Shakespeare's Metrical Art.* Berkeley: U of California P, 1988.

Zimmerman, Susan, ed. *Erotic Politics: Desire on the Renaissance Stage.* London: Routledge, 1992.

Suggestions for Further Reading

MISCELLANEOUS RESOURCES

Allen, M. J. B., and Kenneth Muir, eds. *Shakespeare's Plays in Quarto: A Facsimile Edition.* Berkeley: U of California P, 1981.

Andrews, John F. *William Shakespeare: His World, His Work, His Influence.* 3 vols. New York: Scribner's, 1985.

Bentley, Gerald Eades. *The Jacobean and Caroline Stage.* 7 vols. Oxford: Oxford UP, 1966.

Bergeron, David, and Geraldo U. de Sousa. *Shakespeare: A Study and Research Guide.* 3rd ed. Lawrence: U of Kansas P, 1995.

Bevington, David. *The Goldentree Bibliography of Shakespeare.* Arlington Heights, Ill.: AHM, 1978.

Bulman, James C., J. R. Mulryne, and Margaret Shewring. *Shakespeare in Performance* Series. Manchester: Manchester UP, 1982–.

Chambers, E. K. *The Elizabethan Stage.* 4 vols. Oxford: Oxford UP, 1923.

Harbage, Alfred, Samuel Schoenbaum, and Sylvia S. Wagonheim. *Annals of English Drama, 975–1700.* Rev. ed. London: Routledge, 1989.

Hinman, Charlton. *The Norton Facsimile: The First Folio of Shakespeare.* New York: Norton, 1968.

McManaway, James G., and Jeanne Addison Roberts. *A Selective Bibliography of*

Shakespeare: Editions, Textual Studies, Commentary. Charlottesville: U of Virginia P for the Folger Shakespeare Library, 1975.

O'Brien, Peggy, ed. *Shakespeare Set Free*. 3 vols. New York: Washington Square, 1993–95.

Schoenbaum, Samuel. *William Shakespeare: A Documentary Life*. Oxford: Oxford UP, 1975.

Spevack, Marvin. *A Complete and Systematic Concordance to the Works of Shakespeare*. 9 vols. Hildesheim, Ger.: Georg Olms, 1969–80.

——. *The Harvard Concordance to Shakespeare*. Cambridge, Mass.: Harvard UP, 1973.

Wells, Stanley. *The Cambridge Companion to Shakespeare Studies*. Rev. ed. Cambridge: Cambridge UP, 1986.

——. *Shakespeare: A Bibliographical Guide*. Oxford: Oxford UP, 1990.

Collected Editions

Alexander, Peter, ed. *William Shakespeare: The Complete Works*. London: Collins, 1951.

Barnet, Sylvan, ed. *The Complete Signet Classic Shakespeare*. New York: Harcourt, 1972. Also issued in single-play paperback editions.

Bevington, David, ed. *The Complete Works of Shakespeare*. New York: HarperCollins, 1992.

Evans, G. Blakemore, ed. *The Riverside Shakespeare*. Boston: Houghton, 1974.

Harbage, Alfred, ed. *The Complete Pelican Shakespeare*. Baltimore: Penguin, 1969. Also issued in single-play paperback editions.

Kittredge, George Lyman, ed. *The Complete Works of Shakespeare*. Boston: Ginn, 1936. Rev. ed. by Irving Ribner, 1971.

Wells, Stanley, and Gary Taylor, with John Jowett and William Montgomery, eds. *William Shakespeare: The Complete Works*. Oxford: Oxford UP, 1986.

Single-Play Editions

Bevington, David, ed. *The Bantam Shakespeare*. New York: Bantam, 1980.

Braunmuller, Albert, and Brian Gibbons, gen. eds. *The New Cambridge Shakespeare*. Cambridge: Cambridge UP, 1984–. Replaces *The New Cambridge Shakespeare*. Gen. ed. John Dover Wilson and Arthur Quiller-Couch.

Kastan, David Scott, Richard Proudfoot, and Ann Thompson, gen. eds. *The Arden Shakespeare*. 3rd ed. London: Routledge, 1994–. Replaces *The New Arden Shakespeare*. Gen. ed. Harold F. Brooks and Harold Jenkins.

Mowat, Barbara, and Paul Werstine, gen. eds. *The New Folger Library Shakespeare*. New York: Washington Square, 1990–. Replaces *The Folger Shakespeare*. Ed. Louis B. Wright and Virginia LaMar.

Spencer, T. J. B., gen. ed. *The New Penguin Shakespeare*. Harmondsworth: Penguin, 1967–.

Wells, Stanley, and Gary Taylor, gen. eds. *The New Oxford Shakespeare*. Oxford: Oxford UP, 1982–.

Other

Booth, Stephen, ed. *Shakespeare's Sonnets, edited with analytic commentary*. New Haven: Yale UP, 1977.

Journals

Shakespeare Jahrbuch (Germany). 1946–.
Shakespeare Newsletter. 1951–.

Shakespeare Quarterly. 1950–.
Shakespeare Studies. 1965–.
Shakespeare Survey (England). 1948–.

CONTEXTS: INTELLECTUAL, SOCIAL, IDEOLOGICAL

Baker, Herschel. *The Wars of Truth.* Cambridge, Mass.: Harvard UP, 1952.

Bakhtin, Mikhail. *Rabelais and His World.* Trans. Helene Iswolsky. Bloomington: Indiana UP, 1984.

Black, J. B. *The Reign of Elizabeth, 1558–1603.* 2nd ed. Oxford: Oxford UP, 1959.

Bristol, Michael. *Carnival and Theater: Plebeian Culture and the Structure of Authority in Renaissance England.* London: Routledge, 1985.

Bruster, Douglas. *Drama and the Market in the Age of Shakespeare.* Cambridge: Cambridge UP, 1992.

Byrne, Muriel St. Clare. *Elizabethan Life in Town and Country.* 8th ed. Boston: Houghton, 1961.

Craig, Hardin. *The Enchanted Glass: The Elizabethan Mind in Literature.* New York: Oxford UP, 1936.

Cressy, David. *Literacy and the Social Order: Reading and Writing in Tudor and Stuart England.* Cambridge: Cambridge UP, 1980.

Ferguson, Margaret, Maureen Quilligan, and Nancy J. Vickers, eds. *Rewriting the Renaissance: The Discourses of Sexual Difference in Early Modern Europe.* Chicago: U of Chicago P, 1986.

Frye, Roland M. *Shakespeare and Christian Doctrine.* Princeton: Princeton UP, 1963.

Garber, Marjorie, ed. *Cannibals, Witches, Divorce: Estranging the Renaissance.* Baltimore: Johns Hopkins UP, 1987.

Gillies, John. *Shakespeare and the Geography of Difference.* Cambridge: Cambridge UP, 1994.

Greenblatt, Stephen. *Learning to Curse: Essays in Early Modern Culture.* London: Routledge, 1990.

——. *Renaissance Self-Fashioning: More to Shakespeare.* Chicago: U of Chicago P, 1980.

Hall, Kim F. *Things of Darkness: Economies of Race and Gender in Early Modern England.* Ithaca: Cornell UP, 1996.

Haydn, Hiram. *The Counter-Renaissance.* New York: Scribner's, 1950.

Hendricks, Margo, and Patricia Parker. *Women, "Race," and Writing in the Early Modern Period.* London: Routledge, 1994.

Howell, Wilbur. *Logic and Rhetoric in England, 1500–1700.* Princeton: Princeton UP, 1956.

Jardine, Lisa. *Still Harping on Daughters: Women and Drama in the Age of Shakespeare.* 1983. 2nd ed. New York: Columbia UP, 1989.

Jordan, Constance. *Renaissance Feminism: Literary Texts and Political Models.* Ithaca: Cornell UP, 1990.

Kantorowicz, Ernst. *The King's Two Bodies.* Princeton: Princeton UP, 1957.

Kinney, Arthur. *Humanist Poetics.* Amherst: U of Massachusetts P, 1986.

Kristeller, Paul Oscar. *Renaissance Thought and Its Sources.* Ed. Michael Mooney. New York: Columbia UP, 1979.

Laqueur, Thomas. *Making Sex: Body and Gender from the Greeks to Freud.* Cambridge, Mass.: Harvard UP, 1990.

Levin, Harry. *The Myth of the Golden Age in the Renaissance.* Bloomington: Indiana UP, 1969.

Levy, F. J. *Tudor Historical Thought*. San Marino: Huntington Library, 1967.

Lovejoy, Arthur O. *The Great Chain of Being: A Study of the History of an Idea*. Cambridge, Mass.: Harvard UP, 1936.

Marcus, Leah S. *The Politics of Mirth: Johnson, Herrick, Milton, Marvell, and the Defense of Old Holiday Pastimes*. Chicago: U of Chicago P, 1986.

Peck, Linda Levy, ed. *The Mental World of the Jacobean Court*. Cambridge: Cambridge UP, 1991.

Popkin, Richard H. *The History of Skepticism from Erasmus to Spinoza*. Berkeley: U of California P, 1979.

Quinones, Ricardo J. *The Renaissance Discovery of Time*. Cambridge, Mass.: Harvard UP, 1972.

Shuger, Debora Kuller. *Habits of Thought in the English Renaissance: Religion, Politics, and the Dominant Culture*. Berkeley: U of California P, 1990.

Siraisi, Nancy G. *Medieval and Early Renaissance Medicine: An Introduction to Knowledge and Practice*. Chicago: U of Chicago P, 1990.

Stone, Lawrence. *The Crisis of the Aristocracy, 1558–1641*. Oxford: Oxford UP, 1965.

Tawney, R. H. *Religion and the Rise of Capitalism*. Rpt. Gloucester, Mass.: Peter Smith, 1962.

Thomas, Keith. *Religion and the Decline of Magic*. Rpt. Harmondsworth: Penguin, 1973.

Underdown, David. *Revel, Riot, and Rebellion: Popular Politics and Culture in England, 1603–1660*. Oxford: Oxford UP, 1985.

Woodbridge, Linda. *Women and the English Renaissance*. Urbana: U of Illinois P, 1984.

Wright, Louis B. *Middle-Class Culture in Elizabethan England*. Rpt. Ithaca: Cornell UP for the Folger Shakespeare Library, 1958.

SHAKESPEAREAN PERFORMANCE

Beckerman, Bernard. *Shakespeare at the Globe*. New York: Columbia UP, 1962.

Bentley, Gerald Eades. *The Professions of Dramatist and Player in Shakespeare's Time, 1590–1642*. Princeton: Princeton UP, 1986.

Buchman, Lorne. *Still in Movement: Shakespeare on Screen*. Oxford: Oxford UP, 1991.

Bulman, James C., and Herbert Coursen. *Shakespeare on Television: An Anthology of Essays and Reviews*. Hanover, N.H.: UP of New England, 1988.

Cook, Ann Jennalie. *The Privileged Playgoer of Shakespeare's London, 1576–1642*. Princeton: Princeton UP, 1981.

Crowl, Samuel. *Shakespeare Observed: Studies in Performance on Stage and Screen*. Athens: U of Ohio P, 1992.

Dessen, Alan C. *Elizabethan Stage Conventions and Modern Interpreters*. Cambridge: Cambridge UP, 1984.

Goldman, Michael. *Shakespeare and the Energies of Drama*. Princeton: Princeton UP, 1972.

Granville-Barker, Harley. *Prefaces to Shakespeare*. Rev. ed. 4 vols. Princeton: Princeton UP, 1946–47.

Greg, W. W. *Dramatic Documents from the Elizabethan Playhouses*. 2 vols. Oxford: Oxford UP, 1931.

Jackson, Russell, Robert Smallwood, and Philip Brockbank, eds. *Players of Shakespeare*. 3 vols. to date. Cambridge: Cambridge UP, 1986–93.

Joseph, B. L. *Elizabethan Acting*. 2nd ed. Oxford: Oxford UP, 1964.

Kennedy, Dennis. *Foreign Shakespeare: Contemporary Performance*. Cambridge: Cambridge UP, 1993.

——— . *Looking at Shakespeare: A Visual History of Twentieth-Century Performance.* Cambridge: Cambridge UP, 1993.

Levine, Laura. *Men in Women's Clothing.* Cambridge: Cambridge UP, 1993.

Orgel, Stephen. *The Illusion of Power: Political Theater in the English Renaissance.* Berkeley: U of California P, 1975.

Shattuck, Charles H. *Shakespeare on the American Stage.* 2 vols. Washington: Folger Shakespeare Library, 1976-87.

Styan, J. L. *Shakespeare's Stagecraft.* Cambridge: Cambridge UP, 1967.

TEXT AND LANGUAGE

Abbott, E. A. *A Shakespearian Grammar.* Rpt. New York: Haskell House, 1966.

Blake, N. F. *Shakespeare's Language: An Introduction.* London: Methuen, 1983.

Clemen, Wolfgang. *The Development of Shakespeare's Imagery.* London: Methuen, 1951.

De Grazia, Margreta. *Shakespeare Verbatim.* Oxford: Clarendon, 1990.

De Grazia, Margreta, and Peter Stallybrass. "The Materiality of the Shakespearean Text." *Shakespeare Quarterly* 44 (1993): 255–83.

Edwards, Philip, Inga-Stina Ewbank, and G. K. Hunter, eds. *Shakespeare's Styles.* Cambridge: Cambridge UP, 1980.

Greg, W. W. *The Shakespeare First Folio: Its Bibliographical and Textual History.* Oxford: Clarendon, 1955.

Halliday, F. E. *The Poetry of Shakespeare's Plays.* London: Duckworth, 1954.

Houston, John Porter. *Shakespearean Sentences: A Study in Style and Syntax.* Baton Rouge: Louisiana State UP, 1988.

Joseph, Sister Miriam. *Shakespeare's Use of the Arts of Language.* New York: Columbia UP, 1947.

Kokeritz, Helge. *Shakespeare's Pronunciation.* New Haven: Yale UP, 1953.

Lanham, Richard. *The Motives of Eloquence: Literary Rhetoric in the Renaissance.* New Haven: Yale UP, 1976.

McKerrow, R. B. *An Introduction to Bibliography for Literary Students.* Oxford: Clarendon, 1927.

Onions, C. T. *A Shakespeare Glossary.* Rev. Robert D. Eagleson. Oxford: Oxford UP, 1986.

Parker, Patricia. *Literary Fat Ladies: Rhetoric, Gender, Property.* London: Methuen, 1987.

Partridge, Eric. *Shakespeare's Bawdy.* Rev. ed. London: Routledge, 1969.

Spurgeon, Caroline F. E. *Shakespeare's Imagery and What It Tells Us.* Cambridge: Cambridge UP, 1935.

Vickers, Brian. *The Artistry of Shakespeare's Prose.* London: Methuen, 1968.

Williams, George Walton. *The Craft of Printing and the Publication of Shakespeare's Works.* Washington: Folger Books, 1985.

DRAMATIC FORMS AND INFLUENCES

Baldwin, T. W. *William Shakespeare's Five-Act Structure.* Urbana: U of Illinois P, 1947.

Barber, C. L. *Shakespeare's Festive Comedy.* Princeton: Princeton UP, 1959.

Bate, Jonathan. *Shakespeare and Ovid.* Oxford: Clarendon, 1993.

Belsey, Catherine. *The Subject of Tragedy: Identity and Difference in Renaissance Drama.* London: Methuen, 1985.

Bevington, David. *From "Mankind" to Marlowe.* Cambridge, Mass.: Harvard UP, 1962.

Booth, Stephen. *"King Lear," "Macbeth," Indefinition, and Tragedy.* New Haven: Yale UP, 1983.

Bradbrook, Muriel. *The Growth and Structure of Elizabethan Comedy.* London: Chatto and Windus, 1955.

Bradley, A. C. *Shakespearean Tragedy.* Rpt. New York: St. Martin's, 1967.

Campbell, L. B. *Shakespeare's "Histories": Mirrors of Elizabethan Policy.* San Marino: Huntington Library, 1947.

———. *Shakespeare's Tragic Heroes: Slaves of Passion.* Cambridge: Cambridge UP, 1930.

Carroll, William C. *The Metamorphoses of Shakespearean Comedy.* Princeton: Princeton UP, 1985.

Charney, Maurice. *Shakespeare's Roman Plays.* Cambridge, Mass.: Harvard UP, 1961.

Colie, Rosalie. *The Resources of Kind: Genre Theory in the Renaissance.* Ed. Barbara K. Lewalski. Berkeley: U of California P, 1973.

Doran, Madeleine. *Endeavors of Art: A Study of Form in Elizabethan Drama.* Madison: U of Wisconsin P, 1954.

Evans, Bertrand. *Shakespeare's Comedies.* Oxford: Oxford UP, 1960.

———. *Shakespeare's Tragic Practice.* Oxford: Oxford UP, 1979.

Foakes, R. A. *Shakespeare: The Dark Comedies to the Last Plays.* Charlottesville: U of Virginia P, 1971.

Frye, Northrop. *Fools of Time: Studies in Shakespearean Tragedy.* Toronto: U of Toronto P, 1967.

———. *A Natural Perspective: The Development of Shakespearean Comedy and Romance.* New York: Columbia UP, 1965.

Hodgdon, Barbara. *The End Crowns All: Closure and Contradiction in Shakespeare's History.* Princeton: Princeton UP, 1991.

Hoy, Cyrus. *The Hyacinth Room: An Investigation into the Nature of Comedy, Tragedy, and Tragicomedy.* New York: Knopf, 1964.

Knight, G. Wilson. *The Imperial Theme: Further Interpretations of Shakespeare's Tragedies Including the Roman Plays.* 3rd ed. London: Methuen, 1951.

———. *The Wheel of Fire: Interpretation of Shakespeare's Tragedy.* Rev. ed. New York: Barnes and Noble, 1965.

Long, John H. *Shakespeare's Use of Music.* 3 vols. Gainesville: U of Florida P, 1955–71.

McElroy, Bernard. *Shakespeare's Mature Tragedies.* Princeton: Princeton UP, 1973.

Miola, Robert. *Shakespeare's Rome.* Cambridge: Cambridge UP, 1983.

Mowat, Barbara. *The Dramaturgy of Shakespeare's Romances.* Athens: U of Georgia P, 1976.

Noble, Richmond. *Shakespeare's Biblical Knowledge and Use of the Book of Common Prayer.* New York: Macmillan, 1935.

Ornstein, Robert. *A Kingdom for a Stage: The Achievement of Shakespeare's History Plays.* Cambridge, Mass.: Harvard UP, 1972.

Palmer, D. J. *Shakespeare's Later Comedies: An Anthology of Modern Criticism.* Harmondsworth: Penguin, 1971.

Rackin, Phyllis. *Stages of History: Shakespeare's English Chronicles.* Ithaca: Cornell UP, 1990.

Salingar, Leo. *Shakespeare and the Traditions of Comedy.* Cambridge: Cambridge UP, 1974.

Snyder, Susan. *The Comic Matrix of Shakespeare's Tragedies.* Princeton, 1979.

Spencer, T. J. B., ed. *Shakespeare's Plutarch.* Harmondsworth: Penguin, 1968.

Watson, Robert N. *Shakespeare and the Hazards of Ambition.* Cambridge, Mass.: Harvard UP, 1984.

Weimann, Robert. *Shakespeare and the Popular Tradition in the Theater.* Trans. Robert Schwartz. Baltimore: Johns Hopkins UP, 1978.

Wells, Stanley. "Shakespeare and Romance." Rpt. in *Later Shakespeare.* Ed. John Russell Brown and Bernard Harris. Stratford-upon-Avon Studies 8. London: Edward Arnold, 1966.

Wheeler, Richard P. *Shakespeare's Problem Comedies: Turn and Counter Turn.* Berkeley: U of California P, 1981.

Young, David. *The Heart's Forest: A Study of Shakespeare's Pastoral Plays.* New Haven: Yale UP, 1972.

CRITICAL AND THEORETICAL WORKS

Adelman, Janet. *Suffocating Mothers: Fantasies of Maternal Origin from "Hamlet" to "The Tempest."* London: Routledge, 1992.

Barton, Anne. *Essays, Mainly Shakespearian.* Cambridge: Cambridge UP, 1994.

Booth, Stephen. *An Essay on Shakespeare's Sonnets.* New Haven: Yale UP, 1969.

Bradshaw, Graham. *Misrepresentations: Shakespeare and the Materialists.* Ithaca: Cornell UP, 1993.

Burkhardt, Sigurd. *Shakespearean Meanings.* Princeton: Princeton UP, 1968.

Calderwood, James. *Shakespearean Metadrama.* Minneapolis: U of Minnesota P, 1971.

Cavell, Stanley. *Disowning Knowledge in Six Plays of Shakespeare.* Cambridge: Cambridge UP, 1987.

Colie, Rosalie. *Shakespeare's Living Art.* Princeton: Princeton UP, 1974.

Dean, Leonard F. *Shakespeare: Modern Essays in Criticism.* Rev. ed. Oxford: Oxford UP, 1967.

Dollimore, Jonathan. *Radical Tragedy.* Chicago: U of Chicago P, 1984.

Drakakis, John. *Alternative Shakespeares.* London: Methuen, 1985.

Fineman, Joel. *Shakespeare's Perjured Eye: The Invention of Poetic Subjectivity in the Sonnets.* Berkeley: U of California P, 1986.

Freedman, Barbara. *Staging the Gaze: Postmodernism, Psychoanalysis, and Shakespearean Comedy.* Ithaca: Cornell UP, 1991.

Goddard, Harold C. *The Meaning of Shakespeare.* 2 vols. Chicago: U of Chicago P, 1951.

Goldberg, Jonathan. *James I and the Politics of Literature.* Baltimore: Johns Hopkins UP, 1983.

Howard, Jean E., and Marion F. O'Connor. *Shakespeare Reproduced: The Text in Ideology and History.* London: Methuen, 1987.

Hunt, Maurice. *Shakespeare's Romance of the Word.* Lewisburg: Bucknell UP, 1990.

Kott, Jan. *Shakespeare Our Contemporary.* Trans. Boleslaw Taborski. New York: Norton, 1964.

Lenz, C. S., Gayle Greene, and Carol Thomas Neely. *The Woman's Part: Feminist Criticism of Shakespeare.* Urbana: U of Illinois P, 1980.

Levin, Harry. *The Question of Hamlet.* Oxford: Oxford UP, 1965.

Mack, Maynard. *Everybody's Shakespeare.* Lincoln: U of Nebraska P, 1993.

——— . *King Lear in Our Time.* Berkeley: U of California P, 1965.

McDonald, Russ. *Shakespeare and Jonson/Jonson and Shakespeare.* Lincoln: U of Nebraska P, 1988.

Parker, Patricia, and Geoffrey Hartman, eds. *Shakespeare and the Question of Theory.* London: Methuen, 1985.

Patterson, Annabel. *Shakespeare and the Popular Voice.* Oxford: Blackwell, 1989.

Pechter, Edward. *What Was Shakespeare?: Renaissance Plays and Changing Critical Practice.* Ithaca: Cornell UP, 1995.

Rabkin, Norman. *Shakespeare and the Common Understanding*. New York: Free, 1967.

Roberts, Jeanne Addison. *The Shakespearean Wild: Geography, Genus, and Gender*. Lincoln: U of Nebraska P, 1991.

Rose, Mark. *Shakespearean Design*. Cambridge, Mass.: Harvard UP, 1972.

Rossiter, A. P. *Angel with Horns and Other Shakespearean Lectures*. Ed. Graham Storey. London: Longmans Green, 1961.

Schwartz, Murray M., and Coppélia Kahn. *Representing Shakespeare: New Psychoanalytic Essays*. Baltimore: Johns Hopkins UP, 1980.

Summers, Joseph. *Dreams of Love and Power: On Shakespeare's Plays*. Oxford: Oxford UP, 1984.

Taylor, Gary. *Reinventing Shakespeare: A Cultural History, from the Restoration to the Present*. London: Weidenfield and Nicolson, 1989.

Traub, Valerie. *Desire and Anxiety: Circulations of Sexuality in Shakespearean Drama*. London: Routledge, 1992.

Traversi, Derek. *An Approach to Shakespeare*. Rev. ed. 2 vols. New York: Anchor, 1969.

Turner, Robert Y. *Shakespeare's Apprenticeship*. Chicago: U of Chicago P, 1974.

ACKNOWLEDGMENTS, CONTINUED FROM COPYRIGHT PAGE

CHAPTER 1 (continued)

Map of Stratford-upon-Avon (Eighteenth Century). Reprinted by permission of the Shakespeare Birthplace Trust.

Detail from the "Agas" Map of London (With Shakespeare's Lodging Indicated). Reprinted with permission of Guildhall Library, Corporation of London.

Shakespeare's Will. Text copyright © Honigmann and Brock from *Playhouse Wills* by E.A.J. Honigmann and Susan Brock. Reprinted with permission of St. Martin's Press, Inc., and Manchester University Press. Photo of last page reprinted by permission of The Public Records Office, London. Document reference PROB 1/4.

CHAPTER 2

Map Showing the Playhouses in Shakespeare's Time. From *The Living Monument: Shakespeare and the Theatre of His Time*, by Muriel C. Bradbrook (©1976). Reprinted with the permission of Cambridge University Press.

Henry Peacham, Sketch of *Titus Andronicus*. Reproduced by permission of the Marquess of Bath, Longleat House, Warminster, Wiltshire, Great Britain.

Inventory of Theatrical Costumes (From Henslowe's Papers). Reprinted by kind permission of the Governors of Dulwich College.

Remains of the Rose Playhouse. Reprinted by the permission of Andrew Fulgoni Photography.

Two Plans of the Rose Playhouse. Reprinted with the permission of Cambridge University Press and John Orrell, University Professor of English at the University of Alberta.

C. Walter Hodges, Illustration of the Second Globe. Reprinted from *Shakespeare's Second Globe* by C. Walter Hodges (1973) by permission of Oxford University Press.

Wenceslas Hollar, Detail from *Long View of London*. Reprinted by kind permission of Guildhall Library, Corporation of London.

Philip Henslowe, Log of Plays from His *Diary*. Reprinted by kind permission of the Governors of Dulwich College.

Record of King James's Payment to the King's Men. Reprinted from the Dramatic Records in the Declared Accounts of the Treasurer of the Chamber, 1558–1642. Reprinted by permission of Her Majesty's Stationery Office.

Edward Alleyn, Letter to His Wife. Reprinted by permission of Guildhall Library, Corporation of London.

CHAPTER 3

Illustration of the Folding and Printing Process. Reprinted from G. B. Harrison, *Introducing Shakespeare* (Penguin Books, 1939, 1954, 1966) by permission of David Higham Associates Limited.

Facsimile of a Part of the Play Script of *Sir Thomas More*. Reprinted by permission of The British Library. MS Harley 7368, Addition IIc, f.9.

Title Page of *Titus Andronicus* (First Quarto). Reprinted by permission of the Folger Shakespeare Library.

Title Page and Catalogue of the First Folio. Reprinted by permission of the Folger Shakespeare Library.

Illustration of a Seventeenth-Century Printing Press. Reprinted by permission of the Folger Shakespeare Library.

Facsimile of the Last Page of *King Lear* (First Quarto). Reprinted by permission of the Folger Shakespeare Library.

Facsimile of "To be or not to be" from *Hamlet, Prince of Denmark* (First Quarto). Reproduced by permission of the Huntington Library, San Marino, California, from William Shakespeare's *Hamlet*. London, 1603. RB 69304.

Facsimile of "To be or not to be" from *Hamlet, Prince of Denmark* (1623 Folio). Reprinted by permission of the Folger Shakespeare Library.

A Comparison of the Work of Compositors A and B on the 1623 Folio. From Peter Blayney, *The First Folio of Shakespeare*. Reprinted by permission of the Folger Shakespeare Library.

CHAPTER 4

Giovanni Battista Giraldi Cinthio, From *Gli Hecatommithi* (The Principal Source for *Othello*). From *Narrative and Dramatic Sources in Shakespeare* by Geoffrey Bullough. Copyright © 1957, 1961 by Columbia University Press. Reprinted with the permission of the publisher.

Map from the 1560 Geneva Bible. Reproduced by permission of the Huntington Library, San Marino, California. RB 55362.

From *The Book of Common Prayer* (The Order for the Burial of the Dead). Reprinted by permission of the Folger Shakespeare Library.

Christopher Marlowe, From *Tamburlaine the Great*. Reproduced by permission of the Huntington Library, San Marino, California. RB 136105.

Ovid, From *Metamorphoses*, trans. Rolfe Humphries. Copyright 1955, Indiana University Press. Reprinted by permission.

CHAPTER 5

Aristotle, From *Poetics*. Reprinted from Aristotle's *Poetics*, trans. Ingram Bywater from *The Oxford Translation of Aristotle*, ed. W. D. Ross, vol. II (1925) by permission of Oxford University Press.

Title Page of *Richard III* (First Quarto). Reprinted by permission of the Folger Shakespeare Library.

William Lambarde, From His Notes of a Conversation with Queen Elizabeth I about *Richard II*. Reprinted by permission of The British Library.

CHAPTER 6

Chart of the Relative Proportions of Poetry and Prose in Shakespeare's Plays. From *The Complete Pelican Shakespeare* by William Shakespeare, ed. Alfred Harbage. Copyright © 1969 by Penguin Books, Inc. Used by permission of Viking Penguin, a division of Penguin Books USA Inc.

CHAPTER 7

Thomas Platter, From *Travels in England* (The Thames River), trans. Clare Williams. Reprinted by permission of the Clare Williams Estate and the publishers, Jonathan Cape, London.

Lupold von Wedel, From *Journey through England and Scotland Made by Lupold von Wedel in the Years 1584 and 1585*, ed. Gottfried von Bulow, from *Transactions of the Royal Historical Society* ns 9 (1895). Reprinted by permission of the Royal Historical Society, London.

Gervase Markham, From *The English Husbandman* (Rural Domestic Architecture and Interior Design). Photo courtesy of the Boston Public Library.

CHAPTER 8

Excerpts from Conduct Books. Reprinted with permission from Norbert Elias, *Power and Civility: The Civilizing Process*, vol. II, trans. Edmond Jephcott. Copyright © 1982 by Blackwell Publishers.

Queen Elizabeth I, List of Royal Proclamations, 1596–1601, and Royal Proclamation against Vagabonds and Unlawful Assemblies. Reprinted by permission from James F. Larkin and Paul L. Hughes, *Tudor Royal Proclamations* (New Haven: Yale University Press, 1964–69).

CHAPTER 9

Ermine Portrait of Elizabeth I, by unknown artist. Reproduced by permission of the Marquess of Salisbury.

Portrait of James I, by Paul van Somer, c. 1620. Reproduced by permission of the Royal Collection Enterprises.

King James I, Secret Letter to Sir Robert Cecil. Reprinted by permission of the Marquess of Salisbury. Letter to George Villiers, Duke of Buckingham. Reprinted by permission of G. P. V. Akrigg, the University of California Press, and the Bodleian Library, Oxford. MS. Tanner 72, fol. 14v.

Sir John Harington, Letter Describing the Revels at King James's Court. Reprinted by permission from *Letters and Epigrams of John Harington,* ed. Norman McClure, University of Pennsylvania Press, 1930.

Simon Forman, From His *Diary* (On a Dream about an Encounter with Queen Elizabeth). Reprinted by permission of the Bodleian Library, Oxford. MS. Ashmole 226, fol. 44r.

Index

><

Italic page numbers indicate illustrations and documents reprinted in *The Bedford Companion*.